RETHINKING FRANCE

Rethinking France

Plans for Renewal 1940–1946

ANDREW SHENNAN

CLARENDON PRESS · OXFORD
1989

Oxford University Press, Walton Street, Oxford OX2 6DP
Oxford New York Toronto
Delhi Bombay Calcutta Madras Karachi
Petaling Jaya Singapore Hong Kong Tokyo
Nairobi Dar es Salaam Cape Town
Melbourne Auckland
and associated companies in
Berlin Ibadan

Oxford is a trade mark of Oxford University Press

Published in the United States
by Oxford University Press, New York

© Andrew Shennan 1989

British Library Cataloguing in Publication Data
Shennan, Andrew
Rethinking France: plans for renewal 1940–1946.
1. France. Reform movements history
I. Title
303.4'84
ISBN 0–19–827520–X

Library of Congress Cataloging in Publication Data
Shennan, Andrew.
Rethinking France: plans for renewal, 1940–1946 / Andrew Shennan.
Bibliography: p.
Includes index.
1. France—Politics and government—1940–1945. 2. France—
Politics and government—1945–1958. 3. Political planning—France—
History—20th century. 4. Reconstruction (1939–1951)—France.
5. France—Civilization—Philosophy. I. Title.
DC397.S47 1989 944.081'6—dc20 89–9294
ISBN 0–19–827520–X

Set by Hope Services, Abingdon
Printed in Great Britain by
Bookcraft Ltd.
Midsomer Norton
Avon

Preface

THE six and a half years between the fall of the Third Republic in 1940 and the establishment of the Fourth Republic in 1946 constitute one of the most eventful and controversial periods in France's modern history. The following study, however, does not focus directly on the experiences of invasion, occupation, resistance, collaboration, or liberation. Instead it deals with the ideas of people who self-consciously looked beyond the all-absorbing present, in order to consider what the French nation might or should be like after the deluge. Their ideas took various forms: personal ruminations on France's recent past, on the defects of her pre-war institutions, or on the nature of the modern world; long shopping-lists of hypothetical reforms; legislative proposals, party programmes, and committee recommendations; last but not least, a host of more or less utopian blueprints (some of which remained unpublished, although a surprising number found their way into print). At a time when so much else was happening, this activity might appear a rather marginal subject—remote not only from actual policies or reforms, which usually had to be made under the pressure of events, but also from the major preoccupations of French men and women (politicians as well as *grand public*) during these years.

None the less, there are good reasons for taking this peculiar *discours* seriously. It is clear, first of all, that if reformist ideas by themselves rarely explain the course of reform, they must certainly contribute to an explanation. Political history has its *événements* and its *longue durée*. If events or decisions are the *événements*, the realities of the *longue durée* are the vocabularies and beliefs of the political world. The manner in which new vocabularies and beliefs are articulated and the extent to which they are assimilated into the mainstream are bound ultimately to influence the course of reform. In the present case, many of the wartime and post-Liberation debates which will be discussed below can be shown to have shaped specific post-war innovations. In a broader sense, in so far as they reshaped some of the consensuses of French politics, the debates had a long-term impact which cannot easily be quantified.

Second, it may be contended that, for all its eccentricities, the *discours* of national decline and renewal has considerable intrinsic interest. In France, as elsewhere, the language of the think-tanks and the study commissions captures a good deal of the intellectual and political mood of the 1940s: didacticism and idealism, escapism and optimism, certainty about the errors of the past and insecurity about the world that was being born. It is also a fact that the debate about the future was a significant and continuing feature of French politics throughout the wartime and post-war periods. The numbers of those who contributed actively to it were relatively small, but there was always, within a much larger fraction of both political and non-political élites, a strong sympathy for the proselytizers of renewal.

These are objective grounds for examining more closely the reformist ideas that were produced between 1940 and 1946. At the same time, this book—like most—has a more subjective rationale. To some degree, all historians work by analogy with their own experience. Often the analogy remains implicit or even unconscious, but here, because it has been quite conscious, it can be made explicit. To somebody who has grown up in Britain in the 1970s and 1980s, the vocabulary of decline and renewal that was current in France in the 1940s is a strikingly familiar one. In the 1930s, 1940s, and 1950s France experienced a crisis of decline akin, in many respects, to that which Britain has experienced in the 1960s, 1970s, and 1980s. These crises were not simply periods in which severe problems such as economic stagnation or political instability existed, but rather periods in which such problems were perceived to constitute a fundamental national decline. In both cases decline came to be seen as an inherent feature of the culture: what made these nations distinctively 'French' or 'British' also made them declining powers. In France in the 1940s the cautiousness and conservatism of a peasant psychology were held to be at the root of a demographic and economic 'malthusianism', while the alleged independence and resistance to authority of French citizens (combined with an absence of the Anglo-Saxon communitarian spirit) were felt to have inhibited the development of a functional modern democracy. In Britain four decades later, similar kinds of interpretation are often offered. Instead of a peasant mentality, in

the British case it is usually suggested that the psychological and
social residues of the pre-industrial (or early post-industrial)
nation have caused economic decline. In France the problem was
malthusianism and an *esprit petit-bourgeois*; in Britain it has been
the cult of the amateur and excessive class-consciousness. There
are enough substantive parallels between the French malaise and
the British disease to suggest that it would be a comparison worth
pursuing in greater detail. The real insight that one derives from
actually living through a crisis of decline, however, has nothing to
do with substantive issues. It is simply that national decline is a
subjective as much as an objective phenomenon, a hypothesis as
well as a fact. When one has witnessed at first hand the way in
which a vast journalistic, bureaucratic, and academic industry
monitors the state of a modern nation and churns out prognoses
and remedies, it becomes difficult to disagree with the view of an
eminent historian of a much earlier national decline: 'The constant
interplay between action and perception should form an integral
component of the study of a society "in decline".'[1] What follows is
an attempt to apply this prescription to the history of France
between 1940 and 1946.

During the course of my research, I have accumulated debts of
gratitude in three countries. In the United States, I was fortunate
enough to be able to use the facilities of Harvard University and
Princeton University. Princeton's enlightened policy on the
granting of 'spouse privileges' made my work much easier than it
would otherwise have been. In France, I have been assisted with
invariable patience and courtesy by the staffs of the Bibliothèque
Nationale, the Archives Nationales (and, in particular, Madame
Bonazzi and Madame Poulle in the *section contemporaine*), the
Archives Nationales Section Outre-Mer, the Archives du Ministère
du Travail (in particular, Mlle Bosman), the Archives des
Relations Extérieures, the Office Universitaire de Recherche
Socialiste, the Fondation Nationale des Sciences Politiques, and
the Institut d'Histoire du Temps Présent. In addition, I am
grateful to the Director-General of the Archives Nationales for
permission to consult the series F60 and certain restricted files in
72 AJ, to Janine Bourdin of the FNSP for permission to consult

[1] J. H. Elliott, 'Self-Perception and Decline in Early Seventeenth-Century
Spain', *Past and Present*, 74 (1977), 42.

the archives of the MRP and the UDSR, and to M. Alexandre Kiss of the Institut International des Droits de l'Homme for access to the papers of René Cassin. In Cambridge, my research has been greatly aided at all times by the staff of the University Library.

For their financial assistance, I am deeply grateful to the Commonwealth Fund of New York, the Department of Education and Science, the French Ministry of Foreign Relations, the Twenty-Seven Foundation, and the Master and Fellows of Corpus Christi College, Cambridge.

In the early stages of my work I was assisted by the timely comments and advice of Professor Stanley Hoffmann, Dr Robert Tombs, and M. Jean Charlot. Professors Maurice Larkin and Douglas Johnson, who examined the Ph.D. dissertation on which this book is based, gave very helpful suggestions for revision. Three other people have helped me throughout and, between them, taught me most of what I know about the historical profession. From my undergraduate and postgraduate adviser, Dr Christopher Andrew, I have received almost a decade of encouragement and guidance. Not only did he suggest the idea of studying this topic in the first place, but on numerous occasions since he has sustained my morale and kept me on track. From my mother and my father I have learnt more about history and history-writing than I can possibly express. They made it very easy to follow in their footsteps because they never made me feel as if I was doing so.

Finally, I would like to thank my wife, Elizabeth Doherty, who lived through the writing of this book and then helped me rewrite it. Not only did she give me the benefit of her insight and expertise at every stage of research and writing, but she kindly tolerated some peculiar Parisian accommodation and too many years of transatlantic commuting.

Notwithstanding the assistance that I have received from all of the above (and from numerous other scholars to whose research I am deeply indebted), the responsibility for what follows is entirely my own.

A.S.

Contents

Abbreviations

AN	Archives Nationales
ANC-1	Assemblée Nationale Constituante élue le 21 octobre 1945
ANC-2	Assemblée Nationale Constituante élue le 2 juin 1946
ANSOM	Archives Nationales Section Outre-Mer
BN	Bibliothèque Nationale
CAS	Comité d'Action Socialiste
CDL	Comité Départemental de Libération
CEI	Comité Économique Interministériel
CFLN	Comité Français de Libération Nationale
CFTC	Confédération Française des Travailleurs Chrétiens
CGE	Comité Général d'Études
CGT	Confédération Générale du Travail
CJP	Centre des Jeunes Patrons
CNE	Conseil National Economique
CNF	Comité National Français
CNR	Conseil National de la Résistance
CO	Comité d'Organisation
CSEIC	Conseil Supérieur de l'Économie Industrielle et Commerciale
DGEN	Délégation Générale à l'Équipement National
ENA	École Nationale d'Administration
FFI	Forces Françaises de l'Intérieur
FN	Front National
FRUS	Foreign Relations of the United States
GPRF	Gouvernement Provisoire de la République Française
JO	*Journal Officiel*
MAE	Ministère des Affaires Etrangères
MEN	Ministère de l'Économie Nationale
MLN	Mouvement de Libération Nationale
MRP	Mouvement Républicain Populaire
OCM	Organisation Civile et Militaire
OCRPI	Office Central de Répartition des Produits Industriels
OP	Office Professionnel

OURS	Office Universitaire de Recherche Socialiste
PCF	Parti Communiste Français
PDP	Parti Démocrate Populaire
PRL	Parti Républicain de la Liberté
PS/SFIO	Parti Socialiste/Section Française de l'Internationale Ouvrière
RPF	Rassemblement du Peuple Français
UDSR	Union Démocratique et Socialiste de la Résistance

Introduction

A T six o'clock on the evening of 6 June 1944, as the allied forces of
Operation Overlord were establishing their beach-head on the
coast of Normandy, General de Gaulle, President of the Provisional
Government of the French Republic, broadcast from England to
the people of France:

The supreme battle has been joined . . . Of course, it is the battle of
France and the battle for France! . . . For the sons of France, wherever
they may be and whoever they may be, the simple and sacred duty is to
fight the enemy with every means at their disposal . . . Behind the clouds
so heavy with our blood and tears, we see the sun of our greatness
breaking through![1]

Within hours of de Gaulle's broadcast, the beaches had been
secured. Within a matter of days, a front over one hundred
kilometres long and twenty kilometres deep had been established.
After the initial success of this first week, however, the allied
armies encountered stiff resistance. It was to be almost two
months before a major breach in the German lines was achieved.
Liberation, as and when it came in June, July, and August,
occurred in two ways. In the wedge of territory between the
Normandy coast and Paris (and in the area of the Provençal coast
liberated by Operation Anvil in August), the allied armies were
the liberators. Elsewhere, liberation came through the insurrection
of local Resistance forces. The widespread mobilization of the
maquis which followed in the wake of de Gaulle's 6 June broadcast
proved, in some areas, to be tragically premature. But once
started it could not be reversed, and in many places—especially in
southern and central France, but also in Brittany—it was the
Resistance's Forces Françaises de l'Intérieur (FFI), not allied
armies or gaullist troops, who swept away the vestiges of German
occupation and the Vichy regime. This dualism, which brought
liberation both from above and from below, was symbolized by
events in Paris. There the entry of General Leclerc's second

[1] Quoted by de Gaulle in *Mémoires de guerre: l'unité* (Paris, 1956), 227.

armoured division on 25 August had been preceded by several days of popular insurrection.

The dualism of military authority reflected a political dualism— or, more accurately, a potential dualism. On the one hand, there was de Gaulle's movement, which in four years had evolved from a small contingent of dissidents into a highly organized Provisional Government, recognized by most people inside and outside France (though not yet by the British or American governments) as the only legitimate replacement for the État Français. Several years of painstaking preparation had enabled this Provisional Government, in advance of the landings, to nominate and put in place its agents throughout France: not merely in the central ministries, but in the departmental prefectures and regional *commissariats*. On the other hand, at the grass roots there was the nucleus of a 'second power'—an alternative authority which derived from the clandestine Resistance movements (whose relation to the external, gaullist organization had always been ambiguous). This second power found institutional expression in the Comités de Libération (local committees on which the different movements in each municipality and department were represented).

As soon as he reached the liberated capital on 25 August, de Gaulle set out to curtail this potential dualism and reconstruct a unified and centralized state. On 9 September he reshuffled his Provisional Government and formed a ministry of 'national unanimity' containing two Communists, four Socialists, three Christian Democrats, three Radicals, one Conservative, and nine ministers without party allegiance. This was a carefully adjusted distribution in the best republican tradition. At the same time, de Gaulle included the president of the National Resistance Council (CNR), Georges Bidault, within the government and thus symbolically neutralized the CNR as an alternative focus of allegiance. Two weeks later, a decree issued by the Provisional Government incorporated the FFI into the army. This decree, combined with a later one of 28 October dissolving the so-called *milices patriotiques* (Resistance-run armed police forces), effectively deprived the Liberation Committees of the military arm that might have allowed them to pose a challenge to the central authorities.

While the Liberation Committees rapidly lost ground in their power-struggle with the state, in Paris the political parties re-emerged at the expense of the Resistance movements. In November 1944 the Christian Democratic MRP was created and the Socialist Party held its first post-Liberation gathering. In December a small Radical party congress was held. Lastly and most importantly, with Maurice Thorez's return from Moscow (at the end of November) the Communist party (PCF) renounced any impulse to back the second power in the Liberation Committees and *milices patriotiques*. The PCF fell into line behind de Gaulle and took its place as the strongest political party within the 'first power'. By the early months of 1945 the faint possibility that a major new political force would emerge from the Resistance— either at the base or in Paris—had disappeared.

This meant that the national renewal for which all were clamouring would have to come from above, from the traditional organs of the republican state (government, ministries, parties, parliament). Given the long association of the French state with continuity, many of the more radical *résistants* viewed renewal from above as a contradiction in terms. In their eyes the eclipse of the organized Resistance during the autumn and winter of 1944–5 ended the possibility of a true revolution. It was certainly the end of one kind of revolution. But the restoration of the state and of certain norms of republican politics did not necessarily indicate a complete restoration of the pre-war status quo.[2] The main centres of political power in the restored Republic were all convinced of the necessity of a major transformation. The three political parties which emerged during 1945 as dominant (the Communists, the Socialists, and the Christian Democrats) had committed themselves to implementing the radical programme agreed by the CNR in March 1944—that is, to extensive nationalizations, worker participation, economic planning, and a new social security system (among other items). As for the head of the Provisional Government, his vision of reform proved to be different from that of the parties, but he fully shared in the consensus condemning the 'old' France and proclaiming the need for renovation.

This consensus was not a sudden creation of the Liberation. It had grown out of four years of experiences so extreme that even the French state could not neatly seal them off as a parenthesis. Although the wartime authorities—Vichy, Free France, and the

[2] See on this point René Rémond's observations delivered at a conference on the Liberation: *La Libération de la France* (Paris, 1976), 833–4.

metropolitan Resistance movements—failed to prolong themselves in institutional terms, the emotions and ideas which this period had generated were anything but forgotten at the Liberation. The passionate aspirations of 1944 had been formed after an extended re-evaluation of national attitudes and institutions.

The roots of this re-evaluation of France's post-war future went back to the summer of 1940 and before. During the 'phoney war' months between September 1939 and May 1940 it was often suggested that even if a combination of the French army, the forces of France's allies, and the Maginot line saved France from her enemies (as most people expected that they would), she would still need to be saved from herself. It was symptomatic of this strange period that the first books about the problem of post-war renovation appeared even before the fighting had begun. In one such book, written in the winter of 1939–40, a Catholic intellectual, P.-H. Simon, set out the problem in terms which politicians of all persuasions were to repeat during the following six or seven years:

we not only have to save France today: we shall have to rebuild her tomorrow. One of two things will happen. Either we shall succumb once again to the euphoria of victory and allow France to resume her bad habits . . . to be weakened by discord and lulled by illusions . . . Or, having found a new political, moral, and social style for France, we shall have the strength and the courage to ensure it prevails—and then we shall truly be victors.[3]

One of the reasons that this great debate about post-war reform got off to such a quick start was that it was, in fact, a continuation of a pre-existing debate (as the later chapters of this book will attempt to make clear). During the preceding decade of perpetual crisis, hundreds of intellectuals and politicians had been urging the necessity of reform. Though the catastrophe of May–June 1940 struck a population psychologically prepared only for victory, in many respects defeat had been anticipated for years (not least, as *le Temps* pointed out on 16 June, in the writings of a certain Colonel de Gaulle). In the blueprints for reform which had been produced during the 1930s, the ultimate argument had invariably

---

[3] *Préparer l'après-guerre* (Paris, 1940), 17–18. For a good sample of perspectives on the post-war future during the phoney war, see the two issues which the influential review *Nouveaux cahiers* devoted to the question at the end of 1939: nos. 51 (1 Nov. 1939), 52 (1 Dec. 1939).

been that if the right changes were not introduced—if the birth-rate did not increase, if the economy were not planned, if the executive branch of government were not strengthened, if military strategy were not revised—the nation would be fatally vulnerable.

On 10 May 1940 the German invasion finally began, and within six weeks the worst of the inter-war reformers' fears had come true. The Germans were in Paris, an armistice was signed, and two-thirds of the country was under occupation. In the instant of defeat, a stupefied and numbed population acted more out of reflex than reflection. One reflex was to try to fix blame for the defeat—a reaction that the new regime in Vichy exploited very effectively. Along with recrimination came a second reflex: the frantic search for a silver lining in this blackest of clouds. Paradoxical as it may seem, an immediate consequence of the defeat was the creation of a political atmosphere highly conducive to the rhetoric of renewal.

This rhetoric was, in part, a kind of therapeutic exercise, expressing the natural compulsion to preserve normality in a moment of extreme confusion. The past had come to an abrupt halt and the idea of renewal signified the possibility of a future for France over which the French themselves might still have some control. To discuss the nation's future was a way of believing that it had a future: 'Henceforth, France will be as we want it to be,' wrote one journalist, in the face of overwhelming evidence to the contrary.[4] Talk of renaissance and reconstruction was not merely a ruse of those, like the maurrasians, who saw an opportunity to exploit the 'divine surprise'. Often it expressed an instinctive patriotism, affirming the continued existence of what Jean Guéhenno called 'La France qu'on n'envahit pas'.[5]

It was also, of course, an expression of revulsion against the regime that had been entrusted with the prosecution of the war. In the idiom of mid-1940, words that looked to the future—like renewal and renaissance—carried with them an implicit condem-nation of the past, which meant, first and foremost, the politicians and the 'authorities'.[6] Defence of the status quo was now an impossible, indeed inconceivable, position. The consensus in

[4] Edmond Jaloux, *Le Temps*, 25 June 1940.
[5] *Journal des années noires* (Paris, 1947), 17–19.
[6] See H. R. Kedward, 'Patriots and Patriotism in Vichy France', *Royal Historical Society Transactions*, 5th ser., 32 (1982), 182.

favour of radical reform encompassed more or less the entire republican élite, as became evident at the beginning of July, when the members of the two legislative chambers assembled in Vichy and voted to give Marshal Pétain full powers. When the members of the two chambers were asked on 9 July whether they approved the principle of a renovation of the constitution, there was virtually unanimous approval in both. From all parties individual parliamentarians spoke about the need for reform. The conservative Pierre-Étienne Flandin agreed that constitutional change was essential, but in view of what he termed the 'generalized decadence' he also demanded reform of the press and the bureaucracy.[7] The Radical leader Herriot, President of the Chamber, told deputies: 'We shall have to reform ourselves, to give more backbone to a Republic that we made too weak.'[8] Charles Spinasse, a Socialist deputy from the Corrèze and former minister in the Popular Front government of 1936, offered another *mea culpa*: 'We must break with the past without thought of return. . . . It merely anticipated a future which was beyond our reach.'[9] Spinasse was soon to gravitate towards collaboration with the occupying forces, but others who did not do so shared his premiss about breaking with the past. Typical was a motion which the Radical Vincent Badie and twenty-seven other parliamentarians (including a number of Socialists) tried to present at the meeting of 10 July. Though protesting at the terms of the Pétain government's bill, the Badie motion began as follows: 'The undersigned members of parliament . . . wish to affirm solemnly:—That they are fully aware of all that is blameworthy in the present state of affairs and of the reasons that have brought about our military defeat.—That they appreciate the pressing necessity to conduct . . . the moral and economic *redressement* of our unfortunate country.'[10] Even those who refused Pétain full powers acknowledged the necessity of reform.[11]

[7] See his speech to a closed session of the National Assembly on 10 July, reprinted in Emmanuel Berl, *La Fin de la IIIᵉ République* (Paris, 1968), 304–11.

[8] *JO, Débats parlementaires, Chambre des députés*, 9 July 1940, p. 814.

[9] Quoted by Henri Amouroux, *La Grande Histoire des Français sous l'Occupation*, ii. *Quarante millions de Pétainistes, juin 1940–juin 1941* (Paris, 1977), 69.

[10] Quoted by Amouroux, *Quarante millions de Pétainistes*, p. 78.

[11] See also the declaration of the eight parliamentarians from the department of the Rhône who had voted against Pétain, in Tony Révillon, *Mes carnets (juin–octobre 1940)* (Paris, 1945), 161–6.

It was against the background of this almost universal acceptance of change by the leadership of the *ancien régime* that alternative programmes, which had first been voiced while the regime was still in charge, re-emerged to claim the spotlight. Because there had been such a range of revisionist critiques of the Third Republic, there was no need to create a vocabulary of renewal; the vocabulary—or rather many different vocabularies—already existed. Perhaps the most influential of them was to be the maurrasian ideology of Action Française, which had been losing ground to the newer forces of the extreme right during the 1930s but in the aftermath of defeat enjoyed a sudden resurgence. However, maurrasianism was not without contenders in the battle for the hearts and minds of the new regime. A few examples may suffice to illustrate the diversity of Pétain's ideological suitors. A senator named Jacques Bardoux sent the new head of state a programme of structural reforms which he and his 'Comité technique pour la réforme de l'État' had drafted in 1935–6.[12] A group of neo-socialists and right-wing extremists led by Marcel Déat proposed to Pétain that he integrate a new authoritarian France within a fascist Europe.[13] General Weygand wrote a memorandum for the head of the government, calling for an end to 'l'ancien ordre de choses' and proposing his own version of an intellectual and moral reform.[14] The syndicalist leader René Belin joined the Vichy government in July 1940 with an entirely different agenda in mind: he proposed to forge a new kind of non-antagonistic industrial relations, which might produce a more cohesive society. A few months later, in November 1940, Emmanuel Mounier started up his review *Esprit* once more, and offered its personalist philosophy as the basis for the national renewal which was getting under way.

These were only a few of the many theorists of renewal who saw an opportunity for France in the sudden defeat and who instinctively agreed with Pétain when he told the nation that, while all nations suffer reverses from time to time, 'It is the manner in

[12] For Bardoux's letter see his book, *Journal d'un témoin de la Troisième* (Paris, 1957), 393–8.
[13] See their declaration 'à propos de l'Assemblée Nationale', reprinted in Berl, *La Fin de la IIIe République*, 283–94.
[14] For Weygand's memorandum see *Mémoires: rappelé au service* (Paris, 1950), 298–9.

which they react which shows whether they are weak or strong.'[15]
In the summer of 1940 Pétain adroitly annexed the vocabulary of
reformism. In his early speeches he talked about 'French renewal'
and 'structural reforms'. 'We shall draw the lesson of the battles
we have lost,' he said on 20 June 1940, and a few days later: 'From
now on we must turn our efforts to the future.' The Vichy regime's
National Revolution was the fruit of this rhetoric of renewal.

However, the resonance between National Revolution and national
renewal faded rapidly. Local studies have suggested that popular
enthusiasm for the National Revolution had largely disappeared
by the end of 1940,[16] although many of its acolytes remained
committed to it much longer. It was certainly evident by 1942 that
the National Revolution had stalled and that the likelihood of a
German victory, on which it had been predicated, had receded. As
the military tide turned, it was increasingly Vichy's opponents who
took ultimate victory for granted and began to look beyond it
towards 'renewal' and 'structural reforms'. From 1942 onwards,
gaullists in London and in North Africa were busy debating plans
for post-Liberation reform. In a less structured but uniquely
ardent dialogue, resisters inside France argued over the lessons of
the national crisis and constructed visions of the future.

The motivation behind this concern with the nation's post-war
future was complex. At the back of older minds lurked the
memory of the first 'après-guerre', a settlement which had failed in
part through a lack of intellectual preparation—or so it seemed in
retrospect. To quote one clandestine newspaper: 'From 1914 to 1918,
France remained totally absorbed by her war effort. Suddenly
confronted by the problems of peacetime, for which she did not
have the time to prepare, she allowed herself to be weakened and
divided.'[17] All the anti-Vichy forces were keenly aware of the
danger of winning the war and losing the peace once again.

For the followers of General de Gaulle, an additional stimulus
was provided by all the allied planning which was going on around

---

[15] Speech of 20 June 1940, in Philippe Pétain, *Actes et écrits* (Paris, 1974), 450.

[16] See e.g. John Sweets, *Choices in Vichy France: The French under Nazi
Occupation* (Oxford, 1986), 98; and Pierre Laborie, *Résistants, vichyssois et autres:
l'évolution de l'opinion et des comportements dans le Lot de 1939 à 1944* (Paris,
1980), 176–9.

[17] *Libérer et Fédérer*, 1 (14 July 1942). For the same sentiment, see *La Voix du
Nord*, 14 (20 Sept. 1941), 43 (1 Nov. 1943); *Résistance*, 4 (23 Dec. 1942).

them. Other groups of national exiles in London set up committees to consider post-war issues. More importantly, from early in the war politicians, civil servants, and intellectuals in Britain and America gave urgent consideration to post-war issues. Towards the end of 1942 a writer in the gaullist newspaper *La Marseillaise* listed all the Anglo-Americans who had recently made speeches about post-war reconstruction: the list included virtually every prominent political figure, not to mention the Archbishop of Canterbury and J. B. Priestley.[18] It seemed crucial to keep abreast of these preparations and, wherever possible, ensure that a French contribution was made. Planning for after the war was one way in which an embattled minority in exile could assert France's continuing presence as a force in the world.

To those resisting inside France, thinking about the future was often a welcome distraction from the uncomfortable realities of the present. Resisters and prisoners of war naturally needed to believe that there would be some ultimate justification or recompense for their sufferings. One prisoner wrote of cellmates who 'During long sleepless nights spent side by side in their dark cell . . . tried to forget the horrors of the present by comparing their visions of the future'.[19] As new organizations, Resistance movements also had an institutional self-interest in looking ahead. By stigmatizing national decline and magnifying the tasks of post-war renovation, the movements were creating a long-term role for themselves. One of their aims was to avoid the fate of the *anciens combattants* of the First World War, who had been frustrated in their efforts to influence politics and (in the words of one Resistance tract) had too often ended up 'begging for the post of public-garden attendant'.[20] The resisters' vision of the future was closely connected with their desire to secure their status as a new national élite.

But at the root of the wartime concern with the future lay something stronger than historical analogy, escapism, or self-interest. The catastrophe of May–June 1940 had laid bare a profound national crisis, which had suddenly been manifested in military defeat but was perceived to permeate every aspect of French life—economic, social, demographic, political, even ethical. From the very beginning of the Occupation, it became clear that

[18] No. 18 (11 Oct. 1942).   [19] *Bir-Hakeim*, 2 (Apr.–May 1943).
[20] *Défense de la France*, 21 (1 Nov. 1942).

on one point at least there was agreement between Paris, Vichy, London, and all the centres of the Resistance: the France of the 1930s had disappeared for good. The most striking characteristic of all the wartime planning—a characteristic which was largely passed on to the political leaders of the post-Liberation era—was the desire for a complete break with the pre-war status quo.

To a considerable extent, the issues confronting France at the Liberation resembled those confronting other European nations. Such an immense and costly conflict as the Second World War, following a prolonged period of economic, political, social, and diplomatic crisis, was bound to force all the belligerents to re-evaluate the past. It is scarcely surprising that the re-evaluation that took place in France between 1940 and 1946 echoed—sometimes consciously, sometimes unconsciously—that which occurred elsewhere. Nevertheless, in every country a different experience of war combined with historical, political, or social peculiarities to create a distinct perspective on the future. The various idiosyncrasies of the French perspective are the warp and woof of this study. At the outset, however, it may be helpful to identify its general characteristics.

At the Liberation French élites had one overriding problem which they shared neither with the governments of the victorious 'Big Three' nor with those of the prostrate Axis powers, nor with those of smaller and historically less ambitious European nations. That was the problem of eroding national power: how to preserve the nation not just from external enemies or material distress but from a secular decline in influence and status. The centrality of the idea of decline to the public debate can be clearly seen if one compares the French case with that of Britain. In Britain, which had not undergone a national humiliation like that of 1940, there was no comparable concern about national decadence. The Attlee years were perhaps the last in which decline was *not* an issue.[21] The main focus of British reconstruction policy during and after the war was on ameliorative social and economic reform rather than on bolstering national power.[22] In France, on the contrary, renewal of national power was always a fundamental objective of

---

[21] This is the argument of the most authoritative account of the post-war Labour Government: Kenneth O. Morgan, *Labour in Power, 1945–1951* (Oxford, 1984).

[22] See Paul Addison, *The Road to 1945: British Politics and the Second World War* (London, 1975).

those advocating reform (be it economic or educational, constitutional or colonial).

Along with this tendency to relate all reform to the overarching problem of decline went a grandiose conception of reform itself. Because it is concerned with elucidating the details of public debate, the present study might, at times, give the impression that French reformers viewed renewal as a purely technical problem. That was rarely, in fact, the case. Reformers were at least as interested in *mystique* as in *politique*. One thing that people as diverse as pro-natalists, imperial reformers, and economic planners had in common was a belief that no amount of technical expertise or reformist legislation could be fully effective unless it were accompanied by a collective national *engagement*. In turn, each of the competing political ideologies—Vichy's National Revolution, Resistance socialism, gaullism, patriotic communism—claimed to have discovered the secret of how to mobilize that commitment.

In a period of extreme national disunity and vulnerability, it was hardly surprising that people identified renewal with ideas that transcended—or appeared to transcend—the partisan or the mundane and that promised to unify and galvanize the nation. This was a conception of renewal, furthermore, that came quite naturally to a generation which had reached maturity in the 1930s. In a sense, the debate about national decline that took place after 1940 represented a continuation of the 1930s debate over the crisis of liberal democracy. In both debates the fundamental issue was a comparative one: how could an 'old' country like France mobilize the physical and emotional energies of its citizens to compete with 'modern' totalitarian regimes (like Soviet Russia and Nazi Germany)? The lesson that the French drew from the pre-war German baby boom or the Soviet victory at Stalingrad was the superiority of ideologies that forged a collective will from individual interests. It was felt by many that French republicanism had been such an ideology in 1792 and 1871, but was no longer so in 1940. The rethinking of France between 1940 and 1946 became, to a large extent, the search for a new national mystique.

In the short term, the search proved fruitless (although it may be argued that, in the longer perspective of France's post-war history, the elements of a new mystique of modernity were brought together in this period). This short-term failure may be attributed, in part, to the profound political divisions of the period. These divisions made it impossible for any of the rival mystiques to appeal, in anything but rhetorical fashion, to the whole nation. In 1940 the working class felt excluded; in 1944 the bourgeoisie felt excluded; in 1946 the Resistance and the gaullists felt excluded; in 1947 the Communists felt excluded. An equally important factor, however, were the material conditions in France in these years. In December 1940 the prefect in the Vaucluse reported to Vichy that 'the country's economy and food supply present literally daily problems and are the main preoccupation of the population'.[23] The physical hardships of the Occupation are well enough known. Less well known is the extent to which these hardships persisted after 1944 and preoccupied general public, politicians, and administrators alike. The observation made by the Vichy prefect was made repeatedly by prefects and regional *Commissaires de la République* in the two years after the Liberation. A few excerpts from their reports in 1945 convey the general feeling. In February the *commissaire* in Lyon wrote that 'Everything is dominated by the inadequate food supply and the cold.'[24] In March it was reported from Lille that 'the population remains wholly preoccupied with concerns about food'.[25] In September the *commissaire* in Strasburg reported that the population there 'is obsessed by the worry of feeding, clothing, and housing itself',[26] and the prefect in the Ardèche found 'public opinion almost universally indifferent to anything that does not relate to the essential question of food'.[27] Such official reports were echoed by politicians: a meeting of the Socialist party's National Council was told by one member that, in the sixty meetings he had attended since the Liberation, he had not once been asked about nationalizations or constitutional revision but had been questioned repeatedly about rationing.[28]

This is not to suggest that the French were uninterested in reform. The same government officials cited above reported a considerable, if fluctuating, interest in the progress of reform throughout 1944, 1945, and the early months of 1946. Popular attachment to the Common Programme of the CNR was frequently reported. Occasionally, officials identified a fundamental shift in grass-roots political opinion: in May 1945, for instance, the

[23] AN, F1c III 1195.   [24] AN, F1a 4028.
[25] Ibid.   [26] Ibid. 4027.   [27] Ibid. 4029.
[28] PS/SFIO, *Conseil national du 9 juin 1946, compte-rendu des débats* (Paris, 1946), 117.

commissaire in Poitiers noted that 'since 1939 public opinion has become more favourable to socialist theories on these questions [i.e. nationalizations] and a good many people who would have fiercely opposed them before the war now regard them as natural and justified'.[29] The French public as a whole was receptive to the idea of change, and a sizeable minority had distinct ideas about what kind of change would be desirable. It was not that plans for national renewal did not matter to people. They simply mattered less than food, housing, and clothing.

The following study is divided into two parts. The first examines each of the centres of authority that existed inside and outside France between the fall of the Third Republic and the beginning of the Fourth (Vichy, the metropolitan Resistance, Free France, General de Gaulle, and the three major parties in the post-Liberation period) and considers the various contributions that these groups made to the rethinking of France. In the second part the analysis shifts to a thematic plane. A number of key areas of reformist activity—the state, the empire, the economy, the educational system, and various other aspects of French society— are discussed in greater depth. Although an attempt has been made to maintain a broad perspective, this book does not claim to offer an exhaustive treatment of all areas of reform. Its omissions reflect the limits of its ambitions. It is concerned with the public debate about a perceived national crisis, not with the concurrent debate about an international or European crisis. More specifically still, it focuses on the ways in which the French envisaged reforming themselves in order to reverse national decline. Consequently, it does not treat issues, such as European integration, which offered external solutions to domestic problems. Why confine oneself to internal solutions? The argument of this book is that one of the defining characteristics of public and political debate about the post-war future was precisely the belief that France could not rely on external forces to reverse decline, that what really mattered was whether France (which was assumed to mean the French imperial community) could renew itself domestically.

Even within the area of domestic reform, certain subjects have had to be omitted. Thus, for example, military reform will not be

[29] AN, F1a 4028.

discussed. As a distinguished French historian has recently noted, one of the striking features of political discourse in the years immediately after the Liberation was the general lack of urgency about reconstructing the army which had performed so poorly in 1940.[30] In general, it may be contended that the period after the diplomatic débâcle of the late thirties and the military débâcle of 1940 was one in which traditional sources of national security and power—treaties, alliances, armies, and so forth—were discounted. In these years other factors—such as social vitality and cohesion, strong political leadership, and above all economic strength— were widely regarded as the critical determinants of France's future power. As a result, French reformers devoted a dispro- portionate amount of their attention to such factors and relatively little to issues (like army reform or defence policy) which, on the face of it, might appear more relevant to national power than education or the birth-rate. In the context of the debate about internal regeneration which took place between 1940 and 1946— the context of this book—military reform was relatively tangential.

Two further criteria have been applied in choosing what material to include and what to exclude. The major focus is the national political scene. Both adjectives are used advisedly. The focus is national in the sense that this is a study of the centre rather than the periphery. In the post-Liberation period, it deals with the 'révolution par la loi' directed from Paris rather than with the CDL's activities in the provinces—or, to give a concrete example, with the legislation that established *comités d'entreprises* rather than with the worker management experiments that sprang up spontaneously in many factories in southern France in the late summer of 1944. The history of the post-Liberation period from the perspective of the grass roots remains to be written,[31] but this is not an attempt to write it. On the other hand, the focus is political in the sense that it is primarily the ideas and programmes of governments, ministries, parliamentarians, party officials, and politically active people that are under scrutiny. Many of those

---

[30] S. Berstein, 'French Power as seen by the Political Parties after World War II', in Josef Becker and Franz Knipping (eds.), *Power in Europe?* (Berlin and New York, 1986), 175. For a similar argument see J.-P. Rioux, 'Les Forces politiques et l'armée', in a collection of conference papers entitled *De Gaulle et la nation face aux problèmes de défense (1945–1946)* (Paris, 1983), 61–5.

[31] An interesting attempt at such a study has been made by Grégoire Madjarian in his book *Conflits, pouvoirs et société à la Libération* (Paris, 1980).

who have been seen as the 'modernizers' of post-war France were outside this political world: they were technicians, syndicalists, progressive-minded businessmen.[32] It would be difficult to analyse plans for renewal without recognizing the contribution which non-political figures made to the political debate: wherever possible, this contribution has been noted. But equally it would be impracticable to encompass all those, outside as well as inside politics, who had visions of a modernized France. In any case, after the immense team effort in scholarship deployed by the Fondation Nationale des Sciences Politiques in its 1981 colloquium, 'La France en voie de modernisation, 1944–1952', the need for such a survey is less pressing.

The second criterion is chronological. While it has been recognized that the period 1940–6 should be treated as a whole, there is one moment which has been seen as the crucial one—the Liberation in 1944. Everything, before and after August 1944, has been related to that moment. This, in a sense, flies in the face of the best scholarship about the period. The tendency has been to underline the continuities of this apparently discontinuous period: continuity from the Third Republic to the administration of Vichy, from Vichy to the post-Liberation regime. This scholarship is very convincing in reconstructing the reformist tendencies of the bureaucracy and in tracing the intellectual lineage of reformist ideas. What is sometimes lost, however, is the *sense* of fluidity that existed in the summer and autumn of 1944, not to mention the reality of political—as opposed to intellectual or bureaucratic—discontinuity. The aim here is to restore the Liberation to the centre of the historical frame. In so doing, the emphasis is inevitably shifted somewhat away from Vichy and towards the post-Liberation regime.

[32] René Rémond, 'Les Français voulaient-ils moderniser la France?', *L'Histoire*, 44 (1982), 95.

PART I

Regimes and Renewal

1

Vichy's National Revolution, 1940–1942

IN 1940 and 1941 the vocabulary of national renewal was virtually monopolized by the Vichy regime. Vichy's assumptions were that defeat was a *fait accompli*, that internal regeneration was an absolute pre-condition if France was ever going to recover her independence and freedom, and that such regeneration was possible in spite of the fact that the war was continuing and Germany was occupying much of French territory (including the capital). The new leadership defined its mission as 'the building of the new social, economic, and political edifice which is rising from the storms of the present'.[1] The term that it applied to this process—the 'National Revolution'—appeared in the unoccupied, southern zone in the summer of 1940 and was given a seal of approval by Pétain in a long manifesto that he issued on 11 October. Though the Marshal himself disliked the expression and would have preferred to call it a 'redressement national' or 'rénovation française',[2] the term stuck. Its symbolic overtones gave it a certain appeal in the circumstances of 1940: since the new government was promising to reconcile the nation, it was appropriate that its programme should combine a traditional term of the right ('national') with one of the left ('revolution').

The doctrine of the National Revolution was popularized as the doctrine of the national saviour, Marshal Pétain. It was expounded in a series of twenty or so messages which Pétain delivered in the second half of 1940 and which Robert Aron aptly described as a 'dialogue with the nation'.[3] In fact these messages were generally drafted by others. That is not to imply that the Marshal was without political views of his own. His distaste for freemasons, parliamentarians, secular-minded schoolteachers, and communists, his interest in corporatism and peasantism, his

---

[1] Paul Baudouin, *Neuf mois au gouvernement* (Paris, 1948), 310.
[2] H. du Moulin de Labarthète, *Le Temps des illusions: souvenirs (juillet 1940–avril 1942)* (Geneva, 1946), 158.
[3] 'Qu'est-ce que le Pétainisme?', in Aron, *Dossiers de la seconde guerre mondiale* (Paris, 1976), 164.

paternalist aspiration to eliminate the class struggle while preserving social hierarchy—all qualified him, broadly speaking, as a
maurrasian, although it would seem that he was not well acquainted
with Maurras's books. In general, however, friend and foe agreed
that he was poorly prepared to be the doctrinal leader of a political
movement.[4] He was neither capable of nor interested in developing a
coherent ideology for the National Revolution. Furthermore, his
various speech-writers[5] did not share a conception of what the
National Revolution should be: there were major divergences of
perspective between maurrasians like Henri Massis, personalists
like Robert Loustau, traditional conservatives like Henri du
Moulin de Labarthète, and technocratic types like Yves Bouthillier.

In any case, Pétain's homilies were never intended to provide
more than the rough sketch of a doctrine. They were taken by the
regime's adherents not as the final word but as a stimulus to
further reflection. In response, Pétainists undertook a vast,
inchoate reassessment of the nation's past, present, and future.
Study groups were one of the few growth industries in France in
the period after the defeat. To give an indication of this reformist
zeal, it may be noted that in the area of corporatist organization—
admittedly one of the regime's particular preoccupations—ap-
proximately one hundred proposals reached the government in not
much more than nine months.[6] Some of these proposals emanated
from ministries and agencies within the regime itself, while others
came from various interested parties outside the government. That
pattern held true in other areas of policy. A variety of organizations
were set up under the direct supervision of the government to
think through the principles of the National Revolution that Pétain
had proclaimed. The most elaborate was the quasi-parliamentary
Conseil National, which was established in 1941 with the aim of
bringing together prominent representatives from diverse professional and political backgrounds. This large council considered
a number of the major concerns of the National Revolution

---

[4] Pétain's political shortcomings are recorded in the testimony of many
contemporaries. The point is made, from three quite distinct perspectives, in: Jules
Jeanneney, *Journal politique: septembre 1939–juillet 1942* (Paris, 1972), 115; René
Gillouin, *J'étais l'ami du maréchal Pétain* (Paris, 1966), 35–8; René Belin, *Du
secrétariat de la CGT au gouvernement de Vichy* (Paris, 1978), 181.

[5] A list is given by du Moulin de Labarthète in *Le Temps des illusions*, p. 159.

[6] This statistic is given by Lt.-Col. Cèbe, the Secretary of the Comité de
l'Organisation Professionnelle, in his report of 1 June 1941, AN, F22 1835.

(including constitutional reform and regionalism). However, the experiment of a national representative body, albeit a nominated one, was not successful. Even when it produced tangible results— like the constitutional blueprint that it prepared in 1941—the results were not to the government's liking. With the exception of this abortive pseudo-parliament, Vichy tended to integrate its official study committees more closely within the administration. Some ministries set up advisory councils to canvass expert or interested opinion and act as seed-beds of reformist ideas. Typical of this kind of committee was the Comité Consultatif de la Famille Française that was established to assist the Commissariat Général à la Famille; or the Conseil Supérieur de l'Economie Industrielle et Commerciale (CSEIC), created in 1942 under the auspices of the Secrétariat d'Etat à la Production Industrielle to elucidate 'the doctrine of the new French economy'. Other bodies were given more specific tasks and an identity distinct from any ministry. The Comité de l'Organisation Professionnelle (COP) that was convened in June 1941 was of this kind: staffed by a mixture of ministerial officials (from various branches of the government) and represent- atives from both sides of industry, it was mandated to draw up a final draft for a corporatist Labour Charter. Another kind of organization—similiarly unattached to any particular branch of the bureaucracy but reporting directly to the head of state—was created in April 1941: this was the Délégation Générale à l'Équipement National (DGEN), which was given the task of drawing up investment and retooling plans for the post-war economy. Whatever their institutional form, all these bodies provided for participation from outside the administration (par- ticularly from businessmen and leaders of prominent lobbies). Among such non-official 'representatives', there was considerable overlap from one committee to another. This was particularly true of business representatives: notable *patrons* like Georges Painvin, Pierre Laguionie, Auguste Detœuf, Roger Boutteville, and Jacques Lente all sat on more than one of these government committees. The haziness of any distinction between 'official' and 'unofficial' bodies is illustrated by the fact that these well- connected men were also taking part, alongside senior Vichy officials, in non-governmental bodies like the Comité d'Études pour la France.[7] The Comité d'Études pour la France—a large

[7] Four of the five (Boutteville, Detœuf, Laguionie, Lente) were members of the

think-tank with more than fifty members and an impressive output of studies—was only one of a number of unofficial organizations that were consulted regularly by Vichy and contributed to the dialogue about the National Revolution. Among the most active and influential of these groups were the Centre des Jeunes Patrons, the Institut pour les Problèmes Humains, the Centre d'Études Techniques et Sociales, the Centre de Synthèse des Jeunes, and the Institut d'Études Corporatives et Sociales.

In spite of the ideological diversity of the people who volunteered to define the National Revolution, there were certain common threads in the movement. The most important of these was 'realism'. In their various ways all those who rallied to the National Revolution saw themselves as realists. In the most basic sense, they viewed as an act of *Realpolitik* Pétain's decision to sign the armistice with Hitler and seek national renewal 'by staying put' rather than place his faith in 'a reconquest of our country by allied forces, under circumstances and at a time that are impossible to predict'.[8] The National Revolution was grounded in the belief that, whether or not Germany defeated Britain (which in mid-1940 seemed highly probable), France had been irretrievably defeated and liberation could only occur in the distant future. As the foreign minister Baudouin put it: 'The French people must bow before the German victory, which Germany has deserved.'[9] Vichyite propagandists depicted those who resisted the reality of defeat as (at best) hopeless idealists. 'They no longer see the world as it is', wrote one advocate of the National Revolution, 'and rather than stopping to contemplate and master the tragic reality of our fate, they dream in the abstract of events that are perhaps desirable in themselves but are improbable or unpredictable.'[10] In contrast, the apostles of the National Revolution thought that they were facing up to reality, which, in the exalted language of the period, somehow seemed the first step to 'dominating' or 'transcending' it.

The escape route from the dire circumstances of mid-1940 that

Comité d'Études pour la France. For a discussion of this group, see Philippe Mioche, *Le Plan Monnet: genèse et élaboration, 1941–1947* (Paris, 1987), 15–19.

[8] Pétain's speech to the French cabinet, 13 June 1940, in Pétain, *Actes et écrits*, p. 448.

[9] Memorandum of July 1940, quoted in Baudouin, *Neuf mois*, p. 265.

[10] Sébastien Bijon, *La Leçon des victoires perdues* (Toulouse, 1941), 51.

Pétain offered the nation was itself presented as the path of realism. The National Revolution was realist both in form and in content. In form, it was realist in the sense that it was self-consciously anti-ideological. It denounced specific ideological systems (in particular, Marxism and liberalism) for causing France's élites to lose touch with real issues.[11] In general, it professed itself to be a reaction against abstraction and intellectualism in political life. To quote a Catholic member of one of the progressive fringe-groups that the early phase of the National Revolution inspired (Father Lebret of Économie et Humanisme): 'It is man that we must focus on again, not the man of Rousseau, St Thomas, or Aristotle, but the real man of flesh and blood, the poor bloke in the street, the proletarian masses who fill the neighbourhoods in our cities, and also the bourgeois who have lost their sense of destiny.'[12] Unlike the politicians of the Third Republic (who were characterized by Vichy as thinkers and talkers but never doers), the new élites—typified by Pétain the peasant and soldier—saw themselves as practical, experienced men and their revolution as an empirical solution to the national crisis.[13] The ideology was, as one minister later described it, a 'doctrine of reflective pragmatism'.[14] This pragmatic conceit was one of the bonds between the no-nonsense military men, the corporatist ideologues who insisted that only organic institutions were 'real', and the technocrats in the economic administration.

Here form shaded into content. The National Revolution was not simply the creed of practical men conducting a 'caretaker' administration. The object of the Revolution was actually to promote 'realities' or rather a certain definition of the 'real' France. These realities were what Vichy viewed as the primary

[11] *Le Bulletin de France: organe des comités de propagande sociale du Maréchal*, 28 July 1941 (in AN, 78 AJ 2).

[12] *Vers la révolution communautaire: les journées du Mont-Dore* (Paris, 1943), 184.

[13] Paul Auphan, *Histoire élémentaire de Vichy* (Paris, 1971), 90. An interesting point is the extent to which Pétainism's 'realism' was shaped by popular expectations as much as by the ideological preferences of the Pétainists themselves. Kedward has suggested convincingly that the experience of the 'Exode'—when millions of refugees took to the roads in advance of the German armies—not only discredited the local and national authorities who were perceived as incompetent and even treacherous, but also stimulated an acute desire for decisive, practical, and patriotic leadership—in short, precisely the kind of realism that Pétain appeared to offer. (See H. R. Kedward, 'Patriots and Patriotism in Vichy France', *Royal Historical Society Transactions*, 5th ser., 32 (1982), 182–3.)

[14] Marcel Peyrouton, *Du service public à la prison commune* (Paris, 1950), 124.

social units: family, workplace, profession, region. The National Revolution proposed to shift the focus of public life away from the 'abstract' ideas of citizenship and class to the 'concrete' fact of membership in these communities. In the society that it pledged to construct (or rather reconstruct), natural communities would be freed from the perverting influence of individualism. At every level, social collaboration would be the rule—a rule enforced, if necessary, by the authority of the father, the communal or regional authorities, the foreman, or the corporation. Within the national community, the authority function would be exercised by a strong state. This state would co-ordinate and direct the energies of all the lower communities, acting (to use an expression employed by Jean Bichelonne, the Minister of Industrial Production, in 1943[15]) as the 'chef d'orchestre'. At the same time the scope of the state's activity would be strictly limited; it would guide and arbitrate conflicts but not absorb the functions of other communities.[16]

If the communitarian aspect of Vichy realism had been the only one, it is conceivable that the National Revolution might have retained for longer the credibility that it enjoyed in 1940. The rediscovery of the *pays réel* might then have been seen (as some later tried to interpret it in their own defence) as a tactical *repliement*—a withdrawal into social realities that were invulnerable to the occupier and where the seeds of a future regeneration might have germinated. The vogue that corporatist and regionalist schemes enjoyed under the Occupation—and not just among Pétainists—testifies to the large reservoir of support that existed for a communitarian revolution. Pétain's 16 'principes de la Communauté'—the evil of individualism, the equation of social rights and responsibilities, the primacy of the general interest over individual interests—were notions that would have gained wide acceptance at any point between 1940 and 1946.

However, there were always other dimensions to the National Revolution. Vichy's realism meant more than merely accepting the defeat as a *fait accompli*. It lapsed inexorably into defeatism.

[15] See his interesting speech to the CSEIC's meeting of 6 July 1943, in AN, F12 10143.
[16] For Pétain's views on the role of the state, see his article in the *Revue Universelle*, 1 Jan. 1941 *(Actes de écrits*, pp. 478–81); and his speech to the inaugural session of the Comité d'Organisation Professionnelle, 4 June 1941 *(Actes et écrits*, pp. 495–7).

The domestic policy that epitomized this lowering of national ambition was Pétain's call for a halt to France's industrialization and a return to a more rural and artisanal society. In the eyes of the regime's opponents, the *retour à la terre* quickly became the symbol of all that was most defeatist and retrograde in the National Revolution. As a result, it has often been presented as the product of one wing within Vichy—the traditionalist-corporatist ideologues who wanted to turn the clock back to the *ancien régime*. In fact, the pessimism that the *retour à la terre* expressed infected all factions within the regime. The following recommendation, for example, was drafted by a group of men within the Conseil Supérieur de l'Économie Industrielle et Commerciale, who have been flatteringly portrayed as the 'modernizers' of the État Français:

It would be a great mistake, for example in the sector of heavy industry, to try to work on the same order of magnitude as countries better endowed with raw materials. It would be an equally great mistake to continue to sacrifice that fund of peasant qualities which is the foundation of the French temperament.[17]

The modernizers and the technocrats might have doubted whether it would actually be possible to turn back the clock, but they certainly shared Pétain's assumption about the continuing moral and social importance of a large rural sector and were equally pessimistic about France's chances of competing with such industrial giants as Germany, the Soviet Union, and the USA.

Even more damaging to its claim to be a force for renewal than its defeatism was Vichy's determination to exclude from the *pays réel* large sections of the population (notably Jews, freemasons, communists, and immigrants). The organic community that the National Revolution sought to promote was also a homogeneous, purified community. No text is more revealing in this respect than the radio broadcast that Pétain made on 9 October 1940. In praising the legislative record of the previous few months, the head of state began his enumeration of *achievements* as follows: 'The revision of naturalizations, the law [limiting] access to certain professions, the dissolution of secret societies, the pursuit of those

---

[17] 'La Politique économique et les problèmes du Plan: rapport préliminaire aux travaux de la Commission No 3 [du Conseil Supérieur de l'Économie Industrielle et Commerciale], 25 Juin 1943', 21–2, in AN, F12 10144.

responsible for our disaster'.[18] From the very outset, the National
Revolution relinquished the high ground of national unity by
dividing the population into good and bad, French and anti-
French.[19] The regime of realists innocent of politics and ideology
proved in practice to be the opposite. Maurrasians and other right-
wing ideologues in Vichy were suddenly in a position to act upon
the prejudices and aversions which they had long expressed in
print. They did so with a vengeance. At the same time, the
regime's actions reflected the fact that after the summer of 1940
Vichy derived a disproportionate amount of its support from
certain sectors of society (the church, the bourgeoisie, the
patronat). Given the troubled end of the Third Republic and the
deep divisions in French society—as one Vichy official put it in
1942, 'Neither the *patrons* nor the unions have forgotten 1936'[20]—
the social and political bases of the regime were bound to assert
themselves. From its earliest days, Vichy made clear its intention
to take revenge on the Popular Front[21]—both the leaders like
Blum whom it would attempt to try at Riom and the policies which
it reversed or sought to undermine. In this campaign virtually no
aspect of national life was left unpoliticized. Supporters of the
National Revolution blamed the Republic—and especially the
republican left—for everything from population decline (they
found a correlation between regions which voted left and those
with low birth-rates[22]) to the crisis of the French economy. As for
foreign affairs, vichyites may have continued to believe that their
policy was the only pragmatic one and the only one that could
restore for France 'order as they conceive it and greatness as they
imagine it'.[23] But, even as they were priding themselves on their
realism, events were turning them into perverse idealists. The
reality of the war that they had thought almost finished in June
1940 gradually changed, and they proved unable or unwilling to
make a pragmatic adjustment in policy.

[18] *Actes et écrits*, p. 467.
[19] Henri Michel, *Vichy année 40* (Paris, 1966), 150.
[20] Untitled report by M. Jean Dollfuss concerning a dispute at the SAGEM
factory in Montluçon, mid-1942, in AN, F22 1842.
[21] It is worth noting that, as early as the beginning of July 1940, Pétain was
telling the US ambassador that 'He intended to dismiss every politician who had
been connected with the Blum government' (*FRUS, 1940*, ii. 464).
[22] Maurice Beauchamp, *Pour la rénovation française: bases* (Paris, 1941), 34–6.
[23] Olivier Wormser, *Les Origines doctrinales de la 'Révolution Nationale'* (Paris,
1971), 29.

By mid-1942 the National Revolution had thus received two fatal blows. The État Français had failed in its declared aim of mobilizing the nation behind its vision of renovation-before-liberation (a vision which had seemed feasible to many people in 1940, but by 1942 seemed absurd). Meanwhile, a decisive shift in the likely outcome of the war had undermined one of the regime's original assumptions. If that was not enough, this regime so totally unencumbered with parties, parliaments, and trade unions had proved incapable of transforming its ideological blueprint into reality. No doubt this was partly a consequence of the ideological differences among supporters of the National Revolution: the fifteen months of sterile dispute that preceded the creation of the Labour Charter of October 1941 testified to the damage that such divisions could do. The root cause of the National Revolution's failure, however, lay in the very circumstances that had seemed to make it so necessary in 1940: defeat and occupation. Far from being an ideology of pragmatism, the National Revolution proved to be an ideology undone by pragmatism. At every point that the exigencies of administering a semi-occupied nation came into conflict with the theory of the National Revolution, the latter gave way. The supposedly strong but limited state, for example, came to exercise control over the entire economy. Likewise, the anti-capitalist and anti-trust rhetoric of Pétainist corporatism came to be contradicted by the Comités d'Organisation that Vichy itself had set up in August 1940: these 'temporary' expedients enabled the state and the large capitalist interests, acting in collusion, to direct the economy, while the corporatist institutions of the Labour Charter remained mere phantoms.

The demise of the National Revolution did not stem the flow of ideas about renovation that it had unleashed. If anything, in fact, the regime's failure to realize its ideas only stimulated the planners and theorists. The latter felt compelled, at regular intervals, to 'relaunch' the revolution that Pétain had first launched in 1940. The sentiments that the Secretary-General of one important committee (Gérard Bardet of the CSEIC) expressed at one of his committee's meetings in 1942 were frequently heard in, Vichy think-tanks:

I had the opportunity to go to Vichy some days ago . . . I met there with some very high-ranking people, and I must tell you that there are high expectations of the Conseil Supérieur de l'Économie.

Why? Because in August 1940 professional organization had a truly revolutionary momentum behind it, but in two years . . . it has lost all its force . . .[24]

Caught in this endless cycle of expectation and disillusionment, the ideologues and technicians of the National Revolution were nothing if not tenacious. The thirteenth committee of the CSEIC—dealing with technical research—convened for the first time at the end of June 1944.[25] The economic planners in the DGEN continued to work, despite the indifference of the regime, until the summer of 1944. To the end various figures in Vichy persisted in taking seriously Pétain's constitution-making mandate (granted by the vote of 10 July 1940). Between July and December 1943 a small committee drafted a new constitution which was signed by Pétain in January 1944. Similarly, many of the corporatist and communitarian study groups continued to chew over the principles of the new society that Pétain had announced in 1940. On two occasions in 1943, for example, 200 or so representatives of groups interested in communitarian ideas (syndicalists, small businessmen, Social Catholics, corporatist intellectuals) met at Mont-Dore, in an attempt to synthesize their views into a common programme.[26] As late as May 1944 Pétain's staff were planning another such meeting.[27]

The 200 communitarians who met at Mont-Dore were still willing to operate under the auspices of the regime. Many others who had welcomed the National Revolution in 1940 drifted away from it entirely. Perhaps the most celebrated group of this kind were the personalists associated with Emmanuel Mounier's journal *Esprit*. In 1940 and 1941 *Esprit*'s philosophy came to dominate the National Revolution's 'leadership school' at Uriage. In the summer and autumn of 1940 the views of Mounier and the personalists seemed to converge with aspects of the National Revolution. Both delivered a total condemnation of the Third

[24] 'Réunion générale des rapporteurs: allocution de Monsieur Gérard Bardet, Secrétaire Général', 3 Nov. 1942, in AN, F12 10143.
[25] AN, F22, 1834.
[26] The proceedings of the first meeting were published under the title *Vers la révolution communautaire* (Paris, 1943).
[27] Vice-Amiral Fernet, *Aux côtés du maréchal Pétain: souvenirs, 1940–1944* (Paris, 1953), 239.

Republic. There Mounier was even willing to acknowledge that the maurrasians had been right and *Esprit* wrong:

From the outset, we have not ceased to denounce liberal parliamentary democracy. But it was a sort of courtesy extended to a truth of secondary importance, if not of second rate. We believed that democracy was a parasite on France . . . we did not realize that it was eating away at her like vermin, as surely as the spiritual sickness or the social disorder was eating away at her.[28]

Esprit had the same intuition as the vichyites that it was possible to 'penser la défaite',[29] in other words think through its implications and thereby turn it to France's ultimate advantage. It had the same idea that inter-war France had been living in a dream-world and that the defeat—painful as it was—had at least revealed the true condition of France. 'In yesterday's unreal world, nothing engaged properly: no new beginning was possible, and for almost ten years we had the feeling of not being able to get a grip on our country. . . . The truth, for all its cruelty, liberates. Today's painful France is also a concrete, real France.'[30] Mounier described as 'healthy' the prevailing reaction (which the National Revolution claimed to incarnate) 'against intellectual narcissism, aestheticism, verbalism, and sentimental generalities'.[31] The themes which he offered at the beginning of 1941 as the inspiration for a French youth movement echoed (at least superficially) many of Pétain's precepts: 'we do not look for our salvation from Germany or from England . . . but from ourselves'; 'Our revolution . . . is a discovery of community'; 'We want to restore a civilization of the whole man'; 'We want to restore the taste for a job well done'.[32]

The equation that the founder of Uriage (a Catholic patriot called Pierre de Segonzac) and many others drew between the ideology of the National Revolution and the philosophy of personalism was, therefore, a natural one. As time progressed, however, it became increasingly difficult to sustain the comparison.

[28] Mounier, 'D'une France à l'autre', *Esprit*, 94 (Nov. 1940), 4–5.

[29] Jean Lacroix, 'Nation et révolution', ibid. 11.

[30] Ibid. 13.

[31] 'Programme pour le mouvement de jeunesse français', *Esprit*, 96 (Jan. 1941), 153. The convergence between the realism of the National Revolution and various non-conformist ideologies which had emerged at the beginning of the 1930s (one of which was Mounier's personalism) has been noted by J.-L. Loubet del Bayle, *Les Non-conformistes des années 30* (Paris, 1969), 405–6.

[32] 'Programme pour le mouvement de jeunesse français', pp. 161–7.

As has already been noted, glaring inconsistencies soon appeared
between the rhetoric of national reconciliation and regeneration
and the reality of Vichy policy. The mirage of renovation-before-
liberation faded, while the willingness of Vichy to co-operate with
the occupying authorities caused increasing uneasiness among
patriots like de Segonzac. As a consequence of these factors, 1941
and 1942 witnessed a gradual estrangement between Uriage and
Vichy, which culminated at the end of 1942 with Laval's decree
dissolving the school. Thereafter, the task of elaborating a
doctrine for the spiritual renewal of the nation—one of the tasks
that de Segonzac had assigned to the school in accordance with
Pétain's objective of moral renewal—was continued clandestinely,
ultimately in the *maquis*.[33]

The experience of *Esprit* and Uriage provides only one example
of a trajectory followed by many. As Kedward has noted, even
many resisters, who adamantly opposed Vichy's collaboration with
Germany, initially approved the concept of internal reform.[34] The
history of the National Revolution between 1940 and 1942 is one
of a movement which 'created expectations of change among many
who could not be identified with the nationalist Right' but then
allowed its own sectarianism to destroy this 'broad base of
tolerance'.[35]

There was more to Vichy than the National Revolution. In spite of
its failure to elaborate a coherent doctrine and convert it into
reality, the Vichy regime produced many legislative and administrative innovations. Though the majority of these dealt with
problems that were closely related to the war, it has long been
recognized that some of them had broader or longer-term
implications. The impact of Vichy reforms in particular areas of
policy will be discussed in Part II, but it may be useful at this point
to make some general observations about them.

The extent to which this *ad hoc* and, in the eyes of its successors,
illegitimate regime influenced the course of post-war events is (as
one historian has rightly observed) 'One of the most interesting

[33] W. D. Halls, *Youth of Vichy France* (Oxford, 1981), 308–25, and Raymond
Josse, 'L'Ecole des Cadres d'Uriage (1940–1942)', *Revue d'histoire de la Deuxième
Guerre Mondiale*, 61 (1966), 49–74. The doctrine of renewal that emerged from
Uriage was published after the Liberation: Gilbert Gadoffre, *Vers le style du XXe
siècle* (Paris, 1945).
[34] *Resistance in Vichy France* (Oxford, 1978), pp. 131–2.   [35] Ibid. 90.

debates in contemporary French history'.[36] The intriguing continuities between Vichy policies and post-war reforms were
sketched by Stanley Hoffmann over twenty years ago.[37] He noted
that Vichy's stress on family policy and youth was echoed after
1944 and that the organization of economic and social interests
which Vichy had initiated or accelerated helped to shape post-war
institutions representing *patrons*, farmers, *cadres*, and various
professional groups. He also suggested that, by relying on young
and dynamic businessmen, Vichy helped to promote a new
entrepreneurial and technocratic élite who were to prove vital to
the success of post-war modernization. Subsequently, Hoffmann's
sketch was fleshed out at a number of points. The work of Gordon
Wright and Isabel Boussard demonstrated how crucial Vichy's
Corporation Paysanne was in producing new leaders and new
attitudes in rural France.[38] Richard Kuisel produced evidence of
the link between Vichy's economic planning and the post-war
Monnet Plan. He also emphasized the important short-term
continuity between Vichy's economic control structures and those
operated by the post-Liberation regime.[39]

All these are instances in which what may be regarded as
significant post-war developments had their roots in Vichy
innovation. The État Français did not always have such a
beneficial effect. Within the economic sphere, it is possible to find
major sectors (such as shopkeeping) where Vichy reforms failed to
achieve modernization.[40] In other areas of policy, Vichy's zeal for
renewal was often counter-productive: it not only failed to
produce the effect that it sought but made the task of post-war
reformers more difficult. Might it not have been easier, in 1944, to
break down the left–right schism over Catholic schools, if Pétain's
ministers of education had not started giving them subsidies?
Might it not have been easier to frame a constitution with a strong
executive if the État Français had been a less autocratic regime?
Might not the post-war left have felt more comfortable about
retaining Offices Professionnels (the bodies which acted as

[36] Joseph Jones, 'Vichy France and Post-war Economic Modernization: The
Case of the Shopkeepers', *French Historical Studies*, 12 (1982), 541.
[37] *In Search of France* 2nd edn. (New York, 1965), 34–41.
[38] Boussard, *Vichy et la Corporation Paysanne* (Paris, 1980); Wright, *Rural
Revolution in France* (Stanford, 1964).
[39] *Capitalism and the State in Modern France* (Cambridge, 1981), 128–56.
[40] Jones, 'Vichy France and Post-war Economic Modernization', pp. 562–3.

intermediaries between industrial sectors and the government's economic ministries) if they had not been the successors to Vichy's Comités d'Organisation? These questions will be raised again later, but an issue that will not be raised again provides perhaps the classic instance of Vichy reformism backfiring: this was the case of regional reform.

By a law of 19 April 1941, Vichy had introduced 'regional prefects' to administer police and economic affairs in seventeen regions (groups of departments).[41] The inspiration for this law had been both ideological and pragmatic. On the one hand, it reflected Pétain's rhetoric about decentralization and the reinvigoration of provincial life (a rhetoric influenced by maurrasianism's preference for the organic region over the post-revolutionary department). On the other hand, it was conceived both as a practical response to immediate administrative problems (one that would allow the central authority in Vichy to exert a tighter supervision over the regions) and as a progressive reform replacing an outdated administrative unit with a more modern one. These two sets of aims—the one essentially traditionalist and the other modernizing—were bound to come into conflict, and the contradiction between the two contributed to the failure of this regional experiment. In the longer term, however, both aspects of Vichy regionalism contributed to the general disfavour of regionalist schemes among post-Liberation élites. After 1944, doctrines of administrative decentralization and reorganization were dogged by the image that Vichy had given regionalism—that of a reactionary ideology and a superfluous, inquisitorial bureaucracy. The regional *Commissaires de la République* to whom de Gaulle's Provisional Government entrusted the task of restoring order in the provinces were abolished in 1946, at least in part because they followed in the footsteps of Vichy's regional prefects.[42] This association was frustrating to those, like the *commissaire* Francis-Louis

[41] On Vichy's regionalism see Jean Bancal, *Les Circonscriptions administratives de la France* (Paris, 1945), 198–211; and Pierre Doueil, *L'Administration locale à l'épreuve de la guerre (1939–1949)* (Paris, 1950), 14–37.

[42] There were undoubtedly other factors involved—e.g. bureaucratic in-fighting and the strong desire to reaffirm national unity after four years which had not only divided the Resistance from Vichy but also (until Nov. 1942) the occupied zone from the unoccupied zone. The most thorough account of the *commissaires'* demise is given in Charles-Louis Foulon's fine study, *Le Pouvoir en province à la Libération* (Paris, 1975).

Closon, who believed that a remodelling of France's provincial administration was a vital step towards national renewal: 'It is indeed regrettable that pre-war inertia left Vichy with the privilege of introducing innovation, but the same is true of other creations of the post–1940 period, such as the Ministry of Industrial Production. Who could reasonably reproach this ministry with its original sin?'[43]

In the case of some Vichy reforms, the original sin did not deter post-Liberation élites from accepting change. In other areas—especially where there existed deep divisions among these élites and thus a potential for rapid politicization—the precedent of Vichy reformism could be a vital inhibiting factor. Ironically, in these areas, it might be argued that Vichy reformism did more damage to the cause of long-term renewal than did the divisive ideology of the National Revolution. Because this ideology quickly became associated with a foreign policy of collaboration and submission, it did far more damage to its advocates (especially the extreme Right)[44] than to the cause of renewal which it espoused and then parodied. This cause gradually deserted Vichy, as Vichy deserted it. The failure of the National Revolution was thus a beginning as well as an end: with its effective demise in 1942, both the ideal and the vocabulary of national renewal passed conclusively to those who were committed to the liberation of the *patrie*.[45] Even though aspects of Vichy's ideology and policy were to have a profound and long-lasting effect, it is fair to say that the rethinking of post-Liberation, as opposed to unliberated, France began in earnest in the period 1942–4—in the Resistance and in de Gaulle's Free France.

---

[43] Closon, *La Région, cadre d'un gouvernement moderne* (Paris, 1946), 41.

[44] Hoffmann, *In Search of France*, p. 44.

[45] For some perceptive comments on the transference of patriotic vocabulary from Vichy to the Resistance see Kedward, 'Patriots and Patriotism in Vichy France', pp. 189–91.

2

The Resistance: Liberation and Renovation[1]

EVEN in the early phase of organized resistance to the occupying forces (1940–2), there were certain resisters who combined their activism with an interest in post-war issues. The archives of the Comité d'Histoire de la Deuxième Guerre Mondiale record some of the efforts of such people. In October 1940 several educators created a study group called Maintenir, which drew up plans for reform of the national educational system.[2] In early 1941 a number of intellectuals, including Sartre and Merleau-Ponty, formed the movement Socialisme et Liberté, one of whose aims was to prepare the future constitution of liberated France.[3] In Toulouse, Marcel Abraham (a former aide to the pre-war Education Minister, Jean Zay) joined with Jean Cassou, Georges Friedmann, and Claude Aveline in a discussion group called the Club des Bouches Cousues ('Closed Mouths Club'), which proposed to trace 'the main lines of a sort of Resistance Charter'.[4] At the end of 1941 the Socialist resister André Philip met with prominent Resistance leaders in the southern zone and agreed to set up groups of anti-Vichy intellectuals 'so that they could prepare at once to draw up the political, economic, and social structure of the Fourth Republic'.[5] The network of groups that Philip established— in Grenoble, Montpellier, Avignon, Valence, Grasse, St Raphaël, Toulouse, Marseille, and Lyon—provided some of the personnel and a working precedent for a more ambitious Resistance think-tank, the Comité Général d'Études (CGE), which was created by

---

[1] This chapter will deal with the non-communist Resistance movements. The wartime programmes of the PCF and affiliated organizations will be discussed in ch. 4.

[2] 'Témoignage de M. Claude Bellanger', in AN, 72 AJ 68.

[3] 'Témoignage de Gustave Monod', ibid. 50. Sartre apparently took the task of writing a constitution very seriously: he produced a text of a hundred or so pages (of which, unfortunately, no copy survives). See Annie Cohen-Solal, *Sartre: A Life* (New York, 1987), 169.

[4] 'Témoignage de Marcel Abraham', AN, 72 AJ 55.

[5] 'Témoignage d'André Philip', ibid. 70.

de Gaulle's delegate in France, Jean Moulin, at the beginning of July 1942.[6]

It is important to emphasize, however, that this kind of endeavour was a decidedly minority activity, especially during the first two years of the Occupation. The Resistance was not born as a 'political' movement, that is to say as a movement constructed around a given political programme. For some, resisting was essentially a moral act—a rejection of the immorality of fascism (in the case of a group like the Catholic Témoignage Chrétien) or, as one resister later put it, an assertion of 'the inner law proclaimed by Antigone'.[7] For most people the initial reflex was a patriotic one: resisters wanted to do whatever they could to expel the invader. In its statement of intent the movement Libération-Sud declared:

We have objectives. We do not have a doctrine. We do not wish to have one at the moment. To construct a political system on doctrinal assumptions, there must be a foundation, a substructure: the geographic and economic form of a state, the elements of a nation. But today this foundation does not exist. . . . Tomorrow will be the time for political doctrines. Today our objective must be to escape the wretched condition of a conquered people.[8]

Even after the reactionary nature of the National Revolution and Vichy's slide into collaborationism had begun to politicize the Resistance, the main impetus and unifying force remained that of patriotism. A resister who joined the movement Défense de la France in July 1943 recalled that even then 'political questions did not interest those who joined: they were anti-German patriots, who wanted to inflict damage on the enemy but were scarcely bothered by purely political questions'.[9] This created what Claude Bourdet has called a 'snobisme activiste'.[10] The study of post-war reforms was dismissed by the majority of resisters as irrelevant to the main aim of carrying on the struggle against Germany.

Something of a turning-point in attitudes towards the future did occur in 1942 and the early months of 1943. With the allied

---

[6] On the CGE see Diane de Bellescize, *Les Neuf Sages de la Résistance* (Paris, 1979), *passim*.

[7] Jean Cassou, *La Mémoire courte* (Paris, 1953), 70.

[8] *Libération* (Southern zone), 1 (July 1941).

[9] 'Témoignage de Madame Michaut (Françoise de Rivière)', AN 72 AJ 50.

[10] *L'Aventure incertaine* (Paris, 1975), 390.

landings in North Africa and the Russian victory at Stalingrad, the end of the war suddenly seemed closer at hand. Furthermore, the movements' closer links to de Gaulle (and the latter's conflict in North Africa with the American-backed General Giraud, whose politics were barely distinguishable from those of Vichy) encouraged the Resistance to make its domestic political agenda more explicit. In 1942–3 the CGE began to prepare extensive studies of the various problems which were expected to confront France in the aftermath of liberation. The clandestine Resistance press also reflected the new interest in post-war issues. In November 1942 the newspaper *Défense de la France* asked for the first time: 'What does Défense de la France want to do after the country has been liberated?'[11] Three months later, a clandestine news-sheet announced that 'Already we can foresee the day when the nightmare of occupation will be lifted' and 'We must begin preparing for tomorrow today.'[12] By December 1943, *La Revue Libre* (a review circulated by the movement Franc–Tireur) was able to take pride in the fact that 'in the heat of the battle, amid the terror of the Gestapo and of Vichy . . . essays, political theses, draft constitutions, programmes are springing up almost everywhere, circulating, being read and discussed'.[13]

Nevertheless, even in the final eighteen months of the Occupation (which produced the bulk of the Resistance's post-war planning) the movements never concentrated their energies primarily on drawing up a coherent programme for post-war reconstruction.[14] To the end the Resistance showed a marked reluctance to address this issue. Resisters were torn between two conflicting imperatives. On the one hand, the end of the war was looming ever closer and there were obvious incentives to prepare for its arrival, especially if the non-communist Resistance wished to distinguish itself from the Communist party and prolong its role beyond the Liberation. On the other hand, the conditions of resisters' activity demanded that the broadest possible front be maintained against Germany

[11] No. 21.
[12] *Demain: liberté–égalité–fraternité* (Feb. 1943). 1943 also saw the Catholics of Témoignage Chrétien moving towards 'un engagement pour l'après-guerre'. See Renée Bédarida, *Les Armes de l'esprit* (Paris, 1977), 175.
[13] No. 1, pp. 2–3.
[14] For a statistical analysis of one clandestine paper's output (which confirms the argument made above), see Dominique Veillon, *Le Franc–Tireur* (Paris, 1977), 272.

and Vichy. Disunity was regarded as the ultimate sacrilege and it was recognized that defining specific programmes—in other words making unambiguous political choices—would inevitably produce splits.[15] The more specific the plans, the more difficult it was bound to become to maintain a united front. Furthermore, as resisters were well aware, they had absolutely no control over the timing and extent of liberation. Since there were good reasons not to be too specific and since it was impossible to predict the precise circumstances of liberation, the Resistance tended to pay little attention to how the revolution it advocated would actually come about. It concentrated instead on publicizing the general aspirations which most resisters held in common.

In February 1944, the movement Défense de la France sent a letter to de Gaulle, which defined these aspirations thus: 'the idea of Republic, the idea of Socialism, and the idea of Nation'.[16] The founding charter of the Mouvement de Libération Nationale (MLN), which represented several of the major Resistance organizations—Combat, Franc–Tireur, Libération-Sud, Résistance, and Défense de la France—echoed the formula: 'The Resistance movements which make up the Movement of National Liberation have decided to seek an agreement on a programme for the future founded on the following principles: the Republic, Socialism, the Nation.'[17]

The Resistance's republicanism encompassed a number of ideas. First and foremost, it expressed resisters' commitment to a democratic system of government, a commitment which had wavered in the aftermath of July 1940 but grew progressively stronger as the war continued. Second, it was a demand for a certain kind of Republic: one which ensured an ethical political and public life, which produced efficient government, and which was socially progressive. In short, the Resistance sought 'une quatrième République pure, efficace, sociale'.[18] This republicanism had a strong comparative connotation. The Fourth Republic that the Resistance proposed to establish was envisaged as a system which would avoid the glaring faults of its two predecessors.

[15] See P. Viannay ['Indomitus'], *Nous sommes les rebelles* (Paris, 1945), 78.
[16] A copy of the letter is in AN, 72 AJ 50.
[17] Text in AN, F1a 3755.
[18] Henri Michel, *Les Courants de pensée de la Résistance* (Paris, 1962), 363–75.

Its proceedings would be more disinterested than the sordid machinations of 1930s parliaments or the comings and goings in Vichy's Hôtel du Parc. It would be more concerned to achieve social justice than was the hamstrung Third Republic or the reactionary État Français. At the same time, the example of strong foreign powers with different but equally functional regimes (Soviet Russia, parliamentary Britain, presidential America) seemed to show that an effective system of government was a prerequisite for national power. The Resistance's constitutional and political doctrine emerged in a period of extreme uncertainty and confusion. The parliamentary system had failed France in the inter-war period, and yet resisters found themselves fighting for the human rights and political freedoms which democracy alone seemed to guarantee. In Vichy, a government which, to general approval, had promised to inject more *autorité* into the French constitution had succeeded only in demonstrating why authoritarian regimes were unacceptable in France. All the thinking of the Resistance movements revolved around the problem of finding a system which synthesized personal liberties with the disciplined state apparatus which seemed to have been achieved by other nations.[19] The Fourth Republic was to be this synthesis, combining 'what is efficient in totalitarian systems with what is noble in liberal ideology'.[20]

The Resistance saw three converging routes to this synthesis. The first route was institutional. All the Resistance movements accepted that some of the responsibility for the catastrophe of 1940 lay with the defective institutions of the Third Republic. Some groups, like the Organisation Civile et Militaire (OCM) and Défense de la France, saw these defects as incurable features of French parliamentarianism.[21] Others who were closer to the republican mainstream none the less wondered whether France should experiment with a new form of democracy closer to a

---

[19] For a particularly interesting formulation of these ideas, see the anonymous 'Essai sur les principes directeurs du Gouvernement de la France après sa libération', in AN, F1a 3791.

[20] *Cahiers de Défense de la France*, 1 (Mar. 1944), 7.

[21] For a summary of the OCM's constitutional views see Blocq-Mascart, *Chroniques de la Résistance* (Paris, 1945), 109–30. For the presidential blueprint of Défense de la France, see *Défense de la France*, 44 (25 Feb. 1944). Both are discussed in greater length in ch. 5 below.

presidential system.[22] As the Liberation approached, however, most of these qualms about the parliamentary system disappeared. By 1944 there was relatively broad agreement that the parliamentary regime—with modifications—was the best alternative. This was the view of the Socialist CAS[23] and of the Christian Democrats in the Resistance.[24] It was also the view of the CGE: Michael Debré, the main author of the CGE's constitutional blueprint, dismissed the possibility of an American-style presidential system.[25]

When it came to making specific institutional proposals, the distinction between advocates of a parliamentary regime and those who suggested a presidential system was not, in fact, very significant. Most resisters agreed that ministerial instability and the weakness of the executive branch had been defects in the Third Republic. One remedy—suggested by 'presidentialists' like the OCM and Défense de la France and 'parliamentarians' like Paul Coste-Floret and André Hauriou—was to increase the authority of the President of the Republic by enlarging the electoral college.[26] Another proposal, which gained even more widespread support (including that of the Socialists, the CGE, Combat, Défense de la France, and a number of other Resistance movements), was to encourage the use of a power of dissolution, which would allow the electorate to adjudicate differences between the executive and the legislature.[27] A third idea, perhaps

---

[22] See Léon Blum's essay, *A l'échelle humaine*. His position was echoed by Nicolas Moreau (*nom de plume* of Amédée Dunois) in *Le Populaire*, 18 (1 Apr. 1943).

[23] Charles Dumas, 'Rapport sur le projet de constitution proposé par le Comité Exécutif du Parti Socialiste', in AN, 72 AJ 70. See also the anonymous 'Vers un grand parti du travail', ibid. 3.

[24] Paul Coste-Floret, 'Quelques idées sur la constitution de demain', *Combat* (*Alger*), 7 Aug. 1943. Quoted in Michel and Mirkine-Guetzévitch, *Les Idées politiques et sociales de la Résistance* (Paris, 1954), 280–2.

[25] See Debré's memoirs, *Trois républiques pour une France* (Paris, 1984), 212; and his wartime book (written with Emmanuel Monick under the pseydonyms Jacquier–Bruère) *Refaire la France* (Paris, 1945), 118–20.

[26] See e.g. the CGE's 'Project de constitution', in AN, F1a 3733; André Hauriou, *Vers une doctrine de la Résistance: le socialisme humaniste* (Algiers, 1944), 162–3; an anonymous 'projet politique' (identified only as MUR/18/36600) in AN, F1a 3791; *Cahiers de Défense de la France*, 1 (Mar. 1944), 44; Coste-Floret, 'Quelques idées sur la constitution de demain', in Michel and Mirkine-Guetzévitch, *Les Idées politiques et sociales de la Résistance*, p. 282; Blocq-Mascart, *Chroniques de la Résistance*, p. 127.

[27] See e.g. Dumas's 'Rapport sur le projet de constitution proposé par le Comité Exécutif du Parti Socialiste', AN, 72 AJ 70; MLN, 'Projet de programme', ibid 64;

the most widely canvassed of all, was to reorganize the political system around a small number of disciplined ideological blocs. These three or four parties would separate into a government and an opposition, and ministerial stability would be assured by the continuity of voting within the two sides.[28]

These were not the only institutional suggestions made by the Resistance. The non-communist left (CAS, MLN, Défense de la France) and the technocratic OCM proposed to eliminate the 'reactionary' Senate and institute a single-chamber parliament. The CGE and Combat favoured a bicameral arrangement. Various groups recommended a Supreme Court to control the constitutionality of laws.[29] Some Resistance organs (including *Bir-Hakeim, Libérer et Fédérer, and Combat (Alger)*) had more unorthodox corporatist blueprints.[30] There were suggestions that the parliament or one chamber of it should be chosen by trade-union representatives. Others proposed assemblies which combined elected representatives with nominated experts.[31]

The second of the three routes to constitutional renovation lay through a replacement of political élites. Because it was itself such a minority movement, the Resistance was fascinated by ideas about élites and élite action. It constantly ascribed the defeat of 1940 to the failure of the old ruling class. By ruling class the resisters meant the bourgeoisie in general (including the army command, business and commercial classes, and the press), but they certainly did not spare the political élites of the Third Republic's last parliament. Most resisters placed their main hopes for post-war renewal in a new political élite. In other words, they

Cahiers de Défense de la France, 1 (Mar. 1944), 54–5; 'Projet de constitution établi par le CGE', in AN, F1a 3733; Blocq-Mascart, *Chroniques de la Résistance*, p. 130.

[28] See André Philip's letter of 5 Apr. 1943, in AN, 72 AJ 70; *Le Populaire*, 31 (Feb. 1944); Léon Blum, 'Projet de reconstruction du parti', AN, 72 AJ 70; *Bir-Hakeim*, 4 (14 July 1943); *Résistance*, 19 (5 Nov. 1943); *Défense de la France*, 32 (5 May 1943). The idea was also raised by Jean Moulin at the inaugural meeting of the CNR on 27 May 1943 (according to Daniel Cordier's *conférence* in *Jean Moulin et le Conseil National de la Résistance* (Paris, 1983), 26.

[29] See the 'projet de programme de la Ligue', AN, 72 AJ 70 (the league included the CGT, the Radical party, and the CAS). See also *Défense de la France*, 33 (20 May 1943).

[30] See *Bir-Hakeim*, 10 (Feb.–Mar. 1944); *Libérer et Fédérer*, 15–16 (Feb. 1944), in Michel and Mirkine-Guetzévitch, *Les Idées politiques et sociales de la Résistance*, pp. 164–6; *Combat (Alger)*, 7 Aug. 1943, ibid. 281.

[31] See e.g the anonymous 'Projet de réorganisation politique de la France', AN, F1a 3791.

saw themselves as the nation's best hope for the future: 'In the aftermath of the Liberation, France will ask each of her sons: what did you do in the time of shame and misery? And on the basis of their reply—without taking social class, party, or creed into account—she will designate those who will have the honour of representing her.'[32]

As the Occupation progressed and some of the pre-war parties—especially those on the left—showed signs of reviving, this notion of a Resistance élite hardened into a proposal for a post-war party to represent the Resistance movements. A 'commission de programmes' (including prominent resisters such as Léo Hamon, Philippe Viannay, J.-D. Jurgensen, and Albert Bayet) raised the possibility of a non-communist, socialist third force, as did Défense de la France and the OCM.[33] It was also raised in *Les Cahiers Politiques*, the CGE's review,[34] and by elements of the Socialist party.[35] The attraction of this idea of a progressive but non-communist Resistance party was powerful. To many resisters it appeared the only practicable method of salvaging the organizations which had been established during the Occupation or forestalling the re-emergence of the old political parties.

The Resistance's third route to constitutional renovation involved a moralization of French politics. Without a renewal of civic spirit, it was argued, the general interest would never predominate over individual or factional interest.[36] Typical of much Resistance writing was *La Voix du Nord*'s insistence that institutional change alone would not suffice: 'It will also be necessary . . . to create a new mentality, drive out the false prophets, remove from power the travelling salesmen of politics, the incompetent, and all those

---

[32] *Combat*, 39 (Jan. 1943). For similar sentiments see *Libération* (Southern zone), 32 (1 Aug. 1943); Viannay, *Nous sommes les rebelles*; 'Projet de manifeste de "Ceux de la Résistance" communiqué par M. J. de Vogué', in AN, 72 AJ 42.

[33] 'Suite du témoignage de Léo Hamon', ibid. For *Défense de la France*, see *Cahiers de Défense de la France*, 1 (Mar. 1944), 5–7. For the OCM see the movement's 'Étude sur l'avenir politique de la résistance', a copy of which is in AN, 72 AJ 68.

[34] No. 3 (Aug. 1943), 8.

[35] This was the argument of an anonymous socialist study entitled: 'Vers un grand parti du travail' (a copy of which is in AN, 72 AJ 3). It was also, of course, the argument of Pierre Brossolette.

[36] See e.g. the 'Déclaration du Mouvement de Libération Nationale', in AN, 72 AJ 70.

who regarded politics as a way of making it.'[37] Since the Vichy regime had orchestrated the denigration of the Third Republic's leaders, the Resistance was treading on dangerous ground here. Occasionally it showed that it was sensitive to the danger of echoing Vichy propaganda: 'We have expressed our hostility towards self-serving campaigns directed against the Third Republic,' wrote the editorialist of *Libération*.[38] But in essence the Resistance shared Vichy's low estimate of the ethics of the old political élites.[39] The superiority of the new Resistance élite—according to its own estimate—lay precisely in its personal integrity: 'The revolutionaries of tomorrow are first and foremost men of character, men who are self-controlled, who refuse to feed adoring platitudes to the crowd, who disdain cowardly submission to squalid monetary interests.'[40]

In brief outline, this was the tripartite programme for political renovation proposed by the leadership of the Resistance movements and parties. While it is relatively easy to describe the political doctrines of the Resistance leaders and of the intellectuals who drew up draft constitutions, the extent to which the rank and file held the same views is far more problematical. How widely, for example, were these various ideas about constitutional and political change discussed and how far were they accepted by the mass of resisters?

One source that provides some tentative answers is a set of Resistance responses to a questionnaire which was sent out by the gaullist CFLN's Commissariat à l'Intérieur in October 1943. The thirty-five replies, which were subsequently filed in the papers of the *commissariat*,[41] came from different parts of metropolitan France and were diverse in content. Some were very brief, others extended; some expressed the opinion of one resister, others the views of several resisters, or even (at any rate so it was claimed) those of an entire organization. Taken as a whole, these responses throw an interesting light on the Resistance's political ideology.

---

[37] No. 61 (Oct.–Nov. 1943).

[38] *Libération* (Southern zone), 32 (1 Aug. 1943).

[39] See e.g. *Libérer et Fédérer*, 5 (Jan. 1943).

[40] Robert Tenaille (pseudonym of Robert Salmon), quoted by Michel and Mirkine-Guetzévitch, *Les Idées politiques et sociales de la Résistance*, p. 158.

[41] These thirty-five responses have been found in AN, F1a 3754 and F1a 3756. It is quite possible that other responses (possibly a considerable number) exist somewhere else in the archives, but I was not able to locate them.

What emerged clearly from them was that, although there was overwhelming support for a republic (as opposed to a monarchy or a dictatorship), there were strong traces of anti-parliamentarianism within the Resistance. More than half of the respondents criticized pre-war politicians for their 'inefficiency . . . weakness . . . demagogy'.[42] A characteristic response parodied the resistance record of the old Socialist party militant 'who shouts "death to the Boches" in cafés where there are no Germans, but does not give a penny for resisters on the run.'[43] Several respondents attacked pre-war parties for having degenerated into 'mutual aid societies run at the expense of the general interest'.[44] It was both an attack on prominent republican personalities and on parliamentarianism *tout court*. There was a general hostility towards the 'métier parlementaire',[45] and a good deal of support for non-traditional republican systems: seven respondents recommended at least one legislative 'corporative chamber', and eight others proposed heavily technocratic systems.

The synthesis between authority and liberty which the intellectuals and aspiring constitution-makers wanted to find in the Resistance did not emerge clearly from the responses to this questionnaire. What emerged was closer to schizophrenia. On the one hand, there were elements of a progressive parliamentarianism. A number of respondents echoed the specific proposals which were being published in Resistance newspapers and programmes. Six mentioned the need for greater ministerial stability. Ten recommended increasing the powers of the President of the Republic. Four demanded a party system of three or four groups, while four others suggested that greater use should be made of the right of dissolution. On the other hand, many of the political views which were expressed seem closer to those of Vichy than to mainstream French republicanism. One response recommended that one of the two legislative assemblies should be a 'chambre de techniciens'.[46] Another proposed that the National Assembly should include three hundred members, 'of whom one-third would be elected in political style, one-third would be elected by employer and worker organizations, and one-third would be chosen by the country's moral and spiritual forces'.[47] Five respondents echoed the anti-

[42] QGS/1/35004, AN, F1a 3756
[43] LIA/19/35000, ibid.
[44] QGS/1/35004 bis, ibid.
[45] QGS/1/35003, ibid.
[46] ATE/6/35001, ibid.
[47] QGS/1/35004, ibid.

semitism (and other prejudices) of Vichy: one described Mendès-France as 'Jewish, too clever by half';[48] another demanded 'the relegation of all Jews, freemasons, former generals, and former politicians';[49] while a third wrote that 'The Jews should be kept out of all governmental and public functions. . . . if there is some disapproval of the harassment, deportation, etc., to which they have been subjected, no one wants to see them reappear as before the war'.[50]

Few resisters seem to have believed that a new constitution would solve the nation's problems. Most placed their faith either in a new political élite or in socio-economic structural reforms. The idea that the main focus should be placed on reforming the French economy and French society was mentioned by several of the questionnaire respondents. It was an idea epitomized by the CNR Common Programme of March 1944, which made fifteen proposals for social and economic reform but confined its political programme to the demand for 'a democracy which matches continuity of government action with effective accountability before the representatives of the people'.[51] Perhaps because there seemed no obvious constitutional way forward after the dual failure of the Republic and the État Français, resisters paid more attention to the potential for social and economic change.

Although many resisters had not been socialists before the war, the keystone of their economic and social philosophy was socialism. The sources of this Resistance socialism were diverse. In part it grew naturally out of the view that France had been betrayed by the bourgeoisie in 1940. In part it reflected the prominence of the working class and its representatives within the Resistance and, on the other side, the growing identification between the Occupation forces and French capitalism. On an intellectual level, it reflected the prestige of Soviet planning (especially after 1942) and a lingering sense that the depression of the 1930s had proved the bankruptcy of liberal capitalism. Like the

---

[48] QGS/1/35004 bis, ibid.   [49] MIX/3/35100, ibid.

[50] ATE/13/35000 (VII), ibid. Anti-semitism was not unknown in Resistance publications. See e.g. the OCM's controversial views, as expressed in the first cahier of June 1942.

[51] The text of the Charter has been reproduced in several places, e.g. Claire Andrieu, *Le Programme Commun de la Résistance: des idées dans la guerre* (Paris, 1984), 168–75.

republicanism of its political doctrines, the Resistance's socialism was envisaged as a synthesis. While the republican synthesis combined liberty and authority, the socialist synthesis combined elements of economic liberalism with elements of collectivism. *Libération*, for example, glimpsed it 'Between the last perilous starts of an old moribund capitalism and the youthful excesses of a marxism still too sectarian and rigid',[52] while *Franc–Tireur* pictured it 'as far from capitalist disorder and petit-bourgeois egoism as from totalitarian dictatorship'.[53] It was an economic synthesis, mixing state direction and ownership with varying degrees of autonomy for producers and consumers. But it was also a geo-political synthesis: it reconciled the philosophy of 'revolutionary' systems (notably the Russian one) and the 'conservative' systems of the Anglo-American world.[54]

This synthesis contained two sets of ideas, one relating to the role of individuals—especially the working class—within the socio-economic system, and the other to the role of the state.

The Resistance proposed to alter the economic role of the individual from one that was essentially passive—the worker as cog, the bourgeois as parasite—to one that would be activist. In the new society, the *engagement* of the resister would be a model for all producers. Most Resistance tracts and newspapers advocated increased responsibility for workers and cadres both at the factory and at the company level. The less radical, like René Courtin (author of the CGE's economic report), talked of participation on company boards,[55] or 'an active role in the technical running of businesses . . . as well as a right to consider and advise on their economic and financial management'.[56] The CNR charter, striving for the common ground, demanded 'the right for workers possessing the requisite qualifications to gain access to positions of management and administration within their firm'. The more radical groups like Libérer et Fédérer advocated that all large,

---

[52] *Libération* (Southern zone), 26 (10 Apr. 1943).
[53] No. 29 (1 Mar. 1944).
[54] For this idea of a revolution reconciling East and West, see *Cahiers du Témoignage Chrétien*, 28–9 (July 1944), 21–2; and *Franc–Tireur*, 29 (1 Mar. 1944).
[55] *Rapport sur la politique économique d'après-guerre* (Algiers, 1944), 23–5.
[56] This was the suggestion of Emile Laffon, who was an agent of the Commissaire à l'Intérieur, André Philip. The text of Laffon's 'projet de programme commun' is in Andrieu, *Le Programme Commun de la Résistance*, pp. 141–4.

non-nationalized firms should be run by boards entirely elected by the workers.[57]

An even greater emphasis was put on a democratization of national economic structures. While vilifying Vichy's Comités d'Organisation, almost all elements of the Resistance acknowledged the utility of professional and interprofessional organizations. Ideas on this subject varied from group to group. For some (e.g. Courtin and Défense de la France) the professional organizations would not direct or control economic activity. Their role would be to gather information or act as an advisory body to the government.[58] For others, like the OCM and a group of trade-unionists in Lyon, professional organizations would play a much more active role: this would generally involve acting as the agent either of a National Economic Council or of the state.[59]

In general, the professional organization was one of the most characteristic products of the Resistance's socialist synthesis. Theoretically, it could involve all workers in the process of drawing up and executing a national economic policy. But at the same time it would allow the state to exercise a more stringent and extensive control over the economy than had been possible before the war. This second aim reflected the other main principle of Resistance socialism: what was required, in addition to popular participation, was a greater degree of state intervention in the economy.

The main structural components of the economic reform which the Resistance wanted the post-war state to adopt were national planning and nationalization. A sample of seventeen different proposals for the post-war economy (dating from 1943 and 1944) shows general support for both these measures: all but two groups mentioned planning and all without exception supported some extension of state ownership.[60]

---

[57] Michel and Mirkine-Guetzévitch, *Les Idées politiques et sociales de la Résistance*, p. 166.

[58] For Défense de la France see 'Défense de la France: la politique économique d'après-guerre', AN, 72 AJ 564. See also Courtin, *Rapport sur la politique économique*, pp. 25–6.

[59] For the OCM see Blocq-Mascart, *Chroniques de la Résistance*, pp. 359–72. See also *Exposé et commentaires du projet syndical d'économie moderne dénommé Charte de la Démocratie, dressé et présenté par l'Union Départementale des Syndicats Confédérés de la région lyonnaise* (Lyon, 1944).

[60] The proposals are from the following sources: *Franc-Tireur*, 14 (20 Jan. 1943); Courtin, *Rapport sur la politique économique*; *Libérer et Fédérer* (Feb.

The content of the *planisme* varied considerably. René Courtin argued in favour of a plan for the period of reconstruction, but did not accept the principle of a permanently planned economy.[61] Others, like the OCM, the Socialist Jules Moch, and the trade-unionists in Lyon, believed that planning would be a permanent feature, indeed that it would be the organizing principle of a managed economy.[62] In these projects fully fledged planning structures (albeit different ones) were elaborated. In most other Resistance programmes, there was at least a generalized commitment to the principle of planning. This signified a determination that the scope of state intervention should extend beyond the inevitably restricted field of nationalized industries.

On the question of nationalization, there was a broad measure of agreement about the sectors which would be subject to it. Of the economic programmes mentioned above, fifteen specified the sectors to be nationalized. Of these, thirteen included banking and insurance, ten included gas and electricity (while three others used the expression 'public services', which presumably meant energy and public transport), ten included mining industries, and seven specified the railways or communications. The CNR charter was close to the overall consensus when it recommended the nationalization of energy industries, coal mining, insurance, and banking.

It was envisaged that the effect of these reforms—the establishment of democratic worker participation and professional organization, the introduction of a nationalized sector and of a planned

1944); CAS, *Le Populaire*, 16 (16 Jan. 1943–1 Feb. 1943); CAS (11 Dec. 1943), in Michel and Mirkine-Guetzévitch, *Les Idées politiques et sociales de la Résistance*, pp. 202–8; CAS, 'Programme d'action de la Résistance' (Mar. 1944), in Andrieu, *Le Programme Commun de la Résistance*, pp. 160–7; Front National, 'Ce que veut le Front National', in Michel and Mirkine-Guetzévitch, *Les Idées politiques et sociales de la Résistance*, pp. 162–3; Front National, 'Projet d'une Charte de la Résistance proposée par le FN' (Nov. 1943), in Andrieu, *Le Programme Commun de la Résistance*, pp. 145–8; Émile Laffon, 'Projet de programme commun' (July 1943), ibid. 141–4; CNR, 'Programme d'Action de la Résistance' (15 Mar. 1944); *Combat*, 54 (Feb. 1944); *Bir-Hakeim*, 10 (Feb.–Mar. 1944); MLN, 'Programme' (n.d.), in AN, 72 AJ 64; MLN, 'Programme d'action de la Résistance' (Feb. 1944), in Andrieu, *Le Programme Commun de la Résistance*, pp. 154–9; *Exposé et commentaires du projet syndical d'économie moderne*; OCM, *3ᵉ Cahier* (May 1943); Défense de la France, 'La politique économique d'après-guerre', in AN, 72 AJ 564.

[61] *Rapport sur la politique économique*, pp. 10–13, 61–4.

[62] See Moch's 'projet de reconstruction politique et économique', in Michel and Mirkine-Guetzévitch, *Les Idées politiques et sociales de la Résistance*, pp. 319–20. For the OCM see Blocq-Mascart, *Chroniques de la Résistance*, pp. 313–19.

economy—would be to overturn capitalism. This would be
achieved not merely by destroying the power-base of the great
capitalist interests, but also by orienting production away from the
profit motive and towards the satisfaction of the needs of
producer, consumer, and nation. The Resistance's anti-capitalism
combined an attack on the 'trusts' (which were portrayed as
tyrannizing over workers and democratic governments alike) with
an attack on the profit motive itself.

The notion that production should be regulated by need had
ambiguous implications for the efficiency of the economy as a
whole. Under certain circumstances, depending on the definition
of need, it might eventually have led to the same malthusianism
for which inter-war capitalism was being chastised. In many
movements, however, perceptions that economic backwardness
had been at the root of the defeat of 1940 and that unfettered
liberalism (i.e. the profit motive) had created this backwardness
drew resisters towards an emphasis on the importance of modernizing and rationalizing the economy. For such people structural
reform had a second justification: in addition to producing a more
equitable society, it would produce a more dynamic and efficient
economy. As one clandestine paper wrote: 'We want . . . an
economic policy which breaks the industrial routine and allows
France to make up a frightening retardation.'[63] The study
commission of the clandestine Socialist party stated bluntly that
one of the aims of the post-war *économie dirigée* would be
'gradually to eliminate industries which are unprofitable or too
costly'.[64] The CGE, acknowledging a long-term economic decline,
proposed an investment programme 'not only to compensate for
losses suffered since the war began, but to increase the economic
potential of the country, which must recover the leading position
in the world which it has lost for more than a decade.'[65] Similar
views were expressed by movements such as the OCM, the CAS,
and Défense de la France. However, it should be emphasized that,
whereas some form of anti-capitalism was expressed in almost
every Resistance tract, programme, or report, the same was not

[63] *Lorraine*, 15 (25 Nov. 1943).
[64] 'Aux responsables fédéraux et régionaux' (Apr. 1944), in AN, 72 AJ 70.
[65] 'Rapport établi par le CGE sur les mesures immédiates à prendre par le
Gouvernement Provisoire' (May 1943), 16, ibid., F1a 3733. For similar opinions
see Courtin, *Rapport sur la politique économique*, pp. 27–43.

true of 'anti-malthusianism'. The CNR Common Programme, for instance, merely recommended 'the intensification of the nation's production'. In view of the economic disarray of March 1944, that was not a particularly radical suggestion.

The first two parts of the triptych Republic, Socialism, Nation have been examined in some detail because they expressed the bulk of the Resistance's ideas about post-war renewal. The third element, though it lacked the lengthy programmatic development of the other two, should at least be noted.

It is worth reiterating that the Resistance began as a patriotic reflex and that the nation's liberation remained its essential aim. This aspect of the Resistance was often reflected in its writings. It is not an exaggeration, in the context of Resistance writing, to speak of a rediscovery of the nation. Nowhere was this rediscovery more evident than among socialist resisters.

. . . socialism must declare loudly its national character. The failure of the internationals is indisputable: they have never managed to prevent a war, combat a crisis, or prepare concerted action. On the other hand, as the present war shows, conflicts between nations are far from belonging to a past era. . . . In France, all the socialists in the Resistance have, in some sense, retrieved the patriotism they had lost, quite simply because they have realized that France's defeat was also the defeat of their socialist ideal.[66]

Former trotskyists like Jean Rous admitted having undergone 'a national reaction' and criticized the extreme left for underestimating 'the national problem'.[67] In underground papers there were frequent declarations that the ultimate aim of the Resistance was to restore French power in the world. *Libération*, for instance, wrote that: 'So long as France has not regained her rank as a great sovereign power, so long as she has not collected her empire around her . . . the national Resistance will have its role to play.'[68] *Défense de la France*, *Résistance*, and *Ceux de la Libération* all agreed that the Resistance had expressed 'une volonté de grandeur',[69] while the members of the MLN's executive committee

---

[66] 'Vers un grand parti du travail', 9, in AN, 72 AJ 3.
[67] 'Témoignage de Jean Rous', ibid. 70.
[68] *Libération* (Southern zone), 43 (20 Jan. 1944).
[69] *Défense de la France*, 27 (5 Feb. 1943); *Résistance*, 4 (23 Dec. 1942); *Ceux de la Libération*, 155 (23 May 1944).

declared that 'patriotism has become a living and essential reality in our country once again'.[70]

Most resisters believed that transnational organization (in the form of a revived League of Nations or a European Federation) was the key to a lasting international settlement. Ultimately, however, the national crisis took precedence over the international one. Though not nationalist (in the sense that de Gaulle and Free France might be described as nationalist), the majority of Resistance movements clearly viewed their primary mission as the restoration of France's independence and status.

In a sense it is misleading to talk about a single Resistance philosophy. Not only was there the broad diversity of views which was inevitable in such a diversified movement, but, in a more basic sense, there were two quite different kinds of Resistance thinking about the post-war future.

The first kind consisted of the programmatic productions, of which the CNR charter of March 1944 was the most conspicuous example. The strengths and weaknesses of these programmes reflected the circumstances which produced them. They emerged from a confrontation between a failed past (economic liberalism and parliamentary republicanism), a failing and discredited present (Vichy's National Revolution), and a highly problematic future. The third factor—the immense uncertainty about a future which resisters could do little, in material terms, to influence—is often underestimated. It is easy to be deceived by the sense of moral certainty that the Resistance movements exuded, but this assurance related only to the immediate struggle against the forces of occupation and collaboration. In so far as the shape of post-war events could be read by resisters, it often appeared a threatening future. During the war the two most plausible options for post-war France seemed to be a return to the Western capitalist fold or a communist revolution on the Russian model. Both alternatives were unpalatable to most resisters. As the resister Léo Hamon noted in his diary entry of 29 June 1944: 'our predicament is . . . that we have to find positions which are truly revolutionary without being communist'.[71]

[70] Text in AN, F1a 3755.
[71] 'Journal de Léo Hamon', 152, ibid., 72 AJ 42.

In spite of the complication, if not impossibility, of such a position, the Resistance's programmes did make significant contributions to the creation of a new post-war consensus. Without the Resistance's republicanism, the transition from Pétainism to republicanism would have been far more difficult. In reaffirming the association of patriotic and republican values, the Resistance renewed the tradition stretching back to 1793 and 1871. It thus repaired the damage which the disastrous record of the last decade of the Third Republic had inflicted on the reputation of republicanism. Equally, the Resistance's socialism helped to amplify what in the 1930s had been minority positions: the desirability of coherent state intervention and management of the economy, the advantages of a developed social policy. The larger goals of the Resistance's socialist synthesis—a socio-economic system at the service of the community—were not to be met, but many of the individual proposals were to be realized in the post-war era.

The second type of Resistance response was less intellectualized than the programmatic type and more characteristic of the Resistance as a distinct body of men and women. It may be described as its *ancien combattant* reflex. Resisters instinctively envisaged the post-war world as a continuation, under different circumstances, of their life under occupation. We have already encountered this reflex in a number of guises: for example, in the moralism of their political doctrines and in the obsession with élites, which manifested itself in all aspects of the resisters' political, social, and economic ideology. The Resistance saw itself as a young and dynamic movement which would renew France simply by coming to the helm. This philosophy was perfectly expressed in September 1944 by Jacques Chaban–Delmas (then a general in the FFI):

. . . the disaster of France in 1940 was largely caused by the death of the flower of French youth between 1914 and 1918. . . . [France] had been forced to rely on old men and second-raters. The situation was now different. . . . there had arisen a new element, the youth inside France which would be her salvation. These young men . . . were not the soft, gilded youth of the 1925–1940 period but were tough and hardened by experience and the risks they had taken in the Resistancé. From this youth would come a new patriotic and progressive French leadership.[72]

[72] 'Memorandum of conversation between Douglas MacArthur and General

Whereas the programmes had a considerable effect on post-war policies, this 'voluntarist' side of Resistance ideology exerted much less influence. After a brief moment of glory at the Liberation, the Resistance as a unified moral and political force disappeared. Political life was not moralized. Economic activity did not become a great participatory mission. Even though the new élites generally had some kind of Resistance background, they proved no more infallible than the old ones. The impact of the Resistance on the post-Liberation period was thus ambiguous. The movement symbolized national renewal. In advocating structural reforms, it helped to shape the post-Liberation political agenda. And yet its deepest aspirations were to be swiftly disappointed.

Delmas-Chabon [*sic*], 27 Sept. 1944', in US National Archives, Record Group 59, 851.00 (Doc. No. 9-2744).

3

Free France and the New France

Two main issues are raised *à propos* the role of France Libre[1]—in its various incarnations, from Conseil de Défense de l'Empire Français to Provisional Government—in the rethinking of France. The first concerns the manner in which the organization that de Gaulle created in London in 1940 contributed to the dialogue about reform. This contribution had the potential to be a significant one. Unlike the Resistance, the Free French had the basis of a governmental structure (bureaucracy, ministries, etc.). As exiles they enjoyed a degree of physical security and even leisure which clandestine resisters lacked. Furthermore, unlike the Resistance or Vichy, they were in a position to witness at first hand the extensive planning which allied governments began to undertake as victory grew more imminent. Free French study groups worked alongside those of other nationalities, and their leaders enjoyed the advantage of being able to consult with allied counterparts. In 1941, for example, a leading figure in the Free French organization, René Cassin, was briefed by Sir William Beveridge about the social security plan which the British were contemplating.[2] In this regard, the London *émigrés* were the least isolated members of the national community.

The second issue relates to Free France in its more restricted sense—as a movement of followers of General de Gaulle. At what point and to what extent did wartime gaullists create or define a distinctive vision of France's future? Gaullists themselves were often reluctant (especially before 1942) to acknowledge that there was any such thing as gaullism: 'It is absurd and scandalous to talk about gaullism or anti-gaullism. There are some Frenchmen who do not agree to treat with the enemy, there are others who collaborate. That is all there is to it. De Gaulle is not the leader of a political movement.'[3] Certainly Free France, like the Resistance,

---

[1] In July 1942, France Libre changed its name to France Combattante. For convenience I will use Free France to apply to both periods.

[2] Cassin, *Les Hommes partis de rien* (Paris, 1975), 371.

[3] Radio broadcast, the text of which is in *Documents d'Information*, 13 (1 Mar. 1942), 14–15.

was composed of people from all points of the political and social spectrum: as one gaullist (Pierre Denis) put it to another (René Pleven), 'Beneath the camaraderie of combat, there are deep divergences of political tendency . . . among the members of Free France.'[4] Given this diversity, it was inevitable that gaullist ideology would develop with very rough edges. But this did not mean that no ideology existed. Even if (in order not to appear sectarian) the Free French chose to deny that their movement could be identified with a certain ideology, in objective terms it clearly took on identifiable political characteristics. Its basic message was a powerful and uncomplicated one: the primacy of the national interest, the importance of collaboration between social classes, and the necessity of a post-war renewal of parliamentary institutions and political élites. Like the Resistance, the Free French expressed a radical dissatisfaction with the pre-war regime as well as with Vichy.[5]

In the wake of de Gaulle's *appel* of 18 June 1940, which summoned French servicemen to continue the struggle against Germany, an organization created itself around the dissident general. Ten days after de Gaulle's speech, Churchill published a communiqué recognizing de Gaulle as 'leader of all free Frenchmen wherever they may be'. Important as this recognition was, it was by its very nature an endorsement of de Gaulle rather than an endorsement of his organization.[6] At this point there was still considerable uncertainty as to the form and function of the new organization. One possibility—that preferred by many in the British establishment and also by prominent Frenchmen in London like Jean Monnet—would have restricted Free France to the role of a 'légion combattante', a group of French citizens fighting as a unit within the allied armies. A second option was for it to assume a political form and become a kind of proto-government rivalling that in Vichy. De Gaulle did not hesitate before choosing the second course. From the outset he regarded Free France as *the* legitimate French authority rather than as a group of mercenaries

---

[4] Quoted by Denis in his book, *Souvenirs de la France Libre* (Paris, 1947), 71–2.

[5] For a discussion of Free French ideology, see Henri Michel, *Les Courants de pensée de la Résistance* (Paris, 1962), 15–118.

[6] On the complex negotiations of the weeks following 18 June, see F. Kersaudy, *Churchill and de Gaulle* (London, 1981), 79–84.

fighting for the allied cause.[7] A manifesto which he issued from
Brazzaville four months later made this assumption of provisional
sovereignty official.

Yet in the early phases of its existence Free France manifested
only a limited interest in developing a long-term political agenda.
One of the essential differences between gaullism and vichyism
was the gaullists' insistence that liberation was the prerequisite for
renovation and that, to use Cassin's expression, all Vichy's
reforms 'are built on sand, as long as the enemy occupies our
country'.[8] The gaullist position in 1940 and 1941 was stated with
perfect clarity by General de Larminat, a member of the Conseil
de Défense de l'Empire, which de Gaulle created in 1940:

> We know full well that a nation does not suffer a disaster like ours without
> there being deep-seated causes for this collapse. We know that it is
> necessary to recognize these causes; we know that it will take radical
> reforms to regenerate the country.
>
> But this is not our concern at this moment. When the house is blazing, it
> is not the moment to repair its faulty foundations. One must first put out
> the fire which threatens to engulf everything; it is only when the bulk of
> the structure has been saved that one calls upon the architect to rebuild,
> starting from the foundation if necessary.[9]

During the eighteen months after the *appel* of 18 June, de Gaulle
himself made almost no public mention of the post-war future.
The main themes of his speeches were attacks on the legitimacy of
the Vichy government; assertions that France had lost a battle in a
world war which would continue and which the allies would win;
and, above all, rallying calls to the empire and to all those who
rejected the armistice. In this period when *rénovation* was one of
the bywords of Pétain's National Revolution, de Gaulle only
employed the term to mock Vichy.[10]

A similar concern not to reinforce vichyite propaganda may
have been one of the roots of de Gaulle's initial reticence about
the Third Republic. His speeches in 1940 and 1941 were noticeably

[7] See e.g. the recollections of Jean Monnet, *Memoirs* (Garden City, NY, 1978),
143–7. De Gaulle's own recollection is, of course, the most famous testimony: see
Mémoires de guerre: l'appel (Paris, 1954), 69.

[8] *18 mois de France Libre* (1942), 17.

[9] 'Position des Français Libres vis-à-vis des problèmes nationaux' (18 Feb.
1941), in AN, F60 1728.

[10] See e.g. the speech of 25 Nov. 1940: de Gaulle, *Discours et messages, 1940–
1946* (Paris, 1970), 43.

harsher on the military hierarchy than on the old political élite, which was being vilified by the new regime in metropolitan France.[11] In this period de Gaulle made a number of vague remarks describing the war as 'revolutionary',[12] but these statements were not linked explicitly to denunciations of the Third Republic. During 1940 and 1941 de Gaulle's strategy was as far as possible to avoid discussion of domestic French politics (while condemning Vichy for its collaboration). This policy entailed a non-committal attitude on the issue of France's future regime: on the one hand, his public statements tended to avoid the kind of overt anti-parliamentarianism which was being expressed by Vichy, by many early resisters, and by members of his own organization;[13] while, on the other, he was careful to avoid identifying his movement with the Third Republic, which he perceived to be highly unpopular within France (an unpopularity which he certainly believed it deserved). In a telegram sent to London from Cairo in July 1941 he explained the need for caution:

We must continue to be discreet in expressing our political stance, in spite of the disadvantages that this ambiguity may present for us at the moment in the United States. If we were simply to proclaim that we are fighting for democracy, we would perhaps receive provisional commendation on the American side, but we would lose a great deal on the French scene which is the main one. At the moment, the mass of the French people confuse the word democracy with the parliamentary regime as it operated in France before this war. An overwhelming majority of our own supporters, whatever their political origin . . . are convinced of it. That regime has been condemned by events and by public opinion.[14]

A speech which de Gaulle delivered at the Albert Hall on 15 November 1941 marked the first public deviation from this prudential silence.[15] This speech contained the first suggestion that Free France might have a mission after the war had finished, the

---

[11] This initial conciliatory tone is noted by Cassin, *Les Hommes partis de rien*, p. 133.

[12] See the speech of 3 Aug. 1940 in de Gaulle, *Discours et messages, 1940–1946*, pp. 21–3. He had made a similar point in a memorandum of 26 Jan. 1940 which he had addressed to Gamelin, Weygand, Georges, Daladier, and Reynaud. See de Gaulle, *Trois études* (Paris, 1970), 100–1.

[13] For the pronounced anti-parliamentary strain in Free French ideology, see Michel, *Les Courants de pensée*, pp. 90–3.

[14] De Gaulle, *Lettres, notes et carnets*, iii (Paris, 1981), 384–5.

[15] *Discours et messages, 1940–1946*, pp. 132–8.

most substantial assertion hitherto of the war's revolutionary character, and the first major attack on the Third Republic. At the beginning of the following month, de Gaulle signed a decree which created four study commissions to consider post-war problems. Taken together, these two acts marked the beginning of Free France's interest in the post-war future.

During 1942 there were signs of an increasing concern about such questions in the Free French press. The semi-official Free French newspaper, *La Marseillaise*, ran a series of articles entitled 'Regards sur l'après-guerre'.[16] In September 1942 it printed a controversial article by Pierre Brossolette, a Socialist intellectual and former party deputy, who had recently arrived from France. In this article Brossolette advanced a radical plan for the dissolution of the pre-war parties and the creation of a permanent gaullist movement, which would be socially progressive, economically *dirigiste,* and constitutionally reformist.[17] In another journal, *La France Libre,* Hervé Alphand and Robert Vacher looked ahead to the post-war economy.[18] Two of the four study commissions established by the decree of December 1941 also began their debates during 1942, and the one which was examining economic and social policy made particular progress. Most importantly of all—since de Gaulle was Free France's main spokesman as well as its leader—the general reiterated and expanded on the themes which he had sounded in the November 1941 speech. His most publicized statement came in a declaration of principles which he addressed to the internal Resistance in June 1942 (at the instigation of a Resistance leader, Christian Pineau). This declaration was the first document in which he described Free France's vision of future renovation.[19] It included a pledge to allow all French men and women to elect a National Assembly 'which will determine the country's future in full sovereignty'; a plan of social reform to give working people 'the practical guarantees which will ensure that every citizen has freedom and

---

[16] Nos. 18 (11 Oct. 1942), 19 (18 Oct. 1942), 20 (25 Oct. 1942), 21 (1 Nov. 1942).

[17] 27 Sept. 1942. The article has been reprinted in Gilberte Brossolette, *Il s'appelait Pierre Brossolette* (Paris, 1976), 269–73.

[18] Nos. 16 (16 Feb. 1942), 317–23, and 20 (15 June 1942), 129–36.

[19] *Discours et messages, 1940–1946,* pp. 205–7. The main motivation for the early clarifications of de Gaulle's views was his desire to rally the metropolitan Resistance behind his leadership (thus giving him vital credibility in his struggles with the allies and later with General Giraud).

dignity in his employment and existence'; and 'a dynamic renewal
of the nation's and the empire's resources through a policy of
dirigisme'. Although *La Marseillaise* greeted the declaration of
June 1942 as a manifesto for the new France,[20] it must also be seen
in the context of de Gaulle's other public statements during this
period. On the whole, de Gaulle's 1942 speeches scarcely
mentioned post-war renovation. They concentrated on reviewing
the allies' war effort, on attacking Vichy (and, increasingly, the
Third Republic as well), and on defending the authority and
autonomy of his organization. As was the case with the metropolitan
Resistance, most of Free France's pronouncements about post-war
reform were confined to the final eighteen months of the
Occupation. By then, the manifest bankruptcy of Vichy's 'renovation' had freed its opponents from any lingering inhibitions
about using the term.

As has already been suggested, the gaullist organization had the
capacity to plan post-war reforms in a more systematic way than
was possible for Resistance movements. Rudimentary though its
bureaucracy was, especially in the London period (1940–early
1943), Free France was organized along the lines of a provisional
government. In April 1941 the central administration already had
a staff of 1,631.[21] The ordinance of 24 September 1941, which
created the Comité National Français (the successor to the Conseil
de Défense de l'Empire Français), established a number of
commissariats that were, in effect, embryonic ministries. One of
these ministries, the Commissariat à l'Intérieur, took on the
responsibility of facilitating dialogue between Free France and the
metropolitan Resistance. Initially the Commissariat à l'Intérieur
was headed by André Diethelm, but in July 1942 he was succeeded
by André Philip, a prominent Socialist resister and ex-deputy who
had arrived in London shortly after his fellow Socialist Brossolette.
In Philip, the *commissariat* had a head who was passionately
interested in post-war issues. Philip paid particular attention to
gathering information about allied planning and disseminating the
programmes which were reaching London from France. He also
followed closely the deliberations of the Free French study
commissions and participated directly in some of them. His

[20] No. 3 (28 June 1942), 3.
[21] C.-L. Foulon, *Le Pouvoir en province à la Libération* (Paris, 1975), 38.

supervision of Free France's post-war planning continued after the move to Algiers, where he was appointed Commissaire aux Relations avec l'Assemblée et aux Études in the CFLN (the new organization formed in mid-1943 in a merger between the gaullist CNF and General Giraud's movement in North Africa). In this post Philip was given the specific task of organizing and co-ordinating studies of post-war reform.

The specialized committees, which were the main forums within Free France for the study and debate of post-war reforms, were constituted in two series. The first series was established in London by de Gaulle's decree of 2 December 1941.[22] This decree created four commissions, of which only two ever operated: one dealing with economic, financial, and social affairs, and another with constitutional, electoral, legal, and educational reform. These were large committees (the first had 47 members, the second 28). Their record was a rather mixed one. The head of their secretariat, M. Maisonneuve, was critical of their performance: 'our committees have a tendency to stall, become debating societies, or indeed suspend activity altogether'.[23] Comparing the achievements of the French committees with those of Belgian counterparts, Maisonneuve found the latter far more impressive. Committee members agreed with him.[24] To judge by their minutes, many of the meetings were indeed poorly directed, with committee members raising the issues which were dear to them and generally failing to achieve coherent or useful syntheses.

In the second series of committees, which was formed by the CFLN in North Africa in 1943 and 1944, some of the weaknesses of the London committees were remedied. The increasing sophistication of Free France's organization and the greater number of qualified members who were available made the Algiers committees less like debating societies. Rather than receiving broad and diffuse instructions, the Algiers committees were given clearly defined tasks and a more specialized personnel. An imperial reform committee (composed of political, academic, and administrative experts) was given the specific task of studying the measures which

[22] The main source for my discussion of the London study commissions is AN, 72 AJ 546.
[23] 'Rapport du chef du secrétariat sur la marche des commissions', ibid.
[24] See e.g. the comments of M. Gendrot to a meeting of the *section sociale*, 25 Feb. 1943, ibid.

would be needed to give the colonies due representation in a future constitution.[25] A constitutional reform committee (established by André Philip in February 1944) included fewer than a dozen members, almost all of whom were to play a significant role in the constitution-making process between 1944 and 1946.[26] Unlike the London committee, which had ranged too widely, it concentrated solely on the issue of the Fourth Republic's constitution. An educational reform committee which René Capitant, Commissaire à l'Éducation Nationale, created around the same time, included a more specialized personnel than its counterpart in London and was able to focus its debate more successfully.[27] Similarly, a committee 'for the study of post-war economic problems', which met between January and July 1944, dealt with many of the same issues that the London committee had raised but in a more systematic fashion: this time four sub-committees were formed to examine what Philip had identified as the four most important questions relating to economic reform.[28]

The reports which these various committees drafted tended to be more substantial and useful than those of the London committees. In other respects, however, the Algiers committees replicated the characteristics of the earlier ones. Some of these characteristics were not necessarily bad. Both sets of committees, for example, paid close attention to innovations proposed or implemented outside France. The Algiers education committee began its report characteristically by stating that: 'We cannot be unaware of the development in Russian schools, the threefold revolution which is changing the face of British schools, or the new teaching methods that are also gaining ground in the United States.'[29] The various committees considering economic policy were kept informed by a steady flow of documents about other nations' economic policies. Here, as in the educational and constitutional reform committees, British institutions were particularly carefully scrutinized: background papers explained the working of Joint Production Committees and the British Civil Service, while the Commissariat aux Études produced synopses of

[25] For this committee, see ch. 6, below.
[26] For this committee, see ch. 5, below.
[27] For this committee, see ch. 7, below.
[28] For this committee, see chs. 10 and 11, below.
[29] 'Rapport général', 2, in AN, 71 AJ 63.

the most important books and reports published in Britain during the war.[30] Philip himself, who had long had an academic interest in Britain and had many personal contacts there (especially in Labour Party circles), was particularly impressed by British institutions; in economic policy, as in educational and constitutional affairs, he believed that France had a good deal to learn both from traditional British practices and from the reforms that had been made there during the war.

A second point of similarity with the London committees was the general approach which the later committees adopted towards their brief: in both cases the aim was to air the issues, to suggest various alternative reforms and examine their strengths and weaknesses, but not to make a definitive proposal. In the first half of 1944, Free France was still operating in a provisional capacity. The objections to an unrepresentative committee of Free French politicians, academics, and administrators settling the course of future reform were as valid as they had been in December 1941. To that extent, though the debates were better informed and more sharply focused, the ultimate limitation on them was the same as in London. That was no doubt one reason why many in the Free French leadership were sceptical about the worth of these study groups—a scepticism which was intensified by the personality of the Commissaire aux Études, whose curious physical mannerisms, forgetfulness, and abstract intelligence fitted the stereotype of the absent-minded professor.[31] Here, for instance, is the ironical verdict of a 'practical' man like Passy on this kind of activity:

In the course of 1943, the CGE sent hundreds of studies to London on a whole range of problems (administrative, economic, constitutional, etc.) . . . [The studies] gave rise, in London as well as in Algiers, to passionate debates within the committees and sub-committees assigned to study them—all of which allowed us, at the moment of liberation . . . to be bathed in clarity and harmony![32]

While the study committees were preparing their inevitably rather theoretical studies, the CFLN was coming to the realization that it would also exert a more concrete influence on the period after

---

[30] Some of these synopses are in AN, F1a 3792.

[31] See the descriptions of Philip by Passy, *Souvenirs,* ii (Monte Carlo, 1947), 231–2; and by Soustelle, *Envers et contre tout,* i (Paris, 1947), 286.

[32] *Souvenirs,* ii, pp. 131–2.

liberation. In the empire, where it had a limited power to implement policy, the CFLN was already exerting such an influence by the beginning of 1944: the Brazzaville conference of January–February 1944 and the decree of 7 March 1944 (which gave important political rights to the Muslim population of French North Africa) not only produced significant results in their own right, but placed the whole issue of imperial reform high on the agenda of post-Liberation politics.[33] When it came to reform in metropolitan France, the position was more complex. On the one hand, until liberation actually began, the CFLN could do no more than make provisional plans. On the other, the Free French realized that, though it would be politically impossible to introduce permanent reforms at the instant of liberation (since de Gaulle and his spokesmen had all along insisted that only the free and sovereign nation could sanction such reforms), there was bound to be a hiatus, during which the sovereign nation would be unable to render its verdict and important decisions would have to be taken. Some of these decisions, which only the CFLN would be in a position to take, would inevitably have a bearing on the longer-term future. Free French planning for this transitional phase focused on a number of issues: how to administer an economy which was already in acute crisis and was bound to suffer further as a result of the allied invasion (a problem which the CFLN resolved, in part, by deciding to maintain many of Vichy's economic controls); how to co-ordinate and control military operations involving irregular clandestine forces; and, above all, how to ensure (with or without the official recognition of Britain and America) that the Provisional Government's authority was established at both the central and local levels. The last issue was the most fundamental: the preparations that Free France made for governing the liberated territories determined how and by whom reform would be introduced in the months after liberation.

Active consideration of the transfer of political and administrative power from Vichy to Free France had begun at an early stage. On 30 June 1942, de Gaulle wrote to solicit the advice of a senior parliamentarian, Jules Jeanneney:

Although the outlook is not much brighter, one can now imagine a change in fortune which might allow us to imagine the 'return' of France into the war.

[33] See ch. 6, below.

In this hypothetical situation—and without making any assumptions about the role that circumstances would thrust on this or that person—it would be necessary to resolve, in a provisional way, the problems of the country's government and democratic representation.[34]

From mid-1942 onwards, proposals for administration of the country after liberation were being drafted inside the Free French organization.[35] In the autumn of 1942, the London study-commission started to consider the constitutional issues: when and how a Constituent Assembly could be elected, and what should be the powers of the interim government. In October 1942, de Gaulle created a Commission du Débarquement, a committee whose specific task was to supervise the preparation of all decisions relating to the administration of France in the period of liberation.[36] The process of preparation was to be a lengthy and complex one, stretching from these early initiatives in 1942 to the eve of Operation Overlord. It involved the Commissariat à l'Intérieur and the Commissariat à la Justice; the CGE and delegates of the Provisional Government inside metropolitan France; the Commission du Débarquement; and the Provisional Consultative Assembly, which the CFLN established in North Africa in the autumn of 1943. The details of this complex process need not detain us, but it is important to recognize that several decisions emerging from it were to affect the course of post-war reform. Two of them in particular should be noted.

The first was contained in an ordinance of 10 January 1944. This ordinance created Commissaires de la République, to administer the regions of liberated France on the CFLN's behalf. It gave these *commissaires* enormous discretionary powers for the period of 'exceptional circumstances' which would follow the allies' invasion.[37] The ordinance of 10 January reflected the absolute priority which the Provisional Government attached to securing its own authority inside France, *vis-à-vis* any allied military administration (AMGOT), existing Vichy administration, or potential Resistance authority. In actual fact, in the summer of 1944 the danger of rule by AMGOT or remnants of the État Français quickly evaporated. The major effect of the 10 January ordinance was to reassert the

---

[34] De Gaulle's letter is printed in Jeanneney, *Journal politique: septembre 1939–juillet 1942* (Paris, 1972), 313.

[35] Foulon, *Le Pouvoir en province*, pp. 44–6.   [36] Ibid. 46–7, 57.

[37] On the background to this ordinance, see ibid. 44–60.

power of the centre in the weeks and months after the liberation of Paris and thus to ensure that any 'revolution' which occurred in the wake of liberation would be a 'révolution par la loi'.

A second and equally important ordinance (dated 21 April 1944) established the timetable for a return to democratic government after liberation. Its most important stipulation was contained in the first article: 'The French people will have supreme power to decide their future institutions. To that end, a national constituent assembly will be convened.'[38] This ordinance did not definitively rule out the retention of the constitution of 1875 (and, indeed, in 1945 de Gaulle was to give serious consideration to such an option). But by throwing its weight behind a new Republic, the Provisional Government made such an eventuality far more unlikely. Likewise, the stipulation of a constituent assembly did not mean that a new constitution could not be drawn up by the Provisional Government itself (as the CGE and OCM proposed to de Gaulle.)[39] But once again it made it much more difficult, politically speaking, to justify anything other than a fully sovereign assembly. Finally, in its provisions for departmental and municipal elections the ordinance of 21 April stated that 'women may vote and stand for election in the same conditions as men'. It is almost inconceivable that women's suffrage would not have been introduced in 1945 (so wide was the consensus in favour of it and so preponderant were the parties of the left), but it is also true that this decision by the Provisional Government helped to make it a *fait accompli*. In general, it may be said that it was in this kind of 'caretaker' capacity—be it in constitutional or economic affairs— that the CFLN had its most direct impact on the course of post-war reform.

On the other hand, the gaullist movement signally failed to develop a distinctive reform programme of its own. It has been suggested by some that, in 1942, de Gaulle came close to tying his movement to a specific reformist ideology (basically that of Brossolette and Soustelle). The argument is that the General was forced by tactical considerations (the need to rally a united front

---

[38] *JO, Lois et Décrets*, 22 Apr. 1944, pp. 325–7.

[39] For the CGE, see the 'Rapport établi par le CGE sur les mesures immédiates à prendre par le Gouvernement Provisoire', 6, in AN, F1a 3733. For the OCM, see the document 'Cahiers de l'OCM', in AN, 72 AJ 67.

against General Giraud) to postpone this 'rassemblement' and to sanction the resurrection of the old political parties.[40] Whatever the reason, Free France did not evolve into the clearly defined political movement which the gaullist RPF was to be in the years after 1947. It remained, throughout the war, a broad church. As we have already noted, that is not to say that Free France had no identifiable political message. Henri Michel, who has given the most thorough analysis of Free French ideology, describes it as a series of visions, passing from a fairly reactionary nationalism in 1940 to a republican and 'socialisant'—if not socialist—nationalism by 1943 and 1944.[41] The emergence of pro-republican and socially progressive ideas reflected changes in personnel, a growing awareness of the Resistance's views, and the inevitable moderating of hostility towards the *ancien régime*, as the memory of 1940 was erased by the experience of a worse regime. What occurred was, in fact, an evolution in emphasis rather than a dramatic change of substance. The ideas which Free France had incarnated in 1940— patriotism and imperial integrity—remained the essential elements in the movement's ideology. The 'new republicanism' of de Gaulle's 1943 speeches conveyed essentially the same message as the 'reactionary' speeches of 1941: the post-war democracy must not replicate the errors of pre-war republicanism. Likewise, there had always been a social dimension to the Free French movement. As early as the autumn of 1941 de Gaulle had told Pleven that 'the social issue is the great issue of tomorrow',[42] and a left-wing gaullist (Henry Hauck) had declared that the Free French leadership held a vision of 'a new France where the working class, which by its heroic resistance has won a special place in the nation's gratitude, will see its power, authority, and responsibilities increase'.[43]

The main characteristic of Free French ideology throughout the war was its tendency to relate *all* other interests to the national

[40] This is the argument of O. Guichard, *Mon général* (Paris, 1980), 137–47. A similar argument was made thirty years ago by Nicholas Wahl, in his Ph.D. dissertation: 'De Gaulle and the Resistance: The Rise of Reform Politics in France' (Harvard, 1956).

[41] See Michel, *Les Courants de pensée*, pp. 98–107.

[42] Quoted in de Gaulle's *Mémoires de guerre: l'appel*, p. 482.

[43] 'Extraits d'une allocution prononcée par M. H. Hauck, directeur du travail de la France Libre, à la matinée cinématographique organisée par le Centre Syndical Français en Grande Bretagne le 5 octobre 1941', *Documents d'Information*, 5 (1 Nov. 1941), 7–8.

interest. Thus, whereas the Resistance's ideas about a new 'social' republic tended to assume an intrinsic worth in republicanism and socialism, the Free French subordinated these ideas to the imperatives of national unity and greatness. The theme of revolution which surfaced in de Gaulle's public pronouncements from time to time was not linked by him or his supporters to socialist ideology: even a Socialist gaullist like Brossolette analysed the crisis of the inter-war period in terms of a frustrated search for national unity, not in terms of an inherent class conflict.[44] The *raison d'être* of social reform for the Free French was twofold. First, it would help to replace a bourgeois élite which had failed the nation with a more dynamic élite: as *La Marseillaise* said, in its commentary on de Gaulle's 1942 declaration to the Resistance, 'A century of egoism and its abominable frivolity have condemned [this class]. Its destruction is imperative.'[45] Second, it would reconstitute the national community. The Free French believed that social divisions lay at the root of the defeat of 1940: 'French unity was in the process of disintegrating when this war began. Not in the horizontal or geographic sense . . . But in the vertical or social sense, as the different layers of the population were stratified and tended to become more and more impermeable.'[46] The Free French general, de Larminat, explained how social reform could renew the nation:

> The egalitarian or social ideal truly represents the *idée-force* around which the French people can unite to build a strong and healthy France. The social question was the sole true obstacle to the unity of the French people, and it is by resolving it that we will remake this unity and thereby remake the greatness of our country.[47]

Similarly, the idea of a managed economy or of nationalization was justified primarily in terms of its beneficial effect on the nation and only secondarily with arguments about social justice. The word-order of de Gaulle's indictment of the 'trusts' was symptomatic of his priorities: 'they endangered the nation, introduced foreign interests into it, degraded civic morality, and hindered social progress'.[48] Likewise, the meagre and cryptic comments that

---

[44] See Brossolette's comments at a press conference on his arrival in London, ibid. 27 (1 Oct. 1942), p. 21.   [45] No. 3 (28 June 1942).

[46] E. de Larminat, *Que sera la France de demain?* (n.p., 1943), 6.

[47] Ibid. 17.

[48] *Discours et messages, 1940–1946*, p. 312 (speech of 14 July 1943).

de Gaulle made about the Fourth Republic—a term which only
made its appearance in gaullist oratory in June 1943[49]—dwelt less
on the inherent virtues of democracy than on the need for a
political system which would be an effective instrument of the
national interest.

The only entity other than the nation that had an independent
value for the Free French was the empire. Because they owed
much of their legitimacy to the initial *ralliement* of parts of the
empire and because most of their military activity took place
within the empire, imperial defence (against the Axis or the allies)
was, from the beginning, one of the main themes of Free French
propaganda.[50] But more than this, as attention began to be
focused on the post-war period, the immense expanse and
population of the empire came to seem both a guarantee of—and
a prerequisite for—the nation's future greatness. '[T]here is one
element which, in these terrible trials, has shown the nation that it
is essential to her future and necessary for her greatness,' declared
de Gaulle in a speech of June 1942. 'That element is the empire.'[51]
Eighteen months later, when another of his speeches had heralded
a campaign to reform the empire, *La Marseillaise* commented:
'The building of an imperial France is under way. Only at this price
will France remain a great power in a world where only enormous
empires have the possibility of living in security.'[52] The empire was
the arena in which the gaullist adventure would continue, once the
initial goal of victory over Germany had been achieved. Recounting
a trip through French Africa which he made with Pleven in 1943,
Jacques Soustelle recalled his feeling for 'that immense French
African country, that continent which—if her leaders cared about
it—should be for France what the Far West was for the United
States'.[53]

Speaking at the University of Algiers in 1943, the Commissaire à
l'Éducation Nationale, René Capitant, summed up Free French
aspirations for the Liberation in the following terms:

In every area the liberation of France will have to be accompanied by the
renewal of her institutions. Profound transformations will have to be

---

[49] See Michel, *Les Courants de pensée*, p. 101.   [50] Ibid. 74–8.
[51] *Discours et messages, 1940–1946*, p. 201.
[52] No. 59 (18 Dec. 1943).
[53] Soustelle, *Envers et contre tout*, ii. 277.

accomplished in the political order, the economic order, the social order. It is an illusion to believe that liberation can lead purely and simply to a return to the way things were before the war.

There is no idea that General de Gaulle has expressed more forcefully and insistently. . . . There is no principle which more inspires the actions of Fighting France.[54]

In this general sense, gaullist propaganda reinforced the Resistance's ideology. Both resisted a nostalgia for the pre-war status quo which the Vichy regime's collaboration made increasingly tempting. Throughout the two years before liberation, de Gaulle constantly stressed the need for post-war change. If he used the word renewal rather than revolution, his meaning appeared none the less radical. The condemnations of the État Français and the Third Republic were bitter and sweeping; the demand for change was comprehensive (encompassing political, economic, social, and imperial structures); and the nationalism was as uncompromising as it had been in 1940. Yet by August 1944 the Provisional Government had not transformed this vision of renewal into a programme for action. Neither de Gaulle nor his closest associates had formulated precise plans for reform. The specialized committees which had been set up under Free French auspices had provided some ideas, but many of them were not particularly 'gaullist'. The *Commissariats* of the CFLN had been too absorbed by the day-to-day tasks of a provisional administration to devote enough attention to future plans.[55] In so far as they had planned post-Liberation measures, understandably enough they had focused on the weeks and months after the landings rather than the longer term. A typical instance is provided by the history of the important Comité Économique Interministériel (CEI). The CEI, whose original brief had included the task of defining 'the main lines of government policy in relation to the future economic structure',[56] found that its first months of activity (April–August 1944) were devoted to making contingency plans for the immediate post-Liberation phase.[57]

---

[54] *Alger Républicain*, 19 Dec. 1943.
[55] 'Note pour le général de Gaulle', 22 Jan. 1944, in AN, F60 914.
[56] See 'Note pour le général de Gaulle', 8 Apr. 1944, ibid. 896.
[57] The minutes and papers of the committee's meetings between Apr. and Aug. 1944 are ibid.

4

De Gaulle and the Parties at Liberation

AT the Liberation the competing authorities of the Occupation period were replaced by a single regime. Vichy left certain political and administrative legacies but as an authority it disappeared almost instantaneously in 1944. As Crane Brinton, then working for the OSS, reported to Washington: 'Vichy has faded away, like Lewis Carroll's Cheshire cat, but not even the leer has remained.'[1] To quote Jean Lacouture: 'Suddenly, this "French State", which had aroused so much devotion and rallied most members of France's "élite", sank like a stone in water. Overnight, it lost all its defenders, all its prefects, all its policemen . . . Nothing but hurried escapes, resentments, and nostalgic reminiscences.'[2] On the other side of the wartime divide, the organized Resistance survived for a time in the Comités de Liberation, in the CNR, and in various movements reincarnated as journals or small-scale political groups. But by early 1945 it was clear that utopian hopes of an alternative legitimacy emerging from the Resistance had been dashed. As for Free France/Fighting France, even before the Liberation it had been subsumed within the Provisional Government and in the process had lost much of its specific identity. Although some veterans of the London years like René Pleven and Jacques Soustelle served in de Gaulle's post-Liberation governments, most of the ministers had not been gaullists in 1940. De Gaulle himself refused to endanger his national 'above party' status by endorsing a gaullist party.

On the other hand, of course, the General was still there, at the head of the new regime. Between the Liberation and January 1946 he presided over a series of Provisional Governments. In addition to his colossal figure, three other political forces filled the vacuum left by the disappearance of Vichy and the Resistance: the Communist party, a new Christian Democratic party called the

---

[1] This and other extracts from Brinton's reports have been published in *French Historical Studies*, 2 (1961), 1–27, 133–56.
[2] Lacouture, *De Gaulle: le politique* (Paris, 1985), 33.

Mouvement Républicain Populaire, and the Socialist party. During 1945 and 1946 these three parties dominated French politics to such an extent that it seemed (wrongly, as it transpired) that the multi-party pattern of the pre-war Republic had been permanently transformed. In the general election of October 1945 the three parties received a total of 74.7 per cent of the vote and took over 80 per cent of the seats in the Constituent Assembly. In the election of June 1946, which was precipitated by the electorate's rejection of the First Constituent Assembly's draft constitution, their combined vote was 75.4 per cent and they occupied 421 of the 522 seats in the Second Constituent Assembly. In the Provisional Governments of August 1944–November 1945 the parties had been under-represented (thanks to de Gaulle's preference for a broadly balanced ministry), but after the elections of 1945 and indeed throughout the constituent period (November 1945–October 1946), they dominated French government. They held fifteen of twenty-two places in de Gaulle's last short-lived ministry of November 1945–January 1946 and virtually every portfolio in the Gouin government (January–June 1946) and the Bidault government (June–November 1946). In the two parliamentary commissions set up by successive Constituent Assemblies to draft the Fourth Republic's constitution, they occupied more than three-quarters of the seats.

Together with de Gaulle, these parties—all of which identified fiercely with the Resistance and its aspirations—had the responsibility but also the opportunity to fashion major reforms in French society, in the economy, in the constitutional and educational structures of the country, and in the empire. They were by no means the only ones thinking about such issues, but in 1945 and 1946 they were uniquely well placed to bring about reform. The programmes and ideas that de Gaulle, the MRP, the SFIO, and the PCF elaborated thus merit particular study.

Their contribution to the rethinking of France will be discussed in two stages. This chapter will give a brief introduction to the particular character of each, in so far as it related to the problems of post-war renewal. Then, in Part II, their substantive contribution will be analysed in greater detail.

De Gaulle: The Philosopher of Renewal

Charles de Gaulle left France in 1940 as an experienced army officer, unorthodox military tactician, and recently appointed junior minister. During the final years of the Third Republic he had begun to acquire some influence outside military circles, but he had scarcely become a figure in national politics. His political reputation, such as it was, was that of a staunch nationalist, with affiliations both to the progressive Catholic Amis de Temps Présent and, indirectly, to the maurrasianism of Action Française.[3] When he returned to Paris four years later, he had not only become the undisputed provisional head of state, but was closely and widely identified with an ideology of reform which bore few resemblances to pre-war Christian Democracy and fewer still to maurrasianism. As the Catholic resister Gilbert Dru wrote, a few months before de Gaulle returned in 1944: 'This man not only accomplished a liberating gesture in 1940, he gradually proclaimed a constructive and profoundly revolutionary doctrine.'[4] The doctrine had been articulated through de Gaulle's wartime speeches and statements, many of which had filtered back to France via Resistance newspapers or Free French radio broadcasts. The speeches of 1942, 1943, and 1944 had been forceful and resonant predictions of post-war 'economic and social structural reforms'[5] and of a renovated republicanism. Through his frequent invocations of renewal, de Gaulle had given political currency to the notion that France stood at a parting of the ways and that the only alternative to decline was a comprehensive national renovation. By August 1944 a widespread impression had been created that Charles de Gaulle 'is the incarnation of the French people's will to recover'.[6]

The theme of renewal was always fundamental to de Gaulle's political philosophy. 'Point d'affaire qui dure sans une incessante rénovation,' he had written in 1934.[7] The basic concepts which

[3] On de Gaulle's politics in 1940, see Jean Lacouture, *De Gaulle: le rebelle* (Paris, 1984), 291–3, 408–12.

[4] Dru, 'Projet d'introduction à une action révolutionnaire des jeunes français', 5, in AN, 72 AJ 64.

[5] See e.g. the speeches of 14 July 1943 and 18 Mar. 1944, *Discours et messages, 1940–1946* (Paris, 1970), 309–13, 380–90.   [6] Dru, 'Projet d'introduction'.

[7] *Vers l'armée de métier* (London, 1946), 27.

constituted his thinking about renovation may be reduced to four. These concepts in turn addressed four basic issues which may be described as follows: the problem of France in the twentieth century; the problem of France in the world; the sources of renovation in France; and the role of the national leader.

Before and after 1940 de Gaulle gave considerable thought to the problems which the conditions of the mid-twentieth century posed for a political system—and, to a degree, a society and economy—which were the products of an earlier age. In de Gaulle's view, the precondition of post-war renewal was a realization that France had to live in the present, not in the past. 'Prenons le siècle comme il est,' he told his audience at Bayeux in 1946.[8] De Gaulle's vision of modernization was grounded neither in admiration of other nations (unlike modernizers as diverse as Jean Monnet and André Philip, whose ideas had been shaped by their periods in the US and Britain), nor even primarily in a critique of France's own past failings. First and foremost, it derived from his perception of the changed conditions in which France had to live.

He had established his ideas about the salient characteristics of the modern age well before the war. In his pre-war essay *Le Fil de l'épée* (1932), he had written: 'our century, which is scarcely a third over, will have seen two radically different eras follow one another, with the war as the sole dividing line.'[9] The earlier epoch had been dominated by the ethos of the bourgeoisie—*droits acquis*, *partis traditionnels*, *revenus fixes*, stability, economy, prudence.[10] De Gaulle argued that, by an inexorable process, this stable period had given way to a more unstable time. 'Earning money, covering distances, avoiding the beaten track, these are today's tastes.'[11] The main instrument of this change was the machine. De Gaulle's emphasis on the impact of *machinisme* and his belief that modern technology radically altered not only military realities but also political, economic, and social arrangements were notable features of his pre-war writing.[12] The effect of technology, in de Gaulle's view, was to quicken the pace of change, both within each society and among nations. By creating rapid transformations in the military and economic capacity of

---

[8] *Discours et messages, 1946–1958* (Paris, 1970), 10.
[9] *Le Fil de l'épée* (Paris, 1944), 53.   [10] Ibid. 54–5.   [11] Ibid. 55.
[12] See e.g. *Vers l'armée de métier*, pp. 26–7.

nations, modern industry produced the conditions for constant, indeed accelerating, competition. This in turn made new demands on political and social structures. His observations about the impact of modern industry convinced de Gaulle, as early as 1934, that the French republican tradition was incompatible with great power status in the twentieth century. A system which had functioned well enough in 'the easy times' of the late nineteenth century, when the pace of change had been relatively slow and the state's role limited, could no longer keep abreast of change or preserve the nation's security and status.[13] He was to return to this theme after the Liberation, at the crucial moment when the constituent process was beginning:

A century in which, in every area, life is undergoing the acceleration of mechanization, in which domestic and external problems crop up in ever quicker and more complex rhythm, in which the tasks facing government and its bureaucracy never cease to grow in every dimension, in which modern means of destruction place any ill-defended country at the risk of immediate invasion—this century can no longer put up with a system like the one that we practised at the outset of this war, which suffered from paralysis.[14]

Whereas the issue of *machinisme* had loomed large in de Gaulle's pre-war writing, the question of France's relation to the international system had been relatively tangential. This was not because de Gaulle thought it unimportant, but because the immediate danger to France's security and independence in the 1920s and 1930s seemed localized (i.e. from Germany). One of the first discoveries that de Gaulle made after this danger had materialized in 1940 was that another, more fundamental, threat existed: whatever the outcome of the war, France might become a permanently second-rank power. In the war against Vichy and Germany, in the painful squabbles with the Allies, in the post-Liberation foreign policy, and in the long years of opposition after 1946, the status of France became an overriding consideration for de Gaulle. His philosophy of renovation must be seen in the context of a determination to preserve the status and autonomy of France within the emerging post-war international system. As with his ideas about mechanization, de Gaulle's ideas about France's

---

[13] Ibid. 106–7.
[14] Radio broadcast of 12 July 1945. *Discours et messages, 1940–1946*, p. 582.

position in the world began from an assumption that a critical and irreversible change in the conditions facing the nation was taking place.[15] Once again his message was that 'the easy times' had come to an end. The new order would be harsher than the old, since there now existed an unmistakable disparity between the power and resources of France and those of the superpowers. This disparity created an unprecedented and seemingly permanent threat to the nation's independence—not only the danger of direct aggression, but the more insidious danger of becoming a satellite of one or other (or both) of the superpowers.

De Gaulle identified renewal with an improvement in the status of the French nation in the world as much as (and probably rather more than) an increase in the social harmony or prosperity of the French population. If the Resistance tended to see renewal as renewal of the French rather than of France, de Gaulle tended in the opposite direction. He certainly acknowledged the link between domestic renewal and France's international status. It was obvious to him that a significant improvement in France's international standing could not take place without economic modernization: 'From the moment that armies cease to be the essence of nations, it is the capacity to live, to work, and to produce that becomes at once the most vital condition of a country's independence and influence.'[16] Conversely, he understood that there were certain domestic advantages which might accrue to France from a well-conducted foreign policy: the political and economic benefits to be derived from governing a large and stable empire; coal supplies from Germany; financial aid from America. But more importantly de Gaulle believed that the link between domestic renewal and international standing was an organic one: domestic renewal could only be achieved if there existed a mystique of national *grandeur* reinforcing the incentives of personal or class interest. Not only would domestic renewal without *grandeur* mean self-defeating consumerism, but it would probably mean no renovation at all—if sectional interests continued to overwhelm the general interest—or else a precarious renovation, whose price would be a permanent dependence on others.

[15] The general's most famous discussion of the changing international environment occurred in a speech which he delivered at Bar-le-Duc in July 1946. *Discours et messages, 1946–1958*, pp. 14–15.

[16] Speech of 24 May 1945, *Discours et messages, 1940–1946*, p. 554. See also the speech of 4 Jan. 1948, *Discours et messages, 1946–1958*, p. 167.

Unlike the leaders of the main parliamentary parties, de Gaulle refused to define renewal in terms of a given set of policies. Unlike many in the Resistance, he also refused to define it as a change of political personnel. One of the distinctive features of gaullist philosophy was its attention to the processes of change, in particular to the central role of the state. The first principle of his critique of the Third and Fourth Republics was not an attack on the substance of their policies, but a belief that the regime had fatally undermined the power of the one agency in France—the state—that was capable of initiating and carrying through reform. The belief that France could only be renewed by the state was already evident in the writing of the pre-war staff officer. In March 1935, for example, he had written to the chief parliamentary patron of his strategic ideas, Paul Reynaud, as follows:

Let us not expect the military corps—any more than any other—to transform itself unaided. Experts are too busy with their current service, and also, inevitably, too divided by their theories, their jobs, and even, alas, their rivalries to undertake and see through a reform of this scope without the assistance and prodding of the authorities.[17]

It is clear that the corollary of this faith in the state was a scepticism about the capacity of parliamentarians (as much a *corps*, in his mind, as the Army High Command) to bring about change. This was something more than mere anti-parliamentarianism (although de Gaulle obviously had such instincts). De Gaulle was at times bitterly critical of the Third and Fourth Republics' leaders but ultimately he believed that what mattered was the system within which élites operated, not which ones were in charge. During the war he was able to find extenuating circumstances for the mistakes of Daladier and Gamelin,[18] just as he was later to blame the errors of the Fourth Republic's governments on the 'system'.[19] The notion that the success of a reform should depend less upon the personal qualities of the élites than upon the structure within which they operated—in particular upon the existence of an independent state—set de Gaulle at odds with the 'voluntarist' Resistance.

[17] De Gaulle, *Lettres, notes et carnets*, ii (Paris, 1980), 384. See also de Gaulle's letter of 3 May 1940, ibid. 493–4, which makes the same point.
[18] See the letter to 'Pertinax' (Charles Géraud), ibid., vol. iv (Paris, 1982), 594–6.
[19] For this kind of argument, see his speeches of 7 Apr. 1947, 20 Sept. 1947, 2 Oct. 1949, 15 Apr. 1951, 1 May 1952.

In order for the state to fulfil its role as the agent of change, it had to be given a form of its own, distinct from any parliamentary assembly and yet derived from the nation. De Gaulle believed that this could only be possible if the state were incarnated in the person of a national leader. In one sense this leader was always de Gaulle himself. But even if one resists the temptation to read all his ideas in a personal light, it remains essential to emphasize that he rejected a depersonalized or bureaucratic state. For de Gaulle, the proper exercise of state power was always synonymous with 'le caractère' (one of the chapter headings in *Le Fil de l'épée*).[20] In other words, it consisted less of an organizational structure than of a set of human qualities (such as decisiveness, self-assurance, and high ambitions). The leadership of the individual was thus the very opposite of that of a collective élite, since in the latter, as we have seen, structure counted for far more than personality.

These were the four basic assumptions of de Gaulle's philosophy of renewal: an acceptance of modernity; a preoccupation with France's status within an international system; a vision of the state as independent of all the *corps constitués* of the nation (including parliament) and as the agent of renewal; and, finally, an insistence on the crucial role of the national leader.

How far this philosophy had impressed itself on the French people or on its new leaders by August 1944 is difficult to determine. Certainly the idea—or expectation—that the Liberation would not lead to the restoration of the pre-war *ancien régime* had been firmly established. In economic affairs de Gaulle had indicated his support for nationalization and *dirigiste* methods. On the question of France's future political system, he had made it clear that he wanted no return to the Third Republic, that he advocated a more stable and effective executive, but, above all, that he was committed to letting the nation choose its own constitution. On the details of all these policies, however, he had refused to commit himself before the Liberation. Even after the Liberation, so long as the war was continuing and absorbing most

[20] Since *Le Fil de l'épée* deals with military leadership, its characterizations cannot automatically be translated to the political sphere. There are conflicting opinions among historians as to how much one should read back into de Gaulle's pre-war writings (most of which dealt with military affairs). But the resonances between the philosophy of leadership expounded in *Le Fil de l'épée* and de Gaulle's actual style of leadership after 1940 are too striking to overlook altogether.

of his energies, he made little progress in defining his programme. Almost six months after the Liberation, a committee representing the Socialists and the Christian Democrats told de Gaulle that they supported the government's policy but were 'anxious to learn its main principles'.[21] Between the Liberation and his resignation from office in January 1946, de Gaulle played an active role in the public debate about renewal: in all the areas of social, economic, imperial, and constitutional reform, his voice was prominent (as will be obvious from the following chapters). Yet the essence of his strategy for achieving renovation only emerged fully after the resignation. That essence was his constitutional blueprint. All other reform—be it economic planning, pro-natalist legislation, or worker participation schemes—was hypothetical, in the sense that it could never bear fruit until the renovation of the state had been accomplished.

The MRP: New Movement and Old Ideals

In the post-Liberation era there seemed no clearer demonstration of the profound political changes which the war had produced than the emergence of the Christian Democratic Mouvement Républicain Populaire as a leading and—after the elections of 2 June 1946—*the* leading party in France. Even more than the Communist party, which had already been gaining strength before the war, the MRP epitomized the new élite which was emerging from the Resistance. In the last years of the Third Republic, the largest Christian Democratic party, the Parti Démocrate Populaire (PDP), had held just thirteen seats in the chamber of deputies.[22] During its sixteen-year existence the PDP had claimed no major ministry and headed no government. The contrast with the Fourth Republic could scarcely have been greater: the MRP participated in twenty-three of the twenty-seven governments which held office between 1944 and 1958, and during that period provided three Prime Ministers

---

[21] This resolution was reported to the MRP's executive commission at its meeting of 3 Feb. 1945. AN, 350 AP 45.

[22] Less than 3% of the electorate voted for the PDP in 1936, whereas the MRP's support in the three general elections of 1945–6 fluctuated between 24.9% and 28.1%.

78   *Regimes and Renewal*

('présidents du conseil'), seven deputy Prime Ministers, and numerous ministers.[23]

A number of factors combined to transform the political prospects of this group which, like de Gaulle, had been on the margins of political life under the Third Republic. The first and most important of these factors was the active role which Christian Democrats had played in the Resistance. Inter-war militants had often attributed the relative failure of the PDP (and of the other Christian Democratic party, the more left-wing Jeune République) to the lack of charismatic or nationally renowned political leadership.[24] In the euphoric months after the Liberation this no longer seemed a problem. Georges Bidault had presided over the CNR and in September 1944 became the first post-Liberation Minister of Foreign Affairs. The new government also included two other leading Christian Democratic resisters (François de Menthon and Pierre-Henri Teitgen). These men, and others (such as Maurice Schumann) who had made their names in the gaullist organization outside France, were better known in 1944 than any of the PDP's deputies had ever been. Perhaps as important was the host of lesser names who had made solid reputations through their involvement in Resistance organizations and were to staff the upper echelons of the nascent MRP.

If resistance heroism provided post-war Christian Democrats with the leaders and the immediate access to ministerial office which the pre-war movement had lacked, it also temporarily released the MRP from an ideological burden which its predecessors had been forced to bear. The inter-war PDP's political life had been dominated by its struggle, as a Catholic party, to prove its republican credentials. Through their wartime heroism, the Catholics of the Resistance had momentarily broken through the barrier of acceptability. The MRP began life in November 1944 with a degree of legitimacy as a bona fide republican party which the PDP had never had.[25]

[23] R. E. M. Irving, *Christian Democracy in France* (London, 1973), 13.
[24] R. W. Rauch, *Politics and Belief* (The Hague, 1972), 47; and Marcel Prélot, 'Les Démocrates Populaires Français: chronique de vingt ans (1919–1939)', *Scritti di sociologia e politica in onore di Luigi Sturzo*, iii (Bologna, 1953), 223.
[25] Evidence of this fact was the electoral support which the new party picked up in what had once been Radical party strongholds. See J.-J. Becker and S. Berstein, 'Modernisation et transformation des partis politiques au

Thirdly, the Vichy period had so gravely compromised the most important parties of the right, especially the clerical right, that the MRP encountered far less competition for Catholic votes than the PDP had faced. The collaborationism of the anti-republican right had broken the spell which Action Française and extreme anti-parliamentarianism had exercised on the Catholic bourgeoisie.[26] As for the former parliamentary representatives of Catholic France (like the Republican Federation), with a few notable exceptions they had stayed loyal to Pétain too long to salvage political credibility after the Liberation. The virtual disappearance of the parties of the right gave the MRP a vast reservoir of potential support. In the long term this support was to prove a two-edged sword for a party which proclaimed itself to be revolutionary. In the elections of 1945 and 1946, however, it was clearly the single most important cause of the MRP's success.

Finally, it became clear that the very weakness of the inter-war Christian Democrats was an asset to their post-war successors. At a moment when the nation was anticipating change, when 'new' was the staple of all political rhetoric, the lack of a past to haunt this new party was anything but a disadvantage. The other main parties had to carry the burden of their failings during and after 1940 (notably the parties of the centre and right, but also, to a certain extent, the Socialists), or of their failings before 1940 (in differing degrees all the main parties of the Third Republic), or (in the case of the Communist party) of their failings between 1939 and Hitler's invasion of Russia in June 1941. The MRP capitalized on the notable resistance record of its leaders and on their almost complete absence from power under the Third Republic, by styling itself 'the party of the Fourth Republic'. The theme of the MRP's newness was hammered home incessantly by its electoral candidates, especially in the first post-war general elections of October 1945.[27] The party's guidelines to its speakers began with

début de la Quatrième République' (paper presented to the colloquium, *La France en voie de modernisation (1944–1952)* (Paris, 1981)), 19.

[26] See Stanley Hoffmann, 'The Effects of World War II on French Society and Politics', *French Historical Studies*, 2 (1961), 50–1.

[27] A selection of the MRP's election manifestos may be found in the BN's *Recueil de tracts électoraux, listes, programmes . . . élections générales, 21 octobre 1945*, 4 Le 100.34.

the advice: 'It is important not to forget to locate the MRP as a new party, forged in the Resistance.'[28]

The MRP may have been new to power, but in terms of its ideology and of its leadership it was anything but a new creation. This latest incarnation of the Social Catholic tradition was heir to a century-old history. At the inaugural party congresses of 1944 and 1945, there were frequent invocations of the nineteenth-century fathers (Lamennais, Lacordaire, Montalembert, de Mun), the pioneers of the early twentieth century (Marc Sangnier's *Sillon*), and inter-war precursors (the PDP and the Catholic Action movements). In achieving an unprecedented unification of the disparate elements in this diverse past, the MRP chose its ideas selectively and certainly added new ones of its own. Nevertheless, it soon became clear that many sections of the party's programme were new only in the sense of untried (as opposed to recently acquired). Much of the MRP's constitutional plan for the Fourth Republic—a second chamber representing non-political interests, a reinforced presidency, proportional representation—had long been propounded in Christian Democratic circles and was inherited directly from the PDP.[29] So too its ideas about 'humanizing' the condition of the working class and managing the economy through an extensive network of professional organizations had figured prominently in the pre-war manifestos of the PDP and in the canons of Christian Democratic philosophy.

The new party's programme for post-war France may be seen as the intertwining of this established tradition with a new Resistance tradition (epitomized by the vogue for nationalization and planning). It was a combination that was perfectly illustrated in the collective biography of the MRP élite. Almost all the MRP's deputies and party officials were new to prominence in national politics. In that sense they were products of the Resistance. Yet they were not people for whom the Resistance had been their only formative activism. Most of those who attended the clandestine meeting of 16 January 1944, at which the preliminary programme of the MRP was debated and adopted, were former members of

---

[28] 'Quelques conseils pour un exposé sur le MRP' (Dec. 1945), in AN, 350 AP 93. The MRP's archives are preserved in the AN's series 350 AP.

[29] For summaries of the PDP's programme, see Irving, *Christian Democracy in France*, pp. 46–8, and Raymond-Laurent, *Le Parti Démocrate Populaire, 1924–1944* (Le Mans, 1966), 65–88.

the PDP.[30] Almost half of the MRP's deputies elected in 1945 had belonged to the PDP and many had held national or departmental posts in the pre-war party.[31] Fifteen per cent, of the deputies had belonged to the Catholic trade union movement,[32] while a third major group within the party was comprised of those who had been active in the Catholic Action movement before the war (most of whom had not engaged directly in parliamentary politics).[33] Furthermore, many of the party's élite had been prominent in political or journalistic enterprises during the inter-war period, writing for *La Vie Catholique* or for *L'Aube*, or participating in the Nouvelles Équipes Françaises.

Considering the MRP's policies with one eye on the longer *durée* helps to bring out important elements of continuity. But such an approach also elucidates the ways in which the MRP programme represented a break from or a progression beyond pre-war programmes. The MRP is too often portrayed as a purely conservative party. Such representations are based, implicitly or explicitly, on a comparison between the revolutionary declarations of the founding congress of November 1944 and the increasingly cautious and pragmatic policies pursued by MRP ministers under the Fourth Republic. Certainly the early denunciations of the 'trusts' were toned down. As time passed, MRP speakers made fewer and fewer references to the CNR charter or to the destruction of capitalism. Still, in spite of a perceptible erosion of enthusiasm for certain structural reforms (notably nationalizations), the MRP remained an integral part of the reformist coalition throughout the period leading up to the creation of the Fourth Republic. If comparisons are drawn with the pre-war PDP, it becomes difficult to label the post-Liberation MRP conservative.

Furthermore, it is important to remember that the party began life with more ideals than ideas, and that the 'evolution' of subsequent years was as much as anything a process of definition. Though all resisters found it difficult to translate the revolutionary verbalism of wartime manifestos into peacetime policies, the Christian Democrats found it perhaps hardest of all. For them, the experience of the Resistance had confirmed the predominantly

---

[30] E. Pezet, *Chrétiens au service de la cité* (Paris, 1965), 109.
[31] R. Bichet, *La Démocratie chrétienne en France: le MRP* (Besançon, 1980), 77.
[32] Irving, *Christian Democracy in France*, p. 81.   [33] Ibid. 50, 79.

ethical vision of politics which had always been a feature of Christian Democracy. This was a tendency which the tiny inter-war party had not needed to fight, since it had never been a party of government. The MRP, however, was faced with the task of going beyond ideals to create policies.

'The ideal which motivates us', said one of the MRP's founders in 1945, 'is an ideal of liberation. After the liberation of the country we want the liberation of man.'[34] This meant more than merely restoring political democracy (and extending it to women). The party's first manifesto, drafted before the Liberation by Colin and Simonnet, set the tone for all the MRP's early statements when it declared that it was 'on the economic and social level . . . that the task to be undertaken is greatest'.[35] Christian Democrats had always adopted a progressive attitude on social questions and criticized capitalists for turning workers into slaves of their machines. This disapproval had been reinforced during the Occupation years by what Christian Democrats interpreted as an attempt by Vichy (acting as a proxy for the bourgeoisie) to exploit the German presence in order to repress the working class still further. In November 1944 Christian Democratic demands were more radical than ever before: the MRP heralded a 'socio-economic 1789', a revolution which would liberate workers from the subordinate position assigned to them by liberal capitalism.[36] The new party endorsed the CNR's Common Programme. It proposed to nationalize banking, insurance, gas, electricity, coal, and transport. It accepted the need for a permanently expanded role for the state in the management of the national economy. It advocated a comprehensive social security system and a demo-cratization of the educational system.

The aim of this liberation was not simply to destroy capitalism, but to remove all impediments to the free moral and intellectual development of each individual. This was a communitarian more

[34] André Colin, addressing the party's *conseil national* of 7–8 Apr. 1945, AN, 350 AP 55.
[35] *Lignes d'action pour la Libération* (Paris, 1945).
[36] See e.g. the *projet de manifeste* drafted for the founding congress: 'Pour libérer l'homme et la femme du Peuple des servitudes économiques qui l'écrasent, le MRP entend abattre les trusts et les puissances d'argent. La République sociale qu'il s'agit d'instaurer suppose le renversement de toutes les Bastilles.' AN, 350 AP 12.

than an individualist ideal. Christian Democrats believed that one acquired freedom through participation: 'alone against the state, the individual is doomed to be crushed. By participating in various collective groups . . . the individual protects [his] freedoms alongside his fellow men.'[37] If the destruction of liberal capitalism was a necessary condition for such participation, a second condition—a second ideal for the MRP—was an abundance of thriving intermediary communities (family, factory, profession, etc.) to channel participation. Ironically, at the same time as proposing to carry through a socio-economic 1789, the MRP wanted to undo the *Loi Le Chapelier* and reintegrate the individual into natural communities. All the new party's policies reflected this aspiration: from its unsuccessful campaign to institutionalize the *vote familial* as a way of giving extra power to the parents of large families to its encouragement of closer co-operation between workers and capitalists within the factory and at the sectoral level.

The events of the war fostered within Christian Democracy a third ideal which had existed in a more diffuse form before 1940 but which the trauma of defeat and occupation greatly intensified: the ideal of the nation. '[W]e have been humbled and have come to realize the fragility as well as the necessity of nations.'[38] Socio-economic reform and patriotism went together. A party memorandum of February 1945 expressed this in the following way:

Our economic and social programme is to put the economy at the service of Man and Nation. These two objectives are not opposed to one another; it cannot even be said that they overlap; they are parts of a single whole. It is necessary for the Nation to be free and strong so that the men who live in it can realize their entire vocation as men. It is necessary to improve the human condition so that all men can serve the Nation effectively. The Nation must be, for us, the setting for a revolution serving Man.[39]

Reflecting a widespread view that France's economic decline had contributed to the defeat of 1940, the MRP stressed the importance

[37] Albert Gortais, 'Rapport sur la doctrine du MRP', Third National Congress, 13–16 Mar. 1947, AN, 350 AP 14.
[38] Georges Hourdin, 'La Résistance et les partis dans la France libérée', *Politique* 1 (1945), 40.
[39] 'Note sur les principes et thèmes du programme économique et social', AN, 350 AP 45. For the same argument, see Gortais' 'Rapport sur la doctrine du MRP', ibid. 14.

of industrial modernization as a key to restored national power. It was not afraid to face the implications of such a policy: 'Industrial re-equipment cannot be accomplished without the abandonment of working methods traditional in France. The industrial structure of our country is still in large part of the artisan type. . . . Our only hope today is to abandon an outdated social equilibrium and search for a new equilibrium which is adapted to the demands of the twentieth century.'[40] This represented a significant development beyond the PDP's pre-war policies. The PDP's economic doctrine had been distinctly 'malthusian'—full of foreboding about 'unbridled mechanization' and reluctant to endanger the delicate 'balance' of a stagnating economy. The experience of the war convinced Christian Democrats that over-production was not the problem, that economic power was at the root of national strength, and that France's economy had fallen behind that of her competitors. Characteristic of the new outlook was the fact that the MRP now challenged the financial orthodoxies by which pre-war parties (including the PDP) had operated. In place of the old belief that a balanced budget was the key to economic recovery, the MRP argued the opposite: in an era when modernization was a national imperative, 'l'économique prime le financier'.

The Christian Democrats' fourth ideal was perhaps the most potent of them all: the ideal of themselves as the nation's new élite. Like most of the Resistance, they ascribed the catastrophe of 1940 to the weakness and cowardice of the bourgeoisie which had placed its narrowly defined class interests before those of the nation.[41] How could the Christian Democrats, most of whose leading members were bourgeois,[42] claim to be replacing the bourgeoisie in this revolution? The answer cannot be reduced to simple hypocrisy or hyperbole in the euphoric afterglow of liberation. The members of the new party shared a sense of

[40] 'Les Objectifs économiques de la France' (May 1946), in AN, 350 AP 93.

[41] See e.g. the report of Georges Hourdin to the National Congress of December 1945: 'Il ne faut pas compter non plus sur la bourgeoisie, considérée comme classe dirigeante. Ici, je suis bien d'accord avec M. Léon Blum: la guerre de 1939 et la défaite de 1940 lui ont porté le dernier coup', AN, 350 AP 12.

[42] For the social background of MRP ministers and deputies, see E. F. Callot, *Le Mouvement Républicain Populaire* (Paris, 1978), 420, 428. Among deputies there was a relatively broad spread of professions, although the majority came from the liberal professions, the law, and farming. Among the party élite the bias towards the bourgeoisie was more marked: the liberal professions, the law, and education provided 23 of the 35 MRP ministers.

participating in a national mission, which transcended class distinctions (and allowed them to transcend their class identity). In part this sense derived from the Resistance, which gave those who took part in it a feeling of moral superiority, especially *vis-à-vis* the 'haute bourgeoisie' who had stayed loyal to Pétain. But it also derived in large measure from the Christian Democratic tradition. As a result of their advanced social and political views, Christian Democrats had always felt themselves to be outside the mainstream of bourgeois society. This sense of being outsiders among the *bien-pensants* was strongly expressed at the MRP's founding congress. Pierre-Henri Teitgen's speech to the 1944 congress was perhaps the classic statement of MRP exceptionalism.[43] Teitgen argued that France needed an entirely new élite to take over 'at the controls and at various levels of the administrative hierarchy'. It was the MRP's role—or mission—to provide them. 'In a liberal system, it is easy to find leaders and cadres: all one has to do is appeal to the profit motive. But if we want our reforms to work, we must find men who are capable of doing with altruistic motives, to serve their country, what others did in the past to make money.' If the war had shattered many illusions, it had also fostered the Christian Democrats' greatest illusion: that a disinterested élite could somehow transcend social and political divisions and, through its example alone, reconcile and renovate the nation.

The Socialist Party: Wartime Planning and Post-war Inertia

Since the MRP was only formally created at the Liberation, it was natural that most of its programme for post-war renewal should have been written after 1944. This was not true of the Socialist party. Not only did the post-war party inherit many of the inter-war SFIO's policies, but throughout much of the Occupation there had survived an embryonic party organization—the Comité d'Action Socialiste (CAS)—which had laid the foundations of a programme for the post-war period. In fact, between 1940 and 1944 Socialists

---

[43] The text of this speech is taken from the minutes of the Congress preserved in the MRP archives (AN, 350 AP 12). An abbreviated (and toned-down) version of this speech was reprinted in the MRP manifesto, *Bâtir la France avec le peuple* (Paris, 1944). On the same theme, see Hourdin's report of Dec. 1945 (AN, 350 AP 12).

devoted more energy than any comparable political group to
thinking about what should follow liberation. In May 1941 one of
the first official statements of the CAS instructed party militants to
reflect 'on what you will ask of our future Constituent Assembly,
the one which we will all, men and women, elect as soon as we are
able to do so'.[44] During the following three years the party
responded energetically to this instruction: indeed it was criticized
by the Communist party and by some resisters for doing so too
zealously.[45] Yet the paradox about the Socialist party was that
once the Liberation arrived and the Constituent Assembly that the
party had predicted was in prospect, the interest in reflecting on
what might be achieved there appeared to evaporate. The main
concerns of the party in the period 1944–6 were either tactical or
doctrinal. Though the party's programme was not ignored, it was
no longer the main focus of attention.

The Socialists' wartime concern with post-war issues may be
explained in a number of ways. In part it reflected the political
nature of their resistance. Before the war the Socialist party had
been a far more parliamentary organization than the PCF, and the
PS found it correspondingly more difficult to adapt to the
conditions of clandestine armed conflict. Unlike the Communists,
Socialists also had to contend with the fact that a substantial
section of their party had voted for Pétain in 1940 or defected to
the side of collaboration. Although Socialists comprised almost
half of the parliamentarians who refused to grant Pétain full
powers on 10 July 1940 (thirty-six out of eighty), ninety Socialist
deputies and senators voted in favour of full powers.[46] The party
general secretary, Paul Faure, and an ex-minister, Charles
Spinasse, were among the many prominent party members who
reached an accommodation with the New Order. This split initially
acted as a powerful incentive for Socialist resisters to define an
authentically Socialist programme: under the Occupation, programmatic activity became a means of preserving the party's true
identity. The incentive was all the greater since the Socialist
defectors were themselves energetic ideologues: collaborationist

[44] 'Vive la République', quoted by Marc Sadoun, *Les Socialistes sous l'Occupation*
(Paris, 1982), 128.
[45] See the Socialist party letter to the PCF (dated 20 July 1944) in AN, 72 AJ 3.
See also Claude Bourdet, *L'Aventure incertaine* (Paris, 1975), 178.
[46] Daniel Ligou, *Histoire du socialisme en France, 1871–1961* (Paris, 1962), 469.

journals such as *L'Œuvre*, *La France Socialiste*, *Le Rouge et Le Bleu*, and *L'Effort* were full of programmes and projects to redefine socialism.[47]

As the military tide turned against Germany, the threat that collaboration posed to the reputation and credibility of Socialist resisters became less significant. But other factors emerged to reinforce their interest in post-war planning. Particularly important were the growing commitment of the Resistance as a whole to the ideology of socialism and the rehabilitation of the Socialist party as a major political force (signalled by the party's representation in the CNR and the prominence of Socialists in the CFLN and the Consultative Assembly in Algiers). The first development placed the party in the ideological mainstream of the Resistance. The second compelled the leadership to envisage an active role for the party in the Provisional Government that was expected to rule the country after liberation. Four years after the devastating schism of 1940, the party found itself on the verge of becoming a party of government. In April 1944 a party circular advised regional officials: 'It seems . . . advisable . . . that the PS ready itself for a role in government.'[48] This eventuality—which the leadership of the CAS eagerly anticipated—had important implications:

If the party's position before the war—or at least before 1936—was relatively easy (expounding its doctrine, criticizing the evils of the capitalist system from inside parliament . . .), the present conditions of our struggle have changed.

It is no longer a question of expounding a doctrine, and on current political issues confining ourselves to a critical attitude. Now it is a matter of (1) expounding our deferred solutions to a new world in process of gestation, (2) translating these solutions into reality, (3) possessing men who are capable of applying our conceptions in practice . . .[49]

The realization that the party was in a position to participate in the post-Liberation governments gave an added sense of urgency to the consideration of post-war programmes. It was essential to

---

[47] For a good survey of Socialist collaborators, see Sadoun, *Les Socialistes*, pp. 55–108.
[48] 'Aux responsables fédéraux et régionaux', in AN, 72 AJ 70.
[49] 'Circulaire aux secrétaires départementaux et régionaux, le 20 juillet 1944', pp. 7–8, in AN, 72 AJ 70. A measure of the importance of this memorandum is that it was reprinted in Robert Verdier's *rapport administratif* to the first post-war national congress: PS, *37ᵉ congrès national, 11–15 août 1945: rapports* (Paris, 1945), 35–42.

establish both a maximum and a minimum programme of reforms which would justify the party's participation in de Gaulle's government.

A large proportion of this wartime thinking about the future was done by a small number of prominent party members (notably André Philip, Jules Moch, Vincent Auriol, and Léon Blum himself). On the other hand, the rethinking was not just the work of isolated individuals. The clandestine party organization which Daniel Mayer and a few others had formed by 1941 was actively involved. This involvement took two forms. First, from 1942 onwards, the CAS set up study commissions to consider a broad range of policy issues. The CAS groups produced reports on such critical issues as the constitution of the Fourth Republic and the extent and modes of nationalization. As the Liberation approached, the study commissions' reports were co-ordinated by the party's executive committee to form the basis of a *programme d'action immédiate*.[50] The other manifestation of the CAS's activity was a series of programmes which it produced in the final twenty months of the Occupation. The first one was published in the party's clandestine newspaper, *Le Populaire*, in January 1943.[51] A second was drawn up in England in the spring of 1943 by Daniel Mayer, who relied on a series of reports drafted by Georges Boris, Louis Lévy, and Raymond Haas-Picard.[52] A third draft was approved by the party in December 1943[53] and a fourth was approved in March of the following year.[54] These four programmes offered a Socialist prescription for post-Liberation reform (extensive nationalizations, intensified and co-ordinated economic production, an extension of the 1936 social legislation, profit-sharing). But they were presented less as party manifestos than as syntheses which could unite all elements in the Resistance: they were, in other words, Socialist drafts of a joint Resistance programme.

The party's concern with its programme did not come to a complete halt at the Liberation. The study commissions which had

[50] See Dumas, 'Programme d'action immédiate: rapport au comité exécutif', 15 Aug. 1944, in AN, 72 AJ 70.
[51] No. 16.
[52] Mayer, *Les Socialistes dans la Résistance* (Paris, 1968), 98–9, 218–23.
[53] The programme of December 1943 was reprinted after the war in a party brochure: *Le Parti Socialiste et l'unité française* (Paris, 1944).
[54] For the text of this draft, see Claire Andrieu, *Le Programme Commun de la Résistance: des idées dans la guerre* (Paris, 1984), 160–7.

been established under the Occupation were maintained by the party leadership. Three months after the Liberation, Daniel Mayer told de Gaulle that 'our study commissions [are] going to draw up a programme of nationalizations', and offered to place this programme at the government's disposal.[55] If the highest priority was to prepare these detailed proposals for nationalization of the main sectors of the French economy, the commissions also considered numerous other fields of policy: by mid-1945, twenty-seven groups were in existence, several of which had sub-committees (the agricultural commission alone having fourteen sub-committees).[56] The range of studies that these commissions (which consisted of a small number of specialists[57]) tackled went from public health to administrative reform, from planning to education, from the German problem to fertilizers. Co-ordinating their work was a *comité technique*, whose task was to approve and pass on policy proposals to the parliamentary group and the *comité directeur*. The study groups and *comité technique* included some of the most creative brains in the party: Moch, Philip, Dumas, Salomon Grumbach, and Georges Boris.[58]

The technical contribution which these committees made to substantiating the Socialist party's claim to be a party of government was considerable. However, the specialists' work coincided with an increasingly marked tendency (both within the party leadership and among party militants) to neglect policy issues. Instead, the post-Liberation party focused its attention both above and beneath policy: either on large doctrinal issues raised by Blum's revisionist wartime essay, *A l'échelle humaine*, and his speech to the 37th party congress of 1945 (in which he suggested that the ultimate aim of socialism was to liberate the human person, not merely transform the ownership of the means of production); or on tactical issues raised by the party's participation in de Gaulle's Provisional Government and in the tripartite ministries of 1946. An indication of the party leadership's priorities was the fact that the *comité directeur* did not devote any

[55] Comité Directeur du Parti Socialiste, procès-verbaux (henceforth PV), 22 Nov. 1944, p. 3.
[56] For a list of the study groups and sub-committees, see PS, *37ᵉ congrès national: rapports*, 96–100.
[57] See Moch's report to the 1945 Congress, ibid. 96.
[58] On the membership of the *comité technique*, see PV, 22 Dec. 1944, and ibid., 18 Dec. 1945.

of its weekly meetings to a review of policy until the end of October 1945. For the preceding twelve months the leadership had been absorbed by such questions as its relations with the head of the Provisional Government and its ideological and organizational links with the PCF.

Virtually every public figure in Paris (including 'reactionaries' like the Archbishop[59]) claimed to support some kind of socialism in the autumn of 1944. As one Socialist put it: 'socialism is in style'.[60] If the PS needed to purge its ranks of collaborators, its analysis of capitalism's crisis appeared to have been vindicated. The first post-Liberation gathering of party militants (in November 1944) proclaimed that the Socialist doctrine 'has been confirmed by events'.[61] The post-Liberation PS liked to emphasize the long-term continuity of its views. When it reprinted its clandestine programme of 11 December 1943, it prefaced it with a claim that had not appeared in the original text: 'This proposal largely drew its inspiration from the party's past programmes, notably the Cahiers de Huyghens of 1932 and the programme of the Rassemblement Populaire.'[62] In the post-Liberation elections of 1945 and 1946, Socialist candidates associated their programmes with past Socialist platforms. In October 1945, for instance, the party's candidates in the Gironde endorsed the CNR's Common Programme because it 'revives the provisions which were not accepted in 1936 by our electoral allies of that era, in particular the return to the nation of the large industrial monopolies . . . unemployment insurance, working class involvement in the running of the economy'.[63]

How far was the party deceiving itself or others with this rhetoric? There were certainly important elements of continuity between the pre-war party and the post-Liberation party. But there were also differences, not only at the doctrinal and tactical levels—where they led to the split of 1946 between Blum's revisionism and the marxist orthodoxy of Guy Mollet—but at the

[59] *Le Populaire*, 2 Dec. 1944.
[60] Anonymous paper entitled 'Vers un grand parti du travail', p. 5, in AN, 72 AJ 3.
[61] 'Le Parti Socialiste au peuple de France' in BN collection of socialist party tracts.
[62] *Le Parti Socialiste et l'unité française*, p. 3.
[63] *Recueil de tracts électoraux*, BN, 4 Le 100.34.

programmatic level. The convergence which had taken place within the Resistance and had created the 'socialist' consensus of August 1944 had also modified the meaning of socialism. The post-Liberation reformism was not merely an ideological reorientation but a pragmatic adjustment of policy to external forces that were unique to this period.

Three contingencies had a particular influence on the Socialist programme during and immediately after the Liberation. The first was the libertarian reaction which four years of foreign occupation brought in their wake. As Blum told the party's National Council in June 1946: 'We have . . . been led to accentuate in our publicity that need for freedom which everyone felt in the aftermath of the German occupation and which many felt still more keenly as a result of their reaction against soviet conceptions.'[64] In this period the PS constantly stressed the dangers of statism. 'Building social-ism', declared the party's *Programme d'Action*, 'does not mean subjecting the country to intrusive statism and bureaucratic red-tape.'[65] It rejected state capitalism on the grounds that, though it might plan production efficiently, it 'only directs the economy towards the improved condition of all . . . at the expense of freedoms which socialists do not consent to give up'.[66] These disclaimers (made repeatedly by the PS between 1944 and 1946) were necessary because socialism had come into vogue at a time when the whole concept of *dirigisme* had been discredited, since it was associated with the constraints and hardships of the Occupation.

The second contingent influence on the Socialists' programme was the resurgence of national sentiment which grew out of the experiences of defeat, occupation, and resistance. Socialists, like other people, had joined the Resistance out of a sense of patriotism. An editorialist of *Le Populaire du Midi* summed up the sentiments of Socialist resisters when he wrote: 'The present circumstances have restored to the idea of the nation the freshness and beauty that yesterday's nationalists sullied with their chauvin-ism.'[67] The rediscovery of the tradition of 1792 confirmed a conception of the party as first and foremost a national movement

---

[64] PS/SFIO, *Conseil national du 9 juin 1946: compte rendu des débats* (Paris, 1946), 165.
[65] *Programme d'action du Parti Socialiste* (Paris, 1945), 4.
[66] *Programme d'action du Parti Socialiste* (Paris, 1946), 23.
[67] Special number, 15 Jan. 1944.

and only secondarily part of an international movement.[68] This conception, in turn, encouraged the party to portray a socialist transformation less as the victory of a single class than as the condition of the entire nation's prosperity and *grandeur*.

Associated with their re-evaluation of the national dimension was a perception of France's decline. The idea that France had suffered a national decline before the war figured prominently in Socialist writings during the Occupation. After the Liberation it became one of the party's major preoccupations. Socialist candidates in the June 1946 elections told their constituents: 'It is not only a matter of returning to the situation of 1939. We must totally renovate our country and catch up the lag which existed in economic and social areas between us and the world's other great nations.'[69] As a result of this perception of decline, issues such as those of structural economic change and long-term modernization were far more prominent in post-war Socialist programmes than they had been in the inter-war period. If Socialism was portrayed as serving national as well as working-class interests, reversing decline seemed the prerequisite for an improvement in the condition of working people's lives, as well as a national necessity.[70]

The Communist Party: Resistance and Reformism

During the period between 1943 and 1946 the Communist party was the most powerful party in France. The early war years, in contrast, had been a very difficult time for the PCF. In August 1939 the news of the German–Soviet pact had shocked many members. In its aftermath the governments of the Third Republic had banned Communist newspapers, ejected PCF deputies from parliament, and thrown many Communists into prison. After the defeat of 1940 the need to defend the pact between Hitler and Stalin had caused further consternation and turmoil: although recent scholarship has modified the allegation (often made by anti-

[68] This was a point that Blum made on his return from prison. See Jérôme Jaffré, *La Crise du Parti Socialiste et l'avènement de Guy Mollet* (Paris, 1971), 53.

[69] *Receuil de tracts électoraux, listes, programmes . . . élections générales, 2 Juin 1946* (BN, 4 Le 101.17), Department of Cher.

[70] See e.g. M. Leenhardt, speaking in the Second Constituent Assembly, *JO, Débats*, 1 Aug. 1946, pp. 2887–9.

Communists) that Communists did not enter the Resistance until Hitler's invasion of Russia in June 1941,[71] the party organization's claim to have resisted before mid-1941 remains tenuous. On the eve of Operation Barbarossa the PCF's strength had been depleted by a mixture of external repression and internal dissension. The party's commitment to national resistance after mid-1941 slowly undid the damage. Gradually it identified the PCF with the cause of liberation and built up an immense moral capital for the party among non-Communists. By 1943 the Communists had become the most powerful single force within the Resistance. At the Liberation this increase in support became quantifiable: in terms of party membership (up from 338,127 in 1937 to 544,921 in 1945), party sections (up from 976 to 2,751) and ultimately in parliamentary seats (up from 72 in 1936 to 148 in October 1945).

The resurgence of the party after 1941, and especially after 1943, coincided with a broadening of its political and social appeal. The party muted its specifically marxist discourse and amplified the national discourse which it had first employed during the Popular Front years in the mid-1930s. In the clandestine battle against the occupying forces, communists invoked the necessity of national unity encompassing all classes—rural and urban, bourgeois and non-bourgeois. Wartime propaganda stressed that the aim of communist resistance was not simply to destroy fascism but to make France 'un pays libre, indépendant et heureux'.[72] Party spokesmen stated frequently that the PCF was motivated by only one concern: 'the greatness and independence of France'.[73] After liberation arrived, the themes of national greatness and independence persisted. The 'parti des 75,000 fusillés', as it styled itself in recognition of its resistance heroism, was unfailingly patriotic. The party leadership (which this time, unlike in 1936, agreed to participate in the government[74]) urged the nation to unite and

[71] See e.g. J. C. Simmonds, 'The French Communist Party and the Beginnings of Resistance: September 1939–June 1941', *European Studies Review*, 11 (1981), 517–41.
[72] 'Extraits de la déclaration des 27 députés communistes français faite à Alger, le 12 juin 1943', in Michel and Mirkine-Guetzévitch, *Les Idées politiques et sociales de la Résistance* (Paris, 1954), 86.
[73] Comité Central du PCF, *La Politique économique de la France nouvelle* (n.d.), 4.
[74] In the government which de Gaulle announced on 9 Sept. 1944, Charles Tillon was named Minister of Air and François Billoux Minister of Public Health.

contribute to the allied war effort against Germany. 'Work, fight
for victory, for the greatness of France,' declared the party's
general secretary, Maurice Thorez, on his return to France from
Moscow at the end of November 1944.[75] Throughout 1945 and
1946 the Communist party exhorted workers to produce as much
and as quickly as possible in order to restore France's strength and
independence. It appealed to peasants, shopkeepers, and artisans
as well as to industrial workers. It praised the patriotic commitment
of engineers, managers, and even *patrons*. Rather than focusing
on the conflict between the working class and the capitalist class, it
set the mass of patriotic French men and women against a tiny
minority of traitors and parasites (the trusts or the 'two hundred
families'). Party orators were far more likely to refer to 1793 than
to 1917. Republicanism, democracy, and national renaissance
were the preferred themes of party propaganda.

The question that tends to be asked about this national
dimension is: why did the party adopt it? Because the PCF
proclaimed itself to be a revolutionary party, those aspects of its
policy which deviated from a self-evidently revolutionary course
are usually analysed in terms of their relation to this ultimate
objective. In the present instance the party's deviation has
prompted the following kinds of question. How far was the party
responding to the needs of a Soviet leadership which was seeking
harmonious collaboration with its capitalist allies and, after the
war, was consolidating its grip on Eastern Europe? How far was
the PCF responding to the same patriotic reflex which resisters of
all persuasions felt after 1940? How far was the patriotic and
consensual rhetoric a front behind which the party hoped to
manœuvre itself into power?[76]

One effect of this emphasis on the motivations of party strategy
has been a relative neglect of the content of party programmes.

Communists had occupied the corresponding *commissariats* in Algiers before the
Liberation.

[75] The text of his speech of 30 Nov. 1944 is in *Cahiers du Communisme*, 2 (Dec.
1944), 9–15.

[76] Some subtle and persuasive answers to these questions have been given by
Philippe Robrieux, *Histoire intérieure du Parti Communiste*, ii. *De la libération à
l'avènement de Georges Marchais, 1945–1972* (Paris, 1981), 13–85; Jean-Jacques
Becker, *Le Parti Communiste veut-il prendre le pouvoir?* (Paris, 1981), 127–41; and
Stéphane Courtois, *Le PCF dans la guerre: de Gaulle, la Résistance, Staline* (Paris,
1980), 387–8, 425, 457–9.

Rather than viewing the Communist programme in the light of the party's 'real' (i.e. revolutionary and pro-Soviet) aims, it will be examined here and in the following chapters at its face value. This does not mean making an assumption that the party programme told the entire truth about the party's objectives, any more than it entails the opposite assumption—that it told none of the truth. It is simply to recognize that the Communist programme—like all party programmes—had some independent significance of its own. In the first place, even in a disciplined party like the PCF, the programme was not automatically and entirely subordinated to the party's political strategy. In fact, it may be argued that on occasion the content of the party's discourse shaped its strategy. As Becker and Agulhon have both suggested, one of the reasons the party was unable to create a revolution in 1944 was that it fell victim to its own consensual propaganda. 'It was difficult, after having declared that it was unifying "all Frenchmen in the struggle on a strictly national basis", to make the masses understand that this appeal also had a revolutionary meaning.'[77] Furthermore, whatever the relation between the party's strategy and its programme, the latter contributed to, influenced, and was in turn influenced by a broader political dialogue about national renewal. In the context of this debate, the external dimension of the Communist programme—what Communists said—is more significant than its internal dimension—why they said it or what they meant.

Under the Occupation the PCF was not one of those groups like the OCM or the Socialist CAS which believed that elaborating a programme for post-war reform was an essential part of resistance activity. *L'Humanité* and the rest of the clandestine Communist party press was a 'presse de combat':[78] the themes which it presented to its readership dealt almost exclusively with the armed struggle, the crimes of traitors and collaborators, the feats of resisters, and the need for unified action.[79] Communist intellectuals writing in *Les Lettres Françaises Clandestines* were far more

[77] Becker, *Le Parti Communiste*, p. 144. See also a conference paper by Maurice Agulhon, 'Les Communistes et la Libération de la France', in *La Libération de la France* (Paris, 1976), 67–90.

[78] The expression belongs to Michel and Mirkine-Guetzévitch, *Les Idées politiques et sociales de la Résistance*, p. 219 n.

[79] A collection of clandestine editions of *L'Humanité* was reprinted by the party under the title *L'Humanité clandestine*.

restrained than their non-Communist counterparts in *Combat* or
Franc-Tireur in evoking visions of what a liberated France might
be like.[80] The party leadership criticized the Socialist newspaper
Le Populaire and the executive committee of the PS for being too
preoccupied with post-war issues at a time when 'the Germans and
the *milice* are waging war against Frenchmen, pillaging, burning,
and murdering the best of our youth'.[81] The clandestine party
argued that the only proper aim for the Resistance was to unite in
preparation for a national insurrection which would liberate the
patrie and restore France to the rank of a great nation. Not
surprisingly, given this priority, the party's contribution to the
elaboration of a common Resistance programme emphasized
those measures which would facilitate the national insurrection
and discounted the longer-term measures which socialists and
trade-unionists were pressing on the CNR.[82]

In many respects the PCF's lack of concern with post-war issues
(certainly when compared to the Socialist party's activity) continued
right up to the Liberation. However, in the final year of the
Occupation, the position did change to a limited extent. As the
fact of liberation, if not its precise circumstances, became more
predictable, there was a sudden urgency—both in Algiers and in
metropolitan France—about post-war planning. If only to ensure
that its future options were not closed off, the Communist party
had to begin considering issues which all the other political groups
inside the CFLN and the CNR were actively debating. During the
final months of 1943 and the first half of 1944, elements of a
Communist post-war programme began to appear. It was in this
period, for instance, that the PCF sketched the outline of its
position on the constitutional question. Two documents were
particularly important in this regard: the 'Observations' which the
PCF presented in the late summer of 1943 in response to a
proposal for a common Resistance programme,[83] and the critique
of the OCM's constitutional blueprint which the party circulated in

---

[80] See David Caute, *Communism and the French Intellectuals, 1914–1960* (New York, 1964), 152–3.

[81] Délégation Zone Sud du Comité Central du PCF, 'Notes du Parti Communiste' (May 1944), in AN, F1a 3751.

[82] This emerges very clearly from Claire Andrieu's admirable study of the CNR charter, *Le Programme Commun de la Résistance* (Paris, 1984).

[83] For a discussion of this document (attributed to the former deputy from the Seine, André Mercier), see ibid. 39–41.

September 1943.[84] Around the same time the party's economic programme emerged from another series of replies to other Resistance organizations (the OCM,[85] the CGE[86] and the Socialist party[87]) and from an important party pamphlet entitled 'Un acte d'accusation contre les traîtres', that was circulated shortly before liberation.[88] Henri Michel has dismissed this activity as relatively insignificant: 'they [the PCF] offered their opinion on other people's proposals rather than making their own proposals known.'[89] It is true that most of the Communists' substantive pre-Liberation statements about post-war reform were framed in the context of rejoinders to other groups' proposals. But it is also true that these rejoinders were often extensive and did not restrict themselves to critiques of the opposing view. From them, and from a couple of important policy statements (such as those on economic and educational reform), a position on post-war issues had emerged by mid-1944 which was not much less clearly defined than that which had emerged from the Socialists' more extensive, but also more diffuse, reflections. The PCF was wary of committing itself publicly to a programme of specific reforms which might have limited its tactical room for manœuvre (prematurely cutting off the insurrectionist option) and would have raised difficult ideological issues. But, reading between the lines, it is certainly possible to discern a reformist critique of pre-war institutions and a programme of non-revolutionary change that could be applied *if* a revolutionary situation were not created in the wake of liberation and *if* the party were to take its place within a regime of national reconstruction.

The main theme in all the PCF's wartime statements about the nation's future was 'the war against the trusts'. The line of attack that the party developed against the trusts expressed its highly

---

[84] 'Sur le projet de constitution de l'OCM: premières observations du Parti Communiste Français', in AN, F1a 3791. A comparison of this text with that quoted by Andrieu suggests that the two documents were very similar.

[85] 'Observations du Parti Communiste sur le rapport OCM 10, *La réforme économique*', in AN, F1a 3751.

[86] This rejoinder to Courtin's *Rapport sur la politique économique d'après-guerre* (written by a small committee of party leaders) was printed by the Central Committee under the title *La Politique économique de la France nouvelle*.

[87] 'Observations du Parti Communiste sur le projet de programme commun présenté par le Parti Socialiste à la Résistance', in Michel and Mirkine-Guetzévitch, *Les Idées politiques et sociales de la Résistance*, pp. 218–38.

[88] The copy cited here is in AN, F1a 3751.

[89] *Les Courants de pensée de la Résistance* (Paris, 1962), 694.

visible patriotism. It accused the trusts of having betrayed the nation and demanded their destruction not as a 'socialist' measure but as a 'public and national necessity', 'in the name of public safety'.[90] The trusts' betrayal had been twofold. The first accusation against them dealt with their activity during the previous decade. The PCF alleged that the trusts had handicapped the French war effort (by slowing down production, sabotaging the Franco-Soviet *rapprochement*, and attacking the working class), and after the defeat had collaborated with their capitalist counterparts in Germany. They were, in short, 'the organizers and profiteers of treason'.[91] At the same time the party levelled a second accusation against the trusts. For the past half-century, it argued, these economic barons had inhibited the development and modernization of the French economy: 'The trusts cannot deny that for fifty years French manufacturing equipment and production volume have remained considerably behind those of other major industrialized nations.'[92] The party rejected the argument that it was the lack of industrial concentration which had produced this result: on the contrary, the party suggested that the progression towards concentration after 1870 had gone hand in hand with the stagnation of the economy. The Communists' diagnosis—if not the aetiology—was similar to that made by neo-liberal modernizers:

. . . parasitic mentality instead of constructive initiative and concern for organization, unscrupulous speculation instead of the dedicated search for technical improvement. The machines in our factories are ten or twenty years too old, and it is only by compressing production costs that one envisages meeting foreign competition. Few or no research departments, few or no laboratories with modern equipment, no funds for research. . . . Finally, no serious production plan adapted to the national interest.[93]

The party diagnosed an economic malthusianism in industry and agriculture which, but for a declining birth-rate, would have left the entire population with a steeply falling standard of living.

In so far as this accusation of economic mismanagement (directed against the trusts, not the capitalist system *per se*) raised the issue of the structural defects of the French economy, it was a first step towards the acceptance of structural reforms (such as

[90] 'Un acte d'accusation contre les traîtres', p. 26.
[91] 'Observations . . . sur le projet . . . présenté par le Parti Socialiste', p. 225.
[92] 'Un acte d'accusation contre les traîtres', p. 4.   [93] Ibid. 5.

nationalization and planning) as economically valid and not merely punitive. The pre-Liberation party was certainly uneasy about proclaiming its adherence to the principle of nationalization which the inter-war party—even in its Popular Front stage—had consistently opposed.[94] In the early stages of the drafting of the CNR charter, Communists opposed the inclusion of any specific commitment about nationalization.[95] In his 'Rapport Chardon' (1943), the Communist resister Pierre Hervé wrote off all structural reforms (including nationalization) as 'a new "asiatic mode" which would be created by a wave of the government's magic wand, without any intervention of the popular masses'.[96] But by November 1943 the party was willing to endorse a Front National programme calling for 'the return to the nation of the main means of production'.[97]

As Philippe Robrieux has shown, most of the PCF's public pronouncements in the autumn of 1944 were compatible with the hypothesis of a gradual replacement of de Gaulle's provisional regime by a 'non-partisan' Resistance (in effect in the hands of the party).[98] Robrieux points to the all-pervasive jacobinism, the vitriol of the assaults on those whom the party labelled as 'vichyites' or 'collaborators', and the sub-theme of a new legality in the Resistance. However, this was not the only tone in the party's propaganda. Albeit discreetly, the party maintained its profile as a party of government committed to a renovation of the nation's economy. In the December 1944 volume of the *Cahiers du Communisme* (the party's most important doctrinal periodical), Benoît Frachon called for extensive nationalizations and suggested that they were necessary not merely to punish the treacherous trusts but to ensure that the post-war economy was rebuilt 'on new foundations'.[99] Throughout the final months of 1944, writers in

---

[94] J.-J. Becker, 'Le Parti Communiste Français et les nationalisations', paper presented to the colloquium *Nationalisations et formes nouvelles de participation des ouvriers à la Libération (1944–1951)* (Paris, 1984).

[95] Andrieu, *Le Programme Commun de la Résistance*, p. 41.

[96] Michel and Mirkine-Guetzévitch, *Les Idées politiques et sociales de la Résistance*, p. 146.

[97] 'Projet d'une charte de la Résistance proposé par le Front National', in Andrieu, *Le Programme Commun de la Résistance*, p. 148.

[98] See especially *Histoire intérieure du Parti Communiste*, ii. 66–76.

[99] 'Le Rôle de la classe ouvrière dans la renaissance de la France', *Cahiers du Communisme* (Dec. 1944), 21–5.

L'Humanité demanded the application of the second half of the Common Programme of March 1944 (the 'measures to be applied after the liberation of the country' that the party had been reluctant to approve six months before).[100] The PCF also continued to stress two points which it had made during the Occupation and which were to be corner-stones of Communist rhetoric throughout the period of the party's participation in government (1944–7). The first was the close connection between national power and economic strength, specifically economic modernization. The primer for party members which was circulated in October 1944 stated, for example: 'The war has vividly demonstrated that a state's political independence was dependent on its industrial equipment and on its capacity to produce the *matériel* and consumer goods necessary for its population and its armies.'[101] The second was a critique of inter-war malthusianism (blamed on the trusts): 'We had a backward and routinish industry. We were always one machine behind advanced countries,' wrote Frachon.[102] The party's agricultural affairs spokesman, Waldeck Rochet, launched his call for the modernization of rural France with the following rhetorical question and observation: 'must we confine ourselves to restoring our agriculture to its pre-war level? No! Because French agriculture is technically very backward in comparison with that of other countries.'[103]

None of this foreclosed the revolutionary option, should it have arisen (as some still hoped in the late autumn of 1944). The party's violent attacks on the trusts' collaboration were the most characteristic aspect of its vocabulary. Communist spokesmen and editorialists played down terms like nationalization which smacked of reformism. But the continuing theme of national union and the implicit acceptance of reformism in the constant references to the CNR Common Programme made for a smooth transition to the period after January 1945, when, with Thorez's return, all revolutionary designs were put aside and the party set about consolidating its strength within a regime committed to non-revolutionary reforms.

[100] See e.g. the editions of 11 Sept., 24 Sept., 24 Oct.
[101] *L'École élémentaire du PCF:* 'notions économiques sur la France' (Paris, 1944), 6.
[102] *Cahiers du Communisme* (Dec. 1944), 24.
[103] *L'Humanité*, 3–4 Dec. 1944.

PART II

Themes of Renewal

Part II: Introduction

BEFORE examining reformist thinking thematically, it is worth identifying some of its major idioms and influences. A thematic approach suggests that reformers of all kinds tended to approach the problem of decline in similar ways. The same metaphors, assumptions, and conceptions will be encountered frequently in the chapters that follow.

A first source of vocabulary was an ever-present past. The interpretations that the French placed on their history were diverse. Reformers sometimes used past failures as arguments for change: there were many, for example, who drew their ideas for the Fourth Republic from a critique of the Third Republic's flaws, or who equated the economic stagnation of the 1930s with a financial obsession about balanced budgets. But the past could also be a source of positive inspiration. It is not difficult to see why a pro-Vichy publishing house should have launched a series of books entitled 'Collection des grands redressements de l'Histoire'.[1] Reformers of all shades generally insisted on a continuity between France's past and their vision of her future. Imperial reformers, for instance, waxed eloquent about the humanity of French colonization and depicted the Union française not as an abnegation of France's colonialism but as a return to the truest traditions of her past. The language of the Resistance and the post-Liberation regime was saturated in the imagery of the French republican tradition.[2] The founders of the Fourth Republic peppered their programmes and speeches with allusions to 1789, 1793, 1830, 1848, 1871, 1934, and 1936. The new Republic was presented as a logical extension of all that was best in the past.

Whatever use they made of historical analogy, it was generally to their own history that the French referred. Conversely, when they drew from a second source of vocabulary—foreign models of reform—they looked to the contemporary or near-contemporary era. Social reformers studied Beveridge, Butler, and the proposals

---

[1] The series was published by Sorlot (Clermont, 1941).
[2] For a discussion of the Resistance's identification with the republican tradition, see H. R. Kedward, *Resistance in Vichy France* (Oxford, 1978), 153–60.

of the ILO. Economic modernizers discussed the Russian four-year plans, Keynesian experiments, and the wartime mobilization of the Anglo-American economies. The members of the Constituent Assemblies compared the merits of the British two-party parliamentary system and the American and Swiss presidential regimes. Pro-natalists studied the demographic successes of Nazi Germany. These foreign models were rarely viewed as transferable in their entirety (and those who suggested otherwise—such as the ultra-collaborationists in occupied Paris—tended to be on the fringes). The general view was that Soviet collectivization would be intolerable to French farmers, that the Commonwealth solution would not work in the French empire, that the US Constitution was inappropriate to a French republic, that the Beveridge report was not as urgently needed in France as across the Channel. French reformers proposed to pick and choose among models of modernity, combining those that were appropriate to France with what they regarded as the most dynamic or beneficial of France's own traditions. Renewal was envisaged as an intricate combination of acceptable innovation and usable tradition. More often than not, the word the French used to describe it was *synthèse*. The *synthèse* was seen as the characteristically French method of renovating the nation: it involved reconciling the great dilemmas of modernity—capitalism or collectivism, liberty or authority, stability or growth—through the application of a creative ingenuity.

To guide themselves between the various Scyllas and Charybdes of the modern world, French reformers drew on their own recent experience of reform. The precedents that had been set by inter-war reformism—the abortive re-evaluation after the First World War, the non-conformist movements of the late 1920s and early 1930s, the Popular Front's legislation, the emergency measures introduced in the final months of the Third Republic—were a third important source of ideas and vocabulary. Many of the individuals who figured prominently in post-1940 reformism had played a role in these inter-war experiments. Others had been influenced, intellectually or politically, by them. Whether consciously or unconsciously, the debate about renewal usually started from positions that had been formulated before the defeat.

For those who came to power in 1944 the most recent experience of reform was the National Revolution. Vichy's reformism was a fourth influence and reference-point in the public debate about the future. It was also an ambiguous reference-point. Especially at the administrative level, many of the État Français's innovations were retained at the Liberation and built upon in the post-war era. It was a Communist minister who, in February 1945, announced that Vichy's Commissariat général à la Famille would be preserved because 'numerous patriots have performed useful work inside it'.[3] Most of Vichy's reforms, however, were highly unpopular, and their unpopularity constituted a powerful negative pole in the debate about the nation's future. In some cases the association of ideas or policies with Vichy was a relatively ephemeral one (not lasting beyond the ascendancy of the National Revolution itself): thus, for example, the negative connotation that the concept of European integration acquired as a result of Vichy's incorporation in Hitler's 'new European order' had faded sufficiently by 1943 for it to appear regularly in Resistance tracts.[4] In other areas (ranging from education to economic policy) the shadow that Vichy reformism cast was a longer and more enduring one.

After the war Vichy was absorbed (like the Resistance) into the collective national past. But during the war it had exerted a much more immediate and direct influence on the debate about national renewal. This illustrates a broader point. At no stage between 1940 and 1946 was reformism a purely intellectual exercise. It did not take place in a political vacuum. Throughout the period, ideas about France's national future were shaped by events in the present—not just seismic events such as defeat, liberation, and changes of regime, but countless other occurrences which influenced the way in which reform arguments were framed and even shaped the agenda of reformism. This was the most pervasive and yet elusive kind of influence on the rethinking of France.

[3] François Billoux, in *JO, Débats*, 7 Feb. 1945, p. 21.
[4] On the slow emergence of pro-European themes in the Resistance's ideology, see Walter Lipgens (ed.), *Documents on the History of European Integration*, i (Berlin and New York, 1985), 270–2.

5

Constitutional Reform

IN 1945 a writer called Léone Bourdel published a slightly bizarre little book, *La Mission de la France*, which began with a utopian scheme for reorganizing the French state. Bourdel's ideas, like those of many other visionaries who were encouraged by the Liberation to set down their plans on paper, were idiosyncratic. However, the identification of state reform as crucial to post-war renewal was utterly typical. State reform meant more than merely rewriting the constitution: as Emmanuel Berl pointed out, the number of those who believed that constitutional clauses alone could regenerate the nation was naturally small in a country which had seen so many constitutions come and go.[1] Reformers usually proposed to change party structures and political mentalities as well as the institutions themselves.

Constitutional reformism had its roots in the pre-war years. It developed considerably under the Occupation, especially in the Resistance and in Free France. After the Liberation, however, it lost much of its momentum. By the time the nation's delegates assembled in Paris in November 1945 to draw up a new constitution, the creative period of the reform movement had come to an end. Some of the ideas which had been raised to prominence were incorporated into the constitution of 1946. Many, however, were either watered down or dropped altogether. The long and complicated process of drawing up a new constitution proved to be far more a contest of political personalities and parties than a contest of ideas. Since it is also a contest which has been well-documented elsewhere,[2] the main focus here will be on the intellectual process that culminated as the Constituent Assemblies began their work.

The collapse of 1940 was not an aberration in the history of an otherwise stable regime. It was, on the contrary, the culmination

---

[1] Berl, *La Fin de la IIIe République*, (Paris, 1968), 211.
[2] See, especially, Gordon Wright, *The Reshaping of French Democracy* (New York, 1948).

of a decade or more of increasing political crisis. Under the cumulative weight of the economic depression, the rise of fascism, and the growing strength on the extremes of left and right, the Third Republic had buckled. Ministry had followed ministry after an average span of less than six months. Decree laws, permitted by parliaments unable to maintain the fiction of legislative control, had given these ephemeral executives dangerously large powers. This vertiginous decline of a regime which had emerged victoriously from the First World War prompted two reactions. The first was a wave of anti-parliamentarianism. This drew its ideological inspiration less from foreign fascism than from fertile home-grown traditions of reaction, and was orchestrated by a number of leagues and parties. The anti-parliamentarians' most celebrated attack on the Republic occurred on 6 February 1934, when a right-wing riot threatened the Chamber of Deputies. The second consequence of the Republic's growing crisis was the emergence of reform movements. Unlike anti-parliamentarians, reformers sought a peaceful transformation and consolidation of French republicanism. The major problem that they addressed was the instability and weakness of republican governments. The constitution of 1875 had given the President of the Republic wide powers, but Presidents had been unable to exercise several of them (most crucially, the power to dissolve the legislature). The effective head of Third Republic governments, the Président du Conseil, had not figured in the constitution at all. As a result, the Présidence du Conseil lacked institutional supports (such as a secretariat) and was held in conjunction with one of the major ministerial portfolios. Présidents du Conseil were too burdened by their ministerial responsibilities to co-ordinate government policy effectively. They were also constantly vulnerable to shifts in parliamentary coalitions.

In the 1920s and 1930s reformers came from across the political spectrum, but more commonly from the right than the left. Apart from an influential article that Léon Blum wrote towards the end of the First World War ('Lettres sur la réforme gouvernementale'[3]), the Socialists made few contributions to inter-war reformism. Both the SFIO and the Radical party tended to oppose constitutional reform on the grounds that reformers were undermining parliamentary rights and privileges. That was the position that the

[3] *La Revue de Paris*, 1 Dec. 1917, pp. 449–73; 15 Dec. 1917, pp. 820–52; 1 Jan. 1918, pp. 140–60.

Radicals adopted in response to Gaston Doumergue's reform plan in 1934.[4] The only group within the Radical party whîch actively endorsed constitutional change were the 'Young Turk' Radicals. In the late 1920s and early 1930s they attempted to renovate the party's ideology and, among their other ideas, proposed to strengthen the powers of the Prime Minister and remodel the legislature.[5]

Elsewhere on the political spectrum, advocates of constitutional reform came from among the leading figures in the Republic. In the early 1920s two Presidents of the Republic (Paul Deschanel and Alexandre Millerand) suggested that the independent authority and power of the President of the Republic ought to be increased.[6] A third inter-war President who campaigned for an increase in the power of the executive (in this case, the Prime Minister rather than the President) was Gaston Doumergue.[7] After being called back from retirement in the wake of the riots of February 1934 to head the government, Doumergue proposed a four-point reform programme, which would have written the Président du Conseil into the constitution, given him the right to dissolve the Chamber, and removed from parliament the right to propose budgetary expenditure. A similar plan for giving the government power of dissolution was tirelessly advocated in the mid-1930s by a former conservative Premier, André Tardieu.[8] Tardieu's plan, in fact, was more far-reaching than Doumergue's: it also included equal voting rights for women, the regular use of referenda by the executive, an enlargement of the electoral college which chose the President of the Republic (one of Millerand's ideas), and the creation of a Supreme Court.

The debate about constitutional reform also extended beyond the republican hierarchy. A number of unofficial bodies considered

---

[4] Peter Larmour, *The French Radical Party in the 1930s* (Stanford, 1964), 157–9.

[5] On the Young Turks, see S. Berstein, *Histoire du Parti Radical: crise du radicalisme, 1926–1939* (Paris, 1982), 94–125, especially 109–11.

[6] See Deschanel's article: 'La Politique extérieure de la France', *Revue des Deux Mondes*, 15 June 1922, 721–37. For Millerand's views, see Raymond Recouly, 'Une visite au président Millerand', *La Revue de France*, Nov.–Dec. 1923, 225–37.

[7] For Doumergue's plan, see the text of his 1934 radio broadcast to the nation, in *Le Temps*, 26 Sept. 1934.

[8] For Tardieu's ideas, see his books: *L'Heure de la décision* (Paris, 1934); *La Réforme de l'État* (Paris, 1934); *Sur la pente* (Paris, 1935); *Le Souverain captif* (Paris, 1936).

the issue. In 1927, for example, a group of centrist political and non-political figures calling themselves the Comité du Groupe d'Étude pour l'Organisation de l'État produced a plan to give the cabinet and the Président du Conseil a more central position in the constitution and to revitalize the National Economic Council (a consultative body which had been created by decree in 1925).[9] Both these ideas were frequently advocated by the technocratic groups which abounded in the inter-war period.[10] Among the more influential plans which such groups produced were the *Plan du 9 juillet* (1934), and one devised by the Comité technique pour la réforme de l'État (1936), which included several people who were to play prominent roles in shaping Vichy's constitutional doctrines.[11]

Another natural source of ideas for constitutional reform was the academic community. One of the most lucid reform proposals was made, on the eve of the defeat, by a law professor called Émile Giraud.[12] If Tardieu was a precursor of the post-war gaullist school of Michel Debré,[13] Giraud's plan anticipated other ideas which parliamentary reformers were to advocate in the period after 1940. Giraud proposed to alter the electoral system to encourage the growth of a few organized parties. He suggested that the government ought to solicit a vote of confidence from the Chamber once each year and should thereafter be immovable except in exceptional circumstances. He also recommended that the Senate should no longer have the power to overturn a government and that the President of the Republic should have an effective right to dissolve the Chamber (on the advice of the Président du Conseil).

Giraud's aim—like that of most inter-war reformers—had been to forge a democratic state which could match totalitarian regimes in terms of efficiency. The suddenness and completeness of the

[9] For this plan, see *L'Europe nouvelle*, 17 Dec. 1927, pp. 1673–5.

[10] See Gérard Brun, *Technocrates et technocratie en France, 1918–1945* (Paris, 1985), 117–19.

[11] For a brief discussion of the Comité technique pour la réforme de l'État, see N. Wahl, 'Aux origines de la nouvelle constitution', *Revue française de science politique*, 9 (1959), p. 62.

[12] See Giraud's book, *La Crise de la démocratie et le renforcement du pouvoir exécutif* (Paris, 1938) and his article (written with André Ganem), 'Plan de réformes d'ordre constitutionnel', *Revue du droit public et de la science politique* (1940), 5–57.

[13] This is the argument of Wahl, 'Aux origines de la nouvelle constitution', 60–1.

defeat in 1940 made that seem a lost cause. The final act of the Third Republic's National Assembly, on 10 July 1940, was to entrust Marshal Pétain with the power to draw up a new constitution. It was generally assumed that he would give up the attempt to square the circle of strong but democratic government, and adopt a much more authoritarian model. Pétain subsequently used his constituent power in two distinct ways. First, he promulgated a series of twelve 'constitutional acts', which defined his powers for the interim period until a new constitution was established. The most important acts were the first two (dated 11 July 1940), which stated that Pétain had assumed the functions of Head of State and detailed his powers.[14] These powers consisted of 'la plénitude du pouvoir gouvernemental' and 'le pouvoir législatif'. The only real restriction on Pétain was that he could not declare war without the assent of the legislative assemblies. Second, and rather belatedly, he set about drawing up the permanent constitution, which the vote of 10 July had stipulated. At the beginning of 1941 he created a Conseil National, one of whose functions was to assist him in his constituent task. Within the Conseil National a special committee was assigned the task of writing a new constitution.[15] This committee was chaired by a constitutional law expert, Joseph Barthélémy, and included twenty-three other members (most of them politicians or intellectuals).[16] It held two sessions, the first in July 1941 and the second in October 1941. In the first series of meetings the commission considered a text prepared by Barthélémy, and in the second a similar text (this time amended by Pétain himself). When Laval returned to power in April 1942, the Conseil National fell into abeyance, as did the constitution that the commission had drawn up. It was a year and a half later, in January 1944, that Pétain finally signed a *projet de constitution de la République française*, which had been drafted for him during 1943 by a small committee (including Lucien Romier, Henri Moysset, Yves Bouthillier, and a former right-wing deputy, Le Cour Grand-

---

[14] *JO, Lois et Décrets*, 12 July 1940, pp. 4517–8.

[15] Some very sketchy records of the constitutional commission of the Conseil National are in AN, F60 361.

[16] For the list of the members, see Jacques de Launay, *Le Dossier de Vichy* (Paris, 1967), 57.

maison).[17] By that stage, needless to say, a Pétainist constitution was bound to be a dead letter.

The main principle of the 1944 constitution was that the power of the executive should be increased. The President of the Republic, who was to be elected by the members of parliament and an equal number of provincial councillors, would hold office for ten years and during that time would be virtually uncontrollable. The President would name and revoke the Prime Minister and cabinet, dissolve the parliament, and exercise complete executive authority (except on the issue of declaring war, where the President had to gain the approval of the two chambers). The proposed constitution also granted women the vote and instituted a bicameral legislature, with the Senate including representatives of professional associations and of the 'national élite'. Both these proposals were to appear in more pro-republican draft constitutions before and after liberation. So indeed were a number of the *projet*'s other recommendations: *vote familial* (defended by the MRP), a Supreme Court to protect the constitution (advocated by a range of Resistance movements), and a Conseil d'Empire to represent the empire within the metropolitan constitution (an idea accepted by almost every group after the Liberation). According to some of his closest associates, the similarities between the 1944 *projet* and mainstream republicanism made Pétain uncomfortable.[18] It is clear that the Marshal wanted the role of the assemblies to be diminished much further than this draft allowed.

At roughly the same time that Pétain's National Council began debating the constitution, some of the members of Free France in London were showing an interest in the issue. They began from the same assumption as the councillors in Vichy—that the Third Republic could not be revived. But whereas Vichyites sought to replace a parliamentary regime with a regime whose guiding principle was *autorité*, the Free French sought to inject more *autorité* into a regime which remained within the French parliamentary tradition.

Free France's counterpart to Vichy's National Council was established by a decree of 2 December 1941. It was a series of four

[17] For an account of this process, see Fernet, *Aux côtés du maréchal Pétain* (Paris, 1953), 209–18. For the text see de Launay, *Le Dossier de Vichy*, pp. 78–87.
[18] See the accounts of Admiral Fernet, *Aux côtés du maréchal Pétain*, pp. 219–20, and Admiral Auphan, *Histoire élémentaire de Vichy* (Paris, 1971), 131–2.

study commissions, one of which (the commission juridique et intellectuelle) had a sub-committee to study state reform.[19] This sub-committee, which provided Free France's earliest coherent ideas on the constitutional issue, had twenty-seven members and was chaired by Félix Gouin, a Socialist deputy from Marseille, who in 1946 was to become Prime Minister. The earliest minutes of the sub-committee's meetings to be found in the archives of the study commission secretariat date from July 1942. The sub-committee's last meeting occurred on 7 August 1943. Within that thirteen-month period, it considered a number of problems: the constitutional implications of the modern state's expanded role in the economy (an issue that interested syndicalist members like Henry Hauck and Catholics like Francis-Louis Closon); a revised Declaration of the Rights of Man which the committee drafted under the guidance of Professor René Cassin; and the complex political and constitutional problems which were likely to be raised in the immediate aftermath of Vichy's collapse. The sub-committee did not at first address the broader question of a new constitution. This was apparently on the orders of General de Gaulle: on 17 October 1942 Gouin informed his committee that 'General de Gaulle does not wish the sub-committee to study the drafting of a constitutional *projet*.'[20] However, the instruction appears to have been rescinded because on 26 June 1943 the sub-committee did begin to consider this issue.

Gouin opened the sub-committee's deliberations with an analysis of the Third Republic's weaknesses. Like inter-war reformers, he acknowledged that the most glaring defect had been 'the legislative branch's constant and continual encroachment on the executive'.[21] His explanation for this shortcoming focused on the failure of French parties to create durable and disciplined organizations. His prescription for a more stable post-war system called for four main parties: the Communist party, the Socialist party, a progressive liberal party (the equivalent of the Radical party), and a conservative party. The emergence of these four ideologically coherent parties would be facilitated by an electoral system which favoured nationally organized groups (proportional representation). A paper which Gouin had written a few months earlier illustrated

---

[19] Some of the papers of this sub-committee are in AN, 72 AJ 546 (Papiers Maisonneuve)) and ibid. 520 (Papiers Gouin).
[20] Ibid. 546.   [21] Minutes of meeting of 26 June 1943, ibid.

how this party system would fit within a larger constitutional context.[22] The head of the government, the Prime Minister, would be chosen at the beginning of each legislature by the National Assembly and would remain in office unless the Assembly withdrew confidence (necessitating an immediate dissolution). Other proposals which Gouin made reflected similarities with what was being discussed in Vichy at the same time: he proposed both female suffrage and a system of *vote familial* to give extra weight to parents of large families; he advocated a Supreme Court; he even allowed for the inclusion of national élites in the Assembly—not, as in the Vichy *projet*, through designation, but through the inscription of prominent intellectuals (from the Institut de France, the Collège de France, and the universities) on the national lists of each party. In this respect Gouin expressed a dissatisfaction with the political mores of the Third Republic that was pervasive in the Free French community. He proposed to rectify the situation by artificially raising the intellectual and moral calibre of the parliamentary candidates,[23] and by reducing politics to a bloodless clash of political ideologies, from which personality was entirely banished.

Gouin made no provision for a second legislative chamber. Hostility to the pre-war Senate was a common theme in the sub-committee's meetings.[24] Another point of agreement in the committee was an opposition to an American-style presidential system. Cassin noted that 'Attributing all government prerogatives to the head of state has never been successful in our country: the Vichy regime instituted in 1940 is a new and unfortunate demonstration of the fact.'[25] It was the British model of stable parliamentary government which the sub-committee members wished to emulate. The main thrust of the committee's deliberations

[22] 'Étude théorique rédigée par M. Félix Gouin à l'intention de ses collègues de la section de la réforme de l'État', ibid. 520.

[23] In addition to the stipulation about including intellectual élites, Gouin proposed a *police électorale*, to stamp out undesirable electoral practices: 'les faits de corruption, falsification, injure ou diffamation'.

[24] See the papers of M. Jacquemin ('Programme d'étude de la réforme de l'État'), and Étienne Hirsch, writing under his pseudonym of Commandant Bernard ('Réflexions sur le régime politique de la France'), both in AN, 72 AJ 520. See also Cassin's speech of 10 July 1943, 'Allocution de M. le Professeur Cassin: *la constitution de 1875 et sa réforme*', ibid. 546.

[25] 'Allocution de M. le Professeur Cassin', p. 2.

was directed, therefore, towards the problem of creating stable majorities in a French Assembly.

The 'new draft constitution'[26] which the Gouin sub-committee prepared proposed a single National Assembly of 400 members (aided by a consultative National Council of 250 members). The National Assembly would elect a President of the Republic for a ten-year term. The President would act as a kind of constitutional monarch (representing the permanent interests of the nation as opposed to transient political interests), but not as the effective head of the executive. The Prime Minister, elected by the Assembly for the duration of the legislature, would choose the members of the cabinet and would supervise all government policy. The Prime Minister could be removed by the Assembly, but only after two successive challenges ('interpellations') and a motion of censure voted after a delay of at least twenty-four hours. In the second half of the legislature such a vote of censure would entail an automatic dissolution of the National Assembly. Implicit in the Gouin draft was the assumption of a two- or three-party system. For example, it referred to the 'leader of the opposition' and stated that in the parliamentary commissions, the 'majority' and the 'opposition' would be represented in their due proportions.

By the time that Gouin's committee began to discuss the future constitution, the main locus of what was now Fighting France had shifted from London to North Africa. This, indeed, may have been the reason that the committee had begun to consider a question which de Gaulle had earlier ordered it not to consider. Three months after the Gouin sub-committee held its last meeting in August 1943, the Consultative Assembly which it had helped to create met in Algiers. André Philip, the CFLN commissaire in charge of relations with the Assembly, was also supervising the CFLN's efforts to plan post-war reform. One of the first questions which he chose to consider was the future constitution. To that end, he created, in January 1944, a new study commission (officially entitled the 'commission d'études relatives à la réforme de la Constitution').[27]

---

[26] This text (which is not in AN, 72 AJ 520 or 546) is reproduced in Michel and Mirkine-Guetzévitch, *Les Idées politiques et sociales de la Résistance* (Paris, 1954), 299–301. There is no obvious reason to doubt the identification of this *projet* as that of the Gouin committee.

[27] 'Arrêté intercommissarial du 31 janvier 1944', *JO, Lois et Décrets*, 17 Feb. 1944.

This commission was initially given nine members, none of whom had served on the Gouin committee. However, when this fact was pointed out to Philip, the commissaire added Cassin in order to co-ordinate with the work of the earlier committee.[28] The list of the new commission's members is a very impressive one: in addition to Cassin, it contained two future *rapporteurs* of Constitutional Commissions (Pierre Cot and Paul Coste-Floret), two leading members of the post-Liberation Socialist party (Albert Gazier and Jules Moch), P.-E. Viard (a law professor from Algiers who was to play an important role in the formulation of the MRP's constitutional and imperial doctrines), René Capitant (one of the architects of gaullist constitutional philosophy), and André Hauriou (whose book *Le Socialisme humaniste* was to be perhaps the most influential plea for a Resistance-led 'third force' in French politics).

The commission's function was to co-ordinate the proliferating programmes and constitutional drafts that were appearing inside and outside France. Philip made clear that its role was not to produce a single draft with the imprimatur of the CFLN, but 'to sift out the two or three main tendencies . . . so that the great debate before the French people may take place in total frankness and full clarity'.[29] The commission complied with this request to compare contending hypotheses. But it also made its preferences plain. On the first issue that it discussed—unicameralism versus bicameralism—the majority of the commission argued in favour of eliminating the pre-war Senate. On the second issue—the electoral system—there was almost unanimous hostility to the Third Republic's system of *scrutin d'arrondissement*.[30] The commission took the view that the single-member constituency encouraged the election of local personalities without party affiliation and made deputies the prisoners of powerful local interests. It supported proportional representation, with a view to removing the 'stagnant ponds' created by the *scrutin d'arrondissement* and facilitating the emergence of four or five national parties. Other proposals made by the commission were also intended to contribute to the

[28] The letters exchanged between Philip and Cassin on this question are in AN, 382 AP 72.
[29] *Supplément au JO, 4 Mar. 1944*, séance du 29 février 1944.
[30] 'Avant-projet du rapport de la commission d'études de la réforme de la constitution', 14–16, in AN, 382 AP 72.

consolidation of the parties. It suggested that parties should have sweeping disciplinary powers over their deputies: if a deputy resigned or was expelled from a party, he or she should immediately be deemed to have resigned from the assembly.[31] The third major issue considered by the commission was the role of the President of the Republic.[32] It unanimously ruled out 'all presidential regimes, more or less inspired by the American system of government'.[33] It recommended that the President of the Republic should no longer have the power to choose the Président du Conseil. Some wanted to go further and write the President out of the constitution altogether. But the most popular solution was a middle course: the President should be elected for a very long term (at least ten years, as in the Gouin *projet*) and should have a largely formal role.

This revision in the role of the President would leave the Prime Minister recognized as the real head of the government. The commission equated greater governmental stability with a greater stability in the position of the Prime Minister. Debating these issues at the beginning of 1944, the commission was well aware of the immense economic tasks which were likely to fall on post-war governments and of the need for continuity of policy, if these tasks were to be carried out effectively. The tenure of the prime ministerial office was seen as running parallel with one instalment of an economic plan: in other words, in normal circumstances, the Prime Minister should be elected for four or five years. The main sanction to enforce this rule was a stipulation that a vote of censure on the government would lead to an immediate dissolution of parliament.[34] This idea of more or less automatic dissolution, which had first been proposed to the commission by Moch, encountered opposition both from those who felt it would lead to very frequent dissolutions and from those who argued that it would give *carte blanche* to the Prime Minister.[35] If applied according to the letter, it might have led to either outcome. But, in fact, the commission's interpretation of 'automatic' was flexible. In

[31] 'Avant-projet du rapport de la commission d'études de la réforme de la constitution', 17–18, in AN, 382 AP 72.   [32] Ibid. 20–2.
[33] 'Rapport de la commission d'études de la réforme de la constitution au Président du Gouvernement Provisoire de la République Française', p. 24, in AN, 382 AP 72.   [34] 'Avant-projet du rapport', p. 25.
[35] See minutes of the meeting of 11 Mar. 1944, p. 3, and the 'Rapport de la commission d'études', p. 29.

the first place the commission refused to endorse a proposal (which had been made frequently by people in the Resistance and by some in London and Algiers) that the Assembly should only have the right to challenge a ministry in an annual debate on its policy. The commission upheld the orthodox notion that deputies should have the right to question the government's policy at any moment. It constructed a complicated but purely formal procedure (reminiscent of that in Gouin's draft) to ensure that this right of 'interpellation' would not recreate the pre-war 'cascade of ministries'.[36] Then, in a second clause, the report drafted by the commission expressed the hope that in a case in which the Prime Minister lost a confidence vote and recognized that the majority of public opinion was against him, he would withdraw voluntarily without calling for a dissolution.[37] This was, potentially, a substantial loophole. It was precisely the tendency of Prime Ministers to resign rather than face a defeat in the Assembly which undermined the Fourth Republic's provisions for dissolution.

The report of the Philip commission was handed to de Gaulle at the end of May or beginning of June 1944. It was, broadly speaking, an attempt to remodel French politics in the British manner. The presumption of a majority and an opposition which had appeared in the Gouin *projet* was repeated here. The proposal to make dissolution automatic if a ministry lost the confidence of the Assembly was a device to overcome the greater fragmentation of French political parties. At the same time the commission's report foreshadowed the constituent debates of 1945–6. In particular, in the two reservations applied to automatic dissolution, it is possible to discern the cautious and orthodox *pis aller* which Socialists and Christian Democrats were to adopt, when the threats of gaullism and communism made the idea of a four-year ministry less obviously desirable.

The work of the Gouin and Philip committees clearly cannot be taken to sum up the constitutional views of Free France. From what we know of the subsequent development of de Gaulle's own ideas, it is certain that he for one did not share all (or indeed many) of the proposals adopted by these committees. On the other hand, on at least some of the points raised by the committees, there existed broad agreement. Of the three most obvious models

[36] 'Avant-projet du rapport', p. 25.
[37] Ibid. 25–6.

for a Fourth Republic—an American presidential system, a
'parlement de personnalités' like that of the early Third Republic,
or a parliamentary democracy on the British model—the last
was overwhelmingly the favourite. The necessity of a small
number of coherent parties established around ideological positions
such as socialism, liberalism, and conservatism was, as Jacques
Soustelle noted, widely propounded.[38] Soustelle himself, Pierre
Brossolette, René Cassin, and Raymond Aron were among those
in London who argued along these lines.[39] To find projects which
go beyond this amended parliamentarianism, one must look to a
handful of groups within the metropolitan Resistance.[40]

The most overtly 'presidential' constitution to be suggested was
published by the OCM in its *cahier* of June 1942.[41] This blueprint
passed through a number of revisions which altered aspects of the
original draft but did not revise the fundamental thesis.[42] The
model for the OCM constitution was the American constitution.
The head of the executive was to be a President elected by the
entire nation, not by a restricted college.[43] Like the American
President, he would be able to veto legislation passed in first
reading in parliament and choose the members of his cabinet from
outside the legislature. But unlike the US President, he would not
be compelled to submit his cabinet nominations to the legislative
branch for approval, and he would have the power to dissolve the

[38] Soustelle, *Envers et contre tout,* ii (Paris, 1950), 172.
[39] On Brossolette, see Passy, *Missions secrètes en France, novembre 1942–juin
1943* (Paris, 1951), 30. For Cassin's views, see 'Allocution de M. le Professeur
Cassin', p. 8. For Aron's views, see his article 'De l'instabilité ministérielle', *La
France Libre*, 41 (15 Mar. 1944), 342–9.
[40] A word of explanation should be given about the use of the terms
'presidential' and 'parliamentary'. In French constitutional law these terms have a
precise meaning. The terms will be used here, however, in a looser sense, to denote
systems that tend towards a greater role for the President of the Republic or a
greater role for the parliament (and the Prime Minister). This usage is necessary if
one is to convey the spirit of constitutional proposals as well as their letter: the
gaullist blueprint is perhaps the most obvious instance where a literal description
(which makes it a parliamentary rather than a presidential constitution) is
inadequate.
[41] A summary of this *projet* is in A. Calmette, *L''OCM'* (Paris, 1961), 47–50. A
revised version of the *projet* was republished after the Liberation in M. Blocq-
Mascart, *Chroniques de la Résistance* (Paris, 1945), 109–30.
[42] Two later drafts, dated July 1943 and Oct. 1943, are in AN, F1a 3791.
[43] In the draft of Oct. 1943, which was an attempt to harmonize the OCM *projet*
with that of the CGE, the President was no longer to be elected by popular vote but
by a large electoral college.

National Assembly whenever he saw fit. The OCM saw no place for a Prime Minister: each of the six ministers would be under the direct supervision of the President.

The legislature, in the OCM's proposal, would have a greatly diminished role. Much of the legislative function would be devolved to regional legislatures which would supervise their own budgets and pass all laws relating to their particular region.[44] Even parliament's power to shape national legislation was to be curtailed. Although no law could be promulgated without being passed by parliament, the OCM proposed complex procedural rules which would make it difficult for parliamentarians to introduce their own legislation or to amend that introduced by the head of state.

A second project, which revised the practice of the Third Republic (less so its theory) more drastically than did the Free French study committees, was drafted by Michel Debré in 1942 or 1943.[45] Though Debré did not go as far as the OCM, his proposals were none the less fairly radical. He rejected the OCM's American model, but advocated a head of state elected for a very long period (twelve years) by a college which would include members of parliament, representatives of unions, representatives of local councils, and even delegates from the universities and the magistracy.[46] Although Debré did not specify all the powers of this head of state, they included the power to dissolve the popular assembly (without the necessity for any complex mechanism of the kind proposed by the Gouin and Philip reports) and to name the Prime Minister. Like the OCM, Debré sought to re-establish a clear distinction between the sphere of responsibility of the legislature (in his scheme, a bicameral legislature[47]) and that of the executive. He did this not by impeding the legislature's right to amend or propose bills, but by separating issues which required legislation from those which he deemed to fall within the executive's statutory power ('pouvoir réglementaire').[48] Other

---

[44] The role of the regional chambers was toned down in subsequent drafts.

[45] It was published after the war in a book co-written with Emmanuel Monick and appearing under the pseudonyms Jacquier and Bruère: *Refaire la France* (Paris, 1945).

[46] Ibid. 122–3.

[47] Debré's second chamber was a political chamber, not the socio-economic council advocated by the Christian Democrats (among others).

[48] *Refaire la France*, pp. 131–2.

proposals that Debré made to limit the power of the legislature included a reduction in the number of permanent parliamentary commissions and an increase in the use of the executive's power of dissolution.

Debré's views were also reflected in the draft constitution which was approved by the CGE in 1943 and which was largely Debré's work.[49] According to the CGE's plan, the President would be elected by an enlarged college and would have the power to name all the ministers (including the Prime Minister). As in Debré's book, the President would be empowered to dissolve the Chamber of Deputies. Though the OCM found the CGE's report 'timid',[50] the CGE's President of the Republic was certainly a far more powerful figure than the Third Republic's President. It is significant, for example, that while the CGE report goes into considerable depth describing the powers of the President, it says virtually nothing about the Prime Minister. It was to be the President, 'aided by his ministers', who was charged with the government and administration of France. When the President is accorded the right to dissolve the Chamber, the report says nothing about the advice of the Prime Minister. The power of control which parliament is to exercise in an annual vote of confidence is exercised not over the real head of the executive (the President), but over his ministers, who are merely his agents. Moreover, according to the CGE, the parliament's legislative function would be restricted in all the ways that *Refaire la France* proposed: if, for example, parliament passed a law pertaining to something outside its *domaine réservé*, the President would be able to amend or reverse it two years after it had been passed. Debré's (and the CGE's) proposal lay somewhere between the parliamentary and the presidential models. In so far as the legislature retained the right to overturn a ministry, it was still a parliamentary system. However, the power of the President was large, that of the Prime Minister largely unspecified, and there was at least the possibility that executive power would pass wholly to the President who was not accountable to parliament.

Another Resistance programme which proposed a major rupture with pre-war constitutional practice was one which the movement

---

[49] A draft of the CGE's *projet* (dating from Sept. 1943) is in AN, F1a 3733. The *projet* was reprinted in *Les Cahiers Politiques*, 14 (Oct. 1945), 1–17.
[50] 'Commentaires de l'OCM sur le rapport CGE', p. 21, in AN, F1a 3791.

Défense de la France published clandestinely in early 1944.[51] The *Cahiers de Défense de la France*—in fact the work of two men, Jean-Daniel Jurgensen and Robert Salmon[52]—proposed two complementary solutions for France's constitutional crisis. The first was the by now familiar idea of a unification of multiple parties to form two or three 'grandes tendances'.[53] The second was a more presidential regime. Défense de la France agreed with Debré that the American system of an elected President would not be acceptable in France: the President would be selected by an enlarged college including the members of the National Assembly and representatives of regional, social, and economic interests. What distinguished Défense de la France's 'régime presidentiel atténué'[54] (as the authors described it) from a parliamentary regime was that the ministers were responsible solely to the President of the Republic and could not be removed by the legislature. The most that the latter could do was 'vote individual censure motions on their policy'. In addition, three other powers bolstered the presidency. The President could veto legislation, dissolve the Assembly at his discretion, and appeal to a Conseil Politique de Justice, which could intervene to prevent legislators from systematically rejecting all of his proposals. There was the potential here for a presidency not much weaker than that proposed by the OCM.

It is significant that both Défense de la France and the OCM should have devoted their first *cahiers* to the question of constitutional reform. Like Debré, these movements identified reform of the state as the prerequisite for all other reforms. It was this priority, as much as their specific proposals, that marked these people out from the Resistance mainstream.

Within the Resistance there was only one other group which matched the detailed constitutional planning of the OCM, the CGE, and Défense de la France: that was the Socialist party. As we have seen, Socialists played a prominent role in the two Free French study commissions, chaired respectively by Gouin and Philip. In addition, three leading figures in the party—Vincent

[51] See *Défense de la France*, 44 (25 Feb. 1944) and *Cahiers de Défense de la France*, 1 (Mar. 1944).
[52] 'Compléments au témoignage de M. Jean-Daniel Jurgensen', in AN, 72 AJ 50.
[53] *Cahiers de Défense de la France*, 1, pp. 5–6, 60–1.
[54] Ibid. 54.

Auriol, Jules Moch, and Charles Dumas—made personal contributions to the debate about post-war institutions.[55] Not surprisingly, there was a strong correspondence between the views expressed in the Free French commissions and the opinions of these Socialists.

Auriol's ideas were drafted in France between November 1942 and September 1943, brought by him to Algiers at the end of 1943 and eventually published in Paris in 1945 under the title *Hier . . . demain*.[56] His central criticism of the Third Republic was that it had been characterized by extreme fragmentation within parliament, lack of stable party affiliation, and political opportunism on the part of deputies (especially those of the centre and right) who often had no commitment to a party or set of principles.[57] Auriol's vision of a renovated parliament demanded the consolidation of political opinion into two or three parties with well-defined doctrinal and programmatic bases.[58] This would allow the emergence of a clear majority in the National Assembly, a formalized government facing a formalized opposition.[59]

The executive which Auriol proposed was unitary. The head of state, who was also to be the Président du Conseil, would be elected by the National Assembly at the beginning of each legislature for its duration. The Prime Minister's freedom of action was not, however, unlimited. When he received the initial vote of confidence, he received it for a specific programme of policies,

---

[55] This leaves aside Blum's comments on the constitutional issue in *A l'échelle humaine*, the essay which he wrote in 1941. Although Blum's prison thoughts were highly influential within the CAS, they did not constitute a systematic constitutional blueprint. Furthermore, the constitutional message of *A l'échelle humaine* was ambiguous. In one of the most famous passages of the essay Blum admitted that, as a result of the Third Republic's collapse, he was now inclined to accept presidential systems (on the American or Swiss model) which 'se fondent sur la séparation et l'équilibre des pouvoirs . . . et assurent au pouvoir exécutif, dans sa sphère propre d'action, une autorité indépendante et continue'. (*L'Œuvre de Léon Blum, 1940–1945* (Paris, 1955), 469.) Less often noted was a passage earlier in the essay in which he had tried to explain why a parliamentary system had worked so much less well in France than in Britain. (*L'Œuvre de Léon Blum*, pp. 431–3.) There he had produced essentially the same critique as that of Auriol, Philip, and Moch. What made parliamentary government effective in Britain was the existence of 'partis suffisamment homogènes et disciplinés'. The French bourgeoisie and its political representatives—i.e. the centre and right—had failed to produce such parties and had hence undermined parliamentarianism in France. The constitutional philosophy of post-Liberation *tripartisme* and of the 1946 Constituent Assemblies was as clearly present in *A l'échelle humaine* as the presidentialist *mea culpa* that de Gaulle saw in it. (*Mémoires de Guerre: le salut* (Paris, 1959), 258–9.)

[56] 2 vols. (Paris, 1945).　　　　[57] *Hier . . . demain*, ii. 32–3.
[58] Ibid. 39–52.　　　　　　　　[59] Ibid. 208–9.

which had to be published in the *Journal Officiel* and had to have appeared in the electoral pledges of the party or parties forming the government majority.[60] Auriol's contractual scheme typified the attempt of these war years to find a constitutional system which eliminated the contingent and personal element of politics and recreated it as a mechanical processing of programmes. The other interesting feature of Auriol's book was its espousal of ideas favoured by Christian Democrats. Unlike many Socialists, Auriol preferred a bicameral legislature, with a second chamber including professional and regional representatives.[61] He also advocated the use of regular referendums to ratify new constitutional laws, to arbitrate irreconcilable conflicts between the National Assembly and a government which had lost the Assembly's confidence, and, finally, to adjudicate in instances where the party in government proposed a piece of major legislation which had not figured in its last electoral programme.[62] In 1945, as the constituent process was beginning, *Hier . . . demain* appeared to be a possible compromise between the MRP's constitutional blueprint and the programme of the SFIO—a constitution around which a 'travailliste' ('labourite') alliance of non-communist progressives could be built.

Auriol's proposals had both similarities and dissimilarities with those made by Jules Moch and Charles Dumas. Moch's 'projet de reconstruction politique et économique'[63] proposed a unicameral legislature, but followed Auriol in having a unitary executive and in stipulating that, if the government were denied confidence, the Assembly would be automatically dissolved.[64] Charles Dumas' proposal (drafted for the Executive Committee of the CAS) retained a President of the Republic, but made the Prime Minister the effective head of the government.[65] He too agreed that the Prime Minister should normally hold office for an entire legislature and that dissolution should be automatic in the event of a breach between the government and the Assembly (though only in the

[60] Ibid. 244–5.   [61] Ibid. 204–7, 219.   [62] Ibid. 200–3.

[63] This *projet* had been begun by Moch and his brother (François) in 1942. It had been submitted to representatives of Combat and Libération and sent to Georges Boris in London. In May 1944 it was presented to General de Gaulle. The text is in Michel and Mirkine-Guetzévitch, *Les Idées politiques et sociales de la Résistance*, pp. 304–37.

[64] 'Projet de reconstruction politique et économique', p. 310.

[65] A copy of this *projet* and an accompanying commentary are in AN, 72 AJ 70: 'Projet de constitution' and 'Rapport sur le projet de constitution proposé par le Comité Exécutif du Parti Socialiste'.

second half of the legislature). All three stressed the need for strong party organizations and believed that proportional representation could help to achieve these strong parties. Equally, they all addressed the problem of the growing strains which would be placed on modern legislatures by the vastly increased volume of legislation (especially economic legislation). Auriol proposed to deal with this problem by reorganizing the system of parliamentary commissions.[66] The other two proposed to do so by devolving decision-making either to the government (Dumas)[67] or to representative councils such as a National Labour Council (Moch).[68]

In these various programmes drawn up inside and outside France, it is possible to distinguish two broad tendencies. The first was the tendency expressed in differing degrees in the projects of the OCM, Défense de la France, Debré, and the CGE. There were important differences between these four programmes. The OCM's was unambiguously presidentialist. Défense de la France's tended, much more tentatively, in the same direction. Debré's and the CGE's stayed within parliamentary bounds and professed to be imitating the British constitution.[69] The common denominator, however, was a heavy emphasis on the President of the Republic. This belief in a stronger presidency was also expressed in some form by many with more orthodox parliamentary views (like Hauriou or Coste-Floret). Ten of the thirty-five respondents to the CFLN's October 1943 questionnaire recommended increasing the powers of the President of the Republic.[70] An opinion poll which was published at the beginning of November 1944 found that 58 per cent of Parisians interviewed favoured a stronger presidency, while 22 per cent disapproved.[71]

The other alternative in August 1944 appeared to be a renovation of parliamentary practice along the lines of that proposed by the

[66] *Hier . . . demain*, ii. 212–17.
[67] 'Rapport sur le projet de constitution', p. 15.
[68] Michel and Mirkine-Guetzévitch, *Les Idées politiques et sociales de la Résistance*, pp. 315–16.
[69] D. de Bellescize, *Les Neuf Sages de la Résistance* (Paris, 1979), 168–9. Debré shared the parliamentary reformers' belief that a consolidation of the parties could lead to stable government.
[70] See ch. 2 above.
[71] Institut Français d'Opinion Publique (IFOP), *Bulletin d'informations*, 1 Nov. 1944, p. 9.

Philip and Gouin committees and by the various Socialist party planners. Whereas the first group proposed to increase the role of the head of state, this second group concentrated on building up the power of the Prime Minister. The key to this renovation was to be a revolution in French party structures. As André Philip put it to the members of the CAS: 'I am convinced that in actual fact a real democracy presupposes the alternation in power of two large, well-organized, parties.'[72] The wartime commissions and constitutional architects who remained within the parliamentary tradition devoted most of their energy and ingenuity to devising ways of bringing this two-party system about or—more realistically—compensating for a greater degree of fragmentation.

As with the idea of strengthening the President's powers, this idea of a self-regulating parliament had a broad appeal. The public opinion poll of November 1944 found that a clear majority (58 per cent to 26 per cent) wished the fusion of all the different political groups into just two parties.[73] Many of the various books and articles which were written in the wake of the Liberation contained suggestions for organizing a few disciplined parties and increasing the powers of the Prime Minister. These more marginal works sometimes illuminate the views of the politicians and illustrate how the latter reflected prevailing concerns. For example, Auriol's contractual idea was also expressed by a union activist called Lelache, who suggested that the legislature should only concern itself with the accomplishment of the programme on which it had secured its mandate: every important question not foreseen at the time of the previous elections should have to be submitted to a referendum.[74] Félix Gouin's concern about the quality of professional politicians was taken one stage further by Philippe Antoine, who recommended the creation of an 'École des Parlementaires', where aspiring politicians could receive a professional training. 'It would never occur to anybody to employ as an electrical engineer a man who had not received any specialized training, simply because he offered his personal assurance that he knew the field well from studying it in his spare time.'[75] As for the idea of making parliamentary politics a clash of ideas, not people, this was taken

---

[72] 'Lettre d'A. Philip', 5 Apr. 1943, in AN, 72 AJ 70.
[73] IFOP, *Bulletin*, 1 Nov. 1944, p. 8.
[74] *La Quatrième République* (Guéret, 1945).
[75] *A la recherche de la République* (Paris, 1945), 46.

up by a certain Marc Morguet, whose pamphlet 'Esquisse d'une constitution pour la IVe République' stated that at election time each of the five parties would have its programme printed up at public expense and circulated to all voters. No other form of communication between voter and candidate would be allowed, in case—as Morguet put it—a good speaker might be able to compensate for the weaknesses of his programme.

For a variety of reasons, the chances that either of these reformist models would be successfully introduced diminished during the fourteen months between the Liberation and the first general election of October 1945. To understand how this happened, it is important to examine the attitudes of the politicians who were to play the crucial roles in drawing up the constitution of 1946.

The most damaging development for the parliamentary reform plan was the Socialist party's marked lack of interest in constitutional questions. After liberation the Socialists' main focus was directed towards the economic structural reforms. One of the first indications of this bias was the scant coverage which the main party paper *Le Populaire* gave to the future constitution. Apart from a few articles by Edouard Depreux and Auriol in August and September 1944[76] and occasional references to the necessity of eliminating the Senate,[77] the party newspaper showed little interest in the form of the new Republic. The party as a whole did not begin to formulate its constitutional proposal until the National Congress of 11–15 August 1945.

Party delegates to this Congress adopted a set of constitutional proposals presented to them by Vincent Auriol.[78] Auriol proposed that there should be a single sovereign legislature and, alongside it, a consultative council composed of representatives from all the various 'professions'. The head of the government would be chosen by the Assembly and would then draw up a programme on which the majority of the Assembly could give him confidence. Subsequent disagreements between the legislature and the executive would bring about an automatic dissolution of the legislature. To

[76] *Le Populaire*, 29 Aug., 9 Sept., 21 Sept.
[77] See e.g. Marcel Bidoux's article: 'La Coquille n'est pas l'escargot', *Le Populaire*, 5–6 Nov. 1944.
[78] PS, *37e congrès national, 11–15 août 1945: rapports* (Paris, 1945). For the text of Auriol's report, see *Le Populaire*, 14 Aug. 1945.

strengthen party discipline, Auriol's report proposed a stipulation which would force dissident deputies to resign their seats. This report (which was incorporated into the party's 'Appel au peuple de France') expressed the essence of the PS's constitutional reformism: a unicameral legislature assisted by non-elected chambers; an executive voted into office to carry through a specific programme of policies; strong parties ensuring unambiguous and lasting majorities in the National Assembly. The aim was to create an efficient parliamentary system which would give each government the stability to design and execute a three- or four-year economic plan.

Even this, however, was by no means a comprehensive plan. In *Le Populaire*, Blum acknowledged that the party had left a number of vital constitutional questions unanswered.[79] The manifestos of Socialist candidates in the general election of October 1945 confirmed this impression: most either did not mention the PS's constitutional programme or gave a very sketchy account of it. The substantive point which candidates made most often was the commitment to abolish the Senate. Only a few candidates bothered to describe in detail the party's scheme for guaranteeing stable government by the procedure of automatic dissolution.

It was not until 12 December 1945—almost two months after the elections and sixteen months after the Liberation—that the PS's main executive body, the *comité directeur*, began to consider the constitution. It only did so then in response to an appeal from the chairman of the First Constituent Assembly's Constitutional Commission, André Philip. Philip told the *comité directeur* that Socialist members of the commission had been placed 'in an impossible situation' by the party's failure to settle the details of its constitutional philosophy.[80] Goaded by Philip's intervention, the committee finally discussed the constitution. At that point it became clear that significant differences of opinion existed within the leadership (as among the Socialist deputies in the Assembly). There were disagreements as to whether it was necessary to have a President of the Republic and whether there should be a constitutional mechanism for controlling the constitutionality of

[79] *Le Populaire*, 9, 10, 11 Oct. 1945.
[80] Comité Directeur du Parti Socialiste, procès-verbaux (henceforth PV), 12 Dec. 1945, p. 6.

laws.[81] As for a statute regulating parties—a measure which Philip
had championed and Blum had endorsed[82]—the party's secretary-
general, Daniel Mayer, told the *comité directeur* that he did not
advise 'putting too many unnecessary things in this constitution,
such as . . . the *statut des partis*'.[83]

The immediate consequence of this long delay in drawing up the
PS's constitutional draft was that in the end decisions had to be
made hastily. The conclusion which may be drawn from it is that,
although Socialists were enthusiastic about the idea of a renovated
Republic, they were not particularly interested in the constitutional
clauses that would bring it about. Constitutional reform was an
area in which compromise—so long as it adhered to the French
republican tradition—was acceptable. This willingness to compromise was evident in the draft which the Socialist party
presented to the First Constituent Assembly at the very outset of
the constituent process.[84] Automatic dissolution was already
qualified: it would only apply to the second government of a
legislature, and governments would only be allowed to ask for a
motion of confidence on certain major issues. The various wartime
ideas for reducing the legislature's workload and concentrating its
energies on the most important legislation had disappeared. There
was no *statut des partis*, and little or nothing about the value of
strong parties. In these amendments it is easy to see the effects of
political contingencies—pressure from the Communist party and
mounting hostility towards de Gaulle's style of leadership. The
impact of these contingencies might not have been so great if the
Socialist party had chosen to consolidate the wartime reflections of
Philip, Moch, Auriol, Dumas, Gouin, and Blum. But the weight
of the party's underlying constitutional conformism—many Socialists
continued to view constitutional reform as a right-wing issue—and
the existence of more pressing issues prevented this consolidation.

Not surprisingly, the tendency to concentrate on socio-economic,
as opposed to constitutional, reforms was even more marked in
the Communist party. That is not to say, however, that the PCF
had no constitutional programme. The party's view on this
question had been publicly aired as early as January 1944, when

[81] PV, 12 Dec. 1945, 14 Dec. 1945.   [82] *Le Populaire*, 11 Oct. 1945.
[83] PV, 26 Dec. 1945, p. 5.
[84] The *projet* was published in *JO, Documents de l'Assemblée Nationale Constituante (élue le 21 octobre 1945)*, pp. 58–62.

Fernand Grenier had spoken in a Consultative Assembly debate about the political arrangements for the post-Liberation period.[85] In part this programme overlapped with that of the Socialists. The Communists were unicameralists. They agreed that disciplined, nationally organized parties could help to increase ministerial stability and channel an increased popular participation in politics:[86] Maurice Thorez told the Tenth Party Congress that 'The existence of large parties, conscious of their responsibilities before the nation, is a necessary thing.'[87] On the other hand, the PCF's wartime diagnosis of the Third Republic's failings was different both from that of parliamentary reformists and that of 'presidentialists'. It refused to acknowledge that ministerial instability or executive weakness had been a significant contributor to the Republic's collapse in 1940. In fact, it argued that far from having been too weak the executive under the Third Republic had been too strong: 'Who would seriously maintain that executive instability was the cause of our failure to prepare for the war? One only has to think of the many years spent in his post by that almost immovable minister of war Daladier. . . . In a more general sense, surely governments made more than enough use of decree-laws and full powers?'[88] Rather than strengthening the powers of the President of the Republic or the Prime Minister, the PCF proposed a dual remedy: tighter control of the government by the members of the legislative assembly and tighter control of the assembly by the electorate (through a constitutional provision allowing electors to replace any deputy voting in contradiction to his or her electoral programme). Here again there were strong traces of the contractual principle.

The programme that the PCF took into the Constituent Assembly in October 1945 echoed the themes which the party's clandestine organization had developed.[89] The basis of the new Republic was to be 'national sovereignty'. As far as possible,

[85] *Supplément au JO, 27 janvier 1944*, séance du 21 janvier 1944, p. 3.
[86] 'Sur le projet de constitution de l'OCM: premières observations du PCF' (22 Sept. 1943), 3, in AN, F1a 3791; Georges Cogniot, 'Comment démocratiser la constitution de la France?', *La Pensée*, 1 (Oct. 1944), 125.
[87] *L'Humanité*, 27 June 1945.
[88] 'Sur le projet de constitution de l'OCM', p. 2.
[89] For the most systematic exposition of the PCF's programme, see André Marty, *Idées sur la nouvelle constitution de la République française* (Paris, 1946). The PCF's official constitutional *projet* is in *JO, Documents*, 23 Nov. 1945, pp. 25–8.

government was to be an expression of the popular will: to this end, the trusts would have to be eliminated; the control that the legislature exerted over the executive would have to be unrestricted; deputies would have to be answerable individually to those who had elected them; and the 'grands corps de l'État' would have to be replaced by elected officials. As party speakers liked to point out, the precedent for this radical 'régime d'assemblée' was Hérault de Séchelles' constitution of 1793.[90] The party presented its programme with a combination of nationalistic and moralistic fervour worthy of Jacobins:

. . . we communists want to introduce a new morality into the country's public life, and next Sunday there will be many citizens who . . . will be determined to express their desire to get rid of the old politicking ways and to move forward under the banner of unity towards the restoration of French greatness and the establishment of a true democracy in accordance with the glorious traditions of France.[91]

The Communists never shared the Socialists' aspiration towards a British-style parliamentary democracy. According to the Communist sympathizer Pierre Cot, the British system relied on a more stable party political structure and more consensual political mores than existed in France.[92] The PCF opposed new rules about dissolution. It did not agree with the Socialists and the Christian Democrats that the constitution ought to regulate political parties through a *statut des partis*. Fajon, one of the Communist members of the constitutional commission, told his colleagues that 'the only entities that the constitution has to recognize . . . are the voters, their representatives, and the institutions.'[93] *L'Humanité* reserved some of its most vitriolic remarks for the *statut des partis*, which Pierre Hervé described as 'an invention of the fascist conspirators of the synarchy'.[94] Given the PCF's parliamentary strength in 1945 and 1946, this opposition to some of the fundamental assumptions of the scheme for a renovated parliamentarianism was a critical obstacle to its implementation.

If Socialist adherents of parliamentary reformism were going to find any political support, it was more likely to come from their

[90] See e.g. Marty, *Idées sur la nouvelle constitution*, p. 12.
[91] Jacques Duclos, *L'Humanité*, 10 May 1945.
[92] ANC-2, *Séances de la Commission de la Constitution* (Paris, 1947), 71, 433.
[93] ANC-1, *Séances de la Commission de la Constitution* (Paris, 1946), 69.
[94] *L'Humanité*, 8 Dec. 1945.

right than their left. During the Occupation, Christian Democrats like Gilbert Dru had advocated a three-party system and after the Liberation the newly-formed MRP moved towards a position not far from that of wartime Socialists. The MRP's National Council, meeting just ten days after the Socialist party's National Congress in August 1945, proposed a constitution in which the Président du Conseil ('the emanation of a parliamentary majority') received annual votes of confidence from the National Assembly. The MRP advocated a Chamber of Deputies elected by proportional representation, which would control the government and vote all laws, while a second chamber representing professional and regional interests would have a legislative role but no power over the government.[95] Like Auriol, the MRP proposed an increased use of referendums to modify the constitution or sanction particularly important legislation, and a procedure of more or less automatic dissolution at the fall of any government.[96] In general the MRP shared the Socialists' belief in the value and necessity of political parties.

There were also, however, discrepancies between the MRP and Socialist programmes. The MRP's second chamber occupied a more central position in their philosophy than its counterpart in Socialist programmes. There was also a basic disagreement about whether or not an updated Declaration of the Rights of Man should include a provision for freedom of education, which the Socialists interpreted as a recognition of the rights of Catholic schools. Finally, there was a presidential element in the Christian Democrats' programme which the Socialists (and still more the Communists) opposed. When François de Menthon introduced the MRP's *projet* to the National Council, the issue on which party activists were most emphatic was that the President of the Republic should chair cabinet meetings.[97] Christian Democratic conceptions of the President's role went much further than the Socialists': for example, they wanted the President to be elected by an enlarged college and to have the right to nominate the Prime Minister, whereas one of the fundamentals of the Socialist *projet* was that the Assembly should choose the Prime Minister on its

[95] AN, 350 AP 55, 56.
[96] 'Projet relatif à la constitution de la IVe République, par F. de Menthon', 17–18, in AN, 350 AP 55.
[97] 'Conseil National, séance de la matinée du dimanche 26 août 1945', ibid. 56.

own initiative. In this respect the MRP's views coincided with those of Debré and the CGE's report (perhaps not surprisingly since Debré had been assisted in drawing up the latter by a prominent Christian Democrat, Pierre-Henri Teitgen).[98]

The failure to consolidate a political alliance behind the Auriol/de Menthon model of a party-run parliamentarianism did not mean that the idea itself had been eclipsed. On the contrary, it was still a very popular theme when the first Constitutional Commission began its deliberations in December 1945. MRP and Socialist members of the commission immediately proposed a *statut des partis*,[99] and Philip, the chairman of the commission, restated many of the positions for which he had argued in the wartime study groups. Perhaps the clearest indication that the idea of strong parties organizing a stable parliamentary democracy had not lost its appeal came from the right. At the end of 1945, conservatives, who had been decimated in the October elections, launched a new party, the Parti Républicain de la Liberté. It was remarkable enough that these deputies should have called their organization a 'party' (a term used generally by those on the left or the extreme right). Still more remarkable was the way in which they echoed the ideas of Socialists and Christian Democrats about the importance of party organization (traditionally an unpopular concept on the parliamentary right):

Party tyranny, people will say. But we have to be logical: to want a parliamentary regime and reject parties (with their precise programme and discipline) is to accept, or indeed to court, confusion, disorder, governmental instability, and intrigues and manœuvres necessitated by the personal interest of a few ambitious people who make up not parties but groups and, more accurately, 'swing-groups', always ready to move from one camp to another. There is no true parliamentary regime without organized parties.[100]

The ideas were still circulating. What was missing was a precise constitutional plan or a political consensus. In part, this reflected a preoccupation with other kinds of reform and a relative neglect of the constitutional issue among party leaders. In part also it

[98] Bellescize, *Les Neuf Sages de la Résistance*, p. 170.
[99] ANC-1, *Séances de la Commission de la Constitution*, pp. 56–66.
[100] Joseph Denais, *La Réforme constitutionnelle* (Paris, 1945), 28–9.

reflected the fact that until the late summer of 1945 such debate as had taken place over constitutional issues had been focused on the 'pre-constitutional' problem—the procedure by which the constitution would be drawn up. Above all, it reflected basic political realities: the mutual suspicions of the two Marxist parties and the failure of the Resistance to form the *parti travailliste* which it had aspired to create. In the minds of those who had advocated a two- or three-party system, it had always been assumed that a progressive centre-left party encompassing at least the Socialists and Christian Democrats would be formed. This had been the expectation of the Catholic Dru, the Socialist Auriol, the jurist Cassin. In the months after the Liberation it became clear that the Resistance movements were a spent force and that neither the Socialist party nor the MRP had the political will to form a centre-left group. Equally frustrated were the hopes of leftist members of Fighting France that General de Gaulle might be persuaded to lead a *rassemblement* of socially progressive, non-communist groups[101], which would have greatly simplified the party system in 1945. The re-emergence of party fragmentation had a significant bearing on the problem of constitutional reform. The more parties existed, the more difficult it became to believe in the possibility of a coherent majority and a coherent opposition. That in turn undermined the main assumption of the strong-party system: that it could provide effective, stable government within a conventional parliamentary setting.

Even greater obstacles impeded the development of the other school of thought which identified renewal with an increased role for the President of the Republic. The first, inescapable, burden which the proponents of this kind of reform faced in 1944 was the legacy of Vichy. Anyone who proposed to strengthen the presidency drew immediate accusations of vichyism. In four years the political atmosphere had totally reversed itself. In 1940 nobody could profess sympathy for the Republic; in 1944 nobody could advocate an authoritarian system of government.

Partly as a result of this legacy of Vichy and partly in reaction to de Gaulle's style of leadership, the parties of the left soon lost any lingering sympathy for the idea of a strengthened presidency. At

---

[101] For some wartime reflections on this *rassemblement*, see the reports sent to London in 1943 and 1944, in AN, F1a 3730.

the end of 1945 Socialists and Communists either proposed to eliminate the President altogether or to make him a symbolic national leader without a significant political role. The Radicals, on the surface, appeared a more likely source of support. Like Debré and de Gaulle, the Radicals advocated a bicameral legislature. They were also naturally opposed to the *République des partis* championed by the Socialists and the Christian Democrats. On the other hand, the Radicals were cautious about increasing the powers of the President too much (beyond giving him the right to dissolve the chamber). Their major concern was to preserve the second chamber, and this, rather than the presidency, was the focus of their propaganda in the 1945 general election campaign and in the Constituent Assemblies. In any case, the election results of 1945 so reduced the party's representation that it could have little influence over the constituent process.[102]

Apart from the Radicals, the other major political force at the Liberation which seemed partially sympathetic to the presidential model was the MRP. As we have noted, the MRP's constitutional position was ambiguous. It did support a stronger presidency, but it also favoured aspects of the plan for a party-run parliamentarianism. In the elections of October 1945 few MRP candidates mentioned a more powerful President of the Republic. The reformist alliance which might have been formed between 'neo-liberals' close to de Gaulle and leaders of the MRP like de Menthon[103] never materialized. The MRP had too strong a commitment to its place in the Republican mainstream to risk supporting a presidentialist campaign of the kind launched by de Gaulle in 1946.

A further reason that the idea of a strengthened presidency had made so little headway by the time the constituent process began was the reluctance of de Gaulle to champion it publicly. For better or worse, most people identified the future of the presidency with the future of Charles de Gaulle. An opinion poll taken in the spring of 1945 found that 49 per cent wanted de Gaulle to assume the functions of President after the war was over. The next highest figure was a mere 4 per cent for Edouard Herriot.[104] It is likely

---

[102] In the Chamber of 1936 there had been 108 Radical deputies. In the First Constituent Assembly there were just 23.

[103] Wahl, 'Aux origines de la nouvelle constitution', pp. 44–5.

[104] IFOP, *Bulletin*, 16 May 1945, p. 107.

that many more than 49 per cent assumed that de Gaulle would be President, even if they did not wish to vote for him.

Between September 1944 and January 1946 de Gaulle made no secret of his belief that France needed new political institutions. However, almost to the end of his period of office, he allowed the constitutional debate to remain fixated on the procedural question of how the constituent process should operate. This outcome, it must be said, was fully in accord with de Gaulle's wishes: he had all along maintained that the people ought to decide the institutions which would govern it and in 1945 he scrupulously refused to anticipate the people's verdict by opening the wider debate. As a result, however, the only indication that the public received of de Gaulle's position in this wider and more fundamental debate came from his stance on the procedural issue.

The drift of his constitutional views was clear enough to most politicians: in July 1945 P.-H. Teitgen had predicted that de Gaulle would prefer a constitution 'largely inspired by the wartime programme written by Debré'.[105] On several occasions during Consultative Assembly debates over the government's proposals for the constituent procedure,[106] de Gaulle emphasized that the future constitution would have to guarantee a more stable executive.[107] He also let slip his support for the principle of a bicameral parliament.[108] For many who heard this speech, it must have been tempting to assume that the interim regime which the general was proposing for the seven-month constituent period was a model of what he had in mind for the Fourth Republic. These assumptions were understandable and far from unfounded. In most respects de Gaulle's constitutional views may be deduced from his proposal for the interim regime (which had as its essential aim the limiting of the head of state's accountability before the assembly). But, on the other hand, crucial elements of his constitutional philosophy—notably the powerful head of state outside and above parliament—were missing in 1945. Those who were privy to de Gaulle's hesitations both before and after he

---

[105] AN, 350 AP 45. Since the constitution of the Fifth Republic was to bear many resemblances to that written by Debré during the war, Teitgen's remark was prophetic.

[106] For the original *projet* proposed by de Gaulle (subsequently rejected by the assembly and revised by de Gaulle himself), see *JO, Documents de l'Assemblée Consultative Provisoire*, 17 July 1945, pp. 680–1.

[107] *JO, Débats*, 29 July 1945, pp. 1613–14.   [108] Ibid. 1613.

presented his proposals to the assembly in July 1945 had especially
good grounds for not taking these 'transitional rules' as de Gaulle's
definitive statement on the subject.[109]

The other interpretation of de Gaulle's failure to declare himself
in 1945 is that he had not yet decided on the specific constitutional
arrangement which he favoured. If the broad outline of his
constitutional philosophy was already established, it may still have
been the case that the debates of the Constitutional Commissions
and the decisions of the Constituent Assemblies clarified his mind
on the clause-by-clause issues. An earlier clarification might well
have led to the same split between de Gaulle and the three main
parties, since there was a radical difference between the general's
plan to step outside the parliamentary tradition and even the
MRP's plan to strengthen the executive while staying firmly within
that tradition. But it would certainly have strengthened de
Gaulle's hand in October 1945, by forcing those who stood for
election to the Constituent Assembly to come out in favour of, or
in opposition to, his plans (at a point when gaullism could not have
been caricatured as bonapartism or worse). As it was, de Gaulle's
constitutional views did not figure as an issue in the October
elections. His subsequent resignation in January 1946 was met
with a mixture of indifference and incomprehension.[110] Many
voters could not understand why the national liberator had chosen
to resign over questions like the relationship between the
legislative and executive branches. This reaction testified to de
Gaulle's failure to convey his scheme for national renovation to
the French public, for the essence of this scheme—new and
efficient political institutions—was precisely what he felt to be at
stake in January 1946.

It was only when de Gaulle had left office that he fully expressed
his reform programme. In a speech which he delivered at Bayeux
on 16 June 1946, he gave his diagnosis of French parliamentarianism
and the details of his antidote. The Bayeux speech called for a
strict separation of powers between the legislature ('les partis')
and the executive ('les hommes de l'État').[111] The executive was to

---

[109] For these hesitations, see C. Mauriac, *Le Temps immobile: un autre de
Gaulle* (Paris, 1970), 120–32; Michel Debré, *Trois républiques pour une France*
(Paris, 1984), 363.

[110] See J. Charlot, *Le Gaullisme d'opposition, 1946–1958* (Paris, 1983), 43–4.

[111] The text of the speech is in *Discours et messages, 1946–1958* (Paris, 1970), 5–
11. The characterization of the legislature and the executive is taken from a letter

be two-tiered. The cabinet, led by the Prime Minister, was to be responsible for all the government's policies. Both the cabinet and its head were to be chosen, not by the bicameral parliament, but by the President of the Republic (or 'chef de l'État'). After being elected by a college (including members of parliament but also an unspecified number of others), the President would have the power to promulgate laws, issue decrees, preside at cabinet meetings, dissolve parliament, and call new elections (when parliament persistently refused to place its confidence in the ministers whom the President had chosen). In sum, the role of this very powerful President was to act as a non-political, national arbiter.

As Raymond Aron noted in 1945, the constitution of the Fourth Republic was written 'à froid'.[112] Unlike the constitution of the Second Republic, it did not come in the aftermath of a revolution. Unlike the constitution of the Third Republic, it did not immediately follow a national defeat—or, at any rate, this time victory, carrying with it a partial vindication of the *ancien régime*, had intervened after the initial defeat. Unlike either 1848 or 1871, there was no uncertainty in 1946 about the type of regime: virtually the entire population agreed that it should be a republic. Furthermore—and this perhaps was Aron's point—fourteen months had been allowed to elapse between the point at which constitutional reform had been theoretically possible and the point at which it actually began. During that time, the political class had been preoccupied with the problems of rebuilding, feeding, heating, and clothing a nation emerging from war and occupation. Whatever energies were not absorbed by these tasks had been directed primarily towards transforming the French economy and French society, in accordance with the priorities of the CNR's Common Programme. The interest in constitutional questions had remained high so long as the presence of Vichy gave them a certain pointedness, but it had declined once the authoritarian regime had disappeared.

The aspect of the constitutional debate which has received most attention from historians is that which came to nothing in 1946: the

that de Gaulle wrote to Debré in July 1946: *Lettres, notes et carnets*, vi (Paris, 1984), 202–4.

[112] Aron and Clairens, *Les Français devant la constitution* (Paris, 1945), 84.

OCM's presidentialist model, Debré's semi-presidentialist views, and de Gaulle's Bayeux constitution. The interesting point about these ideas, as Wahl was the first to point out,[113] was that their time would come twelve years later. In 1946, however, these were the views of a minority (and, in the Constituent Assemblies, a very small minority). The majority in the Assemblies professed to be equally reformist, and their reformism has been rather neglected. The reason is clear: because the constitution produced by the Constituent Assemblies of 1945–6 seemed, in retrospect, a step back towards the Third Republic, their reformism has been dismissed as hypocrisy or hot air. It had elements of both. But it was also a muddled attempt to make French democracy more 'modern', while remaining true to itself.

The first principle of this reformism was the value of coherent, nationally organized parties. The practical assumption was that such parties would be able to establish a firm and stable majority in the Assembly through agreeing to a 'contract' of policies. The corollary of this principle was that political activity would become a contest of ideas and programmes rather than one of politicians. This certainly reflected popular expectations. Shortly after the Liberation, when Parisians were polled about their constitutional views, 72 per cent thought that voters should vote for a programme, while 16 per cent thought that they should vote for a person.[114] The idea of a party-organized democracy fed both on the analogy with the British and American democracies and, more generally, on the contemporary vogue for rationalization and large-scale collective activity. Just as the economic planners proposed to rationalize the chaos of a fragmented industrial base, so the constitutional planners proposed to streamline what they saw as an archaic and inefficient party system.

Secondly, the reformers of the centre and left advocated a major remodelling of the legislature. This involved, first and foremost, the unambiguous primacy of the Chamber of Deputies. The disagreements in the Constituent Assemblies between the MRP and the left should not hide the fact that both sides agreed that the second chamber of the Fourth Republic should be much less powerful than the old Senate. These reformers also recognized (as clearly as Debré and the OCM) that a major reorganization of the

[113] 'Aux origines de la nouvelle constitution'.
[114] IFOP, *Bulletin*, 1 Nov. 1944, p. 7.

legislative process was necessary, if the legislature were to carry
out its functions adequately in an age in which the state—as they
were the first to demand—would have an active role in regulating
the economy and society. Though the provisions which they
introduced into the constitution of 1946 were inadequate in this
regard, it is not true to say that the members of the Constituent
Assemblies merely misunderstood the lessons of the 1930s and
mistook decree-laws for causes rather than symptoms of constitutional decay.[115] Even an avowed advocate of a 'régime d'assemblée' like Pierre Cot acknowledged that: 'The procedure of
decree-laws, which was so misused before the war, was in large
part the result of congestion in parliamentary proceedings.
Parliament was not adapted to the new tasks which fell to it,
especially in economic affairs.'[116]

The reformism of 1946 also proposed to alter the relation
between government and parliament by introducing an effective
power of dissolution. Socialists preferred that the dissolution
should operate as an automatic mechanism in the event of either
the legislature or executive breaking their 'contract'. The MRP
preferred to give the power to the President of the Repubic,
although initially the party's representatives in the Constitutional
Commission accepted the Socialists' automatic procedure.[117] They
all assumed that the Président du Conseil would be bolstered by
this device and would finally be acknowledged as the head of the
government.

The model for the constitutional reformers of 1946 was
unmistakably the British system of parliamentary government.
The President was to be the constitutional monarch, the Président
du Conseil the Prime Minister, the National Assembly the House
of Commons, and the much reduced second chamber the House of
Lords. Those who knew the British system reasonably well
(people like Philip and Cassin) were at pains to underline the
absolute necessity of a small number of parties, if the French
republic were going to function as effectively as the British
constitutional monarchy. For all the rethinking of wartime and

---

[115] This is the argument of François Goguel in his paper 'Les Institutions
politiques', presented to the colloquium, *La France en voie de modernisation
(1944–1952)* (Paris, 1981).
[116] ANC-1, *Séances de la Commission de la Constitution*, p. 106.
[117] Ibid. 88.

post-Liberation planners, it was the party system which proved to be the Achilles heel of the new Republic's philosophy. Nobody saw this more clearly than the Fourth Republic's greatest critic, de Gaulle:

[the] presidential system assures the executive strength, endurance, and independence. *In extremis*, we could perhaps achieve this result, as the British do, through a system of two parties. But we have—and will always have—five parties, one of which, furthermore, spoils the game because it is separatist and dictatorial.[118]

[118] Handwritten note (n.d.), in *Lettres, notes et carnets*, vi, p. 225.

6

Imperial Renovation and the Union Française

No issue produced a broader reformist consensus in 1944 than the future of the empire. This consensus had three fundamental components. First, in the harsh modern world of superpowers France *needed* her empire. With a dwindling and ageing metropolitan population, the nation's post-war status depended upon her capacity to speak for one hundred million, not just forty million people. To quote a recent commentator: 'The Empire was a vital element in the restoration of national prestige, just as it had been after 1870. Unless France retained her Empire, she might face the awful fate outlined by Paul Leroy-Beaulieu in 1880, that France would fall below the rank of Spain or Portugal.'[1] It should be noted that this view was as likely to be held in Vichy as in London or Algiers: the État Français propagandized relentlessly about the value of the empire and the extent to which it could compensate for weakness in Europe.[2] Second, the events of the war had demonstrated the empire's commitment to France. Nothing was more engrained in both vichyite and gaullist propaganda than the notion that the empire had stayed loyal to France. Where nationalist groups had tried to exploit the *métropole*'s troubles, foreign interference (in the form of rival British imperialism or American anti-imperialist ideology) was seen as the root of the problem. Third, the era of primitive colonialism had ended. Since 1939 colonial populations had come to demand greater control over their own destinies and to assume that France would satisfy their demands. A new kind of association would have to be created between France and her possessions—a bond which developed the potential of each member while reaffirming their common identity. The catch-phrase of the period was 'federalism', by which was meant less an authentic federal system than an arrangement which preserved France's control

---

[1] Marc Michel, 'Decolonisation: French Attitudes and Policies, 1944–46', p. 83, in P. Morris and S. Williams (eds.), *France in the World* (1985).
[2] For examples of this propaganda, see Charles-Robert Ageron, *France coloniale ou parti colonial?* (Paris, 1978), 269–73.

over the empire, but satisfied the new aspirations of the non-metropolitan peoples.

Out of the consensus on these three points, there developed between 1943 and 1946 a movement to reform France's imperial policy. In some respects this reformism rephrased long-standing aspirations. The suggestion that France ought to be able to exploit her imperial resources more effectively, for the mutual benefit of the *métropole* and the empire, had been frequently made by reformers under the Third Republic (especially after the First World War and again after the onset of the Depression).[3] The concept of an imperial 'community' had been formulated by an inter-war school of 'colonial humanists'.[4] The most striking development in the 1940s was the heavy emphasis on redefining the constitutional form of the empire—a development which may be attributed in part to the pressure of external and internal anti-colonialism, but in part also to the existence of a constitutional vacuum after the collapse of the Third Republic. Before analysing this attempt at redefinition in greater detail, it might be helpful to summarize where the plans came from and who were to be the main influences on their development.

The initial coincidence which triggered the anti-vichyites' interest in colonial reform occurred in the summer of 1940. In the first months after the armistice, the New Hebrides, French Oceania, the five cities of French India, New Caledonia, and much of French Equatorial Africa rallied to the London dissidents.[5] From this founding period, in which the support of a fraction of the empire provided Free France with its strongest claim to legitimacy, the movement retained a mystique of empire at the heart of its ideology. In its early stages this ideology—like Vichy ideology—stressed only the need to preserve the empire's integrity: gaullists warned that Vichy would hand over the empire to the Axis, while Vichy accused de Gaulle of aiding and abetting British imperialism. Until 1943 there was little or no reformist substance, even on the gaullist side. It is true that the first colonial governor to rally to de Gaulle (Félix Éboué in French Equatorial Africa)

---

[3] See C. M. Andrew and A. S. Kanya-Forstner, *France Overseas: The Great War and the Climax of French Imperial Expansion* (London, 1981); and Jacques Marseille, *Empire colonial et capitalisme français* (Paris, 1984).

[4] R. Girardet, *L'Idée coloniale en France* (Paris, 1972), 184–90.

[5] J.-B. Duroselle, *L'Abîme, 1939–1945* (Paris, 1982), 238–42.

had, as early as 1941, begun to canvass major reforms in colonial policy. In a circular dated 8 November 1941 and in a letter which he sent to de Gaulle and his Commissaire aux Colonies, René Pleven, around the same time, Éboué urged greatly increased co-operation with local indigenous élites and a rapid transformation of the social and economic conditions of the native populations.[6] Though many of his suggestions were later echoed at the Brazzaville Conference of 1944, they cannot be said to have initiated the imperial reform movement, since they did not address the question of the empire's overall structure. At this point de Gaulle's speeches evinced a preoccupation with the unity of the empire. He gave no more than an occasional hint about the need for new post-war structures to guarantee this unity.[7] When he did finally make explicit proposals for reform (at Constantine in December 1943), the gaullist newspaper *La Marseillaise* claimed that the idea had been 'studied at length during our exile in London'.[8] If this is true, these preliminary studies have left few traces. Within the study commissions set up in London by de Gaulle's decree of 2 December 1941, a colonial committee had been belatedly created in February 1943. It met three times, produced an agenda, and then fell into abeyance.[9] There is no sign of any other organized activity.[10]

According to a source well-positioned to know (Henri Laurentie, director of political affairs in the Commissariat aux Colonies), the idea of a conference to launch a new imperial era emerged in mid-1943 from conversations between de Gaulle and Pleven.[11] During 1943 and 1944, these two men were the driving force behind the plans to remodel the empire. From 1943 onwards, in fact, the Provisional Governments and their Colonial Ministers directed the process of reformulating imperial policy. Just as it was de Gaulle

[6] Brian Weinstein, *Éboué* (New York, 1972), 270–4.
[7] See, especially, his speech of October 1941 to the Royal African Society in London: *Discours et messages, 1940–1946* (Paris, 1970), 119–21.
[8] No. 59 (18 Dec. 1943).
[9] The papers of the group, chaired by M. Pierre-Bloch (who had been vice-president of the Commission des colonies et de l'Algérie in the last pre-war chamber) are in AN, 72 AJ 546.
[10] The biographer of Éboué has noted that, in spite of the empire's importance to Free France, 'the French National Committee, prior to 1943, had thought very little about definite new directions'. Weinstein, *Éboué*, p. 293.
[11] See C.-R. Ageron, 'De Gaulle et la conférence de Brazzaville', paper presented to the colloquium *De Gaulle, homme d'État* (Paris, 1978).

and Pleven who began the process, so it was a later minister, Paul Giacobbi, who in March 1945 proclaimed the existence of the Union française before it had been formally created. Later still, Bidault's government of 1946 intervened in the proceedings of the Second Constituent Assembly to impose the government's constitutional definition of the Union française.

On the imperial issue, the Provisional Governments did not receive much guidance from the Resistance. Very few Resistance periodicals or pamphlets discussed the future of the empire. The occasional writer who did mention it tended to offer fairly conventional thoughts about the value of French civilization and the importance of mobilizing the resources of the empire.[12] More coherent ideas about the structure of the future Union française followed rather than preceded the Provisional Governments' initiatives.[13]

In some ways the political parties were equally uninterested in the empire. The schemes for a new kind of imperial community produced a favourable echo in the Consultative Assembly and in the three main parties. But in general imperial issues ranked very low on the parties' list of priorities. The silence of the left's electoral manifestos in October 1945 was deafening: only a handful of right-wingers and the occasional Christian Democrat mentioned the future of the empire at all. Another indication of the low priority afforded imperial questions were the empty seats in the chamber whenever the Consultative or Constituent Assemblies debated them.[14] Within each party there were relatively few prominent members who took an interest in imperial affairs. Because the main parties were bound, by virtue of their dominance in the two Constituent Assemblies, to play a crucial role in the formation of the Union française, these individuals— Marius Moutet (SFIO), P.-E. Viard (MRP), P.-O. Lapie (SFIO), and a small number of others—exerted a disproportionate influence over the debate.

Alongside these political specialists, often sitting with them in the same study commissions and writing in the same journals, were

[12] Henri Michel, *Les Courants de pensée de la Résistance* (Paris, 1962), 407–10.

[13] See e.g. the plans for the incorporation of the empire within the new constitution proposed by the movement Défense de la France: *Cahiers de Défense de la France*, 1 (Mar. 1944), 38.

[14] *Le Monde*, 14–15 Apr. 1946. See also René Pleven's speech in the First Constituent Assembly, *JO, Débats*, 23 Mar. 1946, p. 1036.

the specialists of the colonial service. In 1943, when Pleven and de Gaulle decided to convene a conference at Brazzaville, they turned to Henri Laurentie, as head of the political section of the Commissariat aux Colonies, to draw up the programme.[15] From that point onwards, the officials of the commissariat—Laurentie, Georges Peter (the director of economic affairs), de Curton (Laurentie's deputy), and others—were to play a central role in the elaboration of a new imperial doctrine. Laurentie, in particular, was at the heart of the Brazzaville conference, the Algiers study commission set up on the recommendation of the conference, and the various commissions established in Paris in 1945–6. Once back in Paris, he used his position to advise and cajole successive ministers to adopt the kind of Union française which he advocated.

Finally, in addition to the politicians and the technicians, there were those with the most direct stake in the Union française—the *colons*, the colonial lobby in France, and the indigenous populations. In the early stages (1943–5) the impact of these groups was restricted. The Brazzaville conference was a meeting of administrators: no representative of the colonists or the native populations was invited. In Algiers the commission which considered the empire's place in the new French constitution was comprised of politicians, academics, and administrators. It was not until mid-1945, when a study commission proposed a much increased representation of the colonial population within the future Constituent Assembly, that the influence of both sides began to grow. The *indigène* deputies in the First Constituent Assembly— led by Léopold Senghor, Houphouet-Boigny, Apithy, and Lamine-Guèye—were instrumental in maintaining the pressure for reform and keeping the colonial lobby on the defensive.[16] In the Second Constituent Assembly, the deputies of the Parti du Manifeste Algérien, led by Ferhat Abbas, were at the centre of controversy, both because of their uncompromising autonomist views and because parliamentary arithmetic happened to give them a crucial influence in split votes. The influence of the *colons* and the *parti colonial* also increased once the Constituent Assemblies convened.

[15] Laurentie was a protégé of Félix Éboué and had actively supported the latter's *ralliement* to Free France in 1940.

[16] Paul Isoart, 'L'Élaboration de la constitution de l'Union française: les assemblées constituantes et le problème colonial', paper presented to the colloquium *Les Prodromes de la décolonisation de l'empire français (1936–1956)* (Paris, 1984), 11.

In September 1945 an organization called the États Généraux de la Colonisation Française held its founding meeting in Douala. Together with older established colonial lobbies in Paris, like the Académie des Sciences Coloniales and the Comité de l'Empire Français, it was to exert a major influence, especially in the summer of 1946.

Perhaps more than any other issue, imperial reform was a question for experts—experts in the government, in the colonial administration, in the parties, and in the press. Public opinion in 1945 believed that the empire was worth preserving and should be preserved: the idea that the empire in some sense guaranteed France's national status—a message that had been fed to the French people from all sides since 1940—had apparently sunk in. The metropolitan population accepted the need for renovation in the form of a more democratic imperial system, but it did not, so far as one may judge from opinion polls, follow the process of renovation with particular attention or interest.[17] The same was true of many politicians and journalists.[18] For those who placed imperial renewal at the centre of their thoughts, the challenge was twofold: first, to make the Union française a durable, successful institution; and, second, to proselytize about the importance of being 'empire-minded'.

On 13 October 1943, the Commissaire aux Colonies, René Pleven, announced that the CFLN intended to convene an imperial conference. The avowed aim was to reassess French imperial policy, but an underlying purpose was to respond to the challenge of American anti-colonialism, by demonstrating both the CFLN's reformist intentions and its determination to hold on to the empire. The conference of colonial administrators that convened at Brazzaville between 30 January and 8 February 1944 did not settle or even properly define the larger questions about the future of the Union française, but it did make progress in establishing a programme of concrete reforms. The conference proposed to open up a range of professions to *indigènes* and to encourage native

---

[17] See C.-R. Ageron, 'L'Opinion publique face aux problèmes de l'Union française', paper presented to the colloquium *Les Prodromes de la décolonisation de l'empire français (1936–1956)*.

[18] *Le Monde* of 14 July 1945 reported a French official's rueful observation that Giacobbi's important declaration of Mar. 1945 had attracted more attention in the Anglo-Saxon press than in the French press.

élites to take over local political responsibilities. It recommended the extension of education and public health provision and proposed to limit and eventually abolish forced labour. Such recommendations gained widespread approval among foreign observers, at whom they were in large part aimed.

There were also, however, important ambiguities in the recommendations of the Brazzaville conference.[19] There were contradictions between a deeply rooted assimilationist reflex (expressed in proposals 'to develop this indigenous mass in the direction of a more and more complete assimilation with the principles that constitute the common heritage of French civilization')[20] and other recommendations which urged a development of the role of indigenous institutions. There were also contradictory statements about the political form of the empire. Some participants, like Governors Saller, Sautot, and Dagain envisaged increased colonial representation within the metropolitan parliament, while others like Laurentie suggested that granting colonies 'a political personality' logically entailed some kind of federal assembly.

The political recommendations of the conference were very cautious—particularly so the notorious preamble to the conference report, which ruled out 'all idea of autonomy, all possibility of evolution out of the French orbit'.[21] This outright rejection of self-government, even in the long term, went further than the conference programme, which had stated: 'If there is self-government, it can only come at the end of a fairly long and strictly controlled evolution.'[22] When Laurentie, who had drafted the programme, tried to raise the issue of self-government at one of the conference sessions, his attempt was stonewalled by other participants. One governor retorted that it had already been decided that 'the question of self-government was not to be

[19] Ageron has suggested that these ambiguities reflected a fundamental difference of opinion between the liberal Commissariat aux Colonies (especially Laurentie) and the much more traditional-minded governors and governors-general. See his paper: 'La Préparation de la conférence de Brazzaville et ses enseignements', delivered to the colloquium, *De Gaulle et la conférence de Brazzaville* (Paris, 1987).
[20] Ministère des colonies, *Conférence Africaine Française* (Paris, 1945), 39.
[21] Ibid. 32.
[22] 'Programme général de la conférence de Brazzaville', 13. A copy of this programme is in the archives of the Ministry of Foreign Affairs, *Guerre 1939–1945, Alger CFLN–GPRF*, 683.

raised'.[23] By adopting this position on the issue of self-government, the conference thwarted any possibility of discussing the federal concept in any depth—in spite of the fact that just a fortnight before the conference began Pleven had told the Consultative Assembly in Algiers that 'The hour has come . . . to investigate the federal concept thoroughly.'[24]

On the crucial issue of the empire's place within the future constitution, the conference members acknowledged that they were unable to make a recommendation and proposed that the question be studied by a commission of experts appointed by the Provisional Government. Even as they dodged the issue, however, they raised it to a new prominence. In the conference programme the order of the agenda had been: 'politique indigène', 'politique économique', 'organisation politique et administrative', 'représentation des colonies dans la nouvelle constitution française'. In the conference report the priorities were reversed: the constitutional organization of the empire was discussed first. Whether or not this change was deliberate, it was certainly symptomatic of the direction in which the debate was moving. From Brazzaville until the end of the Second Constituent Assembly in the autumn of 1946, the reworking of the empire was closely linked with that of the French constitution.

The first attempt to solve this problem of integrating the empire within the constitution was made, as the Brazzaville report had recommended, by a commission of experts, which met in Algiers between May and July 1944. This commission—officially instructed to 'study measures appropriate to assure the colonies their rightful place in the new French constitution' and informally instructed to consider the various pitfalls and possibilities of federalism—has been largely overlooked by historians.[25] Its debates were none the less important, since they provided the starting-point for the debate which was to be engaged in Paris after the Liberation.[26]

[23] The minutes of this session (4 Feb. 1944) are in the *Archives Nationales Section Outre-Mer* (hereafter ANSOM), Affaires économiques, 101.

[24] *JO, Débats*, 14 Jan. 1944, p. 8.

[25] To my knowledge, only C.-R. Ageron has made (brief) reference to it. See his paper presented to the colloquium, *La France en voie de modernisation (1944–1952)* (Paris, 1981): 'Novation et immobilisme de la politique française vis-à-vis de l'outre-mer dans les premières années de la IVᵉ République.'

[26] The minutes of the commission may be consulted in the Cassin archives, AN, 382 AP 71.

The commission was comprised of three distinct groups. The first and largest category consisted of delegates in the Consultative Assembly, including prominent figures like the Socialist Jules Moch, the Communist André Mercier, and Pierre-Olivier Lapie (the most vocal advocate of federalism in the assembly). Alongside them there were three prominent and politically active jurists (Professors Hauriou, Cassin, and Viard) and, thirdly, a group of colonial administrators. Apart from the chairman, Laurentie, none of the delegates to the Brazzaville conference were present in this commission.

Some members (notably Jules Moch) believed a priori that the federal concept was a poor one. In relatively few parts of the empire, Moch argued, were the populations developed enough to elect a democratic national assembly. Without such assemblies, the delegates whom the majority of colonies sent to a federal assembly would not be chosen by universal suffrage. Since any authentic federation would involve a transfer of power from the metropolitan assembly to the federal assembly, the sovereignty of the people would thus be transferred to an unrepresentative body. Moch summed up his argument in the phrase: 'I do not want Queen Bakoko to have the power to overturn the government.'[27] Moch believed that instead of an instant federalism, France ought to opt for a system closer in the short term to the status quo (but one which could evolve towards federalism). He proposed a large degree of local autonomy for the more developed countries and, for the others, a regime of local representation and devolved decision-making which would build up democracy from below. Above all, he emphasized the need for a new mystique of 'la plus grande France'.[28]

The main protagonist of the federal cause within the commission was Laurentie. He envisaged a system in which there was to be both a federal executive and a federal legislature, which would have jurisdiction over foreign policy, defence, education policy, federal economic plans, and communications between the various member states.[29] Laurentie accepted that the creation of a federal assembly would reduce the powers of the metropolitan assembly, but regarded that as desirable: 'We think that we ought to bring

[27] 'Procès-verbal de la réunion du 16 mai 1944', p. 15.
[28] 'Procès-verbal de la réunion du 4 juillet 1944', pp. 3–7.
[29] 'Procès-verbal de la réunion du 9 mai 1944', p. 6.

the French people to think federally . . . that is to say, abstract itself from its own prejudices so as to envisage all French policy as always applying to the whole federation.'[30]

The other members of the commission fell in between Moch's and Laurentie's positions. Mercier, for example, saw federalism as a means to an end: 'through the idea of a federation we want to fuse together the *métropole* and the whole body of her colonies . . . Federation or not, the word itself does not matter, but we must fuse them together!'[31] Cassin acknowledged the advantages of federalism, but argued that in the present circumstances a true federal system was out of the question. He proposed a more pragmatic arrangement, with a federal assembly constituted in *ad hoc* fashion, along the lines of the Consultative Assembly in Algiers.[32] This piecemeal approach was supported by others on the committee, like Lassalle-Séré (an Inspector-General in the colonial ministry): he advocated an 'assemblée disparate', with varying methods of selection (depending on the colony) and varying degrees of deliberative and consultative power (depending on the issue).

The commission's final report, which was drafted by Laurentie, reflected the views of the pro-federalist majority rather than Moch's minority position. It acknowledged that the idea of a federal assembly. This assembly was to be composed of representatives of the *métropole* (either chosen by the National Assembly evolution.[33] The centre-piece of the report's proposals was a federal assembly. This assembly was to be composed of representatives of the *métropole* (either chosen by the National Assembly or elected by universal suffrage)[34] and representatives from each of the overseas territories. The role of this assembly would be to deliberate on a federal budget and a federal economic plan. On questions relating to defence, foreign policy, and education, Laurentie's report accepted that the metropolitan parliament—at least for the immediate future—would have to retain the ultimate power of decision, but it granted the federal assembly the right to

---

[30] 'Procès-verbal de la réunion du 9 mai 1944', p. 15.
[31] Quoted by Ageron, 'Novation et immobilisme', p. 4.
[32] 'Procès-verbal de la réunion du 27 juin 1944', pp. 2–3, 7.
[33] 'Rapport de la commission chargée d'étudier le moyen d'installer les colonies dans la nouvelle constitution française', p. 4.
[34] The majority favoured the second option.

be consulted compulsorily on these questions.[35] Laurentie was also forced to admit that the uneducated political opinion of metropolitan France and the undeveloped political and economic systems of many colonies made a federal government impracticable in the short term. Instead he proposed an interim solution, in which metropolitan France and the French federation would share a single government. Gradually all the various metropolitan ministries would extend their sphere of activity to the federal level, so that, for example, the Ministry of Public Instruction would ultimately administer the educational system of the entire empire. Perhaps the most radical proposal of all was that the Ministers of Finance and Economy should be responsible forthwith to the federal assembly and not to the metropolitan assembly.[36] This suggestion— and the proposal to grant deliberative powers to the federal assembly—seemed to go beyond what had been agreed in the commission, as various members pointed out to Laurentie.[37]

Between the end of the Brazzaville conference and the beginning of the First Constituent Assembly twenty-one months later, General de Gaulle's Provisional Government played the key role in sustaining momentum behind this idea of an imperial federation. At a press conference in Washington in July 1944, de Gaulle described his vision of the empire's future: 'I believe that every land on which the French flag flies must be represented inside a kind of federal system, in which the *métropole* will be a part and in which it will be possible to harmonize the interests of each member.'[38] Three months later he repeated the same idea: 'I will not use the expression French federation, because one can debate the term, but a French system in which each will have a role to play.'[39] Successive ministers also declared their support for a federal system. The first to do so was Pleven.[40] However, it was his successor at the colonial ministry, Paul Giacobbi, who made the most important and explicit declaration about the future of the empire.

This famous declaration (of 24 March 1945) was specifically concerned with the post-war *statut* of French Indochina.[41] But its

[35] 'Rapport de la commission', p. 5.
[36] Ibid. 6.   [37] 'Procès-verbal de la réunion du 4 juillet 1944', pp. 1–2, 7.
[38] *Discours et messages, 1940–1946*, p. 418.   [39] Ibid. 464.
[40] See Pleven's views, as quoted by Ageron, 'Novation et immobilisme', p. 5.
[41] The text of the declaration of 24 Mar. 1945 may be found, among other

implications for the rest of the empire were immediately evident, especially in the following lines:

The Federation of Indochina, together with France and the other parts of the community, will form a 'French Union', whose interests in the outside world will be represented by France. . . . The nationals of the Indochinese Federation will be citizens of Indochina and citizens of the French Union. In this capacity, they will have access to all federal posts and employments in Indochina and in the rest of the Union, without discrimination as to race, religion, or origin . . .

The rationale for this new form of citizenship and new organization of the empire was explained in a letter which Giacobbi wrote on 21 June 1945 to the Governor-General of French West Africa, P. Cournarie.[42] Giacobbi argued that 'the outlook of the colonial populations has undergone a profound transformation since 1939'. These populations, which had accepted the pre-war status quo as ineluctable, now believed in the possibility of change. The weakness of France, which the defeat of 1940 and the subsequent occupation had demonstrated to the empire, had whetted their appetite for change. Giacobbi also noted the anti-colonialism of American public opinion. While he argued that the American view was misguided (because most of France's colonies were not sufficiently developed, economically and socially, to cope with political independence), he suggested that it would be dangerous simply to ignore it. Giacobbi reminded Cournarie that Free France had already developed its own imperial doctrine (first at Brazzaville and now in the declaration of March 1945), and that this doctrine would permit the satisfaction of colonial aspirations, while heading off foreign interference. It was, therefore, essential to put this doctrine into action.

The message of the letter to Cournarie was reiterated even more forcefully in a circular that Giacobbi sent to all Governors-General and Governors in October 1945.[43] Here Giacobbi again recognized that the British and Americans had designs on the French empire,

places, in ANSOM, Affaires politiques, 214. It was drafted by Laurentie, according to his own recollections in a contribution to a conference: *Le Général de Gaulle et l'Indochine 1940–1946* (Paris, 1982), 236.

[42] A copy of this letter is in ANSOM, Affaires politiques, 214. It was written in response to a note from the Governor-General, reporting a speech made by a prominent African politician, M. Lamine-Guèye.

[43] ANSOM, PA 28, dossier 169.

but warned that foreign powers were exploiting rather than creating France's problems: 'It is because our empire is sick that the British and Americans, posing as doctors . . . are rather tactlessly meddling in it.' It was certain, he wrote, that the great majority of colonial élites aspired, if not to independence, at least to a measure of autonomy. The consequences of this fact were ineluctable for France:

We find ourselves . . . under the moral obligation to prove, by way of effective economic, social, and political reforms, that France moves with her time, understands its demands, and that, far from remaining unappreciative of the aspirations of the peoples whom she governs, she means to integrate these peoples within the nation, but within an enlarged nation, where all will be equal before the law and will be free to choose the institutions which suit their personality and particular needs.

This was the model for the Union française which Giacobbi had outlined in his declaration on Indochina: a flexible federation, with each member having its own degree of autonomy; elected assemblies in every territory, permitting the exercise of a decentralized local power; local élites fully involved in the administration of their countries; greater freedom for all members of the federation to develop economically.

As Giacobbi made clear, this vision of a Union française could only be institutionalized by the Constituent Assembly. Still, the government's hands were not entirely tied. In addition to making both public and private commitments to the concept of a federation, there was one way in which it could directly influence the debate in the Constituent Assemblies: that was by ensuring that the empire was well represented within them.

The Brazzaville conference had suggested, in its very first recommendation, that the colonies should be given a representation in the Constituent Assembly 'equivalent to the colonies' importance in the French community'.[44] The Provisional Government accepted this recommendation and, on 20 February 1945, agreed to form a commission of experts to study the problem of the empire's representation within the Constituent Assembly. This commission, which was chaired by Gaston Monnerville, the chairman of the Consultative Assembly's commission de la France d'outre-mer, included seven members of the Consultative Assembly, *fonction-naires* from the Colonial and Interior Ministries, and—for the first

[44] Ministère des colonies, *Conférence Africaine Française*, p. 33.

time—representatives from both the colonial lobby (the Comité de l'Empire Français and the Académie des Sciences Coloniales) and the various colonial populations.[45]

The report of the Monnerville commission proposed to enlarge colonial representation, both in terms of the numbers of those eligible to vote and the proportion of seats in the assembly.[46] The most far-reaching suggestion was that all those who lived in the empire, male and female, citizen and non-citizen, should be represented within the Constituent Assembly and should be eligible to stand for election. As for the form of election, the majority of the commission recognized that, in the absence of electoral lists of non-citizens, there would have to be two separate systems for citizens and non-citizens. Citizens would elect directly, while non-citizens would choose electors who would vote on their behalf. But this did not mean that the commission was forced to admit the principle of a two-college election. The electors chosen by non-citizens would combine with the body of citizens to elect their representatives together.

The commission was not unanimous in reaching these conclusions. A minority report, signed by an Inspecteur Général des Colonies and two representatives of the colonial lobby, argued that it was premature to apply universal suffrage to non-citizen elections. In addition to the three authors of the minority report, other members of the commission—notably Professors Louis Rolland and Henri Solus—made clear their concern that in enfranchising non-citizens the majority report would deprive citizens of their due representation in the assembly.

It was the majority report which the Consultative Assembly endorsed. At the end of July 1945, acting now as chairman of the commission de la France d'outre-mer, Monnerville commended the proposals of his commission to the assembly.[47] Four days later Roger Deniau, another member of the commission de la France d'outre-mer, proposed a resolution which established that citizens and non-citizens would be represented in the Constituent Assembly and would be eligible for election.[48] This proposal, which more or

[45] The papers of the commission are in ANSOM, Affaires politiques, 214 and 215.
[46] 'Rapport de la commission', ibid. 214.
[47] *JO, Débats*, 29 July 1945, pp. 1611–12.
[48] Ibid., 2 Aug. 1945, pp. 1768–9.

less reproduced the majority report of the Monnerville commission, was approved by the assembly. Though there was some opposition to the exact figures proposed for the number of colonial represent- atives, there was a general consensus on the principle that all the colonial populations—whether citizens or not—should be repres- ented. Giacobbi indicated to the assembly that the government shared in this consensus.[49] When the government eventually published its ordinance, it indeed provided for the representation and eligibility of non-citizens as well as citizens.[50] In other respects, however, the government shied away from the more radical suggestions of the Monnerville commission. It created a two-college system, and in certain territories it limited non-citizens who could vote to restricted social and professional categories. In spite of such restrictions, de Gaulle's claim that the government's decision was 'an immense innovation'[51] was justified. The ordin- ance of 22 August 1945 was the culmination of the Provisional Government's efforts—stretching back to Brazzaville—to ensure that when the constitution was rewritten, the empire should find a prominent place within it.

While the government, on its return to Paris, gave the lead in propagating the idea of a French Union, the process of reformulating the imperial system was carried on in two other places: within the colonial ministry and within the emerging or re-emerging political parties.

The driving force behind imperial reform within the ministry was, as we have seen, Laurentie. The strategy which he recommended to successive ministers was two-pronged.[52] The first consisted of a scheme for political federation. This federation would be flexible enough for member states either to be assimilated totally into metropolitan France or to be given separate political identities.[53] It would find its institutional

---

[49] Ibid., 29 July 1945, pp. 1612–13.

[50] Ordonnance no. 45–1874 (22 Aug. 1945).

[51] 'Conférence de presse faite à l'ambassade de France à Washington', 24 Aug. 1945. *Discours et messages, 1940–1946*, p. 606.

[52] See e.g. an untitled memorandum of mid-1944 in ANSOM, Affaires politiques, 880; and also the 'Conférence par M. le gouverneur Laurentie à l'ouverture des cours d'information sur l'Indochine' (mid-1945), ibid. 214.

[53] One problem with this scheme was that, as Laurentie admitted, much of the empire (including all of Black Africa) could not be placed in one category or the other. His only solution to this was that these territories should remain under

expression in a federal assembly sitting regularly in Paris. The other part of Laurentie's strategy involved granting the colonies economic equality with the *métropole*: 'Not only are the colonies no longer made exclusively for France, but it may be said . . . that they are made for themselves and that France's interest must always come second to the colony's interest.'[54] Laurentie assumed that such 'equality' would require the development of industrial sectors in the colonial economies.

The idea of colonial industrialization had been gaining ground in the administration before the war, but it received sudden momentum as a result of the events of 1940. The defeat and its aftermath highlighted the strategic and economic vulnerability of non-industrialized colonies, as well as the costs of that vulnerability for France.[55] In the Vichy administration and in the rival Free French service, the war produced a parallel evolution in favour of industrialization.[56] The reasoning ranged from the general argument that industrialization was bound to happen and therefore should happen 'with our support' rather than 'in spite of us',[57] to the more concrete arguments that it would raise living standards (thus creating markets for French goods), open up opportunities for local élites, and provide employment for expanding popu- lations.[58] A further point of convergence between Free French and Vichy administrations had been their tendency to link the cause of

French 'tutelle' until they were 'mature' enough to opt for one or the other. This sounded to representatives of the colonized peoples perilously close to a return to the status quo.

[54] 'Conférence par M. le Gouverneur Laurentie à l'ouverture des cours d'information sur l'Indochine', p. 8.

[55] See Jacques Marseille, 'La Conférence de Brazzaville et l'économie im- périale: des "innovations éclatantes" ou des recommandations "prudentes"?', paper presented to the colloquium, *De Gaulle et la conférence de Brazzaville* (Paris, 1987).

[56] For Vichy see C. Coquery-Vidrovitch, 'Vichy et l'industrialisation aux colonies', *Revue d'histoire de la Deuxième Guerre Mondiale*, 114 (1979), 69–94; and Marseille, *Empire colonial*, pp. 337–42; for the Free French, see Marseille, *Empire colonial*, pp. 342–7, and his paper 'La Conférence de Brazzaville et l'économie impériale'.

[57] See the paper prepared in 1942 by Vichy's colonial bureaucracy: 'Les Perspectives de l'avenir industriel des colonies', quoted by both Coquery- Vidrovitch ('Vichy', p. 87) and Marseille ('La Conférence de Brazzaville et l'économie impériale', p. 12). See also DGEN, 'Plan d'équipement national: tranche de démarrage' (1944), p. 24, in AN, F60 659.

[58] The Brazzaville Conference had endorsed a cautious but explicit pro- industrialization position.

industrialization to that of economic planning. Both reports
drafted by Vichy's economic planning agency (the DGEN) had
included colonial industrialization (albeit a modest industrialization)
among the targets of its equipment plan.[59] Recent research has
shown that a similar belief in the state's duty to intervene and plan
industrial development was the dominant ideology of participants
at the Brazzaville Conference.[60] It was an ideology to which
Laurentie certainly subscribed: as he put it in the report of his 1944
study commission, it was possible to conceive of an imperial
economic plan without a federation, but it was impossible to
conceive of a federation without the economic plan.[61]

Laurentie's diagnosis of the colonial crisis—that it had both
political and underlying socio-economic causes—was widely held
within the ministry.[62] It was shared, for example, by assimilationists
like Governor Saller, whose views about the political future of the
empire were different from those of Laurentie.[63] However, during
1945 and 1946, the constitutional form of the Union française was
the main focus of attention. On that issue there were major
divergences between Laurentie's opinion and the opinion of other
experts. These divergences surfaced at the beginning of 1945,
when Laurentie proposed to his minister that he establish a study
group, to consider 'a new colonial charter' for the post-war era.[64]
The group consisted of three professors of the Paris Law Faculty
(MM. Solus, Rolland, and Lampué), three officials of the
ministry's direction des affaires politiques, and M. de Curton
(Laurentie's deputy). At the first meeting of this small committee

[59] For a more detailed assessment of the DGEN's treatment of colonial industrialization, see Coquery-Vidrovitch, 'Vichy', pp. 81–94.
[60] See the excellent comments of Jacques Marseille, in 'La Conférence de Brazzaville et l'économie impériale', pp. 12–16.
[61] 'Rapport de la commission chargée d'étudier le moyen d'installer les colonies dans la nouvelle constitution française', p. 2. AN, 382 AP 71.
[62] See e.g. the views of the director of economic affairs, Peter, as expressed in his article: 'Un empire sans métropole', *Le Monde Français*, 1 (Sept. 1945), 89–114.
[63] For Saller's views, see his note 'Les Réformes nécessaires' (12 June 1945), in ANSOM, Affaires politiques, 214.
[64] A draft of the note to the minister (dated 4 Jan. 1945) is ibid. 215. At this point the idea was to create both a *bureau d'étude* and a commission, whose joint role would be to draw up a constitution for the Union française and the *statut* of each of the overseas territories. The *bureau d'étude* did consider some of these larger issues, but the commission—which became the Monnerville commission—was confined by the minister to drawing up proposals for the representation of the colonies in the Constituent Assembly.

(2 March 1945), the legal experts voiced their opposition to Laurentie's 1944 majority report, which was the starting-point for their discussions.[65] Both Solus and Lampué maintained—as Cassin had suggested in Algiers—that the idea of a federal assembly was impracticable. They pointed out that a federation would lead to conflicts between the federal and metropolitan assemblies and might well be resented by the metropolitan population, since the sovereign assembly would be forced to surrender a portion of its sovereignty. De Curton refused to rule out the possibility of a federal body, but compromised by agreeing to a plan which provided for a purely consultative assembly comprised of the members of the Union *except* France, and occasional joint meetings between the metropolitan assembly and this consultative imperial assembly. However, Laurentie disavowed this compromise.[66] Thereafter, the committee began to consider increasingly baroque schemes. It concluded its work without finding a new imperial formula.

The proceedings of this small and well-qualified committee were ominous. The lawyers' objections to the principle of an instantaneous federation were impressive and were shared by other experienced observers.[67] Furthermore, the fact that these experts could not devise a simple, realistic scheme for the Union française suggested that an assembly of amateurs, largely ignorant about imperial issues, would be unlikely to come up with a successful plan. If the improbable were to happen, it would require the political parties who were to control the majority of seats in the Constituent Assembly to agree on a realistic prescription for imperial reform.

In the area of economic reform, it might be argued that they did make some progress. The Constituent Assemblies took up the concept of state-directed industrialization, which had germinated in the colonial administration immediately before and during the war. In debates over the empire, politicians from all parties placed a heavy emphasis on the importance of economic development:[68]

[65] For the minutes of this and following meetings, ibid. 214.

[66] 'Procès-verbal de la séance du 16 mars 1945', p. 3.

[67] e.g. by Colonel F. Bernard, one of the French delegates to the Hot Springs Conference of the Institute of Pacific Relations (6–17 Jan. 1945) and a leading commentator on colonial issues.

[68] See e.g. the debate on the economic situation in Algeria (1 Mar., 5 Mar. 1946) and the larger debate of 20–6 Mar. 1946.

speakers ranging from Soustelle to the Communist deputy Lozeray said explicitly that development meant industrialization.[69] At the beginning of March 1946 Gaston Monnerville proposed the creation of a ten-year plan to achieve 'the transformation of these [colonial] territories into modern countries'.[70] Both Monnerville and the UDSR group (led by two former colonial ministers, Pleven and Soustelle) made proposals for a fund to modernize the French Union.[71] The tripartite government led by Félix Gouin followed this lead. It established a commission du plan d'équipement des colonies, to work within Jean Monnet's planning commissariat, and on 12 April 1946 announced its intention to create an Investment Fund for Economic and Social Development (FIDES).[72]

On the issue which is central to the present discussion—the constitutional form of the Union française—the parties achieved a less satisfactory result. It was perhaps a kind of consensus, but one based on ambiguity. To describe how this consensus was arrived at, the views of each of the main parties should be briefly sketched.

As with other aspects of the new constitution, the Socialist party at first paid relatively little attention to the issue of an imperial federation. The Extraordinary National Congress, which met in Paris in November 1944, established the outlines of a policy. Its resolution stated that the party's objective was 'the emancipation of the indigenous populations, an emancipation which they will attain through an ever closer unity with a democratic and socialist France'.[73] In other words, the Socialists were committed to securing the emancipation of the colonies from the abuses of 'colonialism', but equally adamantly they opposed 'movements which, under cover of half-digested nationalisms, would tend to keep the overseas peoples in the grip of backward feudalisms or agitators in the pay of foreign powers'.[74] Liberation for the empire

---

[69] See *JO, Débats*, 20 Mar. 1946, p. 908; 23 Mar., p. 1035.

[70] *JO, Documents*, Mar. 1946, p. 563.

[71] Ibid. 562–3, 582–3.

[72] See *JO, Débats*, 12 Apr. 1946, pp. 1757–8. The law creating the FIDES was dated 30 Apr. 1946. To qualify the above, it should be noted that the Monnet plan actually put less emphasis on colonial industrialization than some of the plans which had been drawn up by the Vichy administration (according to Jacques Marseille, *Empire colonial*, pp. 347–8).

[73] *Les Décisions du congrès national extraordinaire* (Paris, 1944), 11–12.

[74] 'La Politique du Parti Socialiste et l'Union française', pp. 2–3, in ANSOM, PA 28, dossier 169.

was unthinkable if it meant liberation from France. This position seemed to be aligned on the recommendations of the Brazzaville conference and the policy of the Provisional Government. But some members of the party were less than enthusiastic about Brazzaville. In the Consultative Assembly Paul Valentino, a delegate from Guadeloupe, declared that 'the Brazzaville conference's conclusion must not become the basis of French policy'. In some colonies, Valentino argued, assimilation would never work and, therefore, self-government could not be ruled out.[75]

There was an underlying divergence within the party between federalists and anti-federalists. The federal approach had been pioneered by Lapie. His scheme called for a federal assembly including both metropolitan and colonial representatives, whose function would be to indicate to France 'the outlines of global strategy'.[76] Within this federation colonies would have increased autonomy to negotiate such matters as trade agreements and even military arrangements,[77] although the last word would remain with France. Lapie's plan was similar to that which Giacobbi and Laurentie advocated. There were also, however, influential opponents of federalism within the Socialist party—spokesmen for the long assimilationist tradition in French socialism. The first expression of this opposition had been made by Moch in the 1944 Algiers commission. Initially, however, federalism had a still more influential opponent within the party: Marius Moutet, who had been the Minister of Colonies in the Popular Front government and who returned in 1946 to head the renamed Ministry of Overseas France. Like Moch, Moutet objected less to the principle of federalism—which he saw as the probable long-term future for the empire—than to the idea of creating it immediately and artificially. At the beginning of the constituent period he observed: 'I do not think that we will make federalism. It forms itself, it emerges historically and politically, but it is not made. One only federates that which already exists . . . . it is all the more impossible to create when one is dealing with profoundly different regions . . .'[78] Rather than attempting a premature federation,

---

[75] *JO, Débats*, 20 Mar. 1945, pp. 579–82.

[76] Ibid., 13 Jan. 1944, p. 14.

[77] 'Pour une politique coloniale nouvelle', *Renaissances* (Oct. 1944), 19.

[78] 'Séance de la commission constituée par M. Soustelle du 10 janvier 1946', pp. 6–7, in ANSOM, Affaires politiques, 215. The papers of all four meetings held by the committee are in this *carton*.

Moutet advocated a more pragmatic arrangement. He proposed an increase in democratic control from below, through devolution of powers to elected local assemblies. But he also argued for assimilationist measures (he once described himself as 'plutôt assimilateur de tendance'[79]) which would aim to extend French citizenship to the colonial populations and also increase their representation within the French parliament. The constitutional proposal which the Socialists introduced at the beginning of the First Constituent Assembly contained elements of both the federal and anti-federal approach.[80] As a result it was, as Moutet frankly admitted, 'rather contradictory and vague'.[81]

A similar ambivalence about federalism existed in the MRP. Like the Socialists, the Christian Democrats were suspicious that federalism would set the empire on the slippery slope to dissolution. Viard, the main MRP authority on imperial affairs, wrote in October 1944: 'It does not seem that France is psychologically ready to accept the idea that Paris . . . should not be the sovereign power and could not, in the final analysis, settle an issue once and for all.'[82] The blueprint which Viard offered in this article was to form the basis of the MRP's policy. Its essential characteristics were as follows. French sovereignty would be fully maintained, since the only legislative body in the empire would be the bicameral parliament in Paris. Representatives of the colonies (excluding the protectorates) would occupy a quarter or a third of the seats in the Senate. (This was a modification of a suggestion which a Communist delegate to the Consultative Assembly had made in January 1944.[83]) The empire would participate in the election of the President of the Republic. A conseil impérial would be established, in which the executives of France, the mandated territories, and the North African protectorates would meet regularly to discuss issues relating to the French community. Finally, the power of local assemblies would be greatly extended. In particular, they would be consulted about all executive decrees

[79] 'Séance de la commission constituée par M. Soustelle du 14 janvier 1946', p. 23.
[80] *JO, Documents*, 29 Nov. 1945, pp. 58–62.
[81] 'Séance de la commission constituée par M. Soustelle du 10 janvier 1946', p. 12.
[82] 'Essai d'une organisation constitutionnelle de la "Communauté française"', *Renaissances* (Oct. 1944), 30.
[83] *JO, Débats*, 14 Jan. 1944,.p. 3.

made in respect of their territory. Both Viard and Robert
Delavignette (the director of the École Coloniale who was the
other architect of MRP policy[84]) criticized the fact that colonies
were still being governed according to a *sénatus-consulte* of 1854,
which had placed all imperial legislation in the hands of the head
of state.

When the MRP met to draw up its programme for the
Constituent Assembly at the end of 1945, it largely followed
Viard's advice.[85] The report presented to the MRP's second
congress began by stating bluntly that no part of the French empire
desired independence. It proposed to create local assemblies,
whose task would be to consider and give advice on decrees of the
French executive. It suggested a limited representation for the
colonies within the metropolitan assembly. Expanding on Viard's
plan, the MRP report advocated an Assembly of the French
Union, where representatives of the local assemblies would sit
with representatives of metropolitan departments. This assembly
would have a legislative role, but would not be a political
chamber.[86]

In general, the symbolism of a French Union—a middle way
between autonomy and dependence—struck a powerful chord
with Christian Democrats whose entire social and economic
philosophy was founded on the possibility of associating those with
conflicting social interests. There was an obvious parallel between
'associating' colonizers and colonized and 'associating' workers
and capitalists. In terms of the content of their federalism, there
was no real difference between the MRP and the Socialists.
Neither showed any enthusiasm for creating an authentic federation.
Indeed, the MRP was even more concerned than the Socialist
party that the introduction of a Union française should not weaken
France's hegemony. When André Philip suggested to the First
Constitutional Commission that the conseil consultatif de l'Union
française might eventually become a proper federal assembly,
Viard scotched even this timid suggestion: 'the later change,
forecast by the chairman, would only be possible if this council

---

[84] For Delavignette's views, see his article: 'L'Union française', *Esprit* (1 July
1945), 214–36.

[85] 'Rapport présenté par le docteur Aujoulat sur la politique coloniale', 2nd
National Congress, 13–16 Dec. 1945, in AN, 350 AP 12.

[86] This concept of a non-political federal assembly was similar to the movement's
plan for a professional assembly in the metropolitan legislature.

reserved at least a half, if not two-thirds, of its total seats for representatives of the *métropole*.'[87] The MRP's fears about undermining the unity of the empire initially drove the party to a more assimilationist position than that adopted by the Socialist party.[88] In the Second Constituent Assembly, however, these fears led the Christian Democrats to espouse an instant federalism, when it suddenly began to appear a better way of preserving the unity of the empire than the open-ended mixture of federalism and assimilation which they had defended during the First Constituent Assembly.

The position of the Communist party at the Liberation was close to Viard's. In a debate in mid-January 1944, the Communist spokesman Mercier had told the Consultative Assembly: 'We declare first of all that the French Republic, *métropole* and overseas territories, is one and indivisible.'[89] Mercier then congratulated de Gaulle on his Constantine speech, especially on the decision to grant citizenship to those 'who demonstrated that they were qualified to participate in the country's political life'. A few months later, a party document which was published secretly in France endorsed both the Brazzaville conference and an important CFLN decree of 7 March 1944.[90] These two statements serve to show how the PCF had abandoned its anti-colonialism of the pre-1936 and 1939–41 periods and placed itself firmly in the reformist mainstream. Like de Gaulle, it regarded the preservation of the empire as crucial to France's standing in the post-war world. Like Free France and all the Resistance groups, it assumed that the empire had demonstrated its attachment to the *métropole*. Like progressive voices inside the colonial ministry and the bourgeois parties, the PCF trumpeted the necessity of developing and industrializing colonial economies and of integrating the empire within the constitutional framework.

The most comprehensive study of the PCF's colonial policy in this period has discerned two distinct phases.[91] In the first phase

[87] ANC-1, *Séances de la Commission de la Constitution* (Paris, 1946), 236.
[88] See Viard's speech in the First Constitutional Commission, ibid. 242.
[89] *JO, Débats*, 14 Jan. 1944, p. 3.
[90] Quoted by Grégoire Madjarian, *La Question coloniale et la politique du Parti Communiste Français, 1944–1947* (Paris, 1977), 51. The decree of March 1944 gave voting rights to all Muslim non-citizens in North Africa, granted citizenship to some 50,000 individual Muslims, and improved the representation of non-citizens within local assemblies in Algeria.   [91] Ibid. 240–1.

(mid-1941 to mid-1945) the party stressed imperial unity and assimilation to the exclusion of all other themes. In the second phase, beginning at the end of the war, the PCF could no longer ignore the existence of nationalist movements within the empire. It began to stress the awakening of national consciousness which was taking place and the need to satisfy this aspiration. The earlier endorsement of Brazzaville disappeared.[92] The party now accused Brazzaville of having been too soft on the trusts and too assimilationist in ruling out so categorically the possibility of self-government. Nevertheless, even in this second phase, there was no rejection of France's imperial role. France could not deny the right of colonies to self-determination, but it was implicit that they would not choose total independence. Like the Socialists, the PCF justified this position by arguing that it was in the colonies' own interests to remain attached to a socialist France rather than become dependent on predatory foreign powers. As a result of their desire to restrict the expansion of Anglo-American influence and to extend to the empire social and political gains made in the metropolis, the Communists fell into the broad consensus, stretching from gaullists to socialists: the empire required political, economic, and social reform, but above all it demanded to remain attached to France. On this fundamental point the PCF agreed with its two main partners in the Constituent Assemblies. As Madjarian has observed, the parties' many divergences over the imperial clauses of the constitution never led to an open rupture of the tripartite alliance. In the end they led to compromise.[93] This reflected both the low political priority accorded to the Union française by the main parties and, at the same time, the broad agreement which existed on the issue.

The conclusion that may be drawn from this examination of party programmes on the eve of the First Constituent Assembly is that the fate of the reform movement was more or less sealed. The proceedings of the two Constituent Assemblies were the end of a process, not the beginning. This is not to say that the constitution of the French Union could not have emerged differently. It is obvious that it would have done, if the draft approved by the First

---

[92] See the speech of Henri Lozeray, *JO, Débats*, 20 Mar. 1946, pp. 908–12, and Lozeray's article in *Cahiers du Communisme*, Apr. 1946, pp. 368–78.
[93] *La Question coloniale*, p. 151.

Constituent Assembly in April 1945 had been ratified by the electorate. What seems clear, however, is that the parameters of the debate were established by the beginning of 1946. During the long and tortuous business of constitution-making, the deputies did not pass beyond these parameters.

Both the making of the constitution and the aspects of it relating to the French Union have been described in detail elsewhere and need not be re-examined here.[94] It is sufficient to summarize this complicated story. The First Constituent Assembly discussed the issue of the French Union in an atmosphere of general goodwill. It produced a draft which was generous to the empire but vague. It granted citizenship to all French nationals but did not specify the kind of citizenship. It was assimilationist in guaranteeing that all overseas territories would send deputies to the National Assembly and that the National Assembly's legislation would be sovereign throughout the empire; but it was 'associationist' in providing for a conseil de l'Union française and in describing the Union as 'freely consented'. The Second Constituent Assembly, which convened in June 1946 after the First Assembly's draft had been voted down, debated in a far less cordial atmosphere. The colonial lobby had revived. The *indigène* representatives, antagonized by the rejection of the generous April draft and by the vocal colonial lobby, had become more radical. The MRP had been influenced by de Gaulle's speech at Bayeux (which had demanded the immediate creation of a federal organization to forestall the total disintegration of the empire) and had itself begun to see the attractions of an instantaneous federalism. Lastly, the negotiations with Vietnamese nationalists and the deteriorating relations between the three main parties in the assembly had soured the atmosphere within the Constitutional Commission. In the early stages of the Second Constituent Assembly an Intergroup of Native Deputies (supported by the left) gained a number of their demands. A draft approved by the Constitutional Commission at the end of July 1946 gave more explicit assurances than the April draft that all the overseas territories would be free to develop as they themselves saw fit. It proposed to create a federal system, but left the federal organizations

---

[94] See, especially, Gordon Wright, *The Reshaping of French Democracy* (New York, 1948); D. Bruce Marshall, *The French Colonial Myth and Constitution-Making in the Fourth Republic* (New Haven, Conn., 1973); and Isoart, 'L'Élaboration de la constitution de l'Union française'.

unspecified. It was this draft that the Bidault government, urged on by the criticisms of a senior parliamentarian (Edouard Herriot) and an ex-President (de Gaulle),[95] intervened to quash, on the grounds that it would provoke the dissolution of the empire. The government then produced its own draft, which went much further towards establishing the federal organs of the Union and defining the rights of the *métropole* within the federation. With a few modifications, this government draft subsequently became *titre VIII* of the Fourth Republic's constitution.

In comparison with the draft of the Native Intergroup and even that approved by the Constitutional Commission at the end of July, the government proposals of September 1946 appeared reactionary. The changes which had been made were undeniably motivated by a desire to strengthen France's grip on the empire and to remove what some had interpreted as inducements to secession. They toned down the 'freely consented' union, assured the white *colon* minorities of special representation, and turned the natives' French citizenship into citizenship of the French Union. In a longer perspective, however, this characterization of the September draft should be revised. Like the April draft, the September draft was an expression of the reformism which had begun at Brazzaville. Its reactionary aspects were as integral a feature of this reformism as the liberal aspects of the First Constituent Assembly's draft. To give one example, it may be noted that Giacobbi's March 1945 declaration on Indochina (widely interpreted as a 'liberal' document) had proposed a citizenship of the French Union, just as Bidault's 'reactionary' proposals of August/September 1946 did.

The reformism had all along been primarily the work of the Provisional Governments. The very expression Union française had been created by ministerial declaration. The concept had been fostered by successive ministers, by Laurentie and the colonial ministry, by de Gaulle's public pronouncements, and by the policies of his governments in Algiers and Paris. When the First Constituent Assembly began to address the task of constitution-alizing this new concept, the government had stepped aside and, in

[95] On the same day that Herriot attacked the Constitutional Commission's new draft (27 Aug. 1946), de Gaulle told the press that the draft was unacceptable. See *Discours et messages, 1946–1958* (Paris, 1970), 18–23.

spite of having made plans to submit proposals to the assembly,[96] had not submitted them. However, the failure of the April draft to give a form to the Union française convinced the government that it should provide the Second Constituent Assembly with a proposal that converted into constitutional form the new imperial policy which it and its predecessors had developed.

The government's intervention in August 1946 was thus the culmination of a long-standing pattern of intervention. On 11 September, when the Minister of Overseas France, Moutet, introduced the government's proposals to the Constitutional Commission, he emphasized that he was not submitting merely his own proposals or those of the present government, but rather 'the result, the synthesis of countless studies carried out by ministerial, interministerial, and parliamentary committees under preceding governments, under the present government, or at Algiers'.[97] Most of the proposals which Moutet made on 11 September had indeed been aired during the meetings of the Algiers and Paris study commissions. They had also been made in a note which Laurentie wrote on 10 June 1946—that is to say, before the radicalization of the native deputies' proposals and before the MRP's conversion to federalism.[98] Although there was an important political aspect to the Bidault government's decision to intervene when it did,[99] it is clear that for the preceding three months the colonial ministry had lobbied for a new draft of the French Union clauses. Four days before Herriot's speech in the assembly precipitated the government's decision to intervene, the colonial ministry's *direction des affaires politiques* had sent a note to the cabinet which had stated bluntly:

The statute of the French Union . . . in so far as it tends to modify France's legal situation in the international order and, on the other hand, brings significant innovations *vis-à-vis* overseas territories and nationals, cannot

---

[96] This was the purpose of the committee which Jacques Soustelle (the then colonial minister) had created in January 1946 and which had included Moutet, Laurentie, Delavignette, and Peter.

[97] ANC-2, *Séances de la Commission de la Constitution* (Paris, 1947), 482.

[98] 'Note sur la nécessité d'une constitution de l'Union française', ANSOM, Affaires politiques, 215.

[99] For the political background to this decision, see Marshall, *The French Colonial Myth*, pp. 208 ff. Bidault's intervention reflected the MRP's political need to appear firm in the face of nationalist demands and pressure from de Gaulle and the right.

be decided without the participation of the government which is responsible for French sovereignty in the world and before the country.[100]

The strengths and weaknesses of the final constitutional draft reflected the strengths and weaknesses of the reform movement stretching back to 1943. On the one hand, the September draft expressed all the liberal ideas of the post-Brazzaville period. It enfranchised the disenfranchised. It fostered local democracy. It ended a juridical regime based solely on the dependence of the colonies on the *métropole*, and put in its place an organization which was more flexible and more equitable. It constitutionalized a federation of peoples. On the other hand, it stopped short of a truly functional federation, which would have given the imperial populations a far greater influence over their own lives and the life of the empire than Paris ever envisaged or desired. Ultimately—as federalists and anti-federalists, assimilationists and associationists had almost all wanted and assumed—it maintained France's control over *her* empire. What was most appealing about the Union française was the idea: it was a synthesis of two traditional approaches to imperialism—association and assimilation—neither of which, by itself, seemed a wholly practical or acceptable way forward in 1946. The benefits of a Union française (in the form of a continued imperial role) were so self-evident that few seem to have asked themselves whether the synthesis was a feasible one.[101] What did it mean to synthesize association and assimilation in the best of circumstances, let alone when a growing number of the empire's inhabitants wanted independence for their countries? The Constituent Assemblies carried wartime reformism as far as it was capable of going. However, if it took a leap of imagination to condemn colonialism in the abstract and conceive a constitutionalized French Union, it would have taken a far greater leap to break free of colonial mythology altogether by recognizing that the empire did not necessarily wish to remain attached to France. Instead, the colonial problem was all along viewed as a domestic problem which could be solved by domestic decisions, in particular by the creation of a new constitutional form for the empire.

[100] 'Note pour le conseil des ministres', 23 Aug. 1946, ANSOM, Affaires politiques, 216.

[101] One person who did ask this question was Colonel F. Bernard. See his articles: 'L'Institution d'un trusteeship international et l'évolution des colonies françaises', *Cahiers du Monde Nouveau*, 1 (1945), 168–75; 'L'Union française: illusions et réalités', *Cahiers du Monde Nouveau*, 2 (May 1946), 46–61; 'Comment peut-on vraiment réaliser l'Union française?', *Cahiers du Monde Nouveau*, 2 (Dec. 1946), 22–33.

7

The New Society I: Educational Reform

W. D. HALLS has observed that 'one of the strangest phenomena of the period immediately after the defeat was the imperative felt by many Frenchmen to beat their breast and condemn their generation'.[1] A consequence of this phenomenon was to focus attention on the educational system that had produced the generation of 1940. In September 1940 a circular issued by Vichy's Ministry of the Interior stated that 'The essential condition for a lasting and profound revival of our country is the reform of the education of young Frenchmen.'[2] Among Vichy's opponents in the Resistance, educational reform (albeit of a very different kind) also had many proponents. To quote Henri Wallon, the chairman of the major post-Liberation reform commission, 'The question of reforms in the university is one of those which has most interested French resisters.'[3] The Provisional Government of General de Gaulle was similarly concerned about the issue and established a series of study commissions between 1942 and 1944 to make proposals for reform. After the Liberation it was de Gaulle himself who reminded the Consultative Assembly of the necessity of 'a profound reform of education'.[4]

As in the early years of the Third Republic, the debate about educational reform was not purely over pedagogical details. On the contrary, precisely because it was stimulated by the catastrophic failure of an entire society, it tended to be linked to other structural reforms in the political, economic, and social spheres. Much of its vocabulary and many of its recommendations were derived from a vigorous pre-war tradition of educational reformism, but the events of 1940 gave it a new urgency. They placed education at the centre of the debate about the nation's future. As Raymond Aron put it in 1945: 'At the present time, when French-

[1] *The Youth of Vichy France* (Oxford, 1981), 161.
[2] Quoted by Halls, *Youth of Vichy France*, p. 196.
[3] Wallon, 'La Réforme de l'enseignement en France', in AN, 71 AJ 64. 71 AJ holds the archives of the Institut National de la Recherche Pédagogique.
[4] *Discours et messages, 1940–1946* (Paris, 1970), 531 (speech of 2 Mar. 1945).

men discuss the recovery of their country, their conversations almost invariably come round to the subject of the birth-rate or the subject of education. A logical enough conclusion: France needs more Frenchmen and, while awaiting this problematic increase in quantity, she needs Frenchmen of a higher quality.'[5]

The cause of educational reform was at least as central to the philosophy of the État Français as to that of Vichy's opponents. 'I urge you, first of all, to an intellectual and moral reform,' Pétain told the nation after broadcasting news of the armistice.[6] Education was a question on which the new head of state had long held fixed views. He reiterated them in an article that was published in the *Revue des Deux Mondes* (15 August 1940). This article was the manifesto of Vichy's educational ideology: it emphasized the importance of discipline and traditional values; it reinforced familial authority; it attacked an excessively 'bookish' pedagogy and advocated more practical and physical education; it proposed to orient the young towards agricultural and artisanal professions; it defended the prerogatives of confessional schools; and, finally, it rejected a pre-war reformism that had sought a unified school system ('école unique').[7] In part the État Français was able to legislate its ideology into reality.[8] In the summer and autumn of 1940 a series of decrees allowed the government to weed out those in the teaching profession whom it considered undesirables. A particular target were the staunchly secular and republican primary school teachers, whom the new regime attacked in a variety of ways (for example, by suppressing the *écoles normales d'instituteurs* where they had been trained). Other legislation restored fees in secondary schools, aided private schools by making them eligible for subsidies, and reintroduced optional religious education into the public schools.[9] A law of 2 November

[5] 'Esquisse des problèmes de la réforme de l'enseignement', *La France Libre*, 54 (15 Apr. 1945), 413.

[6] *Actes et écrits* (Paris, 1974), 454.

[7] Ibid. 485–90.

[8] The following summary is based on Halls, *Youth of Vichy France*; E. Maillard, 'La Réforme de l'enseignement', *Revue d'histoire de la Deuxième Guerre Mondiale*, 56 (1964), 43–64; A. Rosier, 'L'Université et la révolution nationale', in P. Arnoult *et al.*, *La France sous l'occupation* (Paris, 1959), 127–43.

[9] This last measure (adopted by J. J. Chevalier at the beginning of 1941) was rescinded by the next Minister of Education (Jérôme Carcopino).

1941, replacing this earlier legislation on Catholic education, gave private schools a subsidy from departmental budgets.

In general, however, the regime was unable to develop or put into operation a plan of fundamental reforms. As in so many other areas, Vichy's educational reformism was lost somewhere between the rhetoric of the ideologues and the decrees and circulars of a zealous bureaucracy. The failure was a reflection of endemic instability and division in the regime. In the early phase of the National Revolution (while constructive reform was still feasible), there were no fewer than six Ministers of Education: Rivaud, Mireaux, Ripert, Chevalier, Carcopino, and Bonnard. The attack on primary school teachers and the support for confessional schools were primarily the work of the first four (all of whom have been characterized as '"intellectual reactionaries" of Catholic and right-wing persuasion').[10] After a brief interlude of more constructive reform (associated with the tenure of Jérôme Carcopino), the Ministry took an overtly collaborationist and pro-fascist turn, with the arrival of Abel Bonnard in April 1942. With his ideas about reconstructing French education along Nazi lines, Bonnard introduced a brand of reformism—if it can be called such—which was difficult to reconcile with the traditionalism of Pétain's August 1940 article.

Some of Vichy's educational reforms—especially the set of secondary school reforms introduced by Carcopino in 1941—were retained after the war. In a broader sense Vichy had two kinds of impact on the debate about educational reform. The first was a negative one. Vichy's subsidies to confessional schools reopened the old dispute between proponents of a state educational monopoly and defenders of private schools. The implications of this were immediately evident. In 1942, for example, the secretary of the Free French study commissions in London, M. Maisonneuve, noted that 'certain people coming from France are of the opinion that anti-clericalism, which was in the process of dying down before the war, will have a renewed outbreak, once the country has been liberated'.[11] This was indeed to be an issue that divided post-Liberation élites and undermined the cause of educational reform in 1944–6. The second kind of impact that Vichy had was more positive. One of the distinguishing features of Vichy's

[10] Halls, *Youth of Vichy France*, p. 16.
[11] See 'Procès-verbal de la réunion du 27 novembre 1942', p. 2, in AN, 71 AJ 62.

educational policy was its attempt to place 'l'enseignement' (education narrowly defined) within the broader context of a 'youth policy'. The État Français' creation of an administrative organ to co-ordinate this policy—the Secrétariat Général à la Jeunesse (SGJ)—repeated an experiment that had been made briefly by the Popular Front government. The SGJ's emphasis on sports and outdoor exercise and its efforts to encourage participation in youth organizations such as the Chantiers de la Jeunesse and the Compagnons de France struck a responsive chord with many people outside, as well as inside, the regime. All the reformers of this period were in agreement that French education needed to pay more attention to forming bodies and characters as well as intellects.

The ultimate aim of educational reformers in the Resistance was diametrically opposed to that of Vichy. Whereas Vichy focused relentlessly on the child's responsibilities and on creating a social setting which constrained personal development, Resistance reformers focused on the child's right to full self-development. Beneath the rhetorical patina about meritocracy, Vichy envisaged an educational system which preserved the social hierarchy, whereas the Resistance, starting from an assumption that bourgeois society had crumbled in 1940, emphasized the need for the educational system to produce new élites and to do so in a way which 'must not take account of the child's economic background, but of his intellectual potential'.[12] The CNR Common Programme summarized this demand for educational equality when it called for:

The real possibility for all French children to benefit from education and attain the most advanced culture, whatever the economic circumstances of their parents, so that the highest positions should be truly accessible to all those who have the ability to hold them, and so that a true élite should be produced—an élite of merit, not of birth, constantly renewed from the ranks of the people.

This ideal of a democratized education was expressed in more concrete terms in a number of reform programmes written by resisters. It was also discussed in the series of commissions established under the aegis of the Free French regime.

[12] *L'École libératrice*, 5 (July 1944), quoted by H. Michel, *Les Courants de pensée de la Résistance* (Paris, 1962), 404–5.

Of Resistance programmes, two were particularly influential. The first of these was published in the second *cahier* of the Organisation Civile et Militaire (OCM) in September 1942.[13] It was the work of a group of resisters, most of whom were involved professionally in education: Alfred Rosier, Claude Bellanger, Georges Jamati, Georges Lapierre, René Paty, Jean Kréher, André Graetz, François de Lescure, René Sordes.[14] The guiding principles of their reform were twofold: on the one hand, equality of opportunity and the importance of a rounded education (incorporating physical, civic, and vocational training) in contrast to the intellectualism of the pre-war system; on the other, the need for an educational system which would unite the nation rather than divide it along social or ideological lines. The members of the OCM proposed that the new system should be philosophically neutral and should integrate all existing schools into an 'école unique'. Children would make their way through this single school, guided among the various classes and options by a process of 'orientation' rather than selected by competitive examination. The aim of this approach was to ensure that schools concentrated on developing each student's capacities to the fullest extent instead of merely ranking children according to narrowly intellectual criteria and making them carry the consequences of this classification throughout the rest of their lives. Both the idea of the single school (integrating the hitherto largely distinct primary and secondary levels) and the pedagogical notion of orientation had been frequently expressed by inter-war reformers.[15] Two features of the OCM's philosophy none the less stand out as characteristic of wartime attitudes. The first was the movement's attempt to de-emphasize the importance of formal education altogether.

If a man's fate should not be a function of his parents' circumstances, no more should it be determined solely . . . between the ages of 10 and 25. Certainly it is important for his training to be adapted to the course which he appears destined to follow, but he must retain the possibility—if he made a mistake . . . about his preferences and abilities—to change direction in order to join the right path.[16]

[13] Reprinted in Maxime Blocq-Mascart, *Chroniques de la Résistance* (Paris, 1945), 185–269. A slightly different version of the report is in AN, F1a 3733.
[14] Arthur Calmette, *L''OCM'* (Paris, 1961), 55.
[15] A good general account of the inter-war reform movement is John E. Talbott, *The Politics of Educational Reform in France, 1918–1940* (Princeton, 1969).
[16] Blocq-Mascart, *Chroniques de la Résistance*, p. 190.

Extending this argument to the selection of the country's élites, the OCM argued that performance in the 'real world' after education ought to count for at least as much as early academic success. This touches on a second prominent aspect of the OCM philosophy: its insistence that democratization was justifiable not just on grounds of social justice but also in terms of national self-interest. The events of 1940 had shown that French education had failed to produce the leadership and social cohesion that were indispensable for national security.[17]

The other comprehensive programme produced by the Resistance was written by the Communist party's spokesman on educational affairs, Georges Cogniot, and was circulated by the PCF at the end of September 1943.[18] This lengthy 'esquisse d'une politique française de l'enseignement' confirmed the party's interest in educational reform, which had first surfaced in 1936. Until that point the party had dismissed all such reform—including the idea of the 'école unique'—on the grounds that it would merely give working-class children a greater dose of bourgeois culture and weaken their class solidarity. In the aftermath of the Popular Front victory, however, the PCF had revised this assessment and accepted educational reform as a progressive and democratic measure (the same grounds for accepting limited nationalizations).[19] Cogniot's wartime report touched on most of the issues that were being discussed inside Resistance circles. It began by making a series of criticisms of the pre-war system. The most fundamental criticism was the same as that made by all the inter-war reformers and by the OCM. The old system had divided children into two unequal groups. One, comprised of those of modest origins, attended the *école primaire*. Most of them left school by the age of 14, while a minority continued their education at an *école primaire supérieure* or an *école d'enseignement technique*. Only a small fraction made the transition from the primary schools to secondary and higher education. The secondary schools—the *lycées* and *collèges*—were the preserve of the bourgeoisie whose parents could afford to keep them in school when no maintenance grants were available. One of the ways in which bourgeois parents had

[17] See the version of the OCM report in AN, F1a 3733 (p. 5).

[18] A copy of the 'Esquisse d'une politique française de l'enseignement' is in AN, F60 1729.

[19] Talbott, *Politics of Educational Reform*, pp. 217–19.

been able to channel their children into the secondary level was by sending them not to the *école primaire* but to the primary classes of the secondary schools. The remedy that Cogniot proposed involved the opening-up of secondary education to all children. The school-leaving age was to be raised to 16 or 17. The preparatory classes of the *lycées* and *collèges* would be abolished. After a common primary education, children would be assigned, according to their abilities, to a secondary school or to the *école primaire supérieure* or the *école technique*. The decision would be made after a careful assessment of the child's capacities and without regard to parental background: 'it is necessary for the engineer to become accustomed to seeing a son who is more suited for manual labour than for the *polytechnique* "oriented" towards the professional school and not advanced mathematics.'[20] In order that academically gifted children from the working class could afford to prolong their education, Cogniot recommended that their families receive an allowance. Like the OCM, Cogniot justified his proposals by relating them to national needs. '[This country] will no longer be able to permit itself the enormous waste of its assets which it traditionally commits by recruiting the vast majority of its scholars and artists, engineers and doctors, political leaders and powerful civil servants, from only a very narrow section of society.'[21]

The conditions of Resistance life made a structured dialogue about educational reform impracticable. However, within the Free French organization, a more structured debate did take place. In July 1942 a sub-committee of one of the four study commissions established by de Gaulle at the end of 1941 began to consider the question of post-war education. This sub-committee, officially entitled the 'section des questions intellectuelles et de l'enseigne-ment', was chaired by Professor Cathala and had twenty-seven members, including Maurice Schumann, a number of academics (Professors Cordier, Fournier, Génissieux, and Vaucher) and trade-unionists (MM. Hauck and Vangrévelinghe).[22]

The memorandum, which became the basis for this sub-committee's discussions, had two major themes.[23] The first was a

[20] 'Esquisse', p. 29.   [21] Ibid. 27.
[22] The papers of the Cathala committee are in AN, 71 AJ 62.
[23] The authors of the memorandum (dated 30 Sept. 1942) were Fournier, Hauck, Neurohr, Schaeffer, and Schumann.

proposal to 'nationalize' the educational system. The 'nationalized sector' which would be created would have a monopoly of all education, but would be independent of the state and would be administered by a tripartite council (with representatives of the state, of teachers, and of 'consumers'—trade unions, artistic and scientific organizations, parents, and pupils). As the members of the sub-committee acknowledged, this proposal was modelled on the inter-war ideas of the primary school teachers' union, the Syndicat National des Instituteurs.[24] The possibility that the state would allow an autonomous educational establishment to exist beyond its control, while at the same time providing it with most of its resources, struck several members of the sub-committee (including, apparently, the Commissaire à l'Intérieur, André Philip) as implausible.[25]

The other component of the sub-committee's plan was a scheme to unite the conflicting interests of the confessional and public schools. Within the nationalized *école* all the different religions would be permitted 'on a footing of total equality' to give religious instruction to those whose families requested it. This instruction would take place in the school buildings but outside the times reserved for normal instruction. This rearrangement of the curriculum was envisaged by the sub-committee as a gesture of reconciliation: to compensate confessional schools for their inclusion within the nationalized sector, the non-Catholics were admitting the right of the priest to enter any school and deliver religious instruction there. Here again, however, there were obvious difficulties with the sub-committee's proposals. Syndicalists on the sub-committee objected to the idea of optional religious education in state-run primary schools,[26] while other members baulked at the idea of a nationalized monopoly.[27]

The work of the Cathala sub-committee prepared the way for the deliberations of a second committee that met in Algiers in 1944. This later committee was created by René Capitant, the Commissaire à l'Éducation Nationale, to establish a basis for post-

---

[24] 'Procès-verbal de la réunion du vendredi 2 octobre 1942'. For the SNI's nationalization blueprint, see Talbott, *Politics of Educational Reform*, pp. 136–9.

[25] For Philip's comments, see the minutes of a meeting held on 15 Jan. 1943.

[26] See the comments of M. Vangrévelinghe, 'Procès-verbal de la réunion du 27 novembre 1942'.

[27] See the comments of M. Burnay, 'Procès-verbal de la réunion du 13 novembre 1942'.

Liberation educational reforms.[28] It was a committee of twenty-five members drawn from three main sources: the political world (MM. Berlioz, Carrière, Giacobbi, and Prigent); the Commissariat à l'Éducation Nationale; and the universities and faculties (mainly those of Algiers). Since there was almost no overlap with the earlier sub-committee, Capitant and Philip (who had by then become Commissaire d'État aux Études) guided the new committee in a different direction. Capitant tried to keep the discussion off the thorny question of whether or not the state should have a monopoly of education, while Philip brought to the fore British reform projects which had been in the background during the Cathala sub-committee's debates. These projects focused on three issues: first, the necessity of maintenance grants (including free meals and clothing) in order to achieve a functional equality of opportunity (a point which both the OCM and Cogniot had made); second, the advantages of part-time education for adolescents who had left school; third, the need to raise technical and vocational education to a level of esteem comparable with that of humanistic education (a point that everyone, from the Communist party to Vichy, was making).[29] The importance of British reform ideas in the deliberations of the Algiers commission may be judged from its archives, which contain large quantities of information about Britain and virtually nothing about reform in other countries.

Whereas the Cathala sub-committee had tried to produce a new institutional framework for the entire educational system, the Algiers committee concentrated its attention on what was widely regarded as the principal flaw of the old system: the restricted entry to secondary education. After five months of weekly meetings, the conclusions that the committee reached on this and related questions were summarized by the vice-chairman of the committee, Marcel Durry (a senior official in the *commissariat*) in a 'Rapport général sur les travaux de la commission pour la réforme de l'enseignement'.[30]

The main proposal of the Durry report was that secondary education should be free and compulsory for all up to the age of 15 and that those who left school at 15 should continue to receive

[28] The papers of the Algiers reform committee are in AN, 71 AJ 63.
[29] See Philip's remarks in 'Procès-verbal de la séance d'ouverture, 8 mars 1944', 2–3.   [30] A copy of this report is in AN, 71 AJ 63.

part-time education until they reached the age of 18. This change
was intended to have an impact on both primary and secondary
education. Since primary education would become for all pupils a
preparatory stage (rather than, for many, the one and only stage),
there would be less need to cram information and more scope for
field-trips, non-academic lessons, and so forth. Again, since all
pupils would be progressing to some kind of secondary school at
the age of 12, there would be no need for terminal examinations.
Pupils would be oriented towards the section of the secondary
school which best met their needs and capacities. If they left school
at 15, they would not receive a qualification dependent upon
examinations but a document in which the school authorities
would give a detailed evaluation of their performance and
potential.

The Durry report also made other significant proposals. It
stressed the importance of vocational and technical education, 'the
poor relation, the underprivileged section of our school system'.[31]
Though it did not resolve the issue of the school-leaving
examination (the *baccalauréat*), it tentatively recommended replacing it with an achievement record similar to that to be
presented to those who left school at 15. It proposed far-reaching
reforms of higher education, with a two-year preparatory stage
before the *licence* and a major revision in the role of the *grandes
écoles*. Finally, it recommended the creation of an École Supérieure
d'Administration that would prepare the highest state servants and
ensure that they were 'devoted to the republican and democratic
system of government'.[32] The committee recognized that this was
a highly ambitious programme. It would take time to train new
teachers and build new schools and laboratories. The state would
have to find new revenues for these expenses, not to mention to
pay for the maintenance awards that the committee recommended.
The Durry report assumed that a lengthy transition period (of five
to six years) was unavoidable.[33]

[31] 'Rapport', p. 18.
[32] Ibid. 28. The idea of an École d'Administration was a popular one, advocated
by (among others) Georges Cogniot, Jules Romains (writing in the Free French
newspaper *La Marseillaise* in April 1943), the CAS (in its April 1944 circular to
regional officials), the economist Charles Rist (see his diary *Une saison gâtée* (Paris,
1983), 124), and the future architect of the ENA, Michel Debré. A proposal to
create such a school had been made before the war by Jean Zay.
[33] 'Rapport', p. 34.

Before reform could begin, however, there remained to be settled the prior issue of Catholic education and its integration within public education. As we have seen, the Cathala sub-committee had raised this issue, while the Durry committee had shelved it on the grounds that the question of an educational monopoly was 'a political more than an educational matter'.[34] Although Vichy subsidies to private schools had reopened the issue, there had been vague hopes in Resistance circles that the active involvement of progressive Catholics in the Resistance would be the prelude to a post-war reconciliation. This reconciliation did not materialize. An anecdote that Halls recounts illustrates how rapidly the illusions were dashed:

Five days after the invasion [of France in 1944] Maurice Schumann, sent by de Gaulle from London, attended a luncheon at Bayeux in honour of the Resistance. For the first time the members of the various movements discovered that they included Catholics, atheists, freemasons, and even priests. By the end of the meal the assembled company were already quarrelling over subsidies to the confessional schools.[35]

In the wake of the Liberation the Provisional Government made one last effort to achieve a settlement of this problem. It established yet another commission (this time headed by André Philip).[36] Between November 1944 and February 1945 this 'committee to study the relations between public and private education' laboured to find a compromise that both Catholics and non-Catholics could accept. For a time the fundamental differences between the two sides were masked by the personal goodwill of the individuals serving on the commission. They soon emerged, however, when the commission got down to discussing concrete issues: should the state subsidize private schools? In rationalizing the number of schools, should it be the village confessional school or the village public school that closed? On such questions the commission members tended to divide into the two camps. In any case, by the time that the Philip commission's meetings were drawing to a close, the private school subsidy issue had re-entered the political arena, where there was very little chance that a compromise settlement reached by a study commission could have much impact. The parties of the left (especially the Communists)

[34] Ibid. 7.   [35] *Youth of Vichy France*, pp. 101–2.
[36] The papers of the Philip commission are in AN, 71 AJ 66.

were mobilizing forces against any continuation of subsidies, while
the church and its political allies were dramatizing the plight of
Catholic schools deprived of their subsidies. At the end of March
1945 the Consultative Assembly voted to discontinue subsidies.
The fears that Philip had voiced to his commission in January and
February proved justified: 'I will view it as a real catastrophe if the
first major political debate should be over this issue. . . . It would
be to fall into the old rut and into a false political categorization
which threatens to compromise our effort at democratic renovation
at the very outset.'[37]

The position of educational reform at the Liberation might be
described, therefore, as finely balanced. The Vichy subsidies had
brought a latent dispute back to the surface. On the other hand,
the CNR programme had committed its signatories, including the
Resistance movements and all the major political parties, to a
democratization of education. A number of broadly convergent
blueprints had already been written inside and outside France. In
the months after August 1944 the momentum behind reform was
partially sustained. On 8 November a ministerial decree created a
new reform commission, the so-called Langevin–Wallon committee,
whose report (delivered two and a half years later) became a
landmark in the history of French educational reform. Before
considering this report, it may be useful to place it in the context of
the ideas about education that were circulating in political and
non-political circles during the post-Liberation period.

During 1945 and 1946 the political parties did little to enhance
the prospects for educational reform. Before the elections of
October 1945, an occasional Socialist party candidate proposed
the 'nationalization' of education[38] or the raising of the school-
leaving age.[39] The two main parties, the MRP and the PCF, were
ostensibly committed to fairly specific 'democratization' reforms.
The MRP proposed to keep all children in school to the age of 17.
It echoed the concern of all wartime planners to give a greater

---

[37] 'Procès-verbal de la 9ème séance tenue le jeudi 25 janvier 1945', p. 4. See also
Philip's comments at a later meeting: 'Procès-verbal de la 12ème séance tenue le
19 février 1945', p. 7.

[38] BN, *Recueil de tracts électoraux, listes, programmes . . . 21 octobre 1945*,
Charente-Maritime.

[39] Ibid., Hérault.

emphasis to technical or pre-professional training.[40] Both the MRP and the PCF stressed the need to modernize schools. The PCF proposed a massive infusion of capital (adopting Jules Ferry's formula of one-sixth of peacetime budgetary expenditure for education) and with this capital proposed to build new schools, pay teachers higher salaries, reduce class sizes, give scholarships to poorer students, and give free milk, school meals, and elementary medical care to all.[41] The Communists also emphasized the need to democratize access to secondary and higher education. Citing the conclusions of the Durry commission (and criticizing the social élitism and alleged pro-Vichy record of the École Libre des Sciences Politiques), the party proposed to replace the 'Sciences Po' with a democratic École d'Administration.[42]

In all the party programmes, however, the major issue was the confessional school question, and on this issue there was no possibility of the easy convergence that existed over the need to open up secondary education or modernize facilities. Though the MRP accepted that Vichy subsidies were indefensible—'not only because they masked a political manœuvre, but because it was difficult to accept that the state should distribute 500 million francs each year to institutions over which it had neither jurisdiction nor control'[43]—the party was committed to the preservation of confessional schools. It proposed a compromise which would, in effect, have maintained subsidies: private schools that agreed to be integrated within a national educational system would offer free instruction, would have their curriculum supervised by the state, but in return would have the salaries of their teachers paid by the state.[44] The parties of the left rejected this compromise out of hand.[45] They also obstructed the MRP's persistent attempts to include a clause guaranteeing freedom of education in the new constitution. In so far, then, as there was a political dialogue about

[40] For the MRP's educational policy, see Albert Gortais's report to the National Council, 25 Aug. 1945, in AN, 350 AP 55. See also the MRP brochures: *Pour une réforme de l'enseignement* (Paris, 1945) and *Le MRP, parti de la quatrième République* (Paris, n.d.).
[41] Georges Cogniot, *L'École et les forces populaires* (Paris, 1946).
[42] See the Communists' motion in the Consultative Assembly: *JO, Documents*, 20 Feb. 1945, pp. 418–20.
[43] Gortais, 'Rapport', p. 4.   [44] *Le MRP*, pp. 24–5.
[45] See e.g. Cogniot, *L'École et les forces populaires*, pp. 8–9. Opposition to state subsidies of Catholic schools was a prominent theme in Socialist and Communist manifestos before the elections of Oct. 1945 and June 1946.

education in the Consultative and Constituent Assemblies, it revolved around the contentious question of the confessional schools.

Outside the political arena, there was much more reformist activity. A few examples may suffice to convey something of its extent and diversity. At the end of 1944 and beginning of 1945 the review *Esprit* published a series of articles about various aspects of educational renovation. One edition reprinted a 'protoschéma d'un plan de réforme universitaire' written by Henri Marrou during the Occupation.[46] Another published a synopsis of British educational reforms,[47] while a third was devoted to 'The School in post-Liberation France' and contained articles by Roger Gal (a member of the Langevin–Wallon committee) and André Philip.[48] *Esprit* also published excerpts of the programme for 'crystallizing' élites that the remnants of the personalist-influenced Uriage team had drawn up at the Château de Murinais after breaking with the National Revolution. Around the same time, a commission pédagogique parisienne de l'union française universitaire met regularly and produced a report that called for compulsory education for all up to the age of 15 and for the abolition of the 'vertical divisions' preventing many students from passing from primary to secondary to higher education.[49] A group of syndicalists and teachers from Toulouse proposed a similar project in a local paper called *L'Espoir*: three years of compulsory secondary education after the age of 12, complete equality of opportunity for all students, free education at all levels.[50] The États Généraux de la Renaissance Française which met in July 1945 (largely under Communist inspiration) produced a lengthy report about educational reform.[51] They recommended raising the school-leaving age, removing all barriers between primary and secondary education, and reorganizing the curriculum 'so that academic instruction does not remain the chief form of instruction, while civic, social, political, manual, and artistic activities continue to be treated as

---

[46] No. 105 (Dec. 1944), 107–17.   [47] No. 107 (Feb. 1945), 355–72.

[48] No. 108 (Mar. 1945), 492–533.

[49] The commission's report (written by MM. Emeriau and Alquie) is in AN, 71 AJ 64.

[50] The plan appeared in the paper between 16 Sept. and 6 Oct. 1944. A copy is in AN, 71 AJ 64.

[51] États Généraux de la Renaissance Française, Commission de la Jeunesse, 'Rapport de la sous-commission de l'enseignement sur le contenu des cahiers'.

subordinate and lesser activities'. The archives of the Langevin–
Wallon committee contain numerous other reform proposals:[52]
from a committee of professors in Clermont-Ferrand, from the
Fédération Nationale des Associations de Parents d'Élèves des
Lycées et Collèges, from educators who had been imprisoned
together in Stalag 1A, from a study commission in Tunis, from the
Liberation Committee in the Ain. The consensus in these plans
was apparent: they virtually all proposed a unified primary school
system, open access to secondary education, diversification of
training to develop each student's skills whatever they might be,
and greater emphasis on learning through experience.

Combining these post-Liberation projects with those that had
been drawn up under the Occupation and with pre-war reform
proposals (especially the proposals made by the Popular Front
minister Jean Zay in March 1937), the committee that met for the
first time under Paul Langevin's chairmanship on 29 November
1944 had no shortage of documentation. It also had no shortage of
eminent and influential members, including five professors from
the Collège de France (Langevin, Wallon, Henri Pieron, Lucien
Febvre, and Émile Coornaert), several other distinguished academics and teachers, and all the top officials of the Ministry of
Education. The task that this committee of experts was assigned
was immense: the establishment of a comprehensive and detailed
programme of reform.[53] This involved rationalizing institutions
which had evolved haphazardly over a long period.[54] It also
involved modernizing an educational philosophy that had been
conceived before the full onset of industrialization and mechanization. In the 1880s the needs of an incipient industrialization had
led to the introduction of mass elementary instruction. In the
1940s the requirements of a more advanced economy (combined
with greater social awareness) demanded higher levels of education.
Given the dimensions of its brief, it was inevitable that the new
committee would take far longer to conduct its investigation than
its immediate predecessors. Whereas the wartime study commissions
had met for a matter of months, the Langevin–Wallon committee
met frequently over a period of more than two years, either in full

[52] These archives are in AN, 71 AJ 64.
[53] The text of the Langevin–Wallon report has been reprinted in various places.
That used here is: *Le Plan Langevin–Wallon de réforme de l'enseignement* (Paris,
1964), 177–236.   [54] Ibid. 179.

session or in four sub-committees. It did not finally present its recommendations until June 1947.[55]

The principles governing the Langevin–Wallon plan were inherited directly from wartime programmes.[56] They may be summed up as equality and diversity. On the one hand, France's educational system should give all children the opportunity to develop their aptitudes 'whatever their family, social, or ethnic backgrounds'. On the other, it should not create a hierarchy that placed intellectual attainments higher than manual or physical attainments. The aim of education was to nurture the development of each individual personality, while matching each personality with a useful social role. In a modern democratic society the extent to which all human resources were developed and efficiently deployed determined the success or failure of a nation. The blueprint that the committee established on the strength of these by now familiar principles went beyond previous proposals.[57] It proposed that education be made mandatory up to the age of eighteen. The 'enseignement du 1er degré' (incorporating what in the past had been primary and secondary education) would run from the ages of 6 to 18. A first 'cycle' up to the age of 11 would be common to all children; a second 'cycle' (ages 11 to 15) would in part be uniform for all pupils but would include an orientation towards one of the three sections of the third 'cycle' (ages 15 to 18), which were the 'section pratique' (for future manual and skilled labourers), the 'section professionnelle' (for those who would provide middle management), and the 'section théorique' (for those who would go on to higher education and staff the nation's élite). Both the 'enseignement du 1er degré' and higher education were to be free. In addition, all students over 15 would receive a grant to compensate their families for loss of earnings. Like the Durry report, the Langevin–Wallon plan concluded that such a reorganization would have to be gradual and would have to be accompanied by a reassessment of the state's financial commitment to education. In 1946, the plan noted, France devoted only 6 or 7 per cent of her national resources to education.

[55] For a good analysis of the Langevin–Wallon plan, its antecedents and dimensions, see Jacques Mièvre, 'Le Problème de la réforme de l'enseignement à l'époque de la Libération: restauration et modernisation dans la perspective du Plan Langevin–Wallon', paper presented to the colloquium, *La France en voie de modernisation (1944–1952)* (Paris, 1981).

[56] *Le Plan Langevin–Wallon*, pp. 181–3.   [57] Ibid. 184–8.

This placed her in 26th position 'among civilized nations', far behind Britain (20 per cent), the USA (21 per cent), and Russia (25 per cent).[58] If all children were to be kept in school until the age of 18, many more schools, laboratories, and other facilities would have to be built, and many teachers trained and paid. The immense cost of putting the plan into effect (estimated at two hundred billion francs) was a potent argument in the hands of the plan's detractors.[59]

By the time the report was presented, the chances of its successful introduction were slim. In addition to the financial issue, the political context had changed since 1944 (with the break-up of the post-Liberation tripartite coalition). Furthermore, the plan encountered hostility from the teaching profession, especially the secondary school teachers who would have seen their superiority of training, salary, and prestige eroded. It became only the first of a long series of unsuccessful reform projects under the Fourth and Fifth Republics.[60]

The rethinking of French education between 1940 and 1946 did not produce the reforms that it sought. In so far as Vichy and the post-Liberation governments introduced major changes in the system, these changes caught up with the programmes of pre-war reformers: the transformation of the *écoles primaires supérieures* into secondary schools (a measure introduced by Vichy and maintained after the Liberation) was a step towards the *école unique*;[61] the introduction in 1945 of 'classes nouvelles', designed 'to make education a matter of experience, real objects and lifelike situations',[62] followed principles that had been formulated before the war;[63] the creation of the École Nationale d'Administration in October 1945 brought to fruition an idea which had been raised by the Popular Front minister, Jean Zay. However, the more ambitious aspirations to construct a fully unified and diversified education were left unsatisfied.

[58] Ibid. 188.
[59] Mièvre, 'Le Problème de la réforme de l'enseignement', pp. 15–16.
[60] See Donegani and Sadoun, 'La Réforme de l'enseignement secondaire en France depuis 1945', *Revue française de science politique*, 26 (1976), 1125–46.
[61] On the unintended democratization caused by Vichy's transformation of *écoles primaires supérieures* into *collèges*, see Antoine Prost, *Histoire générale de l'enseignement et de l'éducation en France*, iv (Paris, 1981), 229–33.
[62] W. R. Fraser, *Education and Society in Modern France* (London, 1963), 8.
[63] Mièvre, 'Le Problème de la réforme de l'enseignement', pp. 4–5.

Many of these aspirations were not particularly novel. Towards the end of the First World War, a group of educators—'Les Compagnons de l'Université Nouvelle'—had produced a programme of educational reforms which could, in most respects, have been written in 1944.[64] There was the same general aspiration towards a new and more 'modern' society, the same insistence on total educational reform, the same concern that education should provide a worthy national élite and should give France the producers it needed ('Tomorrow's problem is a problem of production'[65]). There was also a similar openness to foreign innovations. But most strikingly of all, there was the same educational philosophy: the importance of democratizing education, removing the barriers between primary and secondary schools, assigning children according to their capacities; and, on the other hand, breaking away from a purely intellectual pedagogy to stress vocational and physical training. The Compagnons' definition of the Université of the future perfectly sums up the philosophy of a generation of reformers who came along twenty years later: 'To keep France alive, she must call upon *all* and *all the resources of each*. The new education will address itself therefore to *all the nation* and to the *whole* man.'[66]

Is this to say that the later generation made no real contribution to educational reformism? On the level of ideas, it would certainly be true to say that the reformism of the Second World War rephrased or at best extended themes that had emerged after the First War and had been widely disseminated in the 1920s and 1930s. Often there was a degree of conscious imitation: the official study groups made explicit reference to the Compagnons and Jean Zay's reform programme of March 1937. However, to see reformism purely in the terms of an intellectual history is perhaps a rather narrow perspective. The reformers of the 1940s did not echo earlier reformers purely because they saw themselves as heirs to a tradition. The main influence on their programmes was their own perception of French education's strengths and weaknesses.

While the strengths and weaknesses remained largely unchanged, the manner in which they were perceived did evolve. It evolved, in part, because of 1940 and the light which the defeat had thrown both on educational institutions and on the young people that they

[64] *L'Université nouvelle*, 2 vols. (Paris, 1919).
[65] Ibid. i, 19.　　　[66] Ibid. 20–1.

had produced. After the First World War it had been a question of replenishing a generation of élites that had been decimated on the western front. After the Second War it was a question of replacing a bourgeois élite that was felt to have failed the nation (hence the deepening of hostility towards institutions such as the *grandes écoles* which were seen as bastions of the old élite). In other ways the outlook of this second post-war generation was quite different from that of the Compagnons. In 1918–19 it had been German reform plans that had caught the attention of French reformers, whereas in 1940–6 it was, more often than not, British plans. In the wake of the First War the link between level of education and economic productivity had been grasped in a fairly abstract way. After the economic débâcle of the 1930s and the defeat of 1940, the connection between economic performance and national strength focused the attention of reformers more directly on this question of social productivity and how it might be increased. This concern was evident in the preoccupation with improving technical education, including the technical training of administrative élites (the latter was one of the main motivations behind the introduction of the ENA[67]). Finally, the social context in 1944 was no longer that of 1919. The society that emerged after the Liberation had higher and more specific expectations of social reform than had the society of 1919. The educational reformers of the first 'après-guerre' thought primarily in terms of creating a unified society (recreating the *union sacrée* of the trenches through the *école unique*). The reformers of the 1940s thought more directly in terms of instituting a social democracy: they were not interested solely in allowing individual workers to rise to the élite through intellectual attainments, but in a collective promotion of the working class. Reformers of the 1940s had yet to grasp the full extent to which social factors have an impact on education (to which, for example, socio-cultural background conditions a child's educational attainment, however 'open' the educational system itself), but they were certainly alert to the social dimension of educational reform. As André Philip wrote in 1944, 'Education is always education by and for a particular society.'[68]

[67] On the founding of the ENA, see *Réforme de la fonction publique* (Paris, 1945); Jean-François Kesler, 'La Création de l'ENA', *La Revue administrative*, 178 (1977), 354–69; Michel Debré, *Trois républiques pour une France* (Paris, 1984), 363–83.

[68] Quoted by Mièvre, 'Le Problème de la réforme de l'enseignement', p. 7.

8

The New Society II: Dissolving Class Conflict

IN the decades before the defeat of 1940 various solutions had
been offered to the problems of social inequality and deprivation.
They may be divided into two categories. The first consisted of
measures—such as educational reform or improved social security
provision—that were designed to open up opportunity for the
disadvantaged or to raise their standard of living. The second
category consisted of measures that had the potential to solve the
social question more radically, by eliminating the antagonism
between classes. Socialism, in its different incarnations, clearly
offered a solution that fell within this second category. Another
such solution, bordering in certain respects that of socialism but
also extending into non-socialist ideologies, was the idea of
associating labour and capital in the cockpit of confrontation, the
work-place. The precise form that such association should take had
never been a point of consensus: views ranged from different
models of profit-sharing to workers' 'contrôle' (the French term
implying supervision of economic performance and management
rather than 'control' in the English sense), from full worker
management ('co-gestion' or 'auto-gestion') to various schemes for
worker representation on company boards. But in general the
notion that class divisions would be broken down by involving
workers in the ownership, management, or profitability of their
companies had been a recurrent theme in French social policy
since the dawn of industrialization. In this area the post-Liberation
period did not produce many new concepts but it did achieve a
significant diffusion and development of once minority ideas: in
the aftermath of liberation, polls indicated that 65 per cent of the
French people (and 79 per cent of working people) wanted workers
to participate in the management of their companies.[1] The issue
was to remain a live one in the future: many of the ideas that were

[1] Institut Français d'Opinion Publique, *Bulletin d'Information*, 16 Nov. 1944,
p. 12.

debated in the 1940s resurfaced at regular intervals in the 1950s and 1960s.[2]

As in educational reform, this tradition, though stretching back into the nineteenth century, began its recognizably modern form in the period during and immediately after the First World War.[3] In 1917 a system of 'worker delegates' had been set up in the munitions industry to provide a regular liaison between workers and management.[4] A law passed in April of that year had permitted limited companies to create 'labour shares', to be distributed to the work-force as a form of profit-sharing which would also have entitled them to seats on the board. Such developments helped to fuel a lively post-war debate about the merits of industrial democracy. In 1919–20 the idea of some degree of workers' control (in the French or the English sense) was discussed not only on the left and in the trade unions but by Social Catholics and even by elements of the *patronat*. However, after the failure of a series of major strikes and the election of a conservative majority in the Chamber, this interest in worker control died down. During the remainder of the 1920s and the early 1930s, the idea of 'company councils' appeared intermittently in technocratic reviews such as *Notre temps*.[5] Worker control also continued to feature in syndicalist programmes, but more prominently in the Catholic CFTC than in the CGT or its pro-Communist offshoot, the CGTU. On the whole, the representatives of labour were more concerned about winning union rights or defending the immediate interests of workers (wages and conditions) than in campaigning for the right of workers to participate in management. When the demand for workers' control reappeared

[2] The post-Liberation debate that will be discussed here had run its course by 1946. However, the issue was to be raised to prominence again within a couple of years, when the gaullist RPF placed the idea of 'association capital–travail' at the head of its programme.

[3] The following synopsis of pre-war association ideas relies primarily on two sources: Institut de Science Économique Appliquée, *La Participation des salariés aux responsabilités et aux résultats de l'œuvre de production*, 2 vols. (Paris, 1945–6); and Émile James, *Les Comités d'entreprises: étude de l'ordonnance du 22 février 1945* (Paris, 1945).

[4] This system was instituted by a series of circulars issued by the Socialist minister of armaments, Albert Thomas, on 5 Feb. 1917, 17 Mar. 1917, 11 June 1917, 25 July 1917, and 5 Sept. 1917. Thomas was a keen advocate of industrial democracy.

[5] See Gérard Brun, *Technocrates et technocratie en France, 1918–1945* (Paris, 1985), 127.

in the mid-1930s, it did so in the context of the CGT's newly adopted plan for nationalization and state economic management. Whereas in 1920 worker participation had been envisaged as operating at the factory level, in the guise of 'factory management councils',[6] in the CGT plan it was envisaged as operating at the national level: a Conseil Supérieur de l'Économie, including union-designated worker representatives, was to supervise the vast plan which would govern the nation's economy.[7] The Popular Front legislation of June 1936 strengthened the power of organized labour and, at the factory level, introduced shop stewards to help enforce collective bargaining agreements, but, like the CGT plan, it did not give workers a role in the management of their own companies. Only the CFTC called unequivocally for that kind of worker participation.

Again like the plans for educational reform, the worker participation projects of the post-Liberation period were formulated against two other kinds of background. The first of these was the ambiguous legacy of Vichy reforms. Theoretically, the whole *raison d'être* of the Labour Charter created by the law of 4 October 1941 had been to institute sincere collaboration between the two sides of industry. The Charter established 'social committees' at the local, regional, and national level, and the function of these 'pre-corporative' bodies was assumed to be economic as well as social. In fact, this elaborate structure of committees never materialized. What did materialize, however, were provisional 'company social committees', which Vichy had included almost as an afterthought (only four of the Charter's eighty articles mentioned them). These were committees in which employers met with representatives of the various categories of employee within each factory, to consider such 'social' issues as the provision of canteens, garden allotments, sick-pay, and so forth. They were excluded from overseeing the economic performance or management of the company. Though strongly tinged with paternalism— especially in those firms (perhaps 20 per cent of the total[8]) where

[6] See e.g. the post-war proposals of the Conseil Économique du Travail—a body composed of delegates from the CGT, the Union Syndicale des Techniciens de l'Industrie, du Commerce et de l'Agriculture, la Fédération des Fonctionnaires, and the Fédération Nationale des Coopératives de Consommation.

[7] The CGT's 1934 Plan may be found in the Confederation's monthly newsletter, *La Voix du Peuple*, Sept. 1934.

[8] A survey of 1,500 *comités sociaux d'entreprises* conducted in the Northern

management was instrumental in appointing the worker representatives—these committees none the less performed valuable
functions in a period of extreme hardship. Their usefulness was
demonstrated by their rapid proliferation—there were 372 of them
at the beginning of 1942, 2,367 six months later, 4,644 at the
beginning of 1943, and 6,728 by the autumn of 1943.[9]

Another influence on post-Liberation reform were the innovations
that had been introduced outside France. The various attempts
which had been made to bring workers and managers together
with a view to increasing productivity—in particular the wartime
Joint Production Committees in Britain and America—were
carefully studied by France's post-Liberation élites. It was no
coincidence that the most important post-Liberation ordinance on
this subject (that of 22 February 1945) began its preamble with a
reference to 'the experiments made during the past four years in
Great Britain, the United States, and Canada'. The lessons that
were drawn from these foreign experiments served to reinforce
perceptions of domestic needs. On the one hand, they appeared to
demonstrate the link between strong economic performance and
harmonious social relations. To quote the anonymous pamphleteer
of the Société d'Éditions Économiques et Sociales: 'in all the great
industrial nations, institutions of worker-management collaboration
are increasingly viewed as improving the economic and human
output of labour'.[10] This belief, in turn, confirmed an intuition that
had been strongly and widely held ever since June 1940: France
had been defeated, at least in part, because of her failure to
develop such collaborative institutions. On the other hand, the
foreign innovations indicated that representatives of the working
class in other countries were emerging from a period in which they
had distrusted the very idea of collaboration with a capitalist
management. After 1940 elements within the French working class
appeared to be moving in the same direction, towards a more
uninhibited acceptance of the principle of association.

Zone in 1943 found that 15% of the committees were nominated by management
and a further 5% directly appointed by the *patron*. See 'Un an de vie des comités
sociaux provisoires d'entreprises: une enquête de l'office des comités sociaux
d'entreprises', *Bulletin de la Charte du Travail*, June 1943.

[9] These statistics are presented in 'Les Comités sociaux d'établissements: état
présent, jugements, et vues d'avenir', *Collection Droit Social*, Dec. 1943, p. 18.
[10] SEES, *Les Conseils d'entreprises et les comités mixtes de production* (Paris,
1945), 41–2.

Against this background, a number of factors combined to bring the issue to the top of the political agenda in 1944. First, the sympathy that large sections of the *patronat* had shown for Vichy naturally rebounded against it in the period after liberation: there was a general acceptance of the need to renew the country's managerial élites. Second, the working class was seen as the natural source of new industrial leadership and the factory as the natural seed-bed for such leadership.[11] Although Vichy had talked about class collaboration, the thrust of its policies—the dissolution of the trade union confederations, the Labour Charter, and the acceptance of German demands to send French workers to the Reich—had clearly singled out the working class as a target. As a consequence, workers had played a prominent role in the Resistance and the idea of a collective promotion of the working class had become a salient feature of Resistance discourse. Among other places, this promotion was to occur within the factory: the 'democratization' of the company was a proposal endorsed by the majority of Resistance groups, from conservative liberals like René Courtin to radical socialists like the Libérer et Fédérer movement. The CNR programme of March 1944 formalized this demand by calling for the right of all workers who possessed the necessary qualifications to gain access to managerial or administrative functions within their company.

If any further incentive were needed to look again at participation schemes, it was provided by the widespread desire in 1944 to restructure the French economy. The first Free French group to consider social questions had noted as early as 1942 that 'The solution which will be given to the problem of workers' participation in the management of businesses will have repercussions on the whole economy.'[12] Two kinds of repercussion were envisaged. On the one hand, it was felt that workers who had a stake in the management and profitability of their companies would produce more efficiently, and everyone agreed in 1944 that higher productivity would be essential to national recovery. On the other hand, worker–capital association was also viewed in the context of a new economic strategy. The kind of intervention in economic

---

[11] See e.g. the comments of the post-Liberation Minister of Labour, Alexandre Parodi, in *Le Peuple*, 2 Dec. 1944.

[12] Section sociale de la commission économique, financière, et sociale, 'Programme des travaux', 7 July 1942, in AN, 72 AJ 546.

management that was being envisaged for the French state in 1944–5 seemed to require the participation of the working class. Without such participation, it was feared, nationalization and planning would descend into bureaucratization and technocracy. Many believed that worker participation in the running of the national economy would be impossible without grass-roots participation at the factory level, since that alone would be able to identify and promote a sufficiently large working-class élite.

It had already become apparent before the Liberation that de Gaulle's Provisional Government was sympathetic to these currents of opinion. In May 1944 the Communist Commissaire à l'Air, Fernand Grenier, issued a decree that created 'joint production committees' in all the factories under the supervision of his *commissariat*. Once back in metropolitan France, the government gave a very high priority to the issue of worker association, making it almost the first major reform to be introduced. This urgency should be attributed not only to support for the principle, but also to the pressure of developments inside French factories. The summer and autumn of 1944 saw a number of audacious and radical experiments in worker participation or 'co-gestion'. In various places throughout southern France (most famously in the Berliet works in Lyon), 'patriotic company committees' or consultative 'management committees' were formed by workers and technicians who wanted to have a say in the economic, as well as social, affairs of their companies.[13] Within months of the Liberation there were a variety of these *ad hoc* worker–management schemes in operation. Some had a legal basis (in extensions of the May 1944 decree), while others resulted from agreements between individual businessmen and groups of workers or between Commissaires de la République and workers.[14] When the Council of Ministers agreed to the principle of *comités d'entreprises* at its meeting of 29 September 1944, the urgent need to put an end to grass-roots initiatives loomed large in their thoughts.[15]

[13] For the latest research on these experiments, see Claire Andrieu, Lucette Le Van, and Antoine Prost (eds.), *Les Nationalisations de la Libération: de l'utopie au compromis* (Paris, 1987).
[14] International Labour Office, *Labour–Management Cooperation in France* (Geneva, 1950), 163–5.
[15] J.-P. Rioux, *La France de la Quatrième République*, i. *L'ardeur et la nécessité* (Paris, 1980), 113; Antoine Prost, 'Le Retour aux temps ordinaires', in Andrieu, Le Van, Prost, *Les Nationalisations de la Libération*, pp. 89–106.

Within two months of the decision in the cabinet, the government presented the Consultative Assembly with its proposal for the creation of *comités d'entreprises*.[16] The proposal disappointed the Assembly. It was much more cautious than had been expected—perhaps because of the hostility of influential ministries. The Minister of National Economy, Mendès-France, wanted to reduce the economic powers of the committees,[17] while officials in the Ministry of Industrial Production were anxious that the government should not appear to be sanctioning what they saw as the 'sovietization' inherent in the southern committees.[18] When the Consultative Assembly debated the issue on 12 December 1944, it voted to approve a counter-proposal, which would have widened the powers of the committees and increased the number of firms in which they would be created (by including all those with more than fifty employees, as opposed to the government's figure of one hundred).[19] The ordinance that the government issued two months later took account of some of the Assembly's criticisms but in most respects preserved the original text.[20] It stipulated that in all firms employing more than one hundred employees a *comité d'entreprise* should be established. The committee was to consist of elected delegates of all the categories of employees (with candidates designated by the most representative *syndicats*) and was to be chaired by the head of the company. The committee had a dual function. It was given a social function akin to that granted to its wartime antecedent: 'The company committee assures or supervises the running of all social works established in the company for the benefit of employees or their families.' The Provisional Government also gave the committee an economic function. This role was only consultative, but it was none the less a potentially significant

[16] *JO, Documents*, 21 Nov. 1944, pp. 36–8.

[17] See Mendès-France's comments on Parodi's *projet d'ordonnance* at a meeting of the Comité Économique Interministériel, 26 Oct. 1944, in AN, F60 897.

[18] See the violent note drafted in the Secrétariat Général à la Production Industrielle for the Minister (11 Oct. 1944), in AN, F12 10147. In this note M. Blum-Picard comments on the latest draft of the *ordonnance*: 'Il ne vous échappera pas que par ce projet c'est la dictature du prolétariat qui s'instaure et que . . . c'est la mainmise de la classe ouvrière qui s'affirme au Comité d'Entreprise. . . . je ne saurais donner mon accord à une telle réforme, qui est une révolution et ne peut cadrer avec l'état général de la France actuelle.'

[19] For the Assembly's counter-proposal, see *JO, Documents*, 5 Dec. 1944, pp. 62–6.

[20] *JO, Lois et Décrets*, ordonnance no. 45-280, pp. 954–6.

one. The committee was granted the right to propose any measure that might increase output or productivity. It was to receive from the management an annual report on the economic performance of the company and, in limited companies, possess powers to review financial information and present their views to the shareholders (for instance, as to how profits should be used). The meetings of the committees were to be at least monthly and it was expected that there would be a frank exchange of views between management, foremen, and workers about all aspects of company performance. The only issue specifically excluded from the committees' agenda was that of wage and benefit claims and grievances. These were to be presented not by the workers' representatives on the committees but by the shop stewards ('délégués').

The ordinance of 22 February was very much a middle route. On the one side, it disappointed those who wanted to see worker representatives on the board or at least given more than a consultative role in economic decisions. On the other, it dis-appointed those who felt that workers had no right to infringe on the prerogatives of capital and that their committees should be confined to the purely social sphere. The grass-roots response was lukewarm. A report of the Ministry of Labour's regional inspector in Saint-Quentin conveyed a common reaction: 'The employers tolerate the company committees; the workers show no enthusi-asm.'[21] In the CGT there were misgivings about the limitations on the committees' economic function: they were summed up by one delegate at the CGT's National Congress, who called for true company committees 'where the delegates will have a different role to play than saying "amen" when the director has given his management report'.[22] The CGT attacked the government for failing to follow the Consultative Assembly's advice. It issued a statement calling for the lowering of the limit on the number of employees required for a committee and demanding that committees should have access to financial information in all companies, not merely the larger ones. The attitude of the PCF was also cool. It

[21] Report of 12 Dec. 1945, in AN, TR 14005.
[22] M. Cochinard, speaking in the debate on the report delivered by Benoît Frachon, in CGT, *XXVIᵉ Congrès national de Paris (8–12 avril 1946)* (Paris, 1947), 35. For other criticisms of the *ordonnance*, see the CGT's newspaper, *Le Peuple*, 3 Mar. 1945, 31 Mar. 1945.

was not until the ordinance was revised (by the Communist Minister of Labour, Croizat, in a law dated 16 May 1946) so as to satisfy the CGT's demands that the reform was acknowledged by the PCF as 'an element of the new democracy'.[23] In ideological terms, the Communists never put much credence in utopian theories of 'co-gestion'.

Still, in general, the February 1945 ordinance was welcomed. The business community—relieved no doubt at the moderation of the measures—expressed its agreement 'in principle' and a minority of businessmen (like Auguste Detœuf) were more enthusiastic than that.[24] Most in the new political establishment supported it. General de Gaulle was perhaps more committed to it than to any other 'structural reform'. In November 1944 he told a Socialist party delegation that he 'was particularly interested in the company councils reform'.[25] The Socialists themselves strongly supported the reform: their spokesman in the Consultative Assembly, Robert Verdier, stated that 'the Socialist group is entirely favourable to the proposal presented by the government'.[26] The MRP was also committed to the virtues of worker participation. Equally importantly, the *comités d'entreprises* had many supporters within the trade union movement. The CFTC was enthusiastic about the committees. Even within the CGT, there was a degree of grudging approval: 'We wanted company committees. In principle, we have received satisfaction.'[27] From the outset the socialist wing of the CGT, represented by Albert Gazier, had been keen advocates of worker participation: though they were disappointed by the scope of the initial legislation, they backed the concept whole-heartedly. Furthermore, as the PCF line became more enthusiastic, so even the pro-Communist wing of the Confederation warmed to the committees, in particular to their contribution in the 'battle for production'. At the CGT's National Congress in April 1946, the critics of the committees did not go unchallenged.[28]

[23] On the PCF's attitude towards the committees, see Irwin Wall, *French Communism in the Era of Stalin* (Westport, 1983), 39–40.

[24] See Henry Ehrmann, *Organized Business in France* (Princeton, 1957), 450.

[25] Comité Directeur du Parti Socialiste, procès-verbal, 22 Nov. 1944.

[26] *JO, Débats*, 12 Dec. 1944, p. 494.

[27] R. Bothereau, 'Choisissons parmi les meilleurs', *Le Peuple*, 17 Mar. 1945.

[28] See e.g. the speech of M. Jourdain (of the Fédération des Métaux), in CGT, *Congrès national*, p. 110.

The real debate, however, was not over the *comités* themselves but over what should come after them. The initial criticism of the press, the unions, and the Consultative Assembly was not so much directed at the content of the ordinance as at its omissions. Conversely, the support that it received on the left and within the *syndicats*, was conditional on further developments. The CFTC saw it as a first step which 'will allow a climate to be created which will open the way later on to bolder reforms'.[29] The MRP and PS also described it as a first step, while in the CGT Gazier and Léon Jouhaux said publicly that the February ordinance represented a transitional stage, beyond which workers would assume more and more responsibility in the management of their companies.[30] The obstacles to such an extension of the *comités* system were considerable. In February 1945 business had still lacked a national organization and had been willing to accept an ordinance that had not materially restricted its authority. In the future, however, a better co-ordinated business community could be expected to put up a very vigorous opposition to any extension of the February 1945 provisions. In fact, the newly established Conseil National du Patronat Français put up just such an opposition to the law of 16 May 1946.[31] On the other side, the Communists and the majority of the CGT remained fundamentally wary of participationist experiments.

In spite of these obstacles, the period between 1944 and 1946 saw a proliferation of schemes designed to achieve the social reconciliation that seemed essential to France's post-war renewal. The political parties were one source of these schemes. The Socialist party's proposal for nationalized *secteurs autonomes* stipulated that each company within the state sector should be run by a *conseil du travail de l'entreprise* representing both managers and workers. Another model of worker participation—for the non-nationalized sector—was offered by the MRP, in the guise of its scheme for a new kind of company called a *société de travail et*

[29] Quoted by Charles Soyez, *Les Comités d'entreprises* (Lille, 1945), 47.
[30] See Gazier's speech to the Consultative Assembly, *JO, Débats*, 12 Dec. 1944, pp. 487–8, and Jouhaux's speech to the CGT national congress, *Congrès national*, p. 183.
[31] See Ehrmann, *Organized Business*, pp. 451–2. For a discussion of the law of 16 May, see Renée Petit, 'Une loi nouvelle en matière de comités d'entreprises: la loi du 16 mai 1946', *Collection Droit Social*, Dec. 1946, pp. 1–21.

d'épargne.[32] These companies would be managed by a *comité de gestion* in which the interests of labour, capital, and all levels of management would be represented. Not only would the scheme give workers a share in management, but they would also receive a fair share of their company's profits and would thus be raised from the 'lowly condition of wage-earner'.[33] The MRP's aim (characteristic of the long-established Social Catholic philosophy of association) was to end the proletarian condition by, in effect, recreating the collaborative relation between masters and apprentices that had existed in pre-industrial workshops. Such notions were also attractive to many elements of the French centre and right (as they had been attractive to the corporatists in Vichy). Shortly after the MRP published its proposal, a similar plan was proposed by three conservative deputies (MM. Brunhes, July, and Legendre).[34] Their plan for 'entreprises en participation' had the same rhetoric about ending the 'artificial' antagonism between labour and capital and giving a new juridical form to the (by nature) collaborative activity of production. It proposed similar arrangements for profit-sharing and for a company council. Yet another scheme of the same kind was proposed by the members of the Radical party in the Second Constituent Assembly.[35] Again, it began with a socialist-sounding indictment of a system which placed workers at the mercy of their bosses, denied them independence and security, and stole their rightful share in the profits of their labour. The Radicals proposed that limited companies should be transformed into 'sociétés à participation ouvrière'. Each year 'labour shares' would be created to an equivalent of 5 per cent of the existing 'capital shares' and would be distributed to those who worked in the company. After twenty years the labour shares and the capital shares would be equal, at which point the process of transformation would have been completed.

A second group of participationist proposals came from elements within the *patronat*, especially from those with Social Catholic connections. One such group was the Centre des Jeunes Patrons, which had been founded before the war with the objective of bringing *patrons* 'towards a new and broader conception of their mission' and was reconstituted after the war with an active

---

[32] This scheme was first published officially in *JO, Documents*, 8 Apr. 1946, pp. 930–2.   [33] Ibid. 930
[34] Ibid., 26 June 1946, pp. 14–16.   [35] Ibid., 6 Aug. 1946, pp. 327–8.

membership of around 2,000.[36] The Jeunes Patrons welcomed the ordinance of 22 February (just as they had welcomed Vichy's 'social committees'[37]) and pledged to apply its principles beyond the letter of the law. They also advocated a generalized system of profit-sharing.[38] Another prominent group of businessmen (whose reform plan was entitled *Plan Commun 44*) had objectives similar to those of the Jeunes Patrons: a share for labour in both management and profits, while preserving the authority of the *patron* and the basic principle of capitalist ownership.[39] The Plan Commun group proposed that representatives of the work-force should be admitted to company boards with a full deliberative voice. It also stressed the importance of profit-sharing, which it described as 'the only method of mitigating the latent conflict between capital and labour'.[40] Other *patrons* argued that experiments that they had introduced into their own firms could be extended to the entire economy. One such innovator was a *jeune patron* called Alexandre Dubois, who had been at Uriage during the Occupation and after the Liberation chaired a small but vocal association called the Union des Chefs d'Entreprises pour l'Association du Capital et du Travail. Dubois argued that a company was not the property of the capitalist or the worker, but a distinct institution, formed by a formal contract between labour and capital.[41] The terms of this voluntary contract—to be renegotiated at regular intervals—would establish the form that 'co-gestion' would take and the percentages of the company's profits that would be distributed to labour and capital. A still more radical scheme was championed by a businessman turned parliamentary deputy, Marcel Barbu.[42] Barbu advocated a 'communitarian' system of production, in which all machinery, tools, assets, and raw materials belonged to the 'communauté de travail'. The members of the community could make use of the means of

[36] Centre des Jeunes Patrons, *Une étape* (Paris, 1945), 7–8.

[37] See CJP, 'Les Comités sociaux d'entreprise' (25 Nov. 1941), in AN, F22 1842.

[38] *Une étape*, pp. 32–53.

[39] *Plan Commun 44: contribution à une réforme de l'entreprise*, 2nd edn. (Paris, 1945).

[40] Ibid. 6.

[41] Dubois, *Pourquoi et comment associer les travailleurs à leur entreprise* (Paris, 1946), 11. In presenting the firm as an institution, Dubois was following a long tradition in France. On this point see Ehrmann, *Organized Business*, pp. 355–6.

[42] See Barbu's *proposition de loi*, in *JO, Documents*, 12 Mar. 1946, pp. 608–16.

production but did not own them. All that they owned—whether they had contributed labour or capital—was their share of the goods that they had produced. This kind of utopian scheme was at one extreme of *patronat* projects. At the other extreme were much more practical but less ambitious plans for profit-sharing, 'salaire proportionnel', and so forth.

One of the reasons that worker–capital association was such a pervasive idea in this period was that virtually every group could read its own interests into it. While the Provisional Government wanted to end the rash of worker-initiated take-overs, resisters and Socialists saw a chance to promote a working-class élite (in that sense, the *comités d'entreprises* were an extension of educational democratization). While many *patrons* and political conservatives saw association as a way of heading off more drastic social up-heavals, others—inside and outside the trade union movement—aspired to worker–management. In the dire economic circumstances of 1944–6, many agreed with the MRP[43] that a participatory work-force would be a productive work-force (and, to a degree, they seem to have been right, at any rate until the strikes of 1947 soured industrial relations[44]). On one point, however, virtually everyone was in agreement in the autumn of 1944: whatever its desirability, this promotion of the proletariat was inevitable. The perceptions that stimulated the vogue for worker association schemes in 1944 and 1945 seemed utterly conclusive and compelling: the proletarian condition was unjust and irrational; working-class hostility to capitalism was unavoidable and—under the existing system—interminable; France could not, as a nation, afford the class struggle any longer; in the Resistance the French working class had demonstrated its readiness to accept the burden of greater national responsibilities. These perceptions added up to an assumption that the time had come to alter the structures of French capitalism in order to accommodate new realities.

Reformers often have difficulty distinguishing their visions of the future from their empirical observations of the present. Fired by Resistance aspirations and by the example of foreign innovations

[43] Ibid., 8 Apr. 1946, p. 930.
[44] See the findings of a Ministry of Labour report: R. Blanc, 'Rapport de synthèse relatif à l'application de l'ordonnance du 22 février 1945 dans l'ensemble du territoire (29 Juin 1948)', 26–7. The report is in AN, TR 14002.

(the significance of which was often exaggerated), indignant at the abdication of pre-war élites, many of the post-Liberation reformers found it impossible to separate their perception of a social and economic crisis from their desire to see a genuine socio-economic democracy take root. As in so many areas, they underestimated the weight of inertia and the tenacity of the old system. A sense of inevitability did not convert ideas into reality. What was missing in 1944–6 was the political will to find a more radical solution than the very cautious first step of the *comités d'entreprises*. There were not enough people willing to fight the hard political battle that would have been necessary to achieve widespread worker 'co-gestion'. The Communists and their allies in the CGT did not see 'co-gestion' as the road to socialism, while the centre and right were far more concerned to preserve capitalism than to see their extravagant blueprints put into operation. The *comités d'entreprises* were a logical and timely measure to encourage higher output and better social relations within the French economy. Yet, even by the time the original ordinance was amended and extended in May 1946, the committees were clearly failing in their broader aim of promoting class collaboration. The reports of Ministry of Labour inspectors suggest that most *patrons* fulfilled their legal obligations but made no effort to encourage worker participation in what they still regarded as their prerogative: management.[45] In 1948 a retrospective report on the performance of the committees concluded that, while they had produced positive results in the social sphere (as the Vichy committees had done) and had, in certain instances, increased productivity and plant efficiency, they had not revolutionized the management of French companies or fundamentally altered the social climate of the work-place.[46] The fate of the *comités d'entreprises* was characteristic of that which befell many of the innovations of 1944 and 1945: the mystique soon dissolved, leaving behind a residue of mundane achievement and a sense of unfulfilment.

[45] The reports are ibid. 14001, 14002, 14005.
[46] Blanc, 'Rapport de synthèse', pp. 11–33.

9

The New Society III: Pro-Natalism and Social Security

IN an essay that he wrote in May 1944, George Orwell noted the broad approval that the Beveridge Report on Social Security had elicited in Britain:

Thirty years ago any Conservative would have denounced this as state charity, while most Socialists would have rejected it as a capitalist bribe. In 1944 the only discussion that arises is about whether it will be adopted in whole or in part. This blurring of party distinctions is happening in almost all countries, partly because everywhere . . . the drift is towards a planned economy, partly because in an age of power politics national survival is felt to be more important than class warfare.[1]

Certainly, the case of post-liberation France would support Orwell's contention that the consensus in favour of greater social equality and solidarity crossed national frontiers. Yet, as Orwell himself went on to admit, the content of the British consensus was necessarily conditioned by peculiarities in British society. The same was obviously true in France and elsewhere. No area of reformism saw such a cross-fertilization of ideas as social policy, but equally no area brought out a nation's idiosyncrasies so strongly. The extremes of both particularity and universality in the French experience may be conveyed by looking at two closely related aspects of social policy: one which was a peculiar preoccupation of French politicians (the issue of the birth-rate) and another (social security reform) where an international trend was perceived to be operating.

If at any point between 1940 and 1946 a poll had been taken to determine the most popular explanation for the nation's problems, it is highly likely that *dénatalité*—the falling birth-rate—would have headed the list. Few statistics were fed to the public more incessantly than those of France's demographic decline: between

[1] 'The English People', reprinted in *The Collected Essays, Journalism and Letters of George Orwell*, iii (New York, 1968), 14.

1800 and 1935 France's share of the European population had halved; before the end of the century France's population would fall below thirty million; each year the equivalent of a town the size of Poitiers was lost to the nation. A recent examination of the pro-natalist movement under the Third Republic has concluded that 'The reason the French placed so much misplaced emphasis on the birth-rate was because it both simplified and justified a process [national decline] they never fully understood.'[2] In the long term the defeat of 1940 focused attention on other, more concrete causes of decline, but in the short term it did not appear to diminish the appeal of the pro-natalists' monocausal thesis. On the contrary, the defeat gave the falling birth-rate a considerable symbolic significance: the reluctance of French men and women to have large families seemed the perfect symbol of that decline in national vitality and ambition which so many rushed to diagnose after the defeat. To reformers of all political persuasions the population problem was, in a literal sense, the fundamental one.

Concern about the relatively low birth-rate (in particular relative to that of Germany) had existed throughout the Third Republic. As early as 1920 the problem had received official recognition, with the creation of a Conseil Supérieur de la Natalité within the Ministry of Health. It was not until the late 1930s, however, that an indefatigable pro-natalist lobby (led by the Alliance Nationale contre la Dépopulation) finally began to have a major impact on government policy. The change was brought about by two factors: a worsening of the demographic position (from 1935 onwards, deaths began outstripping births); and the increasing threat of war (as the head of the CGT, Léon Jouhaux, wryly observed, 'it is above all in periods of international tension that people start talking about the birth-rate, as if the problem consisted solely in assuring France's future supply of soldiers'[3]). In the final months before the invasion the Third Republic rushed to address this problem. In February 1939 the Daladier government established a Haut-Comité de la Population (consisting of ministerial representatives and a small number of outside experts, including three parliamentarians, the president of the Alliance Nationale contre la Dépopulation, and the economist and demographer,

[2] Richard Tomlinson, 'The Politics of Dénatalité during the French Third Republic, 1890–1940' (Ph.D. thesis, Cambridge University, 1983), 290.
[3] *Le Peuple*, 12 July 1939.

Alfred Sauvy). The task of this committee was to co-ordinate the various legislative measures that had been enacted before 1939 to encourage a higher birth-rate, and, if necessary, to suggest new measures. The result of its labour was the *Code de la Famille* of 1939. This was a package of reforms introduced by decree-law which (among other things) improved the provision of family allowances, modified adoption laws, and tightened anti-abortion laws. Around the same time the Conseil National Économique (CNE) (an official consultative body representing the various economic interests in the nation) established its own committee to investigate the demographic crisis, in liaison with the Haut-Comité de la Population.[4] Finally, on 5 June 1940 (in the same ministerial reshuffle that brought de Gaulle into the government), a new ministry was created with the role of overseeing all issues relating to the family. The first Minister of the Family (a senator named Georges Pernot who had been instrumental in the setting-up of the Haut-Comité de la Population) lasted little more than a week in office, but the precedent that he had set was enthusiastically followed by the new regime in Vichy.

It was scarcely surprising that in defeat a national élite which had grown accustomed to associating national weakness with the national birth-rate regurgitated its old lessons. Pétain and General Weygand led a chorus of politicians and journalists castigating the fall in the birth-rate.[5] Their regime quickly established the resurrection of the French family as one of the corner-stones of its ideology. It took a considerable time to give a definitive institutional form to this ideology. In 1940 and 1941 responsibility for pro-natalist and pro-family policies passed from one ministry to another: it was not until September 1941 that a distinct Commissariat Général à la Famille (CGF) was created.[6] Three months earlier

---

[4] The papers of the CNE's commission—as yet unclassified—are in the Section Contemporaine at the Archives Nationales. I am grateful to Madame Poulle of the Section Contemporaine for bringing them to my attention.

[5] See Pétain's speech of 20 June, *Actes et écrits* (Paris, 1974), 450, and Weygand's memorandum of July 1940, repr. in his memoirs, *Rappelé au service* (Paris, 1950), 299.

[6] For detailed chronologies of Vichy's family policy, see Georges Desmottes, 'Le Commissariat Général à la Famille: sa mission—son organisation' (June 1943), in AN, SAN 7730; and 'Rapport sur la politique familiale et la tâche du Conseil Supérieur de la Famille' (4 Jan. 1944) ['Rapport Hourdin'], ibid., F10 4970. The question has been carefully analysed in Aline Coutrot, 'La Politique familiale', in

the government had created a consultative committee (the Comité Consultatif de la Famille Française), which was intended to perform the advisory functions of the pre-war Conseil Supérieur de la Natalité. This Consultative Committee proved to be an ineffectual institution, and was replaced, in mid-1943, by a new body (the Conseil Supérieur de la Famille).

In the midst of these administrative upheavals the CGF pushed through a large volume of pro-family laws and decrees—extending family allowances, modifying tax laws to encourage large families, making demographic studies mandatory in schools, restricting divorce, encouraging pro-family associations. Many of these policies were developments of pre-war legislation. In terms of their presentation, however, the continuity with republican pro-natalism was less marked. Vichy's ideology took its lead from Pétain himself. Whereas the ultimate objective of the pre-war pro-natalist movement had been to increase France's power in the world, the Marshal's attitude towards the demographic issue was defeatist. Pétain believed that France was not so much threatened by decline as in irreversible decline: as he told the head of his *cabinet civil*, 'Demographically, France is no longer a great power.'[7] Under Pétain, pro-natalism lost its aggressive (often explicitly anti-German) slant and, instead, focused on the internal 'health' of French society. This introspection led to two predominant characteristics: a moralizing tone and a cult of the family.[8] Neither of these characteristics was peculiar to the État Français: both had long been features of the heavily Catholic pro-natalist movement. However, Vichy emphasized them to an extent that perceptibly altered the tone of public debate.

Most pre-war advocates of anti-depopulation reform had believed that the falling birth-rate had both material and moral causes. On the one hand, as the Alliance Nationale contre la Dépopulation constantly stressed, the standard of living of those with children was lower than that of childless couples (a problem that could only be solved by linking income in some way to size of family). At the

the collection of conference papers entitled *Le Gouvernement de Vichy, 1940–1942* (Paris, 1972), 245–63.

[7] H. du Moulin de Labarthète, *Le Temps des illusions: souvenirs (juillet 1940– avril 1942)* (Geneva, 1946), 196. On this point see Tomlinson, 'The Politics of Dénatalité', p. 298.

[8] See Coutrot, 'La Politique familiale', pp. 253–4.

same time the falling birth-rate was commonly viewed by pro-natalists as the product of undesirable social attitudes. A frequent assumption was that couples chose not to have children because they suffered from 'moral' weaknesses such as alcoholism or because all that they cared about was their personal standard of living. Different kinds of solution were offered to this moral problem: many Catholics blamed it on a decline in religious practice and suggested that religion was the best guarantee of larger families; others pointed to the success of Nazi Germany's pro-natalist policy and suggested that the Reich offered German parents a collective mystique—something larger than self-interest to stimulate their sense of social responsibility; the majority accepted the need for a moral renovation of the family (which, in practice, involved a re-emphasis of patriarchal values and the return of women to the home and to child-bearing).[9] An opinion poll taken in April 1939 found, however, that economic explanations of *dénatalité* were far more widely held than moral explanations (such as 'egoism' or 'irreligion').[10] It is instructive to compare this pre-war poll to the results of a competition organized by the État Français at the end of 1941. Out of 500,000 responses received in Vichy—itself a testimony to the response that this issue was capable of eliciting—almost half said that absence of religion was the principal cause, of *dénatalité* (compared to a mere 4 per cent in the 1939 survey).[11] The 1941 'concours-référendum' was a propaganda exercise, not a scientific poll, but its results certainly reflected the outlook of Vichy and its supporters. The regime's rhetoric offered a largely one-dimensional and moralistic inter-pretation of the problem. Even Philippe Renaudin, the Commis-saire Général à la Famille who is regarded as having checked the real zealots in the regime, traced the crisis to 'the dissolution of morality, the generalization of a contemptuous attitude towards all hierarchy and restraint' and compared France to Greece and

[9] These examples are taken from the debates of the CNE's 1939 committee. For a discussion of the impact that Vichy's familialism had on women, see Miranda Pollard, 'Women and the National Revolution', in Kedward and Austin (eds.), *Vichy France and the Resistance: Culture and Ideology* (Totowa, 1985), 36–47.

[10] The poll is reproduced in Tomlinson, 'The Politics of Dénatalité', pp. 345–52.

[11] This episode is discussed by Henri Amouroux in *La Grande Histoire des Français sous l'occupation*, ii. *Quarante millions de Pétainistes juin 1940–juin 1941* (Paris, 1977), 287.

Rome—'which had also been undermined by a falling birth-rate, divorce, and moral decline'.[12] The ideologues of the National Revolution presented *dénatalité* as a kind of retribution on industrial society, a blight brought on by secularization, urbanization, and proletarianization. Their solution to the demographic problem formed a part of their larger vision of a return to a rural, pre-industrial, Christian society.

To Vichy this society was synonymous with a society of strong families. It had always been true that pro-natalists were, by their very nature, fervent defenders of the family (and of the rural family, in particular). In 1939 the future Minister of the Family, Pernot, defined the four aims of a pro-natalist policy as follows: (1) protecting the race and the family against scourges that threaten them; (2) creating a climate favourable to the family; (3) ensuring social justice for the family; (4) regenerating the rural family.[13] Under the État Français, however, pro-family policy became an end in itself. The demographic crisis was reduced to being a symptom of a larger crisis—the moral crisis of the family. In Pétainist ideology the family was no longer just the source of a reinvigorated population, but the essential component of a hierarchical, organic society ('the basic social nucleus',[14] 'the very foundation of the social structure'[15]).

In reaction against Vichy's idealization of the family, the Resistance movements and the Free French reinverted priorities and tended to emphasize the demographic aspect of the problem. Resisters stressed the implications of an ageing society for the national interest: the dangers of rule by gerontocracy (which, in the eyes of its opponents, Vichy epitomized); the increasing burden on productive members of society; the lowering of economic expectations and the constriction of economic markets.[16] The focus on demographics as opposed to the family was reflected in official vocabulary: when, for example, the Provisional Government

[12] Renaudin, 'La Famille dans la Nation', 16 June 1943, in AN, SAN 7730.
[13] See Pernot's address to the CNE's committee, 28 April 1939.
[14] See Pétain's article in the *Revue Universelle*, 1 Jan. 1941.
[15] See Pétain's article in *Revue des Deux Mondes*, 15 Sept. 1940.
[16] See e.g. René Courtin, *Rapport sur la politique économique d'après-guerre* (Algiers, 1944), 29–31; Défense de la France, 'La Politique économique d'après-guerre', in AN, 72 AJ 564; Jacquier–Bruère [Michel Debré and Emmanuel Monick], *Refaire la France* (Paris, 1945), 15–29; *Les Cahiers politiques*, 1 (Apr. 1943), 27.

created an inter-commissarial commission to study this issue, its objective was declared to be 'the preservation and development of the population'.[17] Resistance and post-Liberation élites recognized that this cause had been advanced in certain ways by the activity of the CGF. They praised some of the measures that it had introduced (particularly those aimed at protecting pregnant women and infants and instituting a network of local family associations). They also retained much of the administrative structure of the CGF, although significantly they renamed it the Secrétariat Général à la Famille et à la Population and integrated it into a Ministry of Public Health and Population. In general, however, the word 'family' was conspicuous by its absence from Resistance and post-Liberation programmes. The CNR's Common Programme made no mention of the rights of families, but, on the contrary, stressed the rights of individuals—as citizens or workers. Of the major parties in the post-Liberation assemblies only the Catholic MRP made a determined effort to portray itself as 'the party of the French family'.

The new élites viewed the ideal of national *grandeur* (not the ideal of the family) as the context in which the population question had to be considered. De Gaulle led the way with his call, in March 1945, for '*douze millions de beaux bébés*' to restore French greatness.[18] All the major parties echoed the message. The Socialist Jules Moch called the population problem 'the most fundamental of all. . . . [It] threatens to reduce our country, at the end of the century, to the level of secondary powers'.[19] The Communist Minister of Public Health, François Billoux, declared that, barring a solution to the problem, 'It is . . . useless to speak of French greatness.'[20] In the same debate an MRP politician asked: 'with what soldiers, in ten, fifteen, or twenty years, will France mount guard on the Rhine?'[21] The concern was shared by all sections of the post-Liberation press, from Communist *L'Humanité*[22] to progressive *Combat*[23] and conservative *Le Figaro*,[24] but it was

[17] Decree of 11 May 1944.   [18] Speech of 2 Mar. 1945.
[19] Moch, *Arguments socialistes* (Paris, 1945), 74–5.
[20] *JO, Débats*, 7 Feb. 1945, p. 20.
[21] Ibid. 24.
[22] See e.g. Germaine Vigneron, 'Berceaux vides, péril pour le pays', *L'Humanité*, 7–8 Oct. 1945.
[23] Henri Calet, 'L'Immigration et la natalité, *Combat*, 28 Feb. 1945.
[24] Jean Schlumberger, 'Dénatalité', *Le Figaro*, 3 Jan. 1945.

perhaps best expressed by an old warrior in the pro-natalist cause, Georges Pernot:

France wants to become a great nation again. She wants to regain the status which momentarily she lost. Let us not delude ourselves. To achieve this objective it will not be enough for her to have a skilful diplomacy or an army equipped with the most modern weapons. First of all she will need a large population. It is through the fertility of her families that she will demonstrate to the whole world her will to live.[25]

In addition to the continuity in government policy and administrative personnel which has already been noted, the handling of the *dénatalité* issue between 1939 and 1945 was marked by two other kinds of continuity: continuity in the administrative innovations which the regimes introduced to tackle the problem; and continuity in their perception of what kind of problem it was. These aspects of pro-natalist policy are of particular interest because they invite comparison with reformism in other areas. For example, two features of Jean Monnet's philosophy which have often been identified as among his most important and original contributions to the cause of economic planning were his insistence that the *commissariat au plan* should report directly to the head of the government and his belief that the plan could only work if it were to unite the nation behind a collective mystique of modernization. It is worth noting that similar ideas had emerged in response to the demographic crisis.

All three regimes—the Third Republic, the État Français, and the Provisional Government—found it essential not only to give the population problem its own ministry but to establish a direct channel between agencies involved with this issue and the *secrétariat général du gouvernement*. This arrangement had first been used in the pre-war Haut-Comité de la Population. The reasoning behind it was put succinctly by Daladier in 1939:

. . . the efforts of the different ministerial departments constantly come up against . . . difficulties created by their diversity, their dispersion, and the absence of leading ideas. In these circumstances it has seemed to us indispensable to set up under the authority of the Prime Minister a body

[25] 'D'où vient, où va le mouvement familial?', *Pour la vie*, 1 (July 1945), 85.

whose role will be precisely to shape the comprehensive programme meant to remedy the present demographic situation.[26]

De Gaulle employed a similar arrangement in April 1945 when he set up a new Haut-Comité de la Population et de la Famille (he demonstrated the high priority that he himself gave the issue by chairing most of the meetings in person).[27] Vichy had seemed, initially, to follow a different path. Much to the chagrin of its supporters, in 1940 and 1941 the administration in charge of family policy had been modest in size and subordinated to other ministries. By mid-1942, however, the CGF had evolved into a fully autonomous body, responsible to the head of the government (via his Secrétaire d'État, Admiral Platon). The CGF was, of course, a quasi-ministerial body, not an expert committee: in that sense the precedent for it was the Third Republic's Ministry of the Family. It is none the less indicative that the CGF should have reported directly to the head of the government: throughout the period between the end of the Third Republic and the beginning of the Fourth, *dénatalité* and the crisis of the family were felt to be problems that defied conventional bureaucratic categorization and demanded a truly national response, led from the top.

These were also problems which were perceived to be above politics (although Vichy's ideological cult of the family temporarily politicized them). The demographic crisis seemed the archetypal case of a social malaise whose solution required more than merely 'technical' reforms. Reformers of all kinds (from the critics of economic malthusianism to the founders of the new Republic) were saying that what France needed was a change of attitudes as much as a change of structures. The pro-natalists led the way in identifying the nation's problem as one of *mentalités* and in seeking a solution in the form of a new mystique which could galvanize individual members of society (much as the republican mystique had once done and the totalitarian mystique seemed to do in the late 1930s). If one looks at the imagery, rather than the substance, of what pro-natalists were saying, it is apparent that they had a

[26] *JO, Lois et décrets*, 24 Feb. 1939. This was not the first time that such a committee had been formed. As Daladier explained, the arrangement copied that of the Haut-Comité Méditerranéen, which already reported directly to the président du conseil.

[27] See Alfred Sauvy's memoirs, *De Paul Reynaud à Charles de Gaulle* (Tournai, 1972), 177.

great deal in common with reformers in other areas. When Renaudin said that '[family policy] can be a *point of crystallization of energies*, a *point of application for a common effort*,'[28] he was using similar metaphors to those employed, in a different context, by Jean Monnet.

One side-effect of the concern about *dénatalité* was the increasing importance which came to be attached to improving the nation's social security system (particularly but not exclusively family allowances). After the Liberation, the depopulation fears which have been described above combined with several other considerations to lead the Provisional Government to undertake a sweeping reform of this system. The centre-piece of the reform—an ordinance of 4 October 1945, which the government referred to as its 'social security plan'—fixed the legal and administrative framework for a radical rationalization and modernization of past legislation.

Social security was an area in which France's problem was perceived to be one of premature innovation as much as relative backwardness. The first reflex of French reformers who read the Beveridge report was often defensive. They pointed to France's long tradition of mutual aid organizations. They also pointed to the considerable volume of inter-war social legislation in France. A 1932 law had mandated employer-financed family allowances (which some employers had been providing on an *ad hoc* basis for a number of years). Another important law, which was voted by parliament in 1928 and took effect two years later, had established a limited system of social insurance. By the mid-1930s a certain percentage of French workers and their families were receiving benefits for sickness, maternity, old age, death, disability, and unemployment. On further reflection, however, most observers in the 1940s recognized that the pre-war coverage had been very uneven and that the idea of a *plan* pointed up the flaws in France's improvised system. Certain aspects of this system attracted particular criticism: the proliferation of offices insuring different groups against different risks (in a single *arrondissement* in Paris there might be forty or more totally independent offices[29]); the

---

[28] 'La Famille dans la nation', 29 (my emphasis).
[29] This statistic is given by Georges Buisson, as quoted by Georges Lefranc, *Les Expériences syndicales en France de 1939 à 1950* (Paris, 1950), 315.

exclusion of important groups (such as self-employed workers and artisans); and the limitations of the coverage (for example, the lack of unemployment benefit for most of those without work).

In addition to improving family allowances and old-age pensions, the Vichy government had shown some interest in rationalizing the system. A proposal to that effect had been considered by the Minister of Labour, René Belin.[30] In Vichy think-tanks, various proposals were made to limit the number of offices and consolidate them on a regional basis.[31] The cause of reform was also taken up by the Resistance movements and post-Liberation élites. The CNR's Common Programme proposed 'a comprehensive social security plan, aiming to assure all citizens of the means of subsistence in every case where they are unable to secure them by working'. Similarly, the CGE's economic report argued that 'the nation must guarantee the worker a decent and properly-paid job or, in its absence, effective assistance for his family and himself'.[32] Other Resistance organizations which advocated an extension of the social security system included the OCM, the Front National, and the Mouvement de Libération Nationale. The concept of imposing order on the mosaic of existing arrangements was in tune with the new leadership's general philosophy: it appealed to the same rationalizing impulse that stimulated the vogue for economic planning or underpinned the Langevin–Wallon plan. The Welfare State idea also dovetailed with the Resistance's vision of a truly democratic society: only a comprehensive social security system could dispel the financial insecurity that afflicted working people and put them on an equal footing with the bourgeoisie. Finally, the pre-war lineage of social security made it an obvious theme for the 'ouvriériste' Resistance to adopt. The CNR programme echoed a demand which CGT programmes had been making for more than two decades.[33] As early as 1918 the CGT's 'Minimum Programme' had called for social insurance to protect all working people against unemployment, sickness, disability, and old age.

---

[30] Louis Fougère, 'L'Administration et la modernisation de la France de 1944 à 1952', paper presented to the colloquium *La France en voie de modernisation* (Paris, 1981), 19.

[31] See e.g. the minutes of sub-committee 11 of the Conseil Supérieur de l'Économie Industrielle et Commerciale (meeting of 9 May 1944), in AN, F22 1834.

[32] Courtin, *Rapport sur la politique économique d'après-guerre*, p. 27.

[33] For details of the CGT's position in the inter-war period, see CGT, *XXIIIᵉ congrès national* (Paris, 1935), 85–100, 276–83.

During the 1920s and early 1930s the CGT had fought hard to secure passage of the 1928 Social Insurance law (which in itself took the better part of a decade) and later to defend the law against employers and conservatives who tried to whittle down its provisions. In the depression years the Confederation had pressed for an extension of the 1928 legislation—to reduce the percentage of medical costs not reimbursed by insurance, to extend unemployment benefits, to bring more workers into the system, and to streamline the administration. In several of these respects the reforms that were introduced after 1945 fulfilled long-standing trade union demands (although it must be admitted that the pre-war CGT programme was not particularly visible in the public debate over social security in 1945–6).

Overall, it is undeniable that the events of 1940–4 created a perception that liberation had to produce a drastic improvement in the living standard of working people. But it is equally clear that in mid-1944 the issue of social security reform was much less central to the French public debate than it was in other countries (notably Britain). There are several possible explanations for this fact. The extent of pre-war legislation was clearly one factor reducing the sense of urgency over this reform. Another may have been the collective perception of the immediate past: in France, memories of the 1930s were primarily memories of economic stagnation and political polarization, whereas in Britain, the United States, and other countries which had experienced higher rates of unemployment, the dominant recollection tended to be one of social deprivation. The fundamental factor, however, was simply that French resisters and post-war reformers had other priorities. In the socio-economic democracy that resisters dreamed of establishing, a social security plan came well below nationalization or worker participation in strategic importance. Even among strictly social reforms, social security was regarded in 1944 as a less pressing demand than the restoration of a free syndicalism, an increase in wages, or the recovery of the social gains made in 1936 and curtailed by Vichy (such as the 40-hour working week and collective-bargaining rights).[34] In Britain the events of 1940–1944

---

[34] See e.g. the 'Rapport sur les principales mesures sociales à prendre dès la libération', prepared by the Consultative Assembly's Commission des affaires économiques et sociales (n.d., but written by Albert Gazier in Algiers before the Liberation). A copy of this report is in AN, 382 AP 72.

(the wartime political coalition, the social experience of the blitz and evacuation) amplified pre-war demands for social solidarity. In France the events of 1940 and afterwards (the collusion of occupiers and capitalists, the anti-working-class bias of the regime in Vichy) placed punitive measures against capitalism and restoration of working-class rights at the head of the reform agenda. If it is legitimate to cite the instances in which Resistance movements advocated reform of social security provision, it is also essential to place them in perspective. The CNR's commitment to establish a social security plan came near the end of its list of socio-economic recommendations. Several earlier drafts of the Common Pro- gramme had included far less specific commitments. For example, the first political programme for the post-war period—drafted at the beginning of 1943 by Socialists (who were to emerge after the war as perhaps the staunchest supporters of Beveridge-type reform)—made no mention whatsoever about extending social welfare.[35] In every Resistance programme the commitment to establish a social security reform (if it was even made) was overshadowed by commitments to eliminate the trusts or to re- establish the social legislation of the Popular Front.

This low priority persisted after the Liberation. In the final months of 1944 the three major parties were largely preoccupied with the structural economic reforms that the Provisional Govern- ment had pledged to introduce. The CGT leadership followed suit. As one senior CGT official (Robert Bothereau) explained: 'In 1936 we made some social gains, but did not bolster, ground, and consolidate them with reforms in the economic structure, and we know full well that these gains are entirely transitory, entirely provisional, entirely subject to revision . . . unless we take some definite positions in the economic sphere.'[36] The primacy of economic *réformes de structure* (especially nationalizations) was reflected in the CGT press: the Confederation's newspaper, *Le Peuple*, made little or no mention of social security reform in the autumn and winter of 1944–5. It was only after the government announced its intention to act, in June 1945, that the CGT made its position clear: 'We demand, after the fashion of the economic plan, a kind of social plan and a system of comprehensive

[35] See Claire Andrieu, *Le Programme Commun de la Résistance: des idées dans la guerre* (Paris, 1984), 139.
[36] Bothereau, *Applications actuelles du syndicalisme* (Paris, 1945), 8–9.

insurance on behalf of those who are underprivileged.'[37] The political parties of the left reacted similarly: they fell in line behind a policy which hitherto had not been central to their programmes for renewing France. The initiative for the 1945 reform plan came from within the government and, in particular, from the Minister of Labour, Alexandre Parodi, and his *directeur général de la sécurité sociale*, Pierre Laroque. If Parodi and Laroque had not taken the lead by preparing a blueprint for reform and, in June 1945, creating a special commission 'assigned to examine the provisions of a proposal relating to the organization of social security',[38] in order to air their plans, it is entirely possible that the political parties' vague pledges would never have been transformed into legislation.

The main stimulus for the government's action in 1945 (and for the politicians' favourable response to it) came from outside the country. Social security was an area where French reformers were obviously following an international current. In no other area was the emulation so explicit or so self-conscious. The proposals that Parodi submitted to the Consultative Assembly in July 1945 opened in characteristic vein: '. . . all the countries of the world . . . are striving to set up a system of social security for their workers and sometimes even for their entire populations.

'France must also prepare such a system, to the best of her capacity and always bearing in mind her economic and psychological idiosyncrasies.'[39] The Socialist party's proposal, submitted a fortnight after Parodi's, began similarly, with a reference to British and Belgian reforms and a plea that France 'whose history is so rich in social provision, should not be left behind'.[40] The international trend towards a more comprehensive form of social welfare had been publicized at a meeting of the International Labour Organization in Philadelphia in April–May 1944. The Philadelphia Conference had recommended that all member countries provide social insurance to cover the following

---

[37] Id., 'Pour un plan social', *Le Peuple*, 23 June 1945.
[38] The proceedings of this commission (which included a mixture of ministerial experts and interest-group representatives) were analysed thirty years ago by Henry C. Galant in his *Histoire politique de la sécurité sociale française, 1945–1952* (Paris, 1955), 29–38. Its papers are classified under the code AN, SAN 7509, but the *carton* in question is missing from the National Archives at Fontainebleau.
[39] *JO, Documents*, 5 July 1945, p. 665.
[40] Ibid., 17 July 1945, p. 673.

contingencies: sickness, maternity, invalidity, old age, death of bread-winner, unemployment, emergency expenses, and employment injuries.[41] The expression of this trend which attracted most attention in France was undoubtedly the wartime report prepared for the British government by Sir William Beveridge. From the moment that it was issued (in 1942) Beveridge was a constant reference-point in the French debate. At the end of 1942 Henry Hauck (then chairman of the Free French study group on social policy and later a high-ranking official in the Ministry of Labour) described it as 'a new and very important landmark in the study of post-war social problems'.[42] Hauck's committee debated the merits of the report and immediately prepared a précis that was dispatched to various Resistance study groups inside France. Two years later, when the British government moved to legislate on the report, there was a further burst of interest in it, both in the French press and in the government.[43] Whilst some features of the British plan seemed inapplicable in France, the philosophy of a comprehensive welfare system for all citizens was immediately recognized as 'a legislation which will be superior to ours both in the amount of benefits and in the number of risks covered'.[44] The architecture of the 'French Beveridge plan'[45] which the Provisional Government presented to the Assembly in Paris in July 1945 and established by the ordinance of 4 October may be briefly described. Its ultimate objective—to be achieved over a period of years— was a social security system which would cover the entire population against all sources of insecurity. Initially, the plan was to provide wage-earners with social insurance, work disability insurance, and family allowances. But it was stipulated that, as soon as possible, it should be extended to provide unemployment benefit and to cover all citizens (including the self-employed and professional and managerial workers). To work towards that end, Parodi proposed a single unified system—unified both in the sense that one institution

[41] The recommendations of the Philadelphia Conference are reproduced in ILO, *International Labour Conventions and Recommendations, 1919–1981* (Geneva, 1982), 517 ff.
[42] Minutes of meetings of 3 Dec. 1942, in AN, 72 AJ 546. The Beveridge Plan featured prominently in the first publication of the CGE: *Les Cahiers politiques*, 1 (Apr. 1943), 28–30.
[43] See e.g. the studies of the plan prepared inside the Ministry of National Economy, ibid. 16, 17.
[44] Albert Gazier, writing in *Le Peuple*, 7 Apr. 1945.
[45] See *L'Année politique 1944–45*, p. 327.

would provide all types of compensation (though temporarily family allowances were given a separate fund) and in the sense that, within a given geographic area, there would be only one *caisse* (office). The system had three tiers. At the local level companies would pay the lump sum of employer and employee contributions into a 'primary office'. This office would be administered by a board composed of two-thirds *syndicat* representatives (a proportion of whom had to be fathers or mothers) and one-third employers and representatives of family associations. It would cover payments for sickness, maternity, temporary disability pay, and (later) family allowances. Above it there were regional offices and a national office, which would guarantee payments from the local offices and cover expenses that they could not be expected to meet (such as pensions and permanent disability insurance). While the consolidation of the multiple offices which had existed before 1939 could be justified on grounds of administrative efficiency, the management of the offices by those who benefited from them gave the plan a second *raison d'être*. In the past much of the social welfare system had been in the hands of commercial insurance companies or the *patronat*. Laroque and Parodi stressed that their scheme of self-managed social welfare would not only secure the material well-being of workers, but would give them a greater control over their own lives (thus harmonizing with the philosophy of Parodi's earlier ordinance which had established the *comités d'entreprises*[46]).

When the government's plan was debated at the end of July, the Assembly was not particularly well-attended,[47] but the delegates gave the proposals emphatic approval.[48] At the end of a one day debate the Assembly backed the plan by 190 votes to one (the sole dissenter being the conservative Joseph Denais, although there were also 84 abstentions). The Socialist party, which had introduced its own proposal for a comprehensive plan,[49] withdrew it in favour of Parodi's. This was no particular sacrifice, since the main features of the Socialist plan were close to those of the government's plan. The Christian Democratic response was more

[46] See Pierre Laroque, 'Le Plan français de sécurité sociale', *Revue française du travail*, 1 (Apr. 1946), 12–13.
[47] This is according to *L'Année politique*, p. 331.
[48] *JO, Débats*, 31 July 1945, pp. 1673–84, 1686–97.
[49] *JO, Documents*, 17 July 1945, pp. 673–9. For a presentation of the PS's ideas, see Moch, *Arguments socialistes*, pp. 76–8.

ambivalent. The MRP supported much of the philosophy behind the plan. It accepted both the technical rationale for reforming an uncoordinated and inefficient system and the political rationale for stripping social security of its paternalist or commercial character. But Catholics raised three major objections to the plan: first, that its provisions for family allowances were unsatisfactory (in other words, that it was not pro-natalist enough); second, that its insistence on uniformity made it impossible for workers of a distinct religious or professional affiliation to manage their own offices (as they had done in the past), and thus raised the spectre of *étatisation*; and, third, that by stipulating that administrators of the offices would be designated by the most representative union rather than elected directly, the government was severely restricting the democratization of the system.[50] These criticisms reflected the concerns of a vital constituency within the MRP, the Catholic syndicalists of the CFTC. In contrast to the CGT, which welcomed the reforms (not surprisingly, since the CGT was likely to gain substantial control over the boards of the *caisses*),[51] the CFTC was hostile. Its members abstained in the Assembly vote in July, launched an unsuccessful parliamentary campaign in the first half of 1946 to revise the ordinance of October 1945, and initially refused to participate in administering the new system.[52] Catholics were united in their suspicion of *uniformisation* and their belief in 'our democratic freedom to choose our insurer'.[53] However, there were divisions over the extent of their resistance, with hard-line Christian syndicalists on one side and, on the other, more flexible syndicalists (who wanted to 'de-confessionalize' the CFTC) together with many Christian Democratic politicians.[54] On balance, the MRP's position was critical but not unconstructive: 'As a general rule, the movement is prepared to participate in perfecting a system which it does not mean to reject in a huff, because it considers it a partial progress.'[55] This approach bore some fruit in

[50] For these arguments see the MRP's position papers, in AN, 350 AP 93.

[51] See the motion passed at the CGT's national congress in April 1946: *XXVIe Congrès National* (Paris, 1947), 360.

[52] For an analysis of the CFTC's position, see Michel Launay, 'Mise au point: la CFTC et la sécurité sociale de 1944 à 1947', in *La France en voie de modernisation (1944–1952)*.

[53] Centre des Jeunes Patrons, *Le Plan de sécurité sociale* (Paris, 1945), 3.

[54] For the divisions within the CFTC, see Gérard Adam, *La CFTC 1940–1958* (Paris, 1964), 58–68, and Launay, 'Mise au point', pp. 9–10.

[55] MRP, 'La Sécurité sociale' (1 May 1946), in AN, 350 AP 93.

1946: at the end of the Second Constituent Assembly, the Bidault government was able to modify the system so that worker representatives on the boards would be elected rather than designated.

Just as Catholics found it difficult, because of their stake in the status quo, to weigh the merits of a modernized system dispassionately, so in reverse the Communists came to be committed to the reform because of the political benefits that implementation seemed likely to offer. Before the war Communists had often opposed compulsory social insurance as a form of 'collaboration with the bourgeois state'.[56] By 1945 their attitude had evolved. The Communist response to the initial government proposals was supportive but not particularly enthusiastic: *L'Humanité*, for example, gave a factual account of the 31 July debate and did not mention the ordinance of 4 October when it appeared. The party's position on social security was similar to that which it adopted on the issue of the *comités d'enterprises*. Though suspicious of the grandiose claims that non-communist reformers made for such policies, it defended them as elements of the CNR's Common Programme (here again taking reformism further than the party had been willing to go before the war). After the October 1945 general elections, however, there was a marked change in the party's attitude. With the appointment of the Communist Ambroise Croizat to head the Ministry of Labour, the PCF became a vocal advocate of the social security plan as well as of the *comités d'entreprises*. At once Croizat announced that his first priority was to 'ensure implementation of the social security plan voted several months ago by the Consultative Assembly'.[57] Following through on this commitment, he presented a government bill (passed by the First Constituent Assembly shortly before it was dissolved in mid-1946) to extend the provisions of the 4 October ordinance to include self-employed workers and non-wage-earners. With Croizat as minister the social security plan became not merely a source of good publicity for the party but an opportunity to maximize the influence of the Communist-led CGT within the new system.[58]

---

[56] See Galant, *Histoire politique de la sécurité sociale française*, pp. 13–14.

[57] *L'Humanité*, 25 Nov. 1945.

[58] See on this issue Irwin Wall, *French Communism in the Era of Stalin* (Westport, 1983), 41–2.

The remodelling of social welfare policy in the post-war period was the product of synthesis—in this case, a synthesis of foreign reforms, past French reforms, and Resistance idealism. Much of the inspiration came from external innovations which stimulated French reformers to look again at the strengths and weaknesses of French legislation in this area. The kind of system that the government opted for reflected a range of influences. The inclusiveness and uniformity of the system reflected both the example of Beveridge and a rationalizing impulse within the administration. The complex network of autonomous local offices was an attempt to create uniformity without bureaucratizing the system, without eliminating 'that spirit of disinterested mutual aid, that generous tradition of mutual assistance which for a century and a half have given all France's social institutions their particular appearance'.[59] A similar concern to build on previous reforms rather than import alien notions dictated that the new system should continue to be funded directly by workers and employers rather than by the state. A system of state-funded welfare was felt by reformers of all persuasions to be inappropriate to France: first, because of the power that it would place in the hands of the instinctively parsimonious Ministry of Finance; and, second, because it appeared to convert an institution of active self-help into one of passive, hence undignified, charity. By turning over management of the system to those whom it protected, the government was bowing to precedent: organizations like the CGT, which had run their own offices before the war, had always maintained that those who contributed to a *caise* had a *droit de gestion*. At the same time the new system was clearly tapping the 'participationist' ethic of the Resistance. Social security reform was absorbed into the distinctive Resistance philosophy of renewal through engagement.

In practice (as happened with the *comités d'entreprises* which grew out of the same general aspirations), this ideal synthesis was not easily converted into reality. Democratizing the running of the Welfare State also meant politicizing it—as the wrangling between the Communists and the MRP over the first elections to the social security boards demonstrated. Creating a universal social security system proved easier to proclaim and even to legislate than

[59] See Parodi's proposals, in *JO, Documents*, 5 July 1945, p. 666.

to achieve in practice. Contrary to the expectation of the original ordinance, the separate social insurance schemes which several important groups of wage-earners (including miners and civil servants) operated were not dismantled. Furthermore, in spite of the Croizat law of May 1946, successive governments proved unable to bring self-employed and independent workers into the system—an essential step if the system were actually to redistribute wealth among classes. In the end the fate of social security reform resembled the fate of many other post-war reforms. Within two or three years of the Liberation the *élan* of national solidarity had disappeared, sectional and class interests had reasserted themselves, and the momentum for reform had been lost. Reformers had achieved the first stage of their plans more or less successfully, but the second and third stages had had to be shelved. This inevitably gave the reforms an air of incompleteness, like a structure left half-built. Nothing epitomized such an outcome better than the case of unemployment insurance.

The absence of any comprehensive unemployment insurance was the major shortcoming of the 1945 and 1946 reforms. This shortcoming is not easy to explain, since unemployment relief was a cause dear to the political groups which were in the ascendancy in the post-Liberation era. As we have noted, the cause had long been championed by the CGT: both the Confederation's 'Minimum Programme' of 1918 and its Plans of the mid-1930s had included demands for unemployment insurance.[60] The Communist CGTU (which, in general, had opposed the CGT's social insurance views) had been insistent about the need to protect the unemployed.[61] During the war, various Resistance groups revived this pre-war demand.[62] While the CNR's Common Programme did not mention unemployment insurance specifically, it was reasonable to infer it there. The post-Liberation statements of the major parties to the CNR Programme appeared to justify such an assumption.

---

[60] See Val R. Lorwin, *The French Labor Movement* (Cambridge, Mass., 1954), 53, 71; Bernard Georges and Denise Tintant, *Léon Jouhaux dans le mouvement syndical français* (Paris, 1979), 75, 85, 197. For statements of the CGT's position, see the motions passed at the 22nd and 23rd National Congresses (of 1933 and 1935 respectively).

[61] Georges Lefranc, *Le Mouvement syndical sous la Troisième République* (Paris, 1967), 308.

[62] See e.g. the MLN's programme in H. Michel and B. Mirkine-Guetzévitch, *Les Idées politiques et sociales de la Résistance* (Paris, 1954), 377.

The legislative proposal that Socialist party representatives introduced in the Consultative Assembly in July 1945 listed unemployment as one of the risks to be covered.[63] Likewise, the MRP's
programme for social security reform claimed to cover all social
risks, including joblessness.[64] More significant still, the joint
platform signed in November 1945 by the CGT, the Socialists, the
Communists, and the Radicals—a document which was presented
to the public as an authoritative exegesis of the CNR's Common
Programme—also called for unemployment insurance.

Despite these commitments—and despite the government's
recognition of the need to extend its legislation in this respect[65]—
France's post-war Welfare State emerged as one of the few in the
industrialized world that did not provide comprehensive unemployment insurance. A temporary postponement became, by
default, an institutionalized omission. In the absence of more
detailed information about the debates which took place inside the
Ministry of Labour, it would be rash to advance any firm
explanations for this omission. In general terms, however, it would
seem to reflect contemporary perceptions of national priorities. In
1945 the demographic crisis was the major preoccupation of social
reformers: hence the salience of social security reforms which
addressed this crisis. Unemployment was certainly a concern of
reformers. But they generally viewed it as an economic rather than
a social problem: there was far more talk about how to secure full
employment than about how to help those who might fall through
the net, even in times of full employment. Once again it is
tempting to see a connection—admittedly one that cannot be
positively demonstrated, since it was not consciously made—
between the experience of the inter-war depression (specifically
the relatively low levels of unemployment in France) and the
pattern of post-war reform. In Britain the dole queues and hunger
marches of the 1930s formed an essential backdrop to the
Beveridge report: as a result, provisions for unemployment benefit
became an integral part of the British social security plan. In the
debates over the French plan the backdrop was different: it was
formed from the wartime privations and heroics of the working
class (as well as the *dénatalité* problem) far more than from the

---

[63] *JO, Documents*, 17 July 1945, p. 675.
[64] See the MRP brochure 'La Sécurité sociale' (n.d.), in AN, 350 AP 93.
[65] See Laroque, 'Le Plan français', pp. 18–19.

sufferings of the pre-war unemployed. One other point should be noted. If the French government had been introducing its reforms in a period of high or rising unemployment, there might have been greater political pressure to introduce insurance. In fact, after a brief surge around the time of the Liberation, unemployment remained at very low levels through the active phase of the reform movement (so low that by 1946 the Ministry of Labour could conclude that full employment had been achieved).[66] Writing a quarter of a century later, Pierre Laroque indicated that the government's decision had been influenced by its calculation that this low unemployment was likely to persist in the foreseeable future.[67]

The lack of unemployment insurance left a gaping hole in the protection which the new system afforded French workers. Yet it should not be allowed to detract from the solid achievements of the post-war reform. The plan of 1945–6 went a considerable way towards achieving the aims set out in the CNR Programme, not to mention the long-standing objectives of organized labour. It improved the coverage of social security in a variety of ways: for example, under the new system 80 per cent of medical expenses could be reimbursed (instead of highly variable and often lower amounts before the war); and long-term illness was now covered for a period up to three years (as opposed to six months under the old system). The goal of social solidarity was partially met by a system which placed all contributions in a common fund, from which all who contributed could draw the full range of benefits. The goal of democratization was met by the non-bureaucratic form of the offices. The goal of a single system for all was not achieved in the 1940s, but the framework for such a system had been created.

[66] 'Evolution du chômage en France depuis la Libération', *Revue française du travail*, 1 (July 1946), 372.
[67] 'La Sécurité sociale de 1944 à 1951', *Revue française des affaires sociales*, 25 (Apr.–June 1971), 12.

10

The New Economy I: Chronology

DURING his trip to the United States in August 1945, General de
Gaulle attended a banquet given in his honour by the Mayor of
Chicago. Acknowledging the crucial importance of US economic
assistance to French reconstruction, the head of the Provisional
Government declared: 'When, in the midst of our ruins, we say
that we want to build a new France, it is above all the economy
that we are alluding to.'[1] De Gaulle's view that economic
modernization was the crux of national renewal was widely shared
at the time. It has certainly been reflected in the historiography
about this period. The contributions that economic historians have
made to our understanding of pre- and post-Liberation France
have been particularly extensive and illuminating.[2] The general
conclusions of this research have been somewhat paradoxical. On
the one hand, it has demonstrated the many contingencies
(political as well as economic, external as well as domestic) that
shaped innovations such as the introduction of economic planning
and the passing of nationalization legislation—reforms which were
once assumed to have grown almost inexorably out of the war. On
the other hand, historians have reaffirmed an intellectual and—to
a degree—institutional continuity in economic reformism, from
inter-war non-conformity, via wartime experimentation, to post-
war innovation.[3] Both these findings (which are complementary
rather than contradictory) reflect a common purpose among
historians: to trace the roots of France's post-war modernization in

[1] Speech of 27 Aug. 1945, reprinted in de Gaulle, *Lettres, notes et carnets*, vi
(Paris, 1984), 65.
[2] The argument of this and the following chapter owes an obvious debt to the
work of several of these historians (in particular, Philippe Mioche, Richard Kuisel,
Michel Margairaz, and Jean Bouvier).
[3] The limits of this continuity argument (which is mainly associated with the
works of Mioche and Kuisel, cited below) have been well stated by Henry Rousso
in two articles: 'Les Élites économiques dans les années quarante', in *Le Elites in
Francia e in Italia negli anni quaranta* (Paris and Rome, 1983), 29–49; 'Les
Paradoxes de Vichy et de l'Occupation: contraintes, archaïsmes et modernités', in
Patrick Fridenson and André Straus (eds.), *Le Capitalisme français 19ᵉ–20ᵉ siècle:
blocages et dynamismes d'une croissance* (Paris, 1987), 67–82.

the reforms of the post-Liberation era. The intention here is less ambitious: it is simply to convey the range of possible economic futures, as they were perceived between 1940 and 1946, without attempting to link them to the future which did emerge after 1946.

Expressed in its most general form, the question that economic reformers addressed in these years was the following: as the objective realities of economic organization changed (with phenomena such as increasing mechanization, the growing economic role of the state, the increasing size of companies), how could or should the dominant ideology of liberalism be modified to take account of these changes and restore a sense of control over events (something which had largely been lost in the 1930s)? June 1940 was not the first occasion that this question had been posed. The chronology of pre-1940 economic reformism resembles that which has been described in other areas.

As in education or industrial relations, the First World War stimulated a current of ideas about reform that was to be replicated on a larger scale during the Second War. In 1917 and 1918 the Ministry of Commerce (under Étienne Clémentel) proposed a number of permanent innovations for the post-war period:[4] a powerful Ministry of National Economy, 'which would guide private initiatives, co-ordinate their efforts, and actively stimulate production and trade';[5] a Production Office which Richard Kuisel terms an 'incipient planning agency';[6] corporatist arrangements to structure relations between employers, workers, and governments, and to encourage rationalization and expansion; and a network of economic regions. In 1918 the CGT suggested a different kind of reconstruction programme, but one which set an equally influential reformist precedent. The CGT's plan included proposals for nationalization of vital sectors and the creation of a National Economic Council. In order to avoid *étatisation*, the CGT recommended that nationalized industries should be constituted as *régies autonomes* or independent organizations managed by tripartite bodies representing the work-force, consumers and the state. More than a decade later, after the onset of the Depression and under the impact of the reformist economic theories of the Belgian socialist Henri de Man, the CGT added to this minimum

---

[4] See Kuisel, *Capitalism and the State in Modern France* (Cambridge, 1981), 43–7.
[5] Quoted ibid. 47.   [6] Ibid.

programme of 1918–19 a *planiste* gloss. The Confederation's programme of 1934 recommended the formulation of an annual economic plan.

This plan was one of many proposed in the 1930s. The manifest failure of orthodox policies to solve the economic crisis of the mid-1930s—combined with the example of more dynamic policies in Germany, Russia, and America—prompted a scramble for economic alternatives.[7] This scramble threw up many of the ideas that were to be at the centre of debate in the 1940s and many of the people who were to debate them. The reassessment took place across a wide front. On the political left, themes of *planisme* and *rationalisation* were advocated by a minority in the Socialist party (including people such as André Philip, Jules Moch, and Robert Marjolin). In the syndicalist movement, two of the most fervent *planistes* were Robert Lacoste and René Belin (future ministers in the GPRF and the État Français respectively). The new intellectual currents also reached various groups of industrialists and economists. In these groups dissatisfaction with the status quo expressed itself in technocratic solutions (such as that pioneered in the late 1920s by Ernest Mercier's Redressement Français) or in neo-liberal planning. Many of the names associated with this non-socialist revisionism (such as jean Coutrot, Auguste Detœuf, and Gérard Bardet) were to reappear in or around Vichy after 1940.

The echo that these ideas encountered in government circles was minimal. The most politically radical ministry of the inter-war period—the Popular Front government of 1936–7—introduced very limited nationalizations, set up a Ministry of National Economy, and brought a number of *planistes* into the administration. However, Blum's coalition did not make structural economic reform a high priority. Other ministries made a few innovations. In 1925 Herriot established a representative National Economic Council to advise the government about economic issues. In the 1920s and 1930s a series of legislative proposals were introduced for 'plans d'équipement', which were programmes to improve and update the economic infrastructure of the country. The first such proposal was introduced by André Tardieu in November 1929. It was followed by others, sponsored by politicians ranging from

---

[7] The literature on the intellectual new wave of the 1930s is large. It is conveniently summarized by Kuisel, ibid. 98–119.

Vincent Auriol to Adrien Marquet and Pierre Laval.[8] Similar kinds of programmes were adopted with the aim of fostering economic development in the empire. In general, however, what was most striking about the Third Republic's response to the inter-war economic depression was its unadventurousness and conservatism.[9]

The background to wartime and post-war reformism was more ambiguous in economic affairs than in other areas. Intellectually, alternatives to the liberal orthodoxy had abounded. They fuelled the debate after 1940 (although one should never underestimate the capacity of intellectuals or politicians to reinvent old ideas). On the other hand, politically, there had been virtually no reform tradition. Whereas, in most areas of policy, past reforms formed an essential component of the dialogue about future change, in the economic sphere the past presented itself as a tale of almost unrelieved error. Depending on one's perspective, the pre-war regime was perceived to have committed sins of omission (too little coherent intervention or commission (too much counter-productive intervention) or indeed both.

Many of the inter-war alternatives for a new economy had pointed in one of two directions: either towards corporatist arrangements that offered the prospect of social reconciliation and economic 'balance', or towards a *planisme* that proposed to save capitalism by rationalizing and renovating it. Both these alternatives found expression after 1940 in the economic philosophy of the Vichy regime. The official ideology of the État Français was a statist variant of corporatism. Pétain's programme of 11 October 1940 laid down the two essential principles of this ideology. First, the different branches of the economy should be organized into *organisations professionnelles* which 'will deal with everything concerning the profession, but will be limited to this professional domain'.[10] At the same time, the state should intervene and 'co-ordinate' private enterprise, in order to break the power of the 'trusts'. This was a prescription for what the regime's supporters

---

[8] 'Historique des plans d'équipement', *Notes documentaires et études*, 267 (22 Mar. 1946).
[9] On the political response to the Depression, see Julian Jackson, *The Politics of Depression in France, 1932–1936* (Cambridge, 1985).
[10] Pétain, *Actes et écrits* (Paris, 1974), 474.

sometimes labelled a 'Salazarian corporatism'—a system in which
the state exercised a general supervision over the economy, in
which each profession was methodically organized and ran its
affairs within the guidelines established by the state, in which the
proletariat was reintegrated into the national community and
'natural' communities such as the family were reinvigorated.[11]
This ideology was theoretically anti-capitalist and undeniably
antithetical to economic modernization. Its vision of a harmonious,
stable social order involved a glorification of rural life and artisanal
production. It was accompanied by a defeatist assessment of
France's industrial competitiveness. In an article in the *Revue des
Deux Mondes* of 15 August 1940 Pétain wrote: 'The prospects of
the present situation call for a halt, if not even a reversal, in the
process of out-and-out industrialization in which France tried to
rival other nations better provided than herself in size of
population or richness of raw materials.'[12] Pétain's *retour à la terre*
expressed a cultural reaction against modernity (and, in particular,
industrialization) which was widespread in 1940. Many examples
of this reaction could be given but one—from a short brochure
published by a doctor on the evils of the automobile—may suffice
to convey its temperament:

The period of that false prosperity by which we were lured after 1918
and of that economic malaise which followed could have the car as its
symbol. . . . The automobile industry, if not the only one in question,
provides the archetypal case of that feverish and relentless assembly-line
production, whose uproar stimulated artificial needs, artificially satisfied.[13]

The other face of Vichy economics was apparent in its
bureaucracy (particularly in the newly created Ministry of Industrial
Production), among technocratic groups, and in various think-
tanks. In the early stages of the National Revolution—in Alfred
Sauvy's words, 'Le Vichy, première manière . . . vertueux, austère,
civique'[14]—these 'modernizers' established a system of economic

[11] One of the best sources for corporatist ideas under Vichy are the publications
of the Institut d'Études Corporatives et Sociales. A large collection of the IECS's
publications—and other corporatist literature—may be found in AN, F22 1778,
1780.
[12] *Actes et écrits*, p. 488.
[13] F. Debat, *A chacun sa maison et non plus à chacun sa voiture* (Paris, 1941),
4, 17.
[14] *De Paul Reynaud à Charles de Gaulle* (Tournai, 1972), 141.

dirigisme that was designed not only to meet present emergencies but to provide a blueprint for managing the post-war economy. To quote Jean Bichelonne, head of 'the Ministry of Industrial Production between April 1942 and August 1944 and one of the most fervent of the modernizers: 'We are all working to establish for the post-war era the rational economy, the intelligent and human economy, which will allow our country to master the effects of economic competition.'[15] To achieve this rational economy, modernizers believed that the state would have to supervise the performance of the leading economic sectors— 'those which have an impact on the country's position vis-à-vis the outside world'.[16]

Under the regime's auspices, a series of attempts were made to develop this conception of *dirigisme*. Two institutions were particularly prominent in this effort: the Délégation Générale à l'Équipement National (DGEN) which was created in 1941 and produced two lengthy documents (the Ten-Year Equipment Plan of 1942 and the 'Tranche de Démarrage' or 'Starting Section' completed in May 1944);[17] and the Conseil Supérieur de l'Économie Industrielle et Commerciale (CSEIC) which was established by Bichelonne himself in 1942 and produced a number of reports, including one dealing with 'economic policy and the problem of the Plan'.[18] The argument of these reports contained certain common threads. Their starting-point was an assumption that *de facto* liberalism had ceased to function: first, because ever since the First World War governments had been forced to intervene more and more in the running of the economy and, second, because free competition had been restricted by the growth of *ententes* and *monopoles de fait*. In keeping with the new regime's self-image of pragmatism, the DGEN and the CSEIC presented their ideas about the future not as an alternative economic ideology but as a purely practical adjustment to reality. Skirting

[15] Quoted in Henry Rousso, 'L'Organisation industrielle de Vichy (perspectives de recherches)', *Revue d'histoire de la Deuxième Guerre Mondiale*, 116 (1979), 28.
[16] See Bichelonne's remarks to the plenary session of the CSEIC, 6 July 1943, in AN, F12 10143.
[17] The DGEN's plans are ibid., F60 658, 659. They have been discussed by Philippe Mioche, *Le Plan Monnet: genèse et élaboration 1941–1947* (Paris, 1987), 19–30; and Kuisel, *Capitalism and the State*, pp. 146–56.
[18] Particularly useful archives from the CSEIC may be found in AN, F12 10143, 10144. The CSEIC's activities have been briefly discussed by Mioche, *Le Plan Monnet*, pp. 24–5 and Kuisel, *Capitalism and the State*, pp. 151–3.

the question as to whether, in the best possible of all worlds, the state *should* intervene, the Vichy planners simply observed that the state did intervene and therefore ought to intervene rationally rather than irrationally.

The 'plan' which the DGEN and the CSEIC proposed for the French economy had a number of specific objectives. It also had two general, overarching functions. The first of these was to co-ordinate into a coherent policy the many discrete interventions of a complex state in a complex economy. The CSEIC's report stated that 'The Plan is justified above all by the necessity of co-ordinating . . . government interventions.'[19] This was precisely the function that Vichy's own planning agency, the DGEN, took upon itself: 'It is the Délégation Générale's function to take an overall view of the proposals that reach it, and, in the light of a general doctrine, *co-ordinate* them and make a *choice*.'[20] The second function of the plan was counter-cyclical. The DGEN's 1942 report suggested that an Equipment Plan could reduce capital investment in periods of expansion and increase it if the economy appeared to be heading for a depression.[21] The CSEIC's report eagerly embraced this idea,[22] which was more an extension of the inter-war *plans d'équipement* than a conscious Keynesian experiment (although the Tranche de Démarrage did justify budget deficits).[23]

Much of Vichy's planning naturally focused on the conditions that were likely to prevail at the end of the war and the constraints that they would place on France's reconstruction. Both the CSEIC and the DGEN distinguished (as their opponents in the Provisional Government were also to do) between two distinct phases of reconstruction: an emergency phase which would follow the end of hostilities and would be characterized by continued shortages and dislocations; and a more remote phase in which the economy would have regained its peacetime equilibrium.[24] Prescriptions for the first phase were naturally influenced by changing perceptions

[19] 'La Politique économique et les problèmes du Plan: rapport préliminaire aux travaux de la Commission no. 3 (troisième rédaction), 25 Juin 1943', 19, in AN, F12 10144.
[20] 'Plan d'Équipement National' (1942), 30, ibid., F60 658.
[21] Ibid. 41–2.
[22] 'La Politique économique et les problèmes du Plan', p. 20.
[23] Mioche, *Le Plan Monnet*, pp. 22–3, 33.
[24] For the CSEIC, see the paper: 'Les Différents Aspects du problème du plan' (Feb. 1943), 9, in AN, F12 10144. For the DGEN, see the 'Plan d'Équipement National', p. 18.

of what France's situation would be at the end of the war. But prescriptions for the second phase were less constrained by practicalities and, therefore, perhaps a better indication of underlying views. These views are not easily categorized in terms of a straightforward dichotomy between modernizing and reactionary. It may make better sense, as Rousso has recently suggested, to treat the reactionary fantasies and the technocratic visions, as complementary rather than mutually exclusive.[25]

By their emphasis on renewing industrial equipment, the planners inside and outside the Ministry of Industrial Production were implicitly contradicting the traditionalists' vision of a deindustrialized society. It is evident that Vichy officials envisaged a long-term expansion of industry. The CSEIC described the goal of its economic plan as 'a constant raising of the standard of living, that is to say growing material production in as stable a price structure as possible'.[26] Both the DGEN plans recommended substantial investment programmes in industry and communications as well as agriculture. The Tranche de Démarrage warned against the perils of malthusianism and criticized the low levels of inter-war investment.[27] On the other hand, as Mioche has correctly advised, it would be an exaggeration to label either of the DGEN's efforts 'modernist'.[28] The key words in Vichy reports tended to be those—like 'balance' and 'stability'—which echoed the social agenda of Pétainism. 'Modernization' was a word rarely used by these modernizers.

The limitations of their commitment to change are well illustrated by their attitude towards agricultural reform. Techno-crats and planners did not take Pétain's *retour à terre* literally. The DGEN's 1942 plan described it as 'probably utopian',[29] while the later plan (like other reports produced in the final months of the regime's existence) stigmatized it more forcefully as a policy likely to reduce France to the status of a second-rank nation.[30] On

---

[25] 'Les Paradoxes de Vichy', pp. 73, 81.

[26] 'Les Différents Aspects du problème du plan', p. 2.

[27] 'Plan d'Équipement National: Tranche de Démarrage' (1944), 20–52, in AN, F60 659. (Hereafter cited as 'Tranche de Démarrage').

[28] *Le Plan Monnet*, pp. 23, 29.

[29] 'Plan d'Équipement National', p. 84.

[30] On the DGEN, see Mioche, *Le Plan Monnet*, p. 28. For another attack on the *retour à la terre*, see the 'Rapport sur la politique familiale et la tâche du Conseil Supérieur de la Famille' (4 Jan. 1944), 45, in AN, F10 4970.

the other hand, even as they rejected a *retour à la terre* as impractical and dangerous, the authors of the DGEN plans advocated 'un renforcement des valeurs paysannes' and 'un certain retour vers la vie rurale'.[31] To quote a study written by another significant group of modernizers, the Comité d'Études pour la France, 'The moral and material balance of our country has always rested on the existence of a thriving rural population.'[32] This point of view was shared by the members of the CSEIC.[33] More or less all Vichy plans, in fact, began from an assumption that France's large rural population had to be conserved. This assumption of a 'balanced' economy was given an institutional form at the very end of the État Français, when a combined committee was formed by the CSEIC and the Conseil National Corporatif Agricole to discuss how the interests of industry and agriculture could be more closely integrated in the post-war era.[34] The meetings of this joint committee in the summer of 1944 epitomized the peculiar mixture of modernism and conservatism which had run through so much of Vichy. It is worth quoting at length from one of its few documents:

WE HAVE TO CREATE A MODERN NATIONAL ECONOMY. . . . We must admit that our cultivation of a land so wonderfully endowed by nature is several decades behind that of the leading countries in Europe, not to mention neighbouring continents. . . . On the other hand, we are witness to an industrial sector which was rudely awakened . . . by the defeat and invasion and now realizes that it was letting itself slide into inertia and dependence. . . .

A great revolution in our economy is imperative in every area; a new outlook, new methods, new approaches. . . .

THIS ECONOMY MUST BE FOUNDED ON FRENCH REALITIES. . . .

Agriculture constitutes the most important sector of our economy both in the aggregate value of its products and in the numbers of workers devoting themselves to it: it produces goods and workers, but also civilized values. . . .

Let us not wait for a world revolution to suppress the proletarian condition; we must discover and implement at once the French solution to

[31] 'Plan d'Équipement National', p. 84; 'Tranche de Démarrage', pp. 13–14. The study on which the DGEN's 1944 agricultural report was partly based was Robert Préaud, *Sur la politique agricole et rurale de la France*.

[32] 'Étude no. 60: contribution au redressement de l'économie française d'après-guerre (Jan. 1943), in AN, F10 4962.

[33] 'La Politique économique et les problèmes du Plan', pp. 21–2.

[34] The papers of this short-lived committee are in AN, F10 4962.

the painful problem of the French proletariat. This solution will emerge automatically from a close co-ordination of the activities of agriculture and industry.[35]

The impact that Vichy had on the debate about economic reform was as multi-faceted as the regime's own *discours*. A first kind of consequence was unintentional. Pétain's rural idyll demonstrated the very opposite of what the Marshal intended: not the evils of urbanism and industrialism but the impossibility of the 'Portugal option' and the indissoluble link between industrial development and national independence. After the Liberation it was frequently said that the defeat of 1940 had alerted French élites to this reality. In fact, the lessons of the defeat might easily have been obscured, if the anti-industrial rhetoric of a defeatist regime had not hammered them home. Ironically, after impeding the efforts of Vichy modernizers, the *retour à la terre* assisted post-Liberation modernizers.

The bureaucrats, businessmen, and intellectuals who organized and theorized about Vichy's new *dirigisme* also left a number of institutional and ideological legacies to the post-Liberation regime. The first of these was an improved statistical apparatus, headed by the Service National des Statistiques (founded in 1941). The extensive network of bodies monitoring and controlling the wartime economy gave the Vichy state the opportunity to gather more economic data than had been possible before the war. It was during the war, for example, that the outdatedness of French industrial equipment—so central to the future calculations of the Monnet plan—was first verified.[36] The necessity of adequate statistical information, if the state was to manage the economy, was a lesson that post-Liberation governments learned from Vichy.

A second legacy came from Vichy's attempts to draw up economic plans for the post-war period. In a variety of ways these plans established patterns that were to be repeated after 1944. There was, first of all, an institutional continuity. In the summer of 1944 Mendès-France's Ministry of National Economy took over the DGEN's Tranche de Démarrage as its own and Mendès described the Délégation Générale as 'prefiguring the future

---

[35] 'L'Agriculture et l'industrie dans le circuit économique d'après-guerre' (11 July 1944), ibid.
[36] Kuisel, *Capitalism and the State*, pp. 133, 140.

planning office'.[37] There was also a strong continuity in terms of the perceived priorities of reconstruction: both the CSEIC and the DGEN had highlighted the inadequacy of pre-war production of machine tools and capital equipment (a theme that was to be echoed constantly after 1944).[38] Other salient characteristics of Vichy's planning experiment whose echoes could be detected after the Liberation included its bureaucratic form (the fact that the DGEN was initially not attached to any existing ministry and that it had an advisory committee to provide 'a direct contact with the daily economic life of the country'[39]), as well as elements of its vocabulary (such as its emphasis on developing a 'mystique' around the plan[40]). In these areas there were certainly parallels with the system that Monnet was to introduce in 1946, but the parallels should not be assumed to imply causation. As we have already seen, there were varied precedents both for the bureaucratic arrangement of the DGEN and for the metaphor of mystique.

The significance of the statistical and planning innovations made under Vichy was hardly recognized beyond the relatively restricted circle of politicians and administrators involved directly in the management of the post-war economy. The aspect of Vichy's economic policy that had the greatest repercussions in French political life in the months immediately after August 1944 was also one of its most improvised parts: the economic controls that had been hastily introduced in August 1940 with the dual aim of preventing a chaotic scramble for supplies, labour, and markets, and of pre-empting German attempts to establish direct relations with French producers. The Comités d'Organisation (CO) and the Office Central de Répartition des Produits Industriels (OCRPI), which were established by this and later legislation, were the main instruments of the Ministry of Industrial Production's control over the economy. The officials of the OCRPI supervised the distribution of rationed supplies to French industry. Within each sector the CO—composed of private businessmen who were nominated by

---

[37] See Mendès-France's letter of June 1944 to the Secretary General of the CEI, in Mendès-France, *Œuvres complètes*, ii. *Une politique de l'économie, 1943–1954* (Paris, 1985), 43–4.

[38] For the CSEIC, see 'La Politique économique et les problèmes du Plan', p. 20. For the DGEN, see the 'Tranche de Démarrage', pp. 36–40.

[39] 'Plan d'Équipement National', p. 52.

[40] These characteristics have been noted by Mioche, *Le Plan Monnet*, pp. 19, 23–4.

the state and supervised by a government commissioner—had huge powers to gather information, decide production schedules, propose prices, and, in the broad terminology of the law of 16 August 1940, fix 'the rules applying to companies in relation to the general conditions of their activity'. These bodies proved intensely unpopular—not only with corporatist ideologues in Vichy who resented the state's heavy-handed interventionism, but with large sections of the business community (especially small businessmen), with the representatives of labour (since one of the first provisions of the law of 16 August 1940 had been the dissolution of the CGT), and with the Resistance, to whom the CO appeared an instrument of the trusts and a symbol of German domination over the French economy. The problem for the politicians and the Provisional Government that succeeded Vichy was that these organizations or some equivalent ones appeared temporarily indispensable.[41] The shortages that had created the need for a system to allocate resources and regulate production were bound to continue. It was inconceivable that the Provisional Government would be able to construct an entirely new network of control organizations within a matter of weeks of the Liberation. To the government this was only a short-term political problem (albeit an acute one). But to those who were committed ideologically to a radical *dirigisme* and who believed that the French economy should be permanently co-ordinated at the sectoral level, it was fundamental. Vichy's economic control system gave *dirigisme* a bad name at precisely the moment that socialists and radical-minded resisters were contemplating an extension of *dirigisme*. There was an almost insuperable pressure on the new élites to water down the *dirigiste* content of their programmes. Thus, in July 1945 we find the syndicalist leader Albert Gazier prescribing 'un dirigisme qui soit libéral'[42]—a formula that, not surprisingly, appealed to René Pleven[43] and the 'neo-liberals', whose own formula might be described as 'un libéralisme qui soit dirigiste'. In other words, the effect of Vichy was to draw socialists and liberals towards a consensus in favour of certain but limited economic controls.

[41] For an interesting analysis of this problem from the point of view of a post-war Socialist minister who was forced to operate controls inherited from Vichy, see Christian Pineau's speech in the First Constituent Assembly: *JO, Débats*, 21 Feb. 1946, p. 419.

[42] Ibid., 3 July 1945, p. 1281.

[43] Ibid., 4 July 1945, p. 1310.

As has already been suggested,[44] the political forces in opposition to Vichy identified economic renovation as a key area of concern almost from the beginning of the Occupation. Resisters produced numerous programmes for economic renewal. Amid the welter of projects, it is difficult to establish a precise chronology. However, to give an indication of the direction that the debate took, a number of the more official or systematic attempts to rethink the economy may be briefly noted.

Within Free France the first attempt to consider the post-war economy occurred in London in 1942. The economic sub-committee of the CNF's social and economic study commission contained a number of important figures.[45] It was chaired by Hervé Alphand (then the head of economic affairs in the *commissariat* dealing with economic and colonial affairs), and included Etienne Hirsch (a businessman who was later to be a member of Monnet's planning team) and the *planiste* socialist, Georges Boris. After he became Commissaire à l'Intérieur in mid-1942, André Philip also attended the sub-committee's meetings, as did other prominent members of the Free French community like the syndicalist Henry Hauck, Francis-Louis Closon (a future Commissaire de la République), and Robert Marjolin (another future planner).

At the outset the London commission was presented with two documents, which, taken together, give a good indication of the parameters of the debate at this early stage. The first document was a memorandum prepared for the economic sub-committee in July 1942 by Alphand, Boris, Hirsch, and three others.[46] It suggested that future economic reforms would be dictated by a double imperative: the concern to preserve France's stature as a great European and colonial power, and the necessity to provide the highest possible standard of living for all (which meant full employment). The memorandum proposed to achieve these aims by a policy that mixed judicious levels of state intervention with encouragement to private enterprise. On the side of state intervention, the memorandum prescribed a vigorous anti-trust

---

[44] See ch. 2 above.

[45] The sub-committee's papers are in AN, 72 AJ 546. Kuisel has discussed the sub-committee's proceedings in *Capitalism and the State*, pp. 159–63.

[46] 'Problèmes économiques d'après-guerre: un point de vue français', in AN, 72 AJ 546.

policy (either in the form of nationalization or monopoly control) and government regulation of economic activity through indirect methods such as fiscal policy, control of credit and prices, and import duties. The report warned that 'State intervention must not have the consequence of suppressing incentives necessary to economic development and the achievement of higher output.'[47] In terms of institutions, the sub-committee recommended two bodies. The first was to provide the element of democratic control over the state's economic management that was so conspicuously absent in Vichy: it was a revival of the inter-war Conseil National Économique, a consultative body representing all the major economic interests in the nation. The second institution was a complex governmental agency charged with the task of setting a general economic strategy. This body would include a number of sub-agencies: an Institut de la conjoncture to monitor and forecast economic trends; an agency to supervise investment and credit policies; an agency to control and dissolve *ententes*, ensure fair competition in the free sector, and regulate prices of approved monopolies; and various bodies to supervise foreign trade.

The other starting-point for the London commission's deliberations was a report that Philip brought over with him from France in 1942. This report represented the views of various (unidentified) Resistance movements.[48] It shared the assumption of the Alphand report that the conditions of the post-war economy would require an element of *dirigisme*, but there were also important differences between the two documents. Whereas the Alphand report had envisaged three divisions within the economy (a nationalized sector, a 'directed sector' of companies whose prices and production levels would be supervised by the state, and a 'free' sector), the Resistance movements proposed a simple distinction between 'free' industries and industries subject to state *dirigisme*. In each 'free' sector the Resistance movements proposed to establish a National Professional Committee, which was a more democratic version of the CO, bringing together representatives of labour and capital to perform a variety of regulatory functions. In the state-managed sectors the Resistance's report proposed to place industries under the authority of directors named by decree. In

---

[47] Ibid., p. 7.
[48] 'Rapport émanant des organisations de Résistance en France: projet de charte économique et professionnelle', in AN, 72 AJ 546.

reaction against the experience of the CO, many of which were run by managers of the largest firms in the industry concerned, the report stipulated that the state-appointed director would be barred from any association with a company under his administration. Though the report introduced a consultative National Professional Commission as a watch-dog, the director's powers were very broad: he was to decide production programmes, allocate resources, supervise every aspect of the performance of his sector, and, within guidelines set by the government, fix prices of all products and services. Giving officials the job of running whole sectors of the economy went beyond the proposals of Alphand's sub-committee. The sub-committee reacted by suggesting that: 'It would be . . . difficult to find a sufficient number of independent, capable, and experienced officials to direct French economic activity in all its complexity.'[49] On the institutional level the Resistance document proposed a National Economic Council similar to that in the Alphand report, and a Ministry of National Economy which would perform the functions of overall co-ordination and policy-making that Alphand's sub-committee proposed to delegate to its unnamed 'Organisme chargé de la politique économique générale'.

These two projects were confronted within the study commission in two meetings (on 25 August 1942 and 6 October 1942).[50] This confrontation produced a three-way split. First, there were the proponents of the sub-committee's report—notably Alphand—who argued that the state could control the economy by acting 'on certain nerve centres' and without intervening directly 'at every level and in every sector'.[51] Second, there was the Socialist view, represented by Philip, which was wary of indirect systems of control such as those advocated by Alphand and preferred a more direct *dirigisme*. Third, there were the syndicalists (joined on occasion by Hirsch), who rejected both the statist model of the Resistance project and the more indirect but still statist approach of the Alphand report. The Centre Syndical Français argued that the National Economic Council should not be confined to a purely consultative role (as both the Alphand and Resistance reports

---

[49] 'Point de vue du sous-comité économique sur les projets remis par M. André Philip.'
[50] The minutes of both meetings are in AN, 72 AJ 546.
[51] Alphand's words at the meeting of 25 Aug.

recommended) but should draw up the economic plan.[52] The syndicalists in the commission (Hauck, Gendrot, and Vangré-velinghe) contended that the state's proper role was to facilitate the National Council's deliberations and implement its programmes.

In spite of these differences, Alphand was not just being diplomatic when he said that his sub-committee's report 'does not present, in its broad principles, a fundamental divergence with the plan which has just been described [by Philip]'.[53] Everybody agreed that, in the reconstruction phase, the economy would have to be managed by the state and that this would necessitate central control over investment and, for a certain period at least, over prices. The main bone of contention was whether the national economic plan would be produced by the state or by economic actors themselves. Nobody seemed to doubt that there should be a plan.

The Resistance report that Philip presented to the London study commission exhibited the main characteristics of what was emerging as the Resistance's economic ideology—an ideology that was *dirigiste, planiste,* and socialist.[54] However, the more liberal approach of the Alphand sub-committee also had its supporters in the Resistance, the most influential of whom were in the Comité Général d'Études (CGE). The CGE's report on the post-Liberation economy was written in 1943 and was largely the work of a professor from Montpellier called René Courtin. It was a powerful statement of the neo-liberal thesis.[55]

Courtin's report acknowledged the abuses of a 'liberal' capitalism that had ceased to conform to the criteria of liberalism. He recommended the nationalization of sectors that had fallen under the control of monopolies, a reform of company law to limit multiple directorships and restore shareholder power, and state control over mergers. However, his solution to France's inevitable post-war economic crisis did not revolve around grandiose structural reforms. Instead, Courtin recommended that a re-construction plan should be drawn up by an Investment Council

[52] See the 'Rapport du Centre Syndical Français sur le texte communiqué par M. André Philip' (17 Sept. 1942); and 'Note du Commandant H. Bernard' (n.d.).
[53] Meeting of 25 Aug.   [54] See ch. 2 above.
[55] Kuisel, *Capitalism and the State*, pp. 167–73. Courtin's report was published clandestinely in France in November 1943 and reissued in Algiers in 1944. The edition used here is the Algiers one: *Rapport sur la politique économique d'apres-guerre.*

(attached to the Ministry of National Economy). The Council, which would consist of a handful of senior civil servants, would have the dual task of establishing an equipment plan for the public sector and, during the period of reconstruction, guiding investment in the private sector. Courtin envisaged that, in the longer term, the Council would retain only the first role (although it might also perform a counter-cyclical function in times of economic recession). Courtin was no *planiste*: his advocacy of planning applied only to the period immediately following liberation. In general, his clear preference was for a more flexible approach to economic management, in which financial and fiscal policy would be used to orient production and in which most direct controls over prices and production would be dropped.

Similar views were expressed in a work which, by comparison with Courtin's report, has gone virtually unnoticed by historians but which—in the opinion of one prominent resister and member of the CGE[56]—foreshadowed the post-war Monnet plan. *Politique d'abord* (published in 1943) was the work of Roger Langeron, a senior official who had been removed from the post of Prefect of Police in 1941. Langeron had been Prefect in the Nord in the era of reconstruction after the First World War. Drawing on his experiences two decades earlier, he offered what was soon to become a familiar analysis of the failures of inter-war policy. The core of his interpretation was that French policy had been led astray by an obsession with financial soundness and by a 'liberal' orthodoxy that had been espoused by an overwhelming majority within the political and economic élites. This orthodoxy, rejecting state intervention in the functioning of the domestic economy while welcoming—and indeed clamouring for—state protection of the domestic market, had cut short the hopes of those who had argued for the maintenance of wartime controls into peacetime.[57] The first lesson of the First World War's aftermath was that this time the state should resist the inevitable demands to withdraw from economic management. A second, equally important, lesson concerned the direction that state management should take. Quoting the unheeded warnings that Loucheur had given in 1919

---

[56] See Francisque Gay, *Les Démocrates d'inspiration chrétienne à l'épreuve du pouvoir* (Paris, 1951), 77.

[57] See Roger Langeron, *Politique d'abord: souvenirs et anticipations* (Paris, 1943), 42.

about the outdatedness of French industrial equipment, Langeron argued that the first priority of post-war economic policy—indeed of post-war policy *tout court*—should be the renovation of France's plant and equipment. A formidable array of obstacles would be certain to confront the state in its attempt to establish this 'économie d'équipement': a population eager to escape rationing and controls; a shortage of financial resources; the competition of other nations trying to re-equip; and a capitalist class keen to satisfy the sudden surge of domestic consumer demand rather than modernize to achieve international competitiveness. Langeron argued that only the state could impose the stringent discipline that would be required of both producers and consumers. He described modernization of France's industrial base as a 'super-politique', transcending all political and economic philosophies and justified by *raison d'état*.[58] Like Courtin, Langeron suggested that one could recognize the necessity of state intervention in the post-Liberation economy without necessarily opting for *dirigisme* in the long run. He shared Courtin's assessment of the need for a plan of reconstruction to channel investments into the sectors where they would be most productive. He also shared Courtin's suspicion of giving extensive planning powers to the producers themselves.

By the time that Courtin's and Langeron's work was published, the balance of power within what was now Fighting France favoured those who saw *dirigisme* as the Resistance mainstream did—as a means not merely of modernizing the economy but of socializing it. The study commission that André Philip appointed in Algiers in January 1944 to consider post-war economic policy was, on the whole, closer in tune with the Resistance mood than with the Courtin report. The commission included senior civil servants, syndicalists like Gazier and Louis Vallon, politicians like Jules Moch, and (to provide continuity with the London study commission) Hervé Alphand.[59] The commission's brief was twofold. In plenary sessions, it was to discuss the basic principles

---

[58] Ibid. 228.

[59] The records of the Algiers commission may be consulted in the Quai d'Orsay, *Guerre 1939–1945, Alger, CFLN–GPRF*, 686, 687. The commission is briefly discussed by Michel Margairaz, in 'La Mise en place de l'appareil de direction économique (1944–1947): des objectifs lointains aux choix du moment', paper presented to the colloquium *La France en voie de modernisation (1944–1952)* (Paris, 1981).

that were likely to govern the post-war economy. In sub-
committee, it was to consider particular problems that might
presént themselves in the immediate aftermath of liberation.
Philip identified four areas that required particular attention: the
administrative organization of economic policy-making; the organizations that would allocate resources and perform the functions of
the CO; the form that nationalization would take; and the
reorganization of the rural economy. Some of the largely technical
debates that took place in these sub-committees will be referred to
below.

The Algiers study commission did not publish a formal report of
its proceedings. The nearest to a public record was provided by
Philip in a lengthy paper entitled 'Les Réformes économiques de
structure'.[60] This gave both a personal view of the general
principles governing post-war reforms and a partial record of the
specific proposals made by the four sub-committees. Philip's
blueprint called for extensive industrial and agricultural modernization. It recommended Keynesian policies to maintain full
employment, socialization of all the key sectors of the economy, a
planned economy with a Ministry of Economy ('essentially the
Ministry of Planning'[61]) co-ordinating all economic activity.
Within the non-nationalized sector Philip distinguished two kinds
of company. Small businesses and artisan industries would be
restored to almost total liberty as soon as the immediate crisis had
passed. However, companies in important sectors such as steel,
dyes, and cement would continue under close governmental
supervision. This supervision would involve perpetuating industrial
groups like the CO, although in Philip's scheme the groups would
be run by a governmental official (the 'préfet professionnel') not
by representatives of the producers themselves.

As the study commission was holding its meetings and composing
its reports, the Provisional Government itself was focusing
increasingly on the question of the post-war economy. During the
second half of 1944 and most of 1945 de Gaulle's government
played the crucial role in shaping the debate about France's

---

[60] This paper was reprinted in *Études et Documents*, 1 (Mar.–Apr. 1945), 3–58.
An abridged version was printed in Algiers the year before in Philip's pamphlet
Les Réformes de structure (n.d. [1944]), pp. 2–13.
[61] 'Réformes économiques de structure', p. 50.

economic future. Before and after the Liberation there were many active study groups, but even the official ones like the Algiers commission had no real power or public presence. As for the political parties and Resistance movements, it was not until the general elections of October 1945 legitimated their mandate that their influence over the course of economic reform became significant.

The intra-governmental debate about post-war economic reconstruction was joined in the early months of 1944. Its main forum was a committee that de Gaulle established in April 1944 to co-ordinate the action of the various economic *commissariats*. Initially, the Comité Économique Interministériel (CEI) concentrated most of its energies on the practical problems that were certain to face the administration in the aftermath of liberation. But the meetings of the CEI also gave the Commissaire aux Finances, Pierre Mendès-France, an opportunity to unveil his proposals for post-Liberation reform. These proposals, which were first expressed to the Provisional Government in February 1944,[62] were to become the major point of reference in the government's debates about economic reform throughout the remaining months of 1944.

Mendès-France's reconstruction programme contained a number of elements, whose combination did not remain entirely stable between February 1944 and March 1945. The first component—at the beginning the essential one—was monetary rather than economic: Mendès-France argued that an immediate and drastic reduction in the money-supply (which had increased dramatically under the Occupation) was essential if France were to avoid an economically and socially debilitating inflation. This monetary argument was soon accompanied by the theme of *planification*, which had been implicit before the Liberation, but was made quite explicit in the autumn of 1944.[63] Mendès-France advocated a national economic plan which would synthesize a host of individual sectoral plans.[64] The priorities of this *plan d'ensemble* mirrored

[62] These proposals of Feb. 1944 (entitled 'Note sur les questions monétaires et financières (période immédiatement postérieure à la libération)') have been reprinted in Mendès-France, *Œuvres complètes*, pp. 561–72.
[63] Mendès described his programme to the government at its meeting of 17 Nov. 1944: see the 'Exposé au conseil des ministres sur le programme du ministère de l'économie nationale', *Œuvres complètes*, pp. 55–72.
[64] Letter of 22 June 1944, in *Œuvres complètes*, pp. 43–4.

those of the inter-war Soviet plans.[65] In a first stage of reconstruction national resources would be channelled towards machinery, industrial tools, heavy industry, and transportation. In a second stage the priority would shift to encompass semi-heavy industries and building. Only then, after these two phases, would attention be given to industries satisfying consumer needs. France faced a choice not merely between guns and butter, but between guns, butter, and reconstruction.[66] Mendès-France's commitment to *planification* reflected itself in his efforts to establish a strong planning organization within the government. In Algiers he lobbied for the insertion of Vichy's planning services (the DGEN) within his *commissariat*.[67] After the Liberation, newly appointed as Minister of National Economy, he argued—in terms similar to those of Philip's 1944 report—for a Ministry of National Economy that would have overall control of economic policy, prepare the plan, and supervise its execution.

A third element in Mendès-France's reform plan also emerged after the Liberation. In his November presentation to the Provisional Government he argued in favour of major national- izations (coal, electricity, banks, insurance, machine tools) both for political/psychological reasons and for technical reasons (to ensure a rational and well-co-ordinated reconstruction).[68] In the early months of 1945 he amplified this commitment to 'structural reforms', by lengthening the list of sectors to be nationalized (to include others such as air transport, merchant shipping, and steel) and by making the political/psychological rationale more explicit.[69] He argued that if the working class were going to accept the option of reconstruction before consumption, it was necessary for the government to show, via nationalizations and other structural reforms, that the sacrifices were benefiting the national interest rather than the capitalist interest.[70]

By the time that Mendès-France wrote his now famous memorandum of March 1945, in which he explained to his cabinet colleagues these views about the urgency of nationalization, he

---

[65] 'Exposé au conseil des ministres', p. 58.   [66] Ibid. 59.

[67] Margairaz, 'La Mise en place de l'appareil de direction économique', p. 4.

[68] *Œuvres complètes*, pp. 60–1.

[69] See the paper that he circulated to the members of the government at the end of March 1945: 'Les Réformes de structures: limites du secteur à nationaliser; ordre d'urgence', in *Œuvres complètes*, pp. 573–605.

[70] Ibid. 575.

was at odds with most of the other members of the government. In fact, the March memorandum has been interpreted as a last-ditch attempt to win over Communist support for a programme which he had been advocating in vain for more than a year.[71] Whatever his reasoning, the attempt was unsuccessful. Mendès-France was isolated from the rest of the government not just on one issue but on almost his entire programme. The dispute with the Minister of Finance, René Pleven, which precipitated Mendès-France's April 1945 resignation (over the severe measures that Mendès-France proposed to introduce to reduce the money-supply and freeze prices and wages) was the controversy that was made public. Behind the scenes, however, there had been constant opposition to his programme.[72] Several ministers, including the Socialist Minister of Industrial Production, Robert Lacoste, objected to his broad definition of the MEN's role. The liberal René Mayer described the proposal for the MEN that Mendès submitted to the CEI in October 1944 as 'a monstrosity'.[73] The MEN's campaign to nationalize banking was resisted by successive Finance Ministers, Lepercq and Pleven, and its plan for immediate nationalization of coal and electricity was opposed by Lacoste.

Mendès-France's resignation from the government (followed by the appointment of Pleven to head both the MEN and the Ministry of Finance) marked the end of the first governmental attempt to plan medium- or long-term renovation. In the second half of 1945 the issue of a planned modernization dropped down the government's agenda. The planners in the MEN, armed only with the power to allocate resources and monitor prices, were unable to look beyond the very short-term. But Mendès-France's departure and the declining interest in planning did not signify complacency in the government about the state of the economy. De Gaulle himself continued to set the tone, by proselytizing about the necessity of higher production and economic renewal. In a radio broadcast of 24 May 1945, for example, he stressed the link

[71] See Mioche, *Le Plan Monnet*, pp. 47–50.

[72] For a brief but incisive overview of this issue, see Jean Bouvier's book (co-written with François Bloch-Lainé), *La France restaurée* (Paris, 1986), 66–71. Mendès-France himself felt that the opposition of the Banque de France had been particularly decisive: see his bitter condemnation of the Bank's interference in the letter that he wrote to Pleven in April 1945 (repr. in *Œuvres complètes*, pp. 148–50). Mendès-France's opinion is supported by a well-placed observer, François Bloch-Lainé, in Bouvier and Bloch-Lainé, *La France restaurée*, p. 83.

[73] René Mayer, *Études, témoignages, documents* (Paris, 1983), 348.

between economic recovery and national power: '. . . it is no longer only our material ease, our standard of living, but our entire weight and role in the world which depend on our production. Yesterday there was no greater national duty than that of fighting. Today there is none greater than that of producing.'[74] In the first major speech that Pleven made in the Consultative Assembly after succeeding Mendès-France he sounded almost as resolute a modernizer and nationalizer as his predecessor:

The fundamental problem for the future of France is the necessity of modernizing . . . A great country, Great Britain, is in the process of educating its population about the economic necessities which it will have to confront in the future. It gives its people the slogan: 'export or die'. We could take as our slogan: 'modernize or die'. . . . Modernizing France's industrial equipment, modernizing her agricultural equipment is not only a technical problem, it is a psychological problem, a political problem, a moral problem. . . . if we want to modernize France, we must nationalize a certain number of industries and key sectors.[75]

The previous month Pleven had activated the Conseil de l'Économie Nationale that had been created in November 1944.[76] This council represented in some sense an intermediate stage between Mendès-France's philosophy of MEN-guided planning and the more consultative, non-bureaucratic approach that Monnet was to introduce six months later. Like the later Conseil du Plan and modernization commissions, the Council brought together leading members of the *patronat* (such as Ricard, Armand, and Fayolle) with senior trade-unionists (Gazier, Jouhaux, le Brun, Saillant, and Tessier).[77] To quote Pleven: 'For the first time since

[74] *Discours et messages, 1940–1946* (Paris, 1970), 554–5.
[75] *JO, Débats*, 4 July 1945, pp. 1311–12.
[76] See Mioche, *Le Plan Monnet*, p. 58.
[77] Gaston Cusin, 'Les Services de l'Économie Nationale, 1944–1948' (Communication à la réunion de la commission d'histoire économique et sociale, Comité d'Histoire de la Deuxième Guerre Mondiale, 12 Dec. 1977), 26. A copy of this paper is in AN, 72 AJ 383. An interesting wartime forerunner of the Council of National Economy was the Comité d'Études pour la France, which was created at the end of 1941. This committee included Sauvy, André Siegfried, and Auguste Detœuf as well as trade-unionists like Gazier, Saillant, and Tessier, and modernizers from Vichy's economic ministries. (Mioche, *Le Plan Monnet*, pp. 15–19.) Another forerunner was the Musée de l'Homme's Comité d'Etudes established by Paul Rivet at the end of 1944. This committee again included trade-unionists and representatives of the *patronat* in addition to economists and senior civil servants. Several people (Gazier, Boutteville, Sauvy, de Tarde) were members of both these study groups.

liberation, the heads of labour organizations, business leaders, and a few men chosen for their technical expertise are going to be able to sit round a table and get to grips with the great problems that affect the future of the French economy.'[78] The Council's starting-point—establishing an inventory of national resources—was to be the starting-point for Monnet and his team. Its general conclusions were also to be echoed by Monnet: on the one hand, 'Economically, France is in a situation of ageing, weakening, and impoverishment'; but, on the other, 'We can, on condition that we employ more modern methods, carry out an essential recovery.'[79] The Council also declared (as Monnet firmly believed) that France's re-equipment and reconstruction was inconceivable without a new American aid policy to replace lend-lease.[80]

The Council did not progress far beyond an inventory. It was not until Monnet returned from Washington in the autumn of 1945 and composed his recommendations for a plan of modernization that the government finally began to turn all the talk about a planned modernization into action.[81] Most of the ideas that Monnet submitted to de Gaulle at the beginning of December 1945 and reiterated in his report to the first Conseil du Plan in March 1946[82] were hardly new: French industrial equipment was far less modern than that of her major competitors; modernization had to be accompanied by increased productivity; a long-term plan was required to co-ordinate the allocation of resources to those areas where investment would be most beneficial; foreign aid would be needed to provide the capital for an investment drive; the entire nation would have to be mobilized behind the task of modernization. Even those aspects of Monnet's proposals which have often been regarded as innovatory and which Monnet himself memorialized as his 'method'[83] prove to have been modest innovations. The representative composition of the Conseil du

[78] *JO, Débats*, 4 July 1945, p. 1312.
[79] 'Communication de M. le ministre de l'Économie Nationale' (3 Sept. 1945), in AN, F60 901.
[80] The Council's inventory is contained in an appendix to Pleven's paper cited in n. 79.
[81] Monnet's memorandum (dated 4 Dec. 1945) was discussed and approved at a meeting of the CEI on 14 Dec. 1945. It was enforced by a decree of 3 Jan. 1946. The text of both the memorandum and the decree is reprinted by Mioche, in *Le Plan Monnet*, pp. 114–19.
[82] The reports of the 1946 meetings of the Conseil du Plan are in AN, 80 AJ 1.
[83] See Monnet, *Memoirs* (Garden City, NY, 1978), esp. 232–49.

Plan and the modernization commissions, which Monnet created in 1946, differed from the MEN's *étatiste* model. But, as Mioche was the first to point out, it had precedents in the Vichy period.[84] Similarly, the arrangement established by the decree of 3 January 1946, whereby the Commissariat au Plan reported directly to the head of the government, had been employed in the past, both in economic and non-economic areas. It had also been advocated as recently as September 1945 by a leading supporter of Mendès-France and critic of neo-liberalism, Georges Boris.[85] Finally, even Monnet's realization of the symbiotic link between a modernization programme and the negotiation of American credits has had to be re-evaluated. Monnet's belief that the Americans would finance reconstruction if it were presented to them in the right light (in the context of ultimate trade liberalization) was tenacious and prescient. But a recent study has suggested convincingly that the securing of American credits was not the original rationale for the plan, that the idea originated in the Quai d'Orsay, and that the government's initial objective was to increase the supply of coal and coke from the Ruhr.[86]

In all these respects the circumstances of the Monnet plan's creation have been thoroughly demythologized. Yet, notwith-standing all the precedents and contingencies that have been uncovered, it remains the case that the 'Propositions au sujet du plan de modernisation et d'équipement' that Monnet submitted to de Gaulle constituted a major moment—even, it may be argued, a turning-point—in the debate about France's economic future. The main focus of thought and debate between 1940 and 1945 had been on the extent, limitations, and methodology of the state's management of economic activity. The ends towards which economic activity should be organized had certainly been debated, but they had rarely been the primary consideration. In Monnet's

[84] 'Aux origines du Plan Monnet: les discours et contenus dans les premiers plans français (1941–1947)', *Revue historique*, 265 (1981), 416.

[85] Bouvier and Bloch-Lainé', *La France restaurée*, p. 121. It has been plausibly suggested that de Gaulle opted for this arrangement, not because he or Monnet saw its institutional advantages, but in order to prevent the *Commissariat* from falling under the authority of Communist ministers (Billoux in the Ministry of National Economy and Paul in the Ministry of Industrial Production). See Mioche, *Le Plan Monnet*, pp. 89, 91.

[86] This is the argument of the Ph.D. thesis of Frances Lynch, 'The Political and Economic Reconstruction of France, 1944–1947, in the International Context' (Manchester, 1981).

proposal this priority was reversed. It was striking that in the December proposals the word 'modernization' was used thirteen times before the word 'plan' appeared. The essence of Monnet's method was precisely that the method mattered less than the objective. Modernization was, of course, neither a new word nor a new concept. The innovation was not so much substantive as symbolic—a change of focus. It was a shrewd focus to adopt. Modernization was an apolitical term. It was the very opposite of what the National Revolution had seemed to stand for, but neither was it identified too closely with the Resistance or with any ideological position (in the way that *planisme* was). It tapped the aspirations for a new kind of society and dramatized the otherwise rather mundane economic imperatives of retooling and increased productivity. It appealed to the sentiment of national pride that was still in the air scarcely a year and a half after the Liberation. It may even be suggested that it appealed to a perennial French ethic of 'prowess':[87] in the years of post-war growth 'modernity' was to acquire the same kind of cachet—the same sense of being a worthwhile end in itself—that the concept of 'quality' had enjoyed in the pre-war economy.

At the same time as the Commissariat au Plan was being formed, the political debate about the economy was broadening beyond the confines of the government and its ministries. Before the Liberation, the Provisional Government had made the key decisions about post-war policy, with minimal consultation with the metropolitan Resistance or the Consultative Assembly in Algiers. Only on one occasion had the Consultative Assembly had the opportunity to hear the Commissaire à la Production Paul Giacobbi describe the government's economic policies.[88] After the Liberation, though the re-forming parties and the relics of the Resistance movements all had their views on economic reform and pressed them on the government, they were not in a position to influence the course of reform directly. The first full debate on economic policy did not take place in the Consultative Assembly until almost a year after the liberation of Paris.[89] In the summer

[87] For an interesting analysis of the cult of prowess in French society, see Jesse Pitts, 'Continuity and Change in Bourgeois France', in S. Hoffmann *et al.*, *In Search of France* (New York, 1965), 235–304.
[88] 21, 22 July 1944.   [89] 3, 4, 5 July 1945.

and autumn of 1945, however, the parties' economic programmes assumed a far greater prominence, as the election campaign propelled them into the limelight. The victors in the general elections of October 1945—the Communist party, the Socialist party, and the MRP—had pronounced ideas about economic reform, and during most of 1946 the programmes of these three parties dominated the public discussion of France's economic future. They overshadowed Monnet's *Commissariat* and the consultative modernization commissions, which went about their work relatively unobtrusively.

In the political arena the major issue between the Liberation and mid-1946 was not planning or modernization but national-ization.[90] Extensive public ownership had been the crux of the new economy that resisters had envisaged. It was the major economic demand that the new élites formulated in the autumn of 1944. By and large, the demand was to be satisfied in the period of the Consultative and Constituent Assemblies. In December 1944 the coal-mines of the Nord and Pas-de-Calais were nationalized by government ordinance (largely to avert the threat of social unrest in the mines). In January 1945 Renault was taken over (in a symbolic punishment of *patronat* collaboration). In March 1945 the Provisional Government agreed in principle that the nationalized sector should include banking and insurance, iron, steel and aluminium production, coal-mining, electricity, railways, air and sea transportation, and machine tools.[91] By the end of the First Constituent Assembly most (though by no means all) of these commitments had been honoured. The chronology was as follows: Gnome-et-Rhône (May 1945); air transportation (June 1945); the four major banks (December 1945); gas and electricity (April 1946); insurance (April 1946); and coal (May 1946). Since nationalization was the centre-piece of the political consensus throughout the post-Liberation era, the different forms in which it was expressed merit further analysis.

In an important speech at the Palais de Chaillot on 12 September 1944 (interpreted at the time as a 'discours-pro-

[90] The nationalizations of this era have been exhaustively discussed in Claire Andrieu, Lucette Le Van, Antoine Prost (eds.), *Les Nationalisations de la Libération: de l'utopie au compromis* (Paris, 1987).

[91] See the decisions adopted by the government on 9, 13, 16, and 20 Mar. 1945, which are reprinted in Mendès-France, *Œuvres complètes*, pp. 605–7.

gramme'), General de Gaulle pledged to abolish 'the coalitions of interests which have so weighed on the life of ordinary people and the policy of the state' and to ensure that 'the main sources of common wealth are worked and managed not for the profit of a few individuals, but for the benefit of all'.[92] Both before and after liberation, de Gaulle publicly attacked the trusts, in particular for undermining the power of the state. Though he nodded in the direction of social justice arguments, it was this threat that over-mighty capitalist interests posed to the state's independence and to its capacity to direct renewal that constituted, in his view, the main justification for an extension of public ownership. However, in spite of his public commitments (repeated in the Consultative Assembly in March 1945[93]), de Gaulle proved reluctant to carry out major nationalizations until elections had taken place. His delaying convinced many on the left that he was privately opposed to the principle. The evidence, on the whole, suggests otherwise. Apart from the fact that, before leaving office, he did authorize the preparation of nationalization bills for banks, electricity, gas, and coal, it is surely significant that he continued to endorse the post-Liberation nationalizations (with the partial exception of the Renault nationalization) long after he had entered into irreducible opposition to the Fourth Republic.

The other group which supported nationalizations while being suspected of having reservations about them was the MRP. At its founding congress in November 1944 the movement had said plainly that the most urgently needed structural reforms 'consist essentially of the nationalization of the large key industries'.[94] This priority was soon toned down: within three months an internal party document was describing nationalization as merely part of 'a comprehensive policy which must . . . nationalize—that is to say put at the disposal of the nation—the whole economy'.[95] Never-theless, the MRP's pro-nationalization position remained largely unchanged throughout 1945 and the first half of 1946. In a series of documents drafted between April 1945 and May 1946 the Christian Democrats advocated nationalization of banking and

---

[92] *Discours et messages, 1940–1946*, p. 450.
[93] Speech of 2 Mar. 1945, repr. ibid. 521–32.
[94] MRP, *Bâtir la France avec le peuple* (Paris, 1944), 7.
[95] 'Note sur les principes et thèmes du programme économique et social', p. 3, in AN, 350 AP 45.

insurance, gas, electricity, coal, petrol, railways, merchant shipping, steel, and fertilizers.[96] They identified five general categories of industry suitable for nationalization: public services; sectors essential to national reconstruction which would otherwise be unable to increase production in line with the nation's needs; important sectors which private enterprise had failed to develop; firms which threatened the independence of the state; and monopolies.[97] Though they did not deny a certain validity to the punitive and political arguments in favour of nationalization, MRP spokesmen tended to emphasize that the main justification for nationalization lay in the means it gave the state to modernize the economy.[98]

Other politicians gave more or less equal weight to political and economic rationales for nationalization. That had been the thrust of Mendès-France's March 1945 memorandum.[99] It was also the position of the Socialist party, which emerged in the autumn of 1944 as the staunchest advocate of nationalization. In November 1944 the Socialists' Extraordinary Congress listed 'energy, raw materials, heavy industry, transport, insurance, and credit' as prime candidates for nationalization—or 'socialization' as they preferred to call it. These rather vague categories were later defined by the party (in concert with the PCF) to include the following sectors: the major banks, insurance companies, electricity, gas, mining, steel-making, merchant shipping, light metal industries, cement, explosives.[100] In addition to this list the Socialist party's economic experts (notably Jules Moch and André Philip) advocated nationalization of several other sectors: bauxite mines, oil drilling, aluminium production, pharmaceuticals, and sugar refining.[101] The objective of these socializations was, first of all, to consummate a

---

[96] See a party brochure, *La Nationalisation* (Apr. 1945); a policy statement of Aug. 1945 entitled 'La Nationalisation', in AN, 350 AP 93; the 'Programme du Mouvement Républicain Populaire' (8 Nov. 1945), ibid. 1; and a memorandum of May 1946, 'Le MRP et les nationalisations (buts et limites)', ibid. 93.

[97] MRP, *La Nationalisation*, p. 7.

[98] See e.g. François de Menthon's speech in the First Constituent Assembly, *JO, Débats*, 2 Dec. 1945, p. 186; and the 'Note sur les principes et thèmes du programme économique et social' (Feb. 1945), in AN, 350 AP 45.

[99] *Œuvres complètes*, p. 575.

[100] See the *Programme Commun* of Nov. 1945 (signed by the SFIO, the PCF, the CGT, and the Ligue des Droits de l'Homme, and witnessed by the Radical party).

[101] The Socialist *discours* on nationalization has been analysed by Serge Berstein in Andrieu, Le Van, Prost, *Les Nationalisations de la Libération*, pp. 168–84.

political victory over the large capitalist interests (the 'trusts' or '200 families') which the party had traditionally identified as its enemy. One French historian has gone so far as to say that 'The fight against the trusts, for fundamental political reasons, constitutes the chief justification of nationalizations for the Socialists.'[102] This may be a slight exaggeration: the programme which is cited to support it was the joint text agreed with the PCF. In the writings of prominent Socialists like Philip and in the legislative proposals which the Socialist group submitted to the Consultative Assembly for socialization of coal-mining, electricity, insurance, and credit, economic motives were at least on a par with political ones.[103] Socialization was presented as a means of giving the state leverage over the economy in order to plan renovation. The party's bill to socialize the coal-mines argued, for example, that reconstruction could only be achieved satisfactorily if the state were able to control the supply and distribution of vital resources like coal.[104] In the 1946 debates over the various nationalization bills Socialist speakers reiterated this belief that socialization was essential to cope with the present economic emergency.[105] At the same time, surveying France's past economic record, Socialists pointed to a longer-term failure of French capitalism to develop the economy's potential. The theorists of socialization like Jules Moch led the assault on French capitalism's historical failure.[106]

The Communists' endorsement of nationalization came slightly later than that of the MRP or the SFIO. In the final months of 1944 the Communists concentrated on the theme of punishing the trusts rather than nationalizing them. In early 1945, however, as the PCF took on the mantle of the CNR's Common Programme, this non-committal attitude gave way to one of strong support for nationalization. At the beginning of February 1945 *L'Humanité* recognized explicitly that the commitment to the CNR Programme entailed nationalizations.[107] At the end of the same month PCF members of the Consultative Assembly formalized this commitment by

[102] Ibid. 177.
[103] For Philip's views, see *Les Réformes de structure*, p. 7. For the party's *propositions de loi*, see *JO, Documents*, 31 Mar. 1945, pp. 491–508.
[104] Ibid. 491.
[105] See e.g. Paul Béchard's speech in *JO, Débats*, 26 Mar. 1946, p. 1074.
[106] Moch, *Guerre aux trusts: solutions socialistes* (Paris, 1945), 15.
[107] See the report of Thorez's speech to militants from the Paris region, *L'Humanité*, 2 Feb. 1945; and Marcel Cachin's article on 4–5 Feb. 1945.

publishing a resolution which called on the government to nationalize the banks, insurance, electricity, steel, chemical industries, and merchant shipping.[108] As with the party's support for other reformist measures (such as the social security plan and the *comités d'entreprises*), its backing for nationalization reached a peak at the beginning of 1946, when a Communist minister (in this case, Marcel Paul at the Ministry of Industrial Production) was given the opportunity of drafting and introducing the relevant legislation. Though the Communists constantly emphasized that nationalization in a capitalist setting could only constitute a democratic or patriotic (not socialist) measure,[109] this often translated into an economic—and not just political—argument. There was a logical progression from the argument that the trusts had sabotaged the nation's economy to the position that nationalization of these trusts was essential to a programme of economic modernization. From a different starting-point, the PCF thereby reached a position similar to that of many modernizers. In the debate over nationalization of electricity, for example, the Communists argued that an increase in electrical generation (through greater use of hydroelectric plants) was essential if France's industry was to modernize, and that private companies could not be trusted to invest in modernization.[110] Similarly, in its proposal for nationalizing the banks (23 November 1945), the PCF linked public ownership to broader economic objectives: 'Reconstruction must lead to a new economy based on planning and orientation. . . . A plan of extremely urgent projects is necessary, but insufficient: it must be integrated into a general plan relating to the principal sectors of the economy.'[111] In both these cases the PCF's justification for nationalization seemed close to that which Mendès-France had defended some months before.

It should be noted that this consensus among the major political actors (which ensured that all the nationalization bills were passed by large margins) was also reflected outside the assembly. From the Liberation onwards the CGT invoked the precedent of its pre-

[108] *JO, Documents*, 28 Feb. 1945, pp. 435–7.
[109] See Jean-Jacques Becker, 'Le PCF', in Andrieu, Le Van, Prost, *Les Nationalisations de la Libération*, pp. 157–67.
[110] See e.g. Georges Cogniot, 'Pour développer la production hydroélectrique, nationalisation!', *L'Humanité*, 21 Feb. 1946, and Lucien Midol, 'Pourqoui faut-il nationaliser l'électricité?', *Cahiers du Communisme*, Feb. 1946, pp. 148–56.
[111] *JO, Documents*, 23 Nov. 1945, p. 29.

war plans and campaigned for immediate nationalization of banking, insurance, electricity, mining, and steel-making.[112] Within the press there was a general assumption of the necessity and beneficial effect of nationalization: writing in February 1945, the economist Gaëtan Pirou could point to only one newspaper article since the Liberation which had opposed nationalization.[113] This tolerance (if not always outright enthusiasm) extended to the ranks of professional economists: a recent study has found that, in a large sample of articles published in 1945 and 1946, fewer than 3 per cent were hostile to the policy.[114] It was scarcely surprising, therefore, that public opinion polls showed consistently large majorities in favour of nationalization throughout 1944 and 1945.[115]

Without this broad agreement about the necessity of a large nationalized sector the nationalizations of 1944–6 might very well not have occurred. There were plenty of factors to discourage or delay implementation of the Resistance's Common Programme in this area. Several important ministers (including the Minister of Industrial Production Lacoste) had reservations about the policy.[116] Legislation of this complexity could not be conjured instantaneously out of the vague commitments of Resistance programmes: in September 1944, for instance, Mendès-France was informed that neither the Ministry of National Economy nor the Ministry of Industrial Production could muster a single study or proposal relating to nationalization of the electrical industry.[117] There was also administrative foot-dragging among senior *fonctionnaires* suspicious of the idea,[118] not to mention the predictable hostility of the *patronat* and the Bank of France.[119] Finally, there were various political factors that held up the nationalizations. The most

[112] For a list of the CGT's demands, see *Le Peuple*, 3 Mar. 1945. For an analysis of the CGT's contribution to the post-war nationalizations, see the chapter by Alain Bergounioux, in Andrieu, Le Van, Prost, *Les Nationalisations de la Libération*, pp. 129–43.
[113] 'Le Problème des trois secteurs', *Revue d'économie politique*, 54 (1940–1944), 463 n.
[114] L. Le Van-Lemesle, 'Les Économistes officiels, experts ou politiques?', in Andrieu, Le Van, Prost, *Les Nationalisations de la Libération*, p. 213.
[115] See the analysis of Antoine Prost, ibid. 242.
[116] Ibid. 126, 197.
[117] 'Note pour M. le Ministre de l'Économie Nationale' (21 Sept. 1944), in AN, F12 10141.
[118] Andrieu, Le Van, Prost, *Les Nationalisations de la Libération*, p. 239.
[119] See Bouvier and Bloch-Lainé, *La France restaurée*, pp. 116–18.

important of these were General de Gaulle's reluctance to introduce major reforms before elections had been held ('fascistement', as he provocatively put it to the Socialist Daniel Mayer in February 1945[120]), and the Communists' initial reservations about nationalization. In spite of the fact that it took more than a year for these obstacles to be overcome, the momentum behind nationalization increased rather than decreased during 1945. The reason was the same as that which made it possible for Monnet to establish the Commissariat au Plan nine months after the cause of planning had apparently been defeated in the government. There was a convergence of quite different ideologies around the theme of nationalization, just as there was a convergence around the theme of planning.

The convergence was never free from ambiguity or strain. Each of the major parties had quite distinct views about the institutional form that nationalization should take, about the companies that were to be nationalized, and about the extent of compensation for shareholders. The diversity of opinions on such issues had first surfaced in the sub-committee that Philip had established in Algiers, to consider the structure of nationalized companies.[121] Before the Liberation these questions seemed technical and were largely confined to such study groups. But after the Liberation they became highly politicized, as the parties sought to differentiate their conceptions of nationalization and as the political stakes rose. It would be impossible to retrace here the complex political infighting that attended the passage of the nationalization laws of 1945–6. But it should at least be noted that the disagreements between the parties reflected both short-term power struggles and deeper ideological differences.[122] In 1946 the PCF's stance was clearly influenced by its desire to build up Communist control within key nationalized industries (just as the MRP's and the SFIO's attitudes were coloured by their perception of a Communist takeover). Ideologically, it is obvious that the idea of nationalization was not equally central to all parties. Socialists such as Moch and Philip saw 'socialization' as essential to their vision of a

---

[120] Minutes of the SFIO's Comité Directeur, 6 Feb. 1945.

[121] 'Sous-commission d'étude de la structure des sociétés de services publics: séance du 4 mai 1944', in MAE, *Guerre 1939–1945 . . .*, 686.

[122] This point is well made by Bouvier, in Bouvier and Bloch-Lainé, *La France restaurée*, pp. 115–16.

planned, socialized economy, whereas the MRP and the PCF viewed it more as a circumstantial measure (necessary to aid the war effort or economic reconstruction). Nationalization was not, however, an integral feature of Christian Democratic or Communist ideology. This fact may help to explain why the momentum for further nationalizations slipped away so abruptly in mid-1946, once the promises of the CNR's Common Programme ('the return to the nation of the great monopolized means of production . . . sources of energy, underground resources, insurance companies, and major banks') had been, broadly speaking, satisfied. As Antoine Prost has rightly suggested, the nationalizations of 1944–6 belong in the same category of reform as the *comités d'entreprises* and the social security plan of October 1945.[123] They were part of the sacred legacy that the new élites carried with them from the Resistance. Speaking in the First Constituent Assembly's debate over the nationalization of insurance, René Pleven (no longer a minister) explained his support for the bill as follows: 'We will vote for the bill because . . . we have all been elected on the programme of the CNR. At a decisive moment for the nation, this programme has been a pact . . . sacred among all those, whatever their political shade, who belonged to the Resistance.'[124] Like other reforms inherited from the CNR programme, nationalization bore the weight of immense initial expectations—as to its destructive impact on capitalism and its beneficial impact on the working class. It proved to be another reform whose effects were less dramatic than anticipated and which left a bitter after-taste for many of its proponents. But—again like the social security plan and the *comités d'entreprises*—its impact was far from negligible. The nationalizations did not bring about the fall of the socio-economic Bastilles which resisters had anticipated, but, for better or worse, they did significantly extend the economic power of the state.

[123] Andrieu, Le Van, Prost, *Les Nationalisations de la Libération*, p. 246.
[124] *JO, Débats*, 23 Apr. 1946, p. 2146.

11

The New Economy II: Issues

THE rethinking of the French economy between 1940 and 1946 revolved around two basic issues. The first was the issue of renovation. How outdated was the French economy? What had caused its decline? What would be needed to reverse the trend? A second issue was raised by the first. In the Vichy ministries, in the Free French *commissariats*, in the Resistance, in the post-Liberation assemblies, governments, and parties, the assumption was that only the state could counteract decline. But this assumption of state intervention raised questions as well as answering them. What techniques should the state use to direct the economy? What would be the effect of these new techniques on political and governmental institutions? What would be the role of economic planning, of nationalization, of corporatist-type organizations? How could *dirigisme* be reconciled with political and social democracy? Was *dirigisme* a short-term expedient or a permanent necessity?

On his return to France in 1945, Monnet looked at the statistics of French economic performance and recognized what he later termed 'the slow and regular decline of our economy' during the twentieth century.[1] It was this economic retardation, he argued, that was France's fundamental problem. 'Fierce controversies about the neglect of spiritual values in recent years, and the ardent professions of faith in the future made by the country's new leaders'[2] were beside the point. Aided by statisticians and economists like Alfred Sauvy and Jean Fourastié, Monnet was able to gain a clear picture of the low level of pre-war productivity and its underlying cause in low levels of investment. However, the implicit contrast which Monnet draws in his memoirs between a political and bureaucratic establishment blind to the reality of long-term retardation and a small band of clear-sighted economists does not do justice to the Resistance or to post-war political élites.

[1] Monnet, *Memoirs* (Garden City, NY, 1978), 232.
[2] Ibid.

Resisters obviously did not have access to precise statistics, but they were well aware of the French economy's long-term crisis. André Philip's 1944 report, for example, stated flatly that 'in 1940 French industry was far overtaken in the major sectors by its foreign competitors. It had lost the sense of risk and creativity.'[3] From a liberal perspective Michel Debré and Emmanuel Monick reached an identical conclusion: 'for half a century everyone in France has acted instinctively as though differences in the levels of the various sectors of the economy had to be reabsorbed not by a wave of expansion, which evens everything up like a flood tide, but by making the most advanced industries fall back'.[4] In the Consultative Assembly in Algiers Georges Buisson, chairman of the social and economic affairs committee, declared: 'At the moment when the country will have to regroup its forces to assure its livelihood and its future, we will have to speak frankly to it and stop promoting the long-established habits in which our economy was mired. Vichy's policy of return to the land and regression to craft production will have to be abandoned. . . . on the contrary, the country will have to move towards a systematic industrialization'.[5]

Resisters concentrated their attention in particular on the poor economic performance of the 1930s and on the deficiencies of the inter-war state's economic strategy. René Courtin argued that all the governments since 1930 had checked economic activity: governments of the right by their deflationary economic creed, the Popular Front by its insistence on lowering the working week to 40 hours, and Vichy 'by developing the anachronistic myth of a return to medieval corporatism'.[6] Resisters noted how the pre-war regime's protectionism had cut off the stimulus of foreign competition. A Resistance memorandum of 1943 (entitled 'The French Economy of Tomorrow') argued that: 'France must think today on a global scale and not on the scale of eighty-six departments, because it is that economic and intellectual contraction which, in large measure, was responsible for our collapse.'[7] Another theme that was voiced on all sides after 1940 was criticism

---

[3] 'Réformes économiques de structure', *Études et documents*, 1 (1945), 5.
[4] Jacquier-Bruère, *Refaire la France* (Paris, 1945), 45–6.
[5] *JO*, 21 July 1944, p. 206.
[6] *Rapport sur la politique économique d'après-guerre* (Algiers, 1944), 28.
[7] A copy of this document may be found in AN, F1a 3791.

of inter-war governments for sacrificing economic policy to financial orthodoxy. This argument was made with particular force by a former Third Republic minister, Jean Zay. On 17 January 1941 Zay wrote in his prison diary:

When people study the causes of our military unpreparedness and of the decrepitude in parliamentary government, as it functioned in the past few years, they will have to place the financial orthodoxy high on the list.

From 1932 to 1940 . . . one subject was 'taboo': monetary and financial liberalism. . . .

You could cover the head of state and his ministers with dirt. . . . Bravo! Fair enough . . . But you were forbidden to criticize the mystique of the balanced budget, under pain of being considered a traitor . . .[8]

Zay's belief that the cause of economic reform had been crippled by an obsession with balanced budgets became one of the axioms of the new leadership in 1944. From all sides the financial mystique was assailed. A Socialist minister in the Provisional Government suggested that the necessity of eradicating it was the best justification for a Ministry of National Economy.[9] Christian Democrats publicly insisted that there was nothing sacrosanct about balanced budgets and that financial or monetary concerns had to be placed in the larger context of economic performance.[10] The CGT's economic commentator, Jean Duret, attacked the Inspection des Finances and the economic establishment for failing to learn the lessons of Keynesianism and clinging to a discredited ideology.[11] Though the parties of the left (and even, in its early stages, the MRP) often turned this critique of an ideology into a critique of the élite that had subscribed to it, the evidence suggests that even in the bastions of orthodoxy the lessons of inter-war failure were being interpreted in a similar way.[12] This questioning of pre-war attitudes should not be construed as a full-scale

[8] Zay, *Souvenirs et solitude* (Paris, 1946), 41.

[9] See a letter from Tanguy-Prigent to Mendès-France, in AN, F12 10142.

[10] See e.g. a speech by François de Menthon to the MRP's National Council, Mar. 1946, in AN, 350 AP 57. Similar sentiments were expressed by the party's financial experts (André, Debray, Barangé, Buron) at the Second National Congress in Dec. 1945, ibid. 14.

[11] See Duret's articles in *Le Peuple*, 17 Mar. 1945 and 14 Apr. 1945.

[12] On the changing views of the financial establishment, see Michel Margairaz, 'Direction et directeurs du Trésor: de l'orthodoxie à la réforme (1930–1950)', in P. Fridenson and A. Straus (eds.), *Le Capitalisme français 19ᵉ–20ᵉ siècle: blocages et dynamismes d'une croissance* (Paris, 1987), 47–65.

intellectual realignment: it did not mean that French political and economic élites had been converted *en masse* to Keynesianism. But it did reflect the new priorities of the post-Liberation era, in particular the absolute priority attached to economic reconstruction and expansion.

A further criticism of pre-war policy focused on the failure of French industry to keep pace with the most modern equipment and machinery. In January 1945 an official publication of the Provisional Government noted that 'French industry suffers . . . from obsolescent equipment, which . . . even before the war no longer met production needs because of its old age.'[13] In 1938, this study stated, the average age of French machine tools had been nineteen years, compared with seven in Germany, six in Italy, and three in the United States. Such comparative backwardness, compounded by war years in which virtually no modern equipment had been installed, called for 'a general modernization of our machine tools'. This concern can be traced back to Mendès-France's presentation to his fellow ministers in November 1944 ('We shall have to make a particular effort to give France a machine tool industry which she has never hitherto had'[14]) and, further back still, to the reports of the DGEN[15], as well as forward to Monnet's December 1945 memorandum. The theme was also picked up by the parties. The MRP's party pamphlets reproduced more or less the same productivity figures used by Monnet and the Provisional Government to dramatize France's plight: each French farmer feeds five people, while his American counterpart feeds fifteen; the average age of French industrial equipment is twenty-five years, while that of British machines is seven, and that of American machines five.[16] Concern about outdated equipment was expressed with particular force by the Communists (whose productivism was not quite as simplistic as some have suggested).[17] In January 1945 Jacques Duclos lamented the fact that 'In 1931,

[13] Ministère de l'Information, 'Les Besoins de la France en machines-outils', *Notes Documentaires et Études*, 31 Jan. 1945.

[14] 'Exposé au conseil des ministres sur le programme du ministère de l'économie nationale', in Mendès-France, *Œuvres complètes*, ii. *Une politique de l'économie, 1943–1954* (Paris, 1985), 58.

[15] See the 'Plan d'Équipement National: Tranche de Démarrage', 36–7, in AN, F60 659.

[16] 'Les Objectifs économiques de la France' (May 1946), ibid. 350 AP 93.

[17] See e.g. G. Elgey, *La République des illusions* (Paris, 1965), 29; Richard Kuisel, *Capitalism and the State in Modern France* (Cambridge, 1981), 190.

out of a total of 15,411,000 people employed in various productive activities, only 938,000 (that is to say, around 6 per cent) worked in the manufacturing of capital goods.'[18] The party recognized that hard work and long hours were necessary but not sufficient to increase productivity. To quote Maurice Thorez (speaking to the party congress in 1945): 'To become a great and independent industrial power, France must manufacture machine tools.'[19]

In a general sense, it did not take Monnet to tell the Provisional Government that France's economy was in relative decline. In mid-1945 the Conseil de l'Économie Nationale, using the services of the MEN's *direction de la documentation et des études économiques,* identified a picture of economic 'ageing, weakening, and impoverishment'.[20] A couple of days before Monnet sent his memorandum to de Gaulle, the Minister of Finance Pleven told the newly elected Constituent Assembly: 'The French people have understood . . . that the economic and financial framework in which it lived no longer corresponded to the needs of this century.'[21] Introducing the government's bill to nationalize the major banks, Pleven linked the nationalization to a patriotic imperative, 'which consists in modernizing our productive plant, surpassing old results, and adapting French manufacturing processes to scientific advances'.[22] The members of the three parties which made up the majority of Pleven's audience agreed with this diagnosis of a seriously outmoded economy and with the prescription of a thorough modernization.

Modernization was something that it was easy for politicians to advocate in non-specific terms. But it also raised practical implications that were more difficult to avow. For example, many modernizers identified the small scale of French firms as an important contributing factor in the inter-war uncompetitiveness. When André Philip, demanding a systematic industrialization and rationalization of the economy, told the Consultative Assembly that: 'We must go beyond the stage of the small cottage industry, to which France has perhaps remained too attached up to now,'[23] there were shouts of 'très bien'. Outside Paris, however, the

[18] Duclos, *Le Chemin de la renaissance française* (Paris, 1945), 10–11.
[19] *L'Humanité*, 27 June 1945.
[20] See above, ch. 10.
[21] *JO, Débats*, 2 Dec. 1945, p. 158.
[22] Ibid. 159.   [23] Ibid. 25 July 1945, p. 1463.

suggestion that modernization might mean fewer artisans or small companies was politically suicidal. The Communist party was particularly adept at exploiting popular resentment at the big business 'modernizers' in the Organization Committees and any others whom it could tar with the same brush. A typical Communist party pamphlet (from 1945) alleged that 'vichyite' bureaucrats in the Ministry of Industrial Production were writing circulars suggesting that 'the present . . . situation necessitates a reduction in the number of commercial enterprises'.[24] The PCF met head-on the objections of economic modernizers like Philip, who criticized the Communists' support of 'uneconomic' producers. Before a large meeting of shopkeepers and artisans Duclos cited Philip's remarks chapter and verse and declared that the party was proud to be accused of a 'sentimental attachment to all that is small against all that is big!'[25]

The dilemma of those who faced the modernization issue squarely was even more difficult when it came to the future of French agriculture. The low productivity of inter-war agriculture was a fact frequently acknowledged by resisters and post-Liberation politicians (with or without figures to back up their arguments).[26] The CFLN's 1944 study commission and its agricultural sub-committee concluded that French agriculture was characterized by five features: diversity of crops and lack of regional specialization; inefficient production methods; the predominance of family farms; a chronic dependence on government protection; and a lack of rational professional organization.[27] The committee made scathing criticisms of pre-war government policy, which it accused of encouraging French agriculture to remain in a stationary position while much of the rest of the world modernized.[28] It established a simple but radical goal for post-war policy: 'To extract from the soil of France and of her empire the maximum amount of produce with the minimum amount of

---

[24] 'Le Parti Communiste défend la propriété', in BN, *Tracts de propagande du PC*, no. 35.

[25] *L'Humanité*, 16 Oct. 1945.

[26] For some statistics, see a speech given by Jean Bourgoin in the debate on economic policy, *JO, Débats*, 4 July 1945, pp. 1306–8.

[27] 'Vues sur la réorganisation de l'agriculture française' (9 June 1944), in Ministère des Affaires Étrangères (MAE), *Guerre 1939–1945, Alger CFLN–GPRF*, 687.

[28] Commission d'études des problèmes économiques d'après-guerre, 'L'Agriculture' (3 July 1944), MAE, *Guerre 1939–1945 . . .*, 687.

264 Themes of Renewal

labour'.[29] Those who thought at all deeply about this issue recognized, like the commission, that modernization would involve a reduction in the manpower employed in agriculture. In the CGE report Courtin observed: 'In all modern societies the reduction of the importance of agriculture relative to the sum of economic activity must be considered the consequence of the raising of the population's living standard and the increase in productivity.'[30] Philip stated this even more bluntly: 'Rural depopulation, which so many well-meaning people lament, is . . . the very indication of the extent of progress made by agricultural methods.'[31] Modernizers like Philip and Courtin agreed that the state had to take the lead in setting the process of modernization (therefore the *exode rural*) in motion. Sounding remarkably like a neo-liberal, Philip recommended that 'The excessive agricultural protectionism of these last years will have to be abandoned and the only products which will survive will have to be those in which France performs respectably in comparison with other nations.'[32] In London a member of Free France, M. Istel, had proposed the same course: 'we must prepare, through the gradual elimination of tariff protection, the abandonment of uneconomic forms of [agricultural] production'.[33]

Those who advocated such a change in government strategy— from a policy that sheltered a large, inefficient agriculture to one which not only encouraged modernization of methods and organization but, by removing tariff protection, virtually compelled it—were aware of its heretical implications. It was not simply a matter of the large rural population and its political lobby that would be bound to take umbrage at plans to rationalize production and open up competition with more efficient foreign producers. The idea of encouraging an *exode rural* went against the grain of French politics. There was a very widely held assumption (not merely on the right) that the large rural population was an invaluable source of social stability. Even the CFLN's study committee in Algiers admitted that the small family farms represented 'an undeniable social stability'.[34] If convinced mod-

[29] Commission d'études des problèmes économiques d'après-guerre, 'L'Agriculture' (3 July 1944), MAE, *Guerre 1939–1945* . . ., 3.
[30] *Rapport sur la politique économique*, p. 39.
[31] *Les Réformes de structure* (Algiers, n.d. [1944]), 3.   [32] Ibid.
[33] 'Rapport présenté par M. Istel' (7 Mar. 1942), in AN, F1a 3734.
[34] 'Vues sur la réorganisation', p. 2.

ernizers could see the attractions of the rural population's
stabilizing role, it was scarcely surprising that pragmatic politicians
played down the issue of an *exode rural*. Rather than suggesting
that modernization would entail reductions in the rural population,
politicians implied the opposite. Here again the Communist
discours offers as clear an illustration as any. The party acknowledged that 'what characterized pre-war France was the weakness
of the rural sector in our national economy'.[35] The main
spokesman on agricultural issues, Waldeck Rochet, proposed a
range of measures to remedy this situation. In order to raise
productivity from its low pre-war rates, he suggested mechanization,
modernization of rural regions (through electrification and better
water-supply), educational reforms, and a variety of other
measures.[36] On the other hand, the party treated the large rural
population as something which had to be preserved and never as
itself an obstacle to modernization. The other parties followed
suit. To quote Socialist party candidates in the election of October
1945, economic modernization would '*preserve* the magnificent
balance of our economy'.[37]

This was also the pattern of government action. Both under
Vichy and in the post-Liberation governments (in which the
socialist François Tanguy-Prigent was Minister of Agriculture for
an uninterrupted term between 1944 and 1947), significant reforms
were introduced. But the creation of agricultural associations, the
provision of modern machinery, the rationalization of crops, and
the consolidation of subdivided holdings were not intended to
change France's small peasant base.[38] The limits of what might be
called conservative rationalization—an attitude which dominated
the political debate about the future of agriculture throughout the

[35] Duclos, *Le Chemin de la renaissance française*, p. 13.
[36] *L'Humanité*, 3–4 Dec. 1944, 30 June 1945.
[37] BN, *Recueil de tracts électoraux, listes, programmes . . . Elections générales, 21
octobre 1945*, department of the Aisne (my emphasis). For a similar view expressed
by the MRP, see F. de Menthon, *Notre politique économique* (Paris, 1946), 10–12.
De Menthon described the aim of the MRP's economic policy as being the
preservation of 'la structure traditionnelle mi-partie paysanne, mi-partie urbaine et
industrielle de notre pays'.
[38] On Vichy's agricultural policy, see Isabel Boussard's book, *Vichy et la
Corporation Paysanne* (Paris, 1980); and her article, 'Principaux aspects de la
politique agricole française pendant la deuxième guerre mondiale', *Revue d'histoire
de la Deuxième Guerre Mondiale*, 134 (1984), 1–25. On the post-Liberation years,
see Gordon Wright, *Rural Revolution in France: The Peasantry in the Twentieth
Century* (Stanford, 1964), 95–113.

period 1940–6—were succinctly expressed by a senior official of Vichy's Corporation Paysanne: 'It would . . . be simply absurd to want to align our country on Russia or the United States, in respect of our mode of production or cultivation. . . . if we want to throw ourselves into a competition in volume against countries ten, twenty, or one hundred times larger than ourselves, we will very quickly be eliminated from the world map'.[39]

In his history of French planning, Kuisel distinguishes two groups of people whose influence was particularly significant: the neo-liberals (represented by people like Alphand, Courtin, Monnet, and some of the Vichy modernizers) who wanted to renovate the economy by opening it up to international competition and keeping the domestic intervention of the state to a minimum (although a significant minimum); and the socialist—or at any rate *dirigiste*—planners (men such as Philip, Moch, Boris, and Mendès-France) who believed that the state had to intervene at every level of economic activity in order to break long-established and pernicious habits of 'malthusian' liberal capitalism. In the broader perspective of French politics these groups were really on the same side. Both sides were modernizers, in the sense that they all tended to regard the creation of a modern, efficient, and competitive economy as *the* national priority. Neo-liberals and socialists alike insisted that the renewal of the productive potential of French industry had to come before the satisfaction of other needs (apart from the most basic consumer needs). That was what Mendès-France meant in November 1944, when he told the Council of Ministers that the nation should choose *rééquipement* rather than guns or butter.[40] The same argument was made by Philip: 'to the extent that we will be able to do it, we will have to import not the manufactured products that we need, but raw materials and equipment'.[41] It was made by the Communists in their stakhanovite phase,[42] and by the progressive Centre des Jeunes Patrons.[43] This priority of long-term over short-term needs

---

[39] Adolphe Pointier, quoted by Boussard, *Vichy*, pp. 322–3. For another formulation of Vichy's agricultural reformism (involving modernization and rationalization but explicitly protecting the large rural population), see the study prepared for the DGEN by Robert Préaud: *Sur la politique agricole et rurale de la France* (Paris, 1944).

[40] *Œuvres complètes*, p. 59.

[41] *JO, Débats*, 25 July 1945, p. 1464.

[42] e.g. *L'Humanité*, 5 Feb. 1946.   [43] CJP, *Une étape* (Paris, 1945), 23.

and of modernization over reconstruction was emphatically endorsed by Monnet.[44]

The number of post-Liberation politicians who held uncompromisingly modernizing (or, for that matter, anti-modernizing) views was relatively small. The majority in the post-Liberation assemblies were aware of the economic retardation that France had experienced and sympathetic to the argument that modernization was essential to national independence and security. On the other hand, as politicians, they all had their own ideologies, interests, and constituencies. What distinguished them from people like Monnet or Mendès-France was that they had other priorities to balance against the imperative of modernization.

For the parties of the left, for example, there was the potentially conflicting priority of working-class interests. The policy of subordinating imports of consumer goods to imports of industrial equipment was bound to encounter reservations from those who represented the people most likely to be hit by the short supply of such goods. These reservations were expressed at the end of 1945 by the Socialist deputy Christian Pineau:

I understand full well that all the experts in the departments of national economy and finance are agreed in asking that we import as many capital goods as possible, goods which are intended to increase our industrial and agricultural capacity, and as few consumer goods as possible.

I think . . . that it would be appropriate to fix a limit to this policy. Industrial equipment and raw materials are not the only elements which influence a country's production; human labour is the most important of all.[45]

At this stage and during the early months of 1946 the Socialists were willing to accept the bitter medicine of investment before consumption. By mid-1946, however, their reservations (fuelled by their intense rivalry with the PCF) produced acrimonious disputes on the left about the wisdom of fighting a 'battle for production' within a still capitalist economy.[46] For the PCF the

---

[44] See Philippe Mioche, *Le Plan Monnet: genèse et élaboration, 1941–1947* (Paris, 1987), 154–5.

[45] *JO, Débats*, 26 Dec. 1945, p. 376.

[46] On these disputes, see Annie Lacroix-Riz, 'CGT et "Bataille de la Production" après la Libération (Septembre 1944–Novembre, Décembre 1947)', paper presented to the colloquium *La France en voie de modernisation (1944–1952)* (Paris, 1981).

theme of modernization was an effective method of perpetuating the patriotic aura which the 'parti des 75,000 fusillés' had won through its Resistance activity, while condemning 'malthusian' trusts, and basking in the reflected glory of Soviet economic achievements. In the political short term it brought kudos to the party (through its ministerial responsibilities). In the strategic long term it seemed the most effective way of preventing US economic power from 'colonizing' a weakened French economy. However, as the party never tired of stressing, structural reform did not mean socialism. This was a way of saying that the commitment to reformism (including the commitment to modernizing French industry) was, by its very nature, transitory. Once the party's general strategy began to change (in response to domestic and international polarization), the priority that the PCF attached to modernization was bound to decline.

A different kind of tension existed for de Gaulle. To go back to Mendès-France's expression, de Gaulle was unable to make an unconditional choice between reconstruction and guns. As early as July 1945 André Philip had raised the possibility of a conflict between economic modernization and gaullist *grandeur* (typified by the heavy commitment of resources that de Gaulle made to the army between the Liberation and the end of the war):

Should we not raise a cry of alarm over a policy of prestige in military as well as in foreign affairs. . . . For several months we have been witnessing too many troop inspections, military reviews, flashy and superficial displays aiming to create illusions about our strength and not corresponding to the actual reality. . . . It did us no good in 1940 to have five million men under arms. . . . It is . . . industrial power that we must build up first of all . . .[47]

Philip's criticism was to be voiced again at the end of December 1945, when the PS's attempt to trim the military budget almost caused de Gaulle's resignation. Though obviously partisan, Philip's arguments contained a grain of truth. De Gaulle accepted the diagnosis of economic backwardness and may well have recognized that the demands of reconstruction would necessitate reductions in defence expenditure. He himself was instrumental in launching the 'battle for production' (for example in his 24 May 1945 radio broadcast).[48] Throughout his period at the head of the Provisional

[47] *JO, Débats*, 25 July 1945, p. 1463.
[48] *Discours et messages, 1940–1946* (Paris, 1970), 553–7.

Government he stressed the connection between economic power and national power. But it is doubtful that de Gaulle would ever have accepted that economic modernization was the sufficient, as well as necessary, condition of national greatness (as, from their different perspectives, Monnet and Philip regarded it). His argument before and during the war was that what Socialists scornfully called the 'politics of bluster'[49]—an independent and ambitious foreign policy—was essential if France was to retain the ability to act as a great power. His argument during the long years of opposition under the Fourth Republic was that only a renovated state would know how to employ the benefits of a modernized economy.

The general view after 1940 was that, like the Third Republic, economic liberalism had not been killed by the war but had committed suicide. For many years the 'liberal' state had been intervening surreptitiously in the economy. It was generally agreed that for the foreseeable future France would be unable to return to an almost mythical liberalism and that the state would have to face up to its economic responsibilities by formulating a proper policy. In the short term at least (while the domestic economy remained weak and the international system unstable), this economic policy would have to be a *dirigiste* one. In 1942 Alphand's sub-committee had predicted that the state would continue to intervene after the war 'to maintain a level of trading activity which assures full employment for all workers, and, in accordance with an international plan, to stimulate the development of economic activities for which France and her empire are most suited'.[50] Though doubtful about the wisdom of *dirigisme* in the longer term, Courtin's report acknowledged that, during the period of reconstruction, 'An authoritative direction must be imposed on the economy in order for France to recover her power and wealth.'[51] From more pro-*dirigiste* positions, Philip told his 1944 study commission that 'everyone knows that, in the aftermath of war, the French

---

[49] Christian Pineau, as quoted by Robert Frank, 'The French Dilemma: Modernization with Dependence or Independence and Decline', in Josef Becker and Franz Knipping (eds.), *Power in Europe?* (Berlin and New York, 1986), 265.
[50] 'Problèmes économiques d'après-guerre: un point de vue français', 11, in AN, 72 AJ 546.
[51] *Rapport sur la politique économique*, p. 8.

economy will be managed'[52] and Mendès-France told the CFLN's Commissaire à l'Information that 'The impoverishment of the country, the decay of equipment, the general will to carry out a great recovery, all that inevitably necessitates a managed economy.'[53] Irrespective of ideological considerations, *dirigisme* appeared to be dictated by the situation of the economy in 1944. In the immediate future there was the certainty that shortages of all kinds would continue and would require government action to allocate and ration resources. In the slightly longer term the idea of trying to compete, without any central direction, with nations which had recently modernized and expanded their economies seemed a recipe for further disaster. *Dirigisme* was a course that all the world's great powers had followed during the war. It seemed to be the wave of the future: as one commentator wrote in January 1945, 'The success in the war of those countries which were able to organize their economy most rigorously appeared a guarantee of this method's success in peacetime.'[54]

At home, however, *dirigisme* was primarily associated with the Vichy regime. It was associated, in other words, not with a successful war effort, but with occupation and organized repression. After the Liberation it became politically essential for governments to relax—or appear to relax—regulation of the economy. If *dirigisme* was presumed to be unavoidable, it was also presumed that it would not be all-pervasive.

Consequently, the advocates of post-war *dirigisme* began by dividing up the economy into those areas where the state would intervene and those areas where it would not. In certain projects the economy was simply divided into two: the Resistance movement Défense de la France, for instance, suggested a 'secteur dirigé' and a 'secteur libre'.[55] More often it was assumed that three sectors would be created. Albert Gazier called them the 'secteur nationalisé', the 'secteur dirigé', and the 'secteur libre',[56] as did

[52] 'Procès-verbal de la séance du 6 avril [1944]', in MAE, *Guerre 1939–1945 . . .*, 686.

[53] 'Note au Commissaire à l'Information sur la propagande en direction de la France' (1 Apr. 1944), in *Œuvres complètes*, p. 40.

[54] Fernand-Charles Jeantet, 'Des comités d'organisation aux offices professionnels', *Droit Social*, 8 (Jan. 1945), 6.

[55] Défense de la France, 'La Politique économique d'après-guerre', in AN, 72 AJ 564.

[56] 'Sous-commission d'étude de l'organisation professionnelle: séance du 5 mai 1944', in MAE, *Guerre 1939–1945 . . .*, 686.

Paul Giacobbi (speaking for the GPRF)[57]. Others (like a study group set up by Professor Paul Rivet at the Musée de l'Homme,[58] the Minister of National Economy Mendès-France,[59] and the economist Gaëtan Pirou[60]) preferred to call the second sector the 'secteur contrôlé', while Louis Vallon labelled it the 'secteur coordonné'.[61] As Henri Noyelle noted in his influential book *Révolution politique et révolution économique* (1945), this tripartite division was, in any case, rather artificial.[62]

Whatever the nomenclature or the number of sectors, the substance of the argument remained fairly constant. First, there was a general consensus that the state would have to take certain industries into public ownership. Both the Free French study commissions assumed that nationalizations would occur, as did the Resistance movements (including Courtin and the CGE), the pre- and post-Liberation Provisional Governments, and all the main post-Liberation parties. Mirroring the consensus about national-ization was an equally broad acceptance that a large proportion of French producers were not suited to state control. The reasons given for creating a 'free' sector were diverse. Robert Lacoste, the post-Liberation Minister of Industrial Production, said simply that since the prosperity or bankruptcy of these firms would have no repercussions on the overall economy, there was no need to regulate them too closely.[63] Others noted that the long traditions of individualism among France's artisan and small-business sector would make 'caporalisation' (regimentation) unworkable and almost certainly counterproductive.[64] Most believed that it made

---

[57] *JO, Débats*, 21 July 1944, p. 203.

[58] Some of the minutes of this committee that met at the end of 1944 may be found in the Cassin archives, AN, 382 AP 75.

[59] 'Les Réformes de structures: limites du secteur à nationaliser; ordre d'urgence', in *Œuvres complètes*, p. 576.

[60] For Pirou's views, see his article: 'Le Problème des trois secteurs', *Revue d'économie politique*, 54 (1940–1944), 447–66.

[61] 'Sous-commission des comités d'organisation: séance du 21 avril 1944', in MAE, *Guerre 1939–1945* . . ., 686.

[62] pp. 97–9. The division of the 'mixed economy' into various sectors had been commonly employed in *planiste* and technocratic works of the 1930s: see Gérard Brun, *Technocrates et technocratie en France, 1918–1945* (Paris, 1985), 111.

[63] 'Conférence de presse de M. Lacoste, Ministre de la Production Industrielle, le 10 février 1945', *Notes Documentaires et Études*, 7 Mar. 1945.

[64] See e.g. Mendès-France, 'Les Réformes de structures', in *Œuvres complètes*, pp. 575–6.

economic as well as political sense to leave France's small producers alone.

Sandwiched between the nationalized industries and the small producers came the 'controlled' sector. This sector had no obvious boundaries, in the sense that public services such as transport and electricity naturally belonged to the nationalized sector and artisan workshops to the free sector. Lacoste defined it as encompassing those industries which, 'without being as essential as those of the nationalized sector, present a vital interest for the nation', for example because of the volume of their exports.[65] The Alphand sub-committee in London had defined it rather differently as 'all industrial or commercial monopolies in private hands'.[66] In 1945 Pirou observed that both these criteria were also being used to justify nationalization.[67] The distinction, as Pirou rightly concluded, was not between different types of industry so much as different types of state control. More often than not, the controlled sector was defined solely in terms of the nature of the control. Gazier argued that, within the controlled sector, production levels, wages, and prices should be fixed directly by the state, acting through the agents that it would place at the head of each professional group.[68] From a more liberal standpoint the Alphand sub-committee had described it as the sector which would remain in private ownership, but where the state would have a power of surveillance over prices and output.[69]

The underlying issue in the debate about the controlled sector was the future of the sectoral organizations that Vichy had created. If the state was to direct economic activity in the controlled sector, it would clearly need some kind of intermediary body to co-ordinate the companies within an industry and convey instructions to them. This meant, in essence, recycling the CO.

Before the Liberation there had been considerable discussion about what de Gaulle's government should do with the CO. In the CFLN's economic study commission in Algiers, the general view had been that the *theoretical* function of the CO was a valuable one, but that in practice their number had to be reduced (from 150

[65] 'Conférence de presse de M. Lacoste', p. 3.
[66] 'Problèmes économiques d'après-guerre', p. 12.
[67] 'Le Problème des trois secteurs', p. 458.
[68] 'Sous-commission d'étude de l'organisation professionnelle: séance du 5 mai 1944', in MAE, *Guerre 1939–1945* . . ., 686.
[69] 'Problèmes économiques d'après-guerre', p. 12.

to 40) and their form changed, in order to place them firmly under the authority of the government. A draft of the commission's conclusions (later incorporated into Philip's report to de Gaulle) had recommended that each branch of economic activity should be headed by a state-appointed *préfet professionnel*, who would be assisted by a consultative council composed of representatives of management and workers.[70] The Provisional Government's Comité Économique Interministériel did eventually agree to maintain the OCRPI and CO after liberation. However, all that the CEI granted was a stay of execution. The ordinance (dated 22 June 1944) stipulated that the CO were to be retained 'until proceedings lead . . . to their effective dissolution' and that 'provisional administrators' were to be placed in charge of them. After the Liberation the Provisional Government was compelled to revise the original ordinance (by another of 7 October 1944) so as to play down the temporary nature of the CO.[71] As one well-placed commentator observed, the second ordinance transformed the 'provisional administrator' (with its overtone of liquidator) into a 'provisional commissioner'.[72] Four months after the second ordinance, the Minister of Industrial Production, Lacoste, announced that, in the free sector, the CO (now renamed Offices Professionnels (OP)) would be dissolved as and when economic conditions returned to normal. In the managed sector, however, the OP would have a permanent function that would involve implementing the government's policies, while adapting them to the particular conditions of each industry.[73] This announcement was in line with what Philip and his economic study commission had suggested before the Liberation and, more generally, with the Resistance's aspiration to organize and direct capitalism without recourse to total collectivization.[74]

Within a year, however, this potentially radical vision of *dirigiste* sectoral organization had come to nothing. Paradoxically, it was killed by the proponents of *dirigisme* on the left rather than by

---

[70] 'Sous-commission d'étude de l'organisation professionnelle: projet de conclusion', in MAE, *Guerre, 1939-1945* . . ., 686.

[71] For a detailed discussion of the two *ordonnances*, see 'Les Organes de l'économie dirigée: les offices professionnels', *Notes Documentaires et Études*, 27 Dec. 1945, pp. 3–9.

[72] Jeantet, 'Des comités d'organisation aux offices professionnels', 6.

[73] 'Conférence de presse de M. Lacoste'.

[74] See Philip, *Les Réformes de structure*, pp. 10–12.

liberals on the right (although the latter certainly opposed the OP with what little force they could muster). The OP were unable to escape the opprobrium that attached to the CO. As early as November 1944 members of the Consultative Assembly were demanding dissolution of what they scornfully called the 'Disorganization Committees'.[75] In 1945 the Communists began a vociferous campaign against the OP, which they accused of being under the thumb of the trusts and of discriminating against small producers.[76] In the elections of October 1945 candidates from all the three main parties demanded the dissolution of the OP/CO. To quote the Socialist candidates in the department of the Côte d'Or: 'We must get rid as soon as possible of the so-called Organization Committees which, far from serving the nation's interests, have been solely in the service of the trusts and have only succeeded in creating new bureaucrats.'[77] At the beginning of the First Constituent Assembly the PCF introduced a bill to dissolve the OP immediately.[78] Six months later, under a Socialist-led government, the OP, which many Socialist reformers had identified as the key to an effective extension of state control beyond the nationalized sectors, were disbanded.

The idea of using sectoral organizations as instruments of an *économie dirigée* was only one conception of the *profession organisée*. There were many people who saw other uses for it— who believed, for example, that intra-professional associations could stimulate social reconciliation, free producers from state intervention, or magnify the economic role of representative bodies such as management associations and labour unions. All these various views may be loosely termed corporatist.

The first attempt to institutionalize a corporatist form of *organisation professionnelle* came in Vichy's Labour Charter of 1941. Though corporatism was a favorite theme among most of the various factions in the État Français, they found it impossible to agree on its substance. In 1940 and 1941 the process of drawing up the Labour Charter was bedevilled by disagreements between two groups: those who envisaged fully-integrated labour–capital as-

[75] *JO, Débats*, 28 Nov. 1944.
[76] See e.g. the remarks of André Mercier, in *JO, Débats*, 3 July 1945, pp. 1285–7, and Jacques Duclos, ibid., 25 July 1945, p. 1483.
[77] BN, *Recueil de tracts . . . Elections générales, 21 octobre 1945*.
[78] *JO, Documents*, 23 Nov. 1945, pp. 38–9.

sociations, and those (in and around the Secrétariat d'État au Travail) who envisaged collaboration between labour and management associations that would none the less retain their separate identities.[79] The almost total failure of the Labour Charter after 1941 was due, in part, to such internal contradictions. It was also due, of course, to the government's own *dirigisme*. Bichelonne argued that the economic controls that the État Français exercised through the CO and the OCRPI were merely an *ad hoc* response to the 'impact of the immediate post-war phase' and that 'what must govern the economy in the future is article four of the Charter, that is to say the profession administering itself'.[80] The problem for the corporatists was that Vichy never managed to outlive the immediate post-war phase.

Outside the regime, the fiasco of Vichy's non-existent professional committees was usually blamed on the socially reactionary nature of the État Français, which made genuine working-class participation impossible. The Labour Charter tarnished the reputation of the word 'corporatism' but it hardly diminished the appeal of the concept. During the war corporatist ideas were widely discussed in the Resistance: for example, the projects that Philip brought over to England in 1942 included elaborate schemes for professional institutions.[81] Other plans also surfaced in the Free French community in London, where their main advocate was the Centre Syndical Français. The Centre argued that 'the defeat could have been avoided if French industry had made the necessary effort to co-ordinate its production . . . instead of delighting in a total anarchy'. For the post-war period it advocated an extensive network of collaborative organizations bringing together representatives of workers and employers.[82] After the Liberation corporatist ideas continued to be defended by groups which had traditionally been attracted to them. In the political arena their chief advocate was the MRP. In the 1930s the PDP had often stressed the value of *organisation professionnelle* as a means both of encouraging co-operation between labour and capital and of

[79] On this dispute, see Lt.-Col. Cèbe, 'Rapport sur les travaux préparatoires' (1 June 1941), in AN, F22 1835.
[80] Minutes of plenary meeting of CSEIC, 6 July 1943, ibid., F12 10143.
[81] See the 'Rapport émanant des organisations de Résistance en France: projet de charte économique et professionnelle', ibid. 72 AJ 546.
[82] Centre Syndical Français d'Études, 'Rapport sur le syndicalisme—organisation professionnelle' (20 Apr. 1942), ibid., F1a 3734.

regulating the economy without excessive state intervention. At the MRP's early congresses there was always a good deal of grass-roots support for corporatist reforms.[83] Party orators argued that this was Christian Democracy's distinctive contribution to economic theory. Outside parliament, similar ideas were advocated by progressive business groups: organizations like the Centre des Jeunes Patrons and the Confédération Française des Professions viewed corporatist arrangements as the only way of co-ordinating (and thereby preserving) the small businesses that proliferated in France.[84] Though the implicit aim of these plans was to protect small producers against larger competitors, their proponents linked them to the cause of economic progress. The CJP, for example, described the *raison d'être* of a professional association as being: 'to improve the technical, economic, and social qualities of the service which [businesses] jointly provide'.[85] Similar views were expressed by August Detœuf, a businessman who was a notable proponent of *organisation professionnelle* and had enjoyed considerable influence with the Vichy modernizers.

In a country where the dimension of businesses is relatively small, and where they are numerous, in comparison with the size of the market, mutual assistance and association are indispensable. . . . at a moment when exporting is going to become a matter of life or death for the country, many businesses need assistance to launch themselves in that market . . . only a professional organization can offer that to them.[86]

Among the numerous corporatist blueprints produced between 1940 and 1946 there were significant variations. Whereas Catholic programmes (which had as a major aim the reconciliation of class divisions) tended to give *patrons* and workers equal representation in the corporate bodies, economic modernizers like Detœuf insisted that the notion of an *organisation professionelle mixte* was pure sentimentality. Detœuf's organizations were management associations, assisted by consultative worker committees.[87] There was also a division (already noted in the context of the Labour Charter) between syndicalists and what one might call integral

[83] See e.g. the debates at the congress of Dec. 1945, ibid. 350 AP 14.
[84] See e.g. CJP, *Une étape*; *Plan commun 46: pour une organisation de la profession* (Paris, 1946); *Patrons 46: cahiers de la Conféderation Français des Professions* (Paris, 1946). [85] *Une étape*, p. 26.
[86] *Passé, présent, avenir de l'organisation professionnelle* (Paris, 1946), 23–4.
[87] Ibid. 26–7.

corporatists. Syndicalists envisaged the corporate body as a formalized setting in which worker and management organizations would meet on a separate but equal basis: René Belin's concept of *organisation professionnelle* involved, as he put it, the 'institutional-ization' of French unions.[88] In the early months of the Vichy regime (before Belin applied the law of 16 August 1940 and dissolved the CGT and the CFTC) this notion appears to have attracted union leaders (including the Comité Confédéral National of the CGT and the Comité d'Études Économiques et Syndicales).[89] Integral corporatists, on the other hand, saw the corporation in precisely the opposite light—as a means of eliminating separate class organizations and creating joint labour–capital associations.

Among resisters and post-Liberation élites, corporatism was no more fashionable a term than liberalism or *étatisme*. One after another, post-war advocates of *organisation professionnelle* be-moaned the damage that Vichy's innovations (introduced in a period of extreme constraint and deprivation) had done to their cause.[90] On the other hand, the *profession organisée* remained a highly seductive notion. Its attractions were threefold. First, it addressed the technical problem of the small scale and dispersion of French firms: for groups like the Christian Democrats, it resolved the problem of how to modernize economically primitive sectors without transforming a mode of production which, for social and political reasons, needed to be protected.[91] Second, it provided a possible arena for co-operation between representatives of the working class and representatives of the *patronat*. Third, it promised to allow the state to plan the economy's reconstruction and development without resorting to oppressive controls. Courtin noted acutely that enthusiasm for the *profession organisée* was fed by a desire somehow to avoid a bureaucratized or collectivist form of *dirigisme* at a time when *dirigisme* itself was generally felt to be unavoidable.[92] Professional organization squared the circle by

[88] See Belin's remarks to the colloquium, *Le Gouvernement de Vichy* (Paris, 1972), 195.
[89] Jacques Julliard, 'La Charte du Travail', ibid. 157–65.
[90] See e.g. Detœuf, *Passé, présent, avenir*, pp. 4–5; *Cahiers de la Confédération Française des Professions*, pp. 110–11; Jean Lobstein, *La Révolution sociale et économique* (Paris, 1944), 5. Lobstein had been a leading figure in a pre-war corporatist group called the Comité Central de l'Organisation Professionnelle.
[91] See an interesting position paper prepared for MRP electoral candidates: 'Le MRP et l'artisanat', in AN, 350 AP 93.
[92] *Rapport sur la politique économique*, p. 17.

combining the advantages of competition with the advantages of co-ordination.[93]

As Mendès-France ruefully observed after the failure of his attempt to found a powerful MEN, all modern nations, faced with the obligation of managing their economies, had taken time to evolve a satisfactory division of labour among the various economic ministries and organs of state. 'Everywhere the solution in the end involved giving one minister . . . an effective authority over the heads of the other ministerial departments affected.'[94] In the USSR it had been the Gosplan, in Germany the Ministry of Armaments, in England the Chancellor of the Exchequer. In France the expectation at the Liberation had been that the MEN would take on this role. An ordinance of 23 November 1944 did give the MEN important powers, but within six months the Ministry of Finance had reasserted its predominance.

The institutional dimension of *dirigisme* was something of which Vichy, the Resistance, and the Provisional Government had all been aware. Vichy's planning body, the DGEN, had been conceived as a small corps of technocrats operating outside the ministries, co-ordinating information provided by the separate departments of the government, and relying on the authority of the head of the state to diffuse bureaucratic objections to its decisions.[95] This approach had been criticized by some in Vichy: the CSEIC argued that the DGEN had insufficient information about, or control over, the economy to plan it effectively. The CSEIC suggested that planning could only be undertaken by a powerful Ministry of National Economy, which could directly supervise various Secrétariats d'État (Industrial Production, Communications, Agriculture, Labour, and Finance).[96] The concept of a Ministry of National Economy was defended by others in the regime, for example by René Perrin, an advisor to Pétain who was briefly considered as a possible Minister of Industrial Production.[97]

---

[93] Noyelle, *Révolution politique et révolution économique*, pp. 103–4.

[94] 'La Réorganisation des ministères économiques' (7 Nov. 1945), in *Œuvres complètes*, p. 158.

[95] See 'Plan d'Équipement', pp. 29–31, 509–11, in AN, F60 658.

[96] 'La Politique économique et les problèmes du Plan: rapport préliminaire aux travaux de la commission no. 3' (25 June 1943), 42–5, ibid., F12 10144.

[97] See Perrin's article: 'Problèmes et organisation économiques d'après-guerre', *Production: Revue Technique de l'Organisation Professionnelle*, 3 (Aug. 1943), 15.

Around the same period Courtin concluded his CGE report with a discussion of this difficult issue.[98] Since the rest of the report had been notable for its clarity, this conclusion was strikingly tentative. It suggested a number of possible solutions. The first was an economic 'superministry', with authority over all the other economic ministries (including the Ministry of Finance) and with a bureau du plan under its direct supervision. Courtin ruled out this solution for a variety of reasons: the superminister would rival the Président du Conseil and would be beyond the control of parliament; the risk of technocracy would be considerable; and the upper echelons of the Ministry of Finance would resist such an obvious subordination. Another possibility was that all the various economic ministries should preserve their existing roles, while their policies would be harmonized by an independent ministry whose function would be purely one of co-ordination. However, as Courtin himself acknowledged, 'Experience has . . . shown that a minister without department had only an insufficient authority with his colleagues.'[99] The solutions that Courtin considered most seriously fell somewhere between these two extremes of super-ministry and co-ordinating agency. In the option which he eventually chose, an expanded MEN would contain three sub-departments: a co-ordinating section, which would be in charge of gathering economic statistics and forecasting; an international department to negotiate commercial agreements, supervise exchange controls and the like; and a *direction générale de l'économie intérieure*, which would take over some of the Ministry of Industrial Production's functions such as allocation of resources (OCRPI) and controlling prices and wages.

Other institutional proposals were made by one of the sub-committees of the 1944 Algiers study commission. The two main views expressed in the sub-committee came from the two Socialist politicians, Philip and Moch. Their ideas had certain elements in common with Courtin's. Both men were aware, like Courtin, of the objections to a superministry.[100] Philip's Ministry of Economic Life was to have three services similar to those that Courtin had attributed to his MEN. It was to perform a similar function of co-

On Perrin, see Henry Rousso, 'Les Élites économiques dans les années quarante', in *Le Elites in Francia e in Italia negli anni quaranta* (Paris and Rome, 1983), 35.

[98] *Rapport sur la politique économique*, pp. 107–9.   [99] Ibid. 108.

[100] See e.g. Philip, 'Réformes économiques de structure', p. 51.

ordinating the activity of ministries that remained otherwise autonomous.[101] However, the Ministry of Economic Life which Philip and Moch envisaged was far more powerful than Courtin's MEN. Moch emphasized, for example, that the Ministry should have clear precedence over the Ministry of Finance.[102] The precedence was not merely a bureaucratic distinction. The system of economic planning that Moch and Philip proposed—in which a four- or five-year plan would become the *de facto* national budget over that period—naturally elevated the institution that was in charge of drawing up this plan (the MEN) and demoted the Ministry of Finance, whose function became that of supervising the less important annual portions of the long-term budget. Such an MEN would be more than merely *primus inter pares*: it would establish the guidelines for all the other economic ministries, and they in turn would be restricted to executing their part of the plan.[103]

Mendès-France, to whom de Gaulle assigned the new MEN after the Liberation, had a similarly powerful ministry in mind. He acknowledged that a superministry was not feasible. However, he believed that the MEN had to be able to exercise some sort of central control over the direction of economic policy. In order to exercise this control, Mendès felt that the MEN would have to include four main departments:[104] the planning agency ('Which certain people envisage placing with the head of the government to increase its independence but which ought logically to belong to the Ministry of National Economy'); a department in charge of allocating resources and setting production levels (merging parts of the old Ministry of Industrial Production and MEN); the Treasury department dealing with the Bank of France (formerly a part of the Ministry of Finance); and a department supervising prices.

Within the Provisional Government there was widespread sympathy in 1944 with the notion that the MEN should co-ordinate economic policy and draw up an economic plan. This sympathy extended from economic liberals like René Mayer, the Minister of

[101] Philip, *Les Réformes de structure*, pp. 12–13.
[102] 'Note sur le ministère de l'économie', copies of which are in MAE, *Guerre, 1939–1945 . . .*, 686, and AN, F1a 3792.
[103] Philip, *Les Réformes de structure*, p. 13.
[104] 'Le Réorganisation des ministères économiques', *Œuvres complètes*, p. 159.

Transport,[105] to Socialists like the Minister of Agriculture, Tanguy-Prigent.[106] In mid-1944 the relatively liberal Commissaire à la Production, Paul Giacobbi, described his vision of an MEN in terms akin to those of Moch, Philip, or Mendès-France.

It will be necessary to have recourse to the creation of a true Ministry of National Economy . . . which will not be a superministry, but will co-ordinate the efforts of all the ministries concerned with economic affairs. . . .

In addition, and independently of this effort to co-ordinate policy, this ministry will have among its functions the control of foreign trade, the control of prices, and the planning office.

This ministry will be the one which determines . . . the plan to be submitted to the government . . .[107]

However, Giacobbi's plan was not the all-embracing plan that Moch and Philip had in mind. It would have its own budget, but this budget was not synonymous with the entire national budget. None of the other ministers (Giacobbi included) was willing to accept that the MEN's *co-ordinating* function should evolve into a *supervisory* one. Throughout the crucial last months of 1944 each of the ministries with economic responsibilities resisted what they interpreted as the MEN's attempts to infringe on their right to execute policy.

This resistance to Mendès-France's ambitious project was successful. With his resignation and the absorption of the MEN within the Ministry of Finance under Pleven, the status quo seemed to have re-established itself. But the issue of the MEN did not altogether die. In 1945 and 1946 the MRP continued to advocate a ministry which was similar to that which Mendès-France had championed. It was on substantive issues (chiefly on monetary policy) that the MRP parted ways with Mendès-France, not over the institutional framework which he had created. Indeed, eight months after Mendès had left office, the MRP was still clinging to its belief that the economic plan should be drawn up by the MEN, not by some independent agency. The Christian

[105] See e.g. Mayer's diary entry of 26 June 1944, noting the general agreement within the CEI as to the necessity of the MEN after the Liberation. Extracts from this diary are in Mayer, *Études, témoignages, documents* (Paris, 1983), 291–375.
[106] See the undated letter from Tanguy-Prigent to Mendès-France, in AN, F12 10142.
[107] *JO, Débats*, 21 July 1944, p. 203.

Democrats' initial coolness towards the Commissariat au Plan was motivated by a suspicion that the new institution would undermine the MEN. This suspicion was clearly stated by the MRP's spokesman in the First Constituent Assembly:

We have . . . a Ministry of National Economy. We hope that it will remain what it is, or, more exactly, that it will become what it ought to be.

Don't we all have the impression that it is not yet that great ministry, that first-rank ministry, which . . . should give the lead to the other ministries? . . .

Well, I think I can sound a first alarm. We have just learned, very recently, of the creation of a Commissariat du Plan outside the Ministry of National Economy.

It seemed to many of us that a Commissariat du Plan . . . ought not to be outside the Ministry of National Economy, but integrated into this ministry.[108]

Such suspicions were only gradually allayed. In the debate on the Washington Agreement (the Blum–Byrnes treaty) in mid-1946, the MRP was still reserving its judgment on Monnet's scheme.[109]

The Socialists had a similar commitment to the MEN and in 1946 they were briefly in a position to reverse the bureaucratic current and re-establish the MEN's control over planning. When André Philip became Minister of Finance and National Economy in January 1946, he made an attempt to subordinate Monnet's Commissariat au Plan to his ministry and reorganize the MEN 'in order to permit it really to co-ordinate the drawing-up of the Plan'.[110] This attempt was successfully headed off by Monnet, with the assistance of the Communists who had no fondness for Philip's concept of a centralized planning ministry.

In general, however, the issue of the MEN's powers remained a matter of bureaucratic politics and never fully engaged attention in the broader political arena. This outcome was significant, since in reality the institutional question had wider significance than a mere contest of ministries fighting to protect their turf. The failure in 1944–5 to create a political and bureaucratic consensus behind the MEN determined the manner in which planning was finally

[108] Marcel Poimbœuf, ibid., 28 Dec. 1945, p. 488.

[109] Ibid., 1 Aug 1946, pp. 2871–910. See also de Menthon, *Notre politique économique* (Mar. 1946). As late as the Congress of 1949 a spokesman was calling for the MEN to implement the plan: see R. E. M. Irving; *Christian Democracy in France* (London, 1973), 111.

[110] See Philip's speech to the CEI, 18 Feb. 1946, in AN, F60 902.

institutionalized in 1946—which is to say, as a temporary *ad hoc* creation that was tied to the *présidence du conseil*.

A more open discussion about the MEN might have helped to sharpen the focus of the wider political debate about planning. Among political élites and the general public, there was a strong but very diffuse sympathy for the idea of a plan. In the Consultative and Constituent Assemblies, as Philippe Mioche has noted, it was considered politically expedient to offer ritual incantations to this idea.[111] All the major political parties did so from time to time. In addition, the Socialists and the Christian Democrats both developed rather grandiose schemes for drawing up and implementing a plan (involving a Ministry of National Economy, a consultative National Economic Council, and various corporate bodies).[112] The Communists were wary of such schemes: as over nationalization, they took considerable pains to distinguish 'planisme bourgeois' from socialist planning.[113] It was precisely their ideological reservations that attracted the Communists to Monnet's pragmatic (and, it was assumed at the time, *pro tempore*) solution;[114] whereas the MRP and the SFIO—with their higher expectations about planning—were initially lukewarm.

The particular contribution that Monnet made was, in a sense, to bridge the gulf between the experts, on the one hand, and the politicians and public, on the other. He did so by presenting *planification* not merely as a set of institutions and procedures (as most of the *planistes* had seen it) but also in metaphorical terms— as a symbol of concerted national action and a test of patriotic resolve. The political atmosphere of the post-Liberation era was not particularly conducive to institutional innovation (as the unhappy experiment of the MEN and the initial suspicions of the Commissariat au Plan demonstrated), but it was conducive to an attempt to infuse a new ethos into both the economy and the political economy. To quote Monnet himself: 'The time was

[111] *Le Plan Monnet*, p. 58.
[112] For the MRP's planning ideas, see two pamphlets by François de Menthon: *Vers la Quatrième République* (Paris, 1946) and *Notre politique économique*. For the SFIO's proposals, see its *Programme d'action du Parti Socialiste* (1945, 1946 edns.) or the various wartime writings of Philip and Moch.
[113] See e.g. Marcel Dufriche, 'Plans quinquennaux soviétiques et planisme bourgeois', *Cahiers du Communisme*, Sept. 1946, pp. 807–18.
[114] The attitude of the PCF towards the Monnet plan has been carefully analysed by Mioche, *Le Plan Monnet*, pp. 185–90.

propitious for experiments in collective effort: the patriotic impulses released by the Liberation were still powerful, and they had not yet found an adequate outlet. . . . Everyone felt that progress was possible, but no one knew precisely what to do.'[115]

One of the main lessons that the French drew from their experiences in the Second World War was a sharpened sense of how, in modern states, the economy had become the crux of national strength and economic policy the major responsibility of government. The years of enforced spectatorship induced the French to compare their economic performance with that of both their allies and their enemies. Except for a few experts, the comparisons were made at the most general level. They were in fact impressions rather than comparisons. The two major impressions reinforced what we have described as the two major preoccupations of French thinking about economic renewal: the necessity of modernization and the necessity of *dirigisme*. On the one hand, the French perceived an immense technical gulf between French equipment and methods and those of other nations, especially the US and the USSR. On the other, they linked the technical backwardness of the French economy to a lack of the systematic state intervention that they observed in these more 'successful' countries. Free French resisters and others (like Monnet) who had passed the war outside France were able to watch at close quarters, as traditionally liberal Anglo-American economies were mobilized to meet the challenges of war. Inside France Vichy technocrats witnessed the power that a state-controlled economy had given Nazi Germany. Their respect for its economic achievements was only matched by the veneration in which the post-Liberation generation held the Soviet economy after Stalingrad. The Soviet victory on the eastern front, which was perceived in France as a victory of Russian industry, contributed a great deal to the aura that surrounded the word 'plan' in post-Liberation France. 'You come back . . . from a country', Léo Hamon told General de Gaulle on his return from meeting Stalin in December 1944, 'where, in spite of the distance, the enthusiasm of France has followed you and where a new economy has proved its might.'[116] Six months earlier another resister had told the Consultative

---

[115] *Memoirs*, p. 239.
[116] *JO, Débats*, 27 Dec. 1944, p. 610.

Assembly: 'Oh! yes, the different schools of economists have debated at length about the merits and drawbacks of planning. For us the debate has been settled . . . since the extraordinary Soviet experience which, in twenty years, took Russia . . . from the darkness of the middle ages to the light of the twentieth century.'[117] During his months as Minister of National Economy Mendès-France made frequent references to the Soviet plan, which was held up as the starting-point for French *planification*.

Ironically, the generation which saw so clear a connection between national independence and economic strength was forced to admit that, in the short term, the restoration of France's economic power necessitated foreign (which, in the geo-political circumstances of 1945, meant American) assistance. Before the Liberation some had warned that the socialist society which resisters sought was incompatible with the likely course of Anglo-American policy. In July 1942 the socialist Georges Boris wrote a paper in which he predicted that in the post-war period the US would try to impose on the nations of Europe a 'neo-liberalism' which he defined as 'a regime of economic *laissez-faire* very slightly tempered by some concerns with social security'.[118] To resist this attempt, Boris argued that Europe would have to show a united front. Henry Hauck made a similar point at a meeting of the London study commissions in August 1942: 'France must take the lead in Europe and not be afraid to be at the head of new ideas at the risk of causing displeasure to a certain Anglo-American capitalism.'[119] After the Liberation the apprehension that France would need generous assistance was fully confirmed. The period after August 1944 saw a growing realization of the outdatedness of French industry and the physical damage that had been inflicted as a result of the Occupation and the war. By August 1945, in advance of de Gaulle's transatlantic trip, the French government was conveying to Washington the message that its economic strategy 'is largely dependent upon present and future American trade and financial policies'.[120] One of the main assumptions that Monnet started from was that a programme of modernization

[117] Ibid., 22 July 1944, p. 218.
[118] 'Politique américaine: les données fondamentales du problème', in AN, F1a 3734.
[119] 'Réunion mixte . . . 25 août 1942', 4, ibid. 72 AJ 546.
[120] 'The Ambassador in France (Caffery) to the Secretary of State, Aug. 17, 1945', in *FRUS, 1945*, iv. 705–7.

could not go forward without US aid. This assumption was accepted by the Socialist-led government that adopted Monnet's plan in 1946 and sent him and Blum to negotiate with the Americans for the necessary credits. André Philip, who had been appointed to succeed Pleven as Minister of National Economy and Finance, had had premonitions of US imperialism during the war, but in 1946 he was no longer discussing a hypothetical future. As he told the First Constituent Assembly, the present situation left the nation with no option: 'France is not in a position to pursue a plan of reorganization and re-equipment, such as the one we have proposed, without serious foreign assistance.'[121]

The French discourse about economic renewal was marked, therefore, by a basic ambiguity. There was a strong sense of the nation's vulnerability—to unwelcome adjustments associated with modernization (such as the *exode rural*) and—in Vichy as in the post-Liberation epoch—to an inescapable dependence on the resources of foreign powers and on unpredictable changes in the international economic order. Yet no other aspect of policy produced such an outpouring of optimism, not only about the possibility of renovating the national economy and raising living standards, but in general about the possibility of acting effectively to shape economic activity. Because pre-war economic policies had been so frequently dictated by non-economic factors, because the state's intervention had been so haphazard, because the perception was that France had never had an economic policy as such, the potential for change—if these defects could be remedied—seemed as incalculable as the productive potential of modern industry itself.

[121] *JO, Débats*, 25 Apr. 1946, p. 2282.

Conclusion

SINCE 1945 the Liberation has had an ambivalent place in the French collective memory. On the one hand, the events of 1944 and their aftermath symbolized the dramatic regeneration of a nation humiliated in 1940. They brought to power a new élite (80 per cent of the members of the two Constituent Assemblies had come to prominence in the Resistance[1]) and, with it, the ideal of social and political transformation and reforged national unity that the Resistance had come to represent.[2] On the other hand, the Liberation quickly disappointed those who had visions of a new era. The major socio-economic reforms that the provisional regime instituted (nationalizations, the introduction of economic planning, social welfare reform, the *comités d'entreprises*, and so forth) did not transform capitalism. The constitution of the Fourth Republic replicated the flaws of its pre-war predecessor. For many resisters, whose organizations were dismantled by the state or the political parties even as they themselves were being lionized for their wartime heroism, the post-Liberation period was an abrupt and traumatic descent from *mystique* to *politique*. The nation as a whole—confronted by continuing material hardships and revived political and geopolitical tensions—shared in the disillusionment: less than three years after the euphoria of the Liberation, the French polling organization reported that 93 per cent of the French people thought that 'things were going badly' in France, while a mere 4 per cent thought they were going well.[3]

For a long time historical accounts tended to portray the period in terms of a retreat from revolution to restoration. During the past decade, however, the historiography of these years has come of age. The mass of research that has been undertaken (aided by an ever increasing availability of archival sources) has rephrased

[1] See J.-P. Rioux, 'A Changing of the Guard? Old and New Elites at the Liberation', in J. Howorth and P. Cerny (eds.), *Elites in France* (London, 1981), 85.

[2] See Pierre Laborie, 'Opinion et représentations: la Libération et l'image de la Résistance', *Revue d'histoire de la Deuxième Guerre Mondiale*, 131 (1983), 65–91.

[3] Institut Français d'Opinion Publique, *Sondages*, 1 July 1947, p. 129.

the revolution/restoration issue in terms of reform or gradual change.[4] The revolutionary rhetoric of the Resistance is taken much less seriously than it used to be. The potential for a decisive rupture with capitalism or with liberal democracy in 1944 or 1945 is now regarded as far less significant than it once was: all kinds of factors (political, economic, social, psychological, external) are seen as having restricted the possibilities for radical transformation. As historians have come to play down the likelihood of a revolution, so the restoration has appeared in a different light. Instead of being construed as a series of virtual betrayals, the continuities in post-Liberation history have increasingly been depicted as natural (an unavoidable 'return to normalcy') and even as beneficial (the continuities between Vichy and post-Liberation reformism providing the context for French capitalism's remarkable renovation in the 1950s and 1960s). The new history of the 1940s subscribes neither to the revolutionary illusions of 1944 nor to the exaggerated despondency of 1947. Its more prosaic reading depicts the period as one of significant reform, whose influence lay at the root of many of the successes of succeeding decades. Perhaps not surprisingly, French historians have tended towards a whig interpretation of this era immediately preceding 'les trente glorieuses'.[5]

The foregoing study might be considered an attempt to bridge these two views of the Liberation: that of modern historical scholarship and that of the Resistance generation itself. It has recognized the constraints on change and, at various points, underlined the naïveties and inadequacies of the ideologies that claimed the right to reshape the nation. It has also recognized that the achievements of the post-Liberation period were more substantial than disillusioned contemporaries credited. On the

---

[4] It would be redundant to cite all the works that have contributed to this re-evaluation (since many of them have been cited in the preceding pages). Two works which summarize the recent literature are: F. Bloch-Lainé and J. Bouvier, *La France restaurée, 1944–1954* (Paris, 1986) and J.-P. Rioux, *La France de la Quatrième République*, i. L'Ardeur et la nécessité, 1944–1952 (Paris, 1980). The 1981 colloquium, *La France en voie de modernisation*, was the forum in which much of the research was first presented.

[5] This expression (describing the economic growth of the post-war decades) was popularized by Jean Fourastié's book of the same title. One important work which has a whiggish bias is Richard Kuisel, *Capitalism and the State in Modern France* (Cambridge, 1981). This was noted by Julian Jackson, in his review of Kuisel's work, in *Historical Journal*, 28 (1985), 493.

other hand, in studying its objective significance, historians should not lose sight of the Liberation as subjective experience. It may be fair to say that the 'révolution manquée' is a 'false problem',[6] in that there was no objective possibility of revolution in 1944 or 1945. But it is impossible to deny either the general assumption among élites that 'in order to survive, [France] had to undergo a profound transformation on all levels, political, economic, social, cultural',[7] or the public confidence (in 1944–5) that France was capable of achieving such a transformation.[8] It is equally undeniable that, whatever the objective constraints, the less than total fulfilment of these aspirations was perceived by most people (not just by marginalized ex-resisters) as an almost total failure.

Shorn of both the determinism of modern historiography and the manichaeism of the Resistance generation's perspective, the Liberation period appears characterized by the collision of very strong but opposed forces—a period in which irresistible pressure for change met irresistible pressure for continuity.

The strongest force militating in favour of change was the widespread desire for renewal which was prompted by defeat in 1940 and again, four years later, by liberation. The root of this desire was a perception that France did not have the option of returning to the past, because the past was synonymous with national decline. The force that such a perception could acquire is well illustrated by the case of 'malthusianism', one of the great bogies of the 1940s. The consensus of economic historians today is that French capitalism had never been inherently malthusian and that a sharp distinction between pre-war and post-war entrepreneurship is untenable.[9] In the context of the post-Liberation

---

[6] The expression belongs to Richard Kuisel. See his review of Bloch-Lainé's and Bouvier's *La France restaurée*, in *French Politics and Society*, 5, 1–2 (Feb. 1987), 52.

[7] René Girault, 'The French Decision-Makers and their Perception of French Power in 1948', in Josef Becker and Franz Knipping (eds.), *Power in Europe?* (Berlin and New York, 1986), 57.

[8] See Pascal Ory, 'Introduction to an Era of Doubt: Cultural Reflections of "French Power" around the year 1948', in Becker and Knipping, *Power in Europe?*, pp. 397–407. Ory argues that 'the decisive . . . break in French self-confidence . . . came less in 1940 or in 1945 . . . than between 1946 and 1948—the events of 1947 being of particular importance in this process but not the whole story' (pp. 399–400).

[9] For a convenient summary of the revisionist literature about the supposed malthusianism of the French economy, see Jean Bouvier's introduction: 'Libres

period, however, the more important fact is that élites *believed* that the past had been malthusian.[10] This 'myth' of endemic malthusianism played a crucial role in the conversion of a rising generation of technocrats, economists, and politicians to the new gospels of growth and modernization. In all areas of policy the period before and after liberation saw the emergence of similarly reformist orthodoxies. Some of them have been analysed in preceding chapters. The era of imperial domination was perceived to be ending and an era of fruitful co-operation beginning. The financial shibboleths of the 1930s were challenged by a new orthodoxy which stressed the primacy of economic factors. The backwardness of French industry and agriculture had become a matter of public debate. Nationalization and state economic management were acceptable to many on both left and right who previously had had their doubts. The notions of worker participation and 'professional organization' enjoyed an unprecedented vogue. There was no single source for these ideas: they were neither wholly the product of the war nor wholly the culmination of pre-war trends. The wartime rethinking certainly involved a diffusion of ideas which had emerged in the inter-war era among a small avant-garde: for instance, the concepts and vocabulary of economic reformism (*réformes de structure, économie dirigée, économie mixte*, nationalization, planning, etc.) were those of inter-war nonconformism, reinforced and amplified by the events of the early 1940s. In other respects, however, the events of the war reversed (at least temporarily) the current of reformism. The victory of Britain and America, the experience of Vichy, the growing appreciation of Nazism's horrors, all tended to dispel the aura of modernity which anti-parliamentarianism and totalitarianism had once had. The crisis of liberal democracy had not been fully resolved, but in 1944 or 1945 many felt that it could be resolved without recourse to the kind of drastic solutions recommended in the 1930s. If Soviet Russia was one model of modernity, progressive and consensual Britain was suddenly another. Finally in yet other respects the war highlighted new areas of concern for

propos autour d'une démarche révisionniste', in P. Fridenson and A. Straus (eds.), *Le Capitalisme français 19ᵉ–20ᵉ siècle: blocages et dynamismes d'une croissance* (Paris, 1987), 11–27.

[10] This point has been made by François Bloch-Lainé, in *La France restaurée*, p. 49.

reformers. The Union française and the social security plan are obvious examples of themes which were central to the dialogue about modernity in 1945, but would have evoked less of a response a decade earlier.

The desire for renewal was reinforced by institutional factors, which temporarily seemed to favour change. The period between the Liberation and the consecration of the Fourth Republic at the end of 1946 was one of great institutional, as well as intellectual, fluidity. For fifteen months between August 1944 and October 1945 the Provisional Government was able to introduce reform by ordinance (as it introduced the *comités d'entreprises*, the social security plan, the ENA, and the first wave of nationalizations). During these months, there was no real legislative check: in so far as the Consultative Assembly criticized the government's reforms, it generally criticized them for not going far enough. Even during the life of the Constituent Assemblies between November 1945 and September 1946 conditions favoured reform. There was only one legislative chamber (and hence no possibility of legislation being delayed in the shuttle from one chamber to another, as had so often happened to reform legislation during the Third Republic). Furthermore, this chamber was controlled by three powerful parties which, in spite of their differences, shared a fundamental adherence to the CNR programme. In political terms the opposition to reform was far weaker than it had been in 1936: the parties of the centre–right and right were decimated in the elections of 1945 and 1946. The significance of this fact may be put counterfactually: if the right and the Radicals had not been so politically weakened, it is quite likely that the immobilism which developed later in the Fourth Republic (after their resurgence) would have occurred in 1946.

If the forces favouring change are relatively simple to describe— new orthodoxies, new élites, and new parliamentary arithmetic— the constraints that operated to counteract these forces were diverse and complex. Some of the major constraints were circumstantial. For example, the fact that the Liberation and the end of the war did not coincide was crucial. During the months between August 1944 and May 1945 the war not only absorbed a large percentage of the nation's scarce resources, but also the attention of the government (and of General de Gaulle in particular). Above all, it sapped the popular *élam* that had been sparked by liberation. Similarly sapping were the bitter residues of four years' occupation: the dislocation of economic activity, the rationing and ever-present black market, the *épuration* of collaborators (and its various scandals of excess or lenience). These problems—which may be termed the problems of recuperation—not only distracted political and public attention from the issue of long-term reform. They could also circumscribe the possible scope of reform. The economic crisis necessitated the maintenance of Vichy's economic controls and impeded a radical *épuration* of financial or administrative élites. It also made ministers nervous about structural reforms whose immediate impact was difficult to foresee. In many areas the legacy of the National Revolution restricted the options for reform in 1944: the unpopularity of economic *dirigisme* and presidentialist regimes, the rekindling of the confessional school dispute, the popular and political hostility to regional reform or corporatist arrangements, were all fruits of the État Français' abortive 'revolution'.

Other constraints were embedded in the political context of the period. An important political factor was the attitude of the head of the Provisional Government. The proponents of the 'révolution manquée' argument have long seen de Gaulle as the arch-reactionary in 1944 and argued that his determination to reassert the central authority of the state in the weeks after liberation killed the possibility for a grass-roots transformation of France. But for present purposes (focusing on the fate of reformism rather than that of a hypothetical revolution), the more significant decision that de Gaulle made came in 1945. That was his refusal to anticipate the popular will by introducing large-scale reforms before the general elections (a commitment which he had first made in London during the war). The cost of such a commitment had been anticipated by André Philip before the Liberation: 'Everything can be done *in the first year following the Liberation*, that is even before elections to the Constituent Assembly. What is not done in the first year will never be done, because by then all the old habits will have been resumed.'[11] There can be little doubt that, by refusing to move precipitately when the political situation was more fluid (although, as we have seen, the government did introduce a number of important reforms before the elections),

[11] *Les Réformes de structure* (Algiers, n.d. [1944]), 24.

de Gaulle restricted the extent to which Resistance aspirations could be fulfilled.

On the other hand, notwithstanding Philip's prediction, the general elections of October 1945 returned an assembly overwhelmingly committed to the CNR's Common Programme. The limits of reform were, at least in part, due to the limitations of the three parties who shared power with de Gaulle in November 1945 and held it without him after January 1946. Each of these parties hindered, as well as furthered, the cause of reformism. The MRP—increasingly a prisoner of its right-wing voters—diluted the radicalism of its founding congress. The Socialist party failed to bring to maturity the progressive ideas that it had developed under the Occupation: instead, it became hypnotized by its relations with the Communist party and by internal ideological divisions. The Communist party did as much as any group to introduce reforms, but, paradoxically, it did so without ever altering its fundamental suspicion about reformism in a bourgeois society. Its commitment was bound, therefore, to be circumstantial.

It is a simple matter to identify other constraints on change: for example, the resistance of financial or administrative élites (who helped to block Mendès-France's ambitious plans) or the extreme dependence on foreign economic assistance (and the consequent imperative not to offend the Americans). Even the calendar could act as a constraint (in areas such as educational reform where lengthy preparation was required). There is an obvious force to such arguments. At the same time there is a risk that they may become alibis for reformers who were unable to institutionalize their blueprints. As François Bloch-Lainé has pointed out, *à propos* the failure to introduce socialist-style planning in 1946 (and it is a point that could be extended to other areas of reform): 'Jean Monnet's team . . . filled a gap more than it displaced something already there.'[12]

In the end the numerous plans and programmes generated by six years of rethinking did not add up to a coherent or feasible alternative to the amended status quo which emerged in 1945 and 1946. It would be harsh to attribute this failure solely to intellectual timidity or inertia (as Bloch-Lainé does[13]). In quantity and in quality, the intellectual planning that was done in France

[12] Bloch-Lainé and Bouvier, *La France restaurée*, p. 105.
[13] Ibid. 55–6, 75, 137.

stands comparison with that done elsewhere in Europe. In so far as it lacked originality or realism, its limitations were as much as anything a reflection on the two decades of inter-war reformism, from which so many of the wartime ideas and so many of the reformers themselves—including Bloch-Lainé—had come. In any case, there are more useful ways of understanding the shortcomings of wartime reformism than by postulating hypothetical 'alternatives' which reformers failed to discover. The most fundamental limitations on reform were those inherent in the outlook of reformers themselves. Two such limitations have suggested themselves repeatedly during the course of the preceding study.

The first relates to the rethinkers' whole conception of what the problem was. National decline was viewed as a holistic crisis that demanded a holistic remedy. The issue of the economy certainly loomed largest. There was a general recognition (which had not existed to the same extent before the war) that economic strength—not military force or cultural prowess—had to be the foundation of French power in the world.[14] But there were relatively few people in 1944 (far fewer than in later decades) who believed that economic modernization alone could restore France to greatness or indeed that economic modernization would be possible without other kinds of transformation. The generation of 1940–6 saw signs of decadence and renovation everywhere. For example, as we have seen, it believed that France could retain an imperial role and that imperial renewal would underwrite national power far into the future. It believed that France could never recover until she had reintegrated the working class within the nation: in 1945 the *comité d'entreprise* (which received a higher approval rating in opinion polls than a new constitution or nationalization of the coal-mines[15]) seemed a crucial development. It also frequently depicted decline as a moral or cultural problem. In retrospect, such assumptions proved unfounded, but they are nevertheless significant because they illustrate the dispersion and confusion of reformist opinion at the Liberation: before the Monnet plan, decolonization, and the Fifth Republic (not to

[14] This point has also been made by Robert Frank in his article: 'The French Dilemma: Modernization with Dependence or Independence and Decline', in Becker and Knipping, *Power in Europe?*, pp. 263–80.
[15] See IFOP, *Bulletin d'informations*, 16 Nov. 1944, 1 Dec. 1944; *Sondages*, 16 Aug. 1945.

mention the emergence of 'modernization theory'), there was no obvious or agreed path to modernity.

Confronting a future full of imponderables, the French sought a restoration in both senses of the term: a return to something familiar and a renewal of something close to collapse. Change and continuity, in other words, were complementary rather than contradictory ends. Here was a second inherent limitation on reformism. Virtually all the plans and programmes to 'renew' France assumed and sought a substantial degree of continuity. Sometimes those who drew up the programmes were conscious of this paradoxical need for stability. On his return from Germany in May 1945, Blum told party officials that the problem facing the PS was the problem facing the nation: 'We must at the same time give the impression of continuity and the impression of renewal. We must show at one and the same time that we are still the Socialist party, the same Socialist party, and that we are also a renewed, rejuvenated, transformed Socialist party.'[16] A year earlier Adolphe Pointier, *syndic national* of Vichy's Corporation paysanne, had made a similar point before that organization's third National Council: 'On the one hand, we must integrate all the technical progress; on the other, we must integrate this progress while respecting our rural civilization.'[17] Often the search for stability was unconscious, but it was none the less there at the back of most minds. The desire to preserve a constitutional tradition was at least as strong as the desire to transform it. The projects to renew the empire were conceived and presented as a means of resisting decolonization. Economic modernization was an acceptable theme only because it promised to preserve what could be preserved of the old economy: one need only think of the Communists (and others) preaching the modernization of agriculture in order to *avoid* a rural exodus.

For a nation of deeply-rooted traditions, renewal could never mean overturning all the existing structures—even if, for political and psychological reasons, that was the rhetorical form in the summer of 1944. It should be viewed not so much as a single act, accomplished once and for all or not accomplished at all, but as a continuing act of will, by which the French sought to adapt their

[16] *Le Populaire*, 22 May 1945.
[17] Quoted by Isabel Boussard, *Vichy et la Corporation Paysanne* (Paris, 1980), 322.

national identity to the demands of the mid-twentieth century, without abandoning the former or failing to live up to the latter. It is an obvious but neglected truth that many of the 'failures' of the post-Liberation years were as willed as the 'successes'.

Bibliography

Bibliographical material has been arranged according to the following scheme:

1. Primary Sources

   I. Archives (France)
  II. Archives (US)
 III. Official Publications
 IV. Newspapers and Periodicals
  V. Memoirs, Diaries, Speeches
 VI. Published Primary Sources (Contemporary Plans, Treatises, etc.)

2. Secondary Sources

   I. Books
  II. Articles
 III. Conference Papers
 IV. Dissertations

1. Primary Sources

I. ARCHIVES (FRANCE)

(a) Archives Nationales

F1a 3730, 3733, 3734, 3750, 3751, 3754–6, 3791, 3792, 3818, 4027–9
  (archives of Free French Commissariat à l'Intérieur)
F1c III 1135–98 (prefectoral reports, 1940–4)
F10 4962, 4970, 5049, 5126 (archives of the Ministry of Agriculture)
F12 9970, 9972, 10141–4, 10147 (archives of the Ministry of Industrial
  Production)
F22 1510, 1778, 1780, 1834, 1835, 1842 (archives of the Ministry of
  Labour)

F60 359–61, 423, 498, 501, 606, 658, 659, 896–8, 901, 902, 914, 1717, 1723, 1728, 1729, 1737, 1742 (archives of the Secrétariat Général du Gouvernement)
71 AJ 62–4, 66 (archives of the Musée Pédagogique)
72 AJ 3, 16, 17, 42, 43, 50, 55, 59, 60, 64, 65, 67, 68, 70, 383, 520, 546, 563, 564, 568, 577 (archives of the Comité d'Histoire de la Deuxième Guerre Mondiale)
78 AJ 2, 14, 15 (miscellaneous material relating to Vichy)
80 AJ 1 (archives of the Commissariat au Plan)
350 AP 1, 12–15, 45, 55–7, 93 (archives of the MRP)
382 AP 70–2, 75 (archives of René Cassin)
412 AP 1 (archives of the Union Démocratique et Socialiste de la Résistance)
SAN 7545, 7547, 7730, 7731 (archives of the Ministry of Labour)
TR 14000–2, 14005, 14039 (archives of the Ministry of Labour)
Unclassified: Conseil National Économique, commission chargée de l'étude du problème démographique, 1939 (2 cartons in the Section Contemporaine)

(*b*) *Archives Nationales Section Outre-Mer*
Affaires politiques 214–16, 391, 875, 877, 880, 2146, 2288
Affaires économiques 101
PA 28, carton 8 (Papiers Marius Moutet)

(*c*) *Ministry of Foreign Affairs*
Guerre 1939–45. Alger CFLN–GPRF 683, 686, 687

(*d*) *Office Universitaire de Recherche Socialiste*
Parti Socialiste, procès-verbaux du Comité directeur, 1944–6

II. ARCHIVES (US)

National Archives
Record Group 59, 851.00, 1944–6 (Department of State Archives)

III. OFFICIAL PUBLICATIONS

Assemblée Nationale Constituante élue le 21 octobre 1945, Séances de la Commission de la Constitution (Paris, 1946).
Assemblée Nationale Constituante élue le 2 juin 1946, Séances de la Commission de la Constitution (Paris, 1947).
Journal Officiel de la République Française. Débats. Assemblée Consultative Provisoire, 1943–5.

Journal Officiel de la République Française. Débats. Assemblée Nationale Constituante élue le 21 octobre 1945, 1945–6.

Journal Officiel de la République Française. Débats. Assemblée Nationale Constituante élue le 2 juin 1946, 1946.

Journal Officiel de la République Française. Documents. Assemblée Consultative Provisoire, 1943–5.

Journal Officiel de la République Française. Documents. Assemblée Nationale Consituante élue le 21 octobre 1945, 1945–6.

Journal Officiel de la République Française. Documents. Assemblée Nationale Constituante élue le 2 juin 1946, 1946.

Journal Officiel. Lois et Décrets, 1940–6.

Ministère des Colonies, *Conférence Africaine Française. Brazzaville 30 janvier 1944–8 février 1944* (Paris, 1945).

Ministère du Travail, *Social Security in France* (Paris, 1952).

Recueil des textes authentiques des programmes et engagements électoraux des députés proclamés élus . . . 1936 (Paris, 1939).

Recueil de tracts électoraux, listes, programmes . . . Elections générales, 21 octobre 1945. (BN: 4 Le 100.34)

Recueil de tracts électoraux, listes, programmes . . . Elections générales, 2 juin 1946. (BN: 4 Le 101.17)

Réforme de la fonction publique (Paris, 1945).

IV. NEWSPAPERS AND PERIODICALS

(a) Resistance and Free France Newspapers, 1940–1946

L'Aurore
Bir-Hakeim
Les Cahiers: études pur une révolution française
Cahiers de Défense de la France
Cahiers de Libération
Cahiers du Témoignage Chrétien
Les Cahiers Politiques
Ceux de la Libération
Ceux de la Résistance
Combat
Courrier Français du Témoignage Chrétien
Défense de la France
Documents d'Information (renamed *Les Cahiers Français* after 1943)
Le Franc-Tireur
La France Libre
L'Humanité
L'Insurgé
Les Lettres Françaises

Libération (Northern zone)
Libération: organe du directoire des forces de libération françaises, organe des Mouvements Unis de Résistance (Southern zone)
Libérer et Fédérer
Liberté
Lorraine
La Marseillaise
MOF (Mouvement Ouvrier Français)
La Nouvelle République. Patriam Recuperare
Les Petites Ailes de France
Le Populaire (Northern zone)
La Quatrième République
Renaissances
Résistance: le nouveau journal de Paris
Socialisme et Liberté
Valmy
Vérités
La Voix du Nord
Volontaire pour la Cité Chrétienne

(b) Post-Liberation Newspapers and Periodicals, 1944–1946

L'Aube
Bulletin de l'Institut Français de l'Opinion Publique (Sondages)
Cahiers du Communisme
Cahiers du Monde Nouveau
Les Cahiers Politiques
Carrefour
Combat: de la résistance à la révolution
Droit Social
Esprit
L'Humanité
Le Monde
Le Monde Français
Notes Documentaires et Études
Politique
Le Populaire
La Vie Intellectuelle

V. MEMOIRS, DIARIES, SPEECHES

ALPHAND, HERVÉ, *L'Étonnement d'être: journal (1939–1973)* (Paris, 1977).
ARON, RAYMOND, *Le Spectateur engagé* (Paris, 1981).

ASTIER DE LA VIGERIE, EMMANUEL D', *Seven Times Seven Days* (London, 1958).

AUPHAN, PAUL, *Histoire élémentaire de Vichy* (Paris, 1971).

BARDOUX, JACQUES, *Journal d'un témoin de la Troisième* (Paris, 1957).

BAUDOUIN, PAUL.*Neuf mois au gouvernement, avril–décembre 1940* (Paris, 1948).

BELIN, RENÉ, *Du secrétariat de la CGT au gouvernement de Vichy* (Paris, 1978).

BIDAULT, GEORGES, *D'une résistance à l'autre* (Paris, 1965).

BILLOUX, FRANÇOIS, *Quand nous étions ministres* (Paris, 1972).

BLOCH, MARC, *Strange Defeat* (New York, 1968).

BLOCH, PIERRE, *Mes jours heureux* (Paris, 1946).

BLOCH-LAINÉ, FRANÇOIS, *Profession: fonctionnaire* (Paris, 1976).

BOOD, MICHELINE, *Les Années doubles: journal d'une lycéenne sous l'Occupation* (Paris, 1974).

BORIS, GEORGES, *Servir la République* (Paris, 1963).

BOUNIN, JACQUES, *Beaucoup d'imprudences* (Paris, 1974).

BOURDET, CLAUDE, *L'Aventure incertaine: de la Résistance à la Restauration* (Paris, 1975).

BOUTHILLIER, YVES, *Le Drame de Vichy*, 2 vols. (Paris, 1950–1).

CARCOPINO, JÉRÔME, *Souvenirs de sept ans, 1937–1944* (Paris, 1953).

CASSIN, RENÉ, *Les Hommes partis de rien: le réveil de la France abattue (1940–41)* (Paris, 1975).

CASSOU, JEAN, *La Mémoire courte* (Paris, 1953).

CAZAUX, YVES, *Journal secret de la Libération, 6 juin 1944–17 novembre 1944* (Paris, 1975).

CERF-FERRIÈRE, RENÉ, *Chemin clandestin* (Paris, 1968).

—— *L'Assemblée consultative vue de mon banc, novembre 1943–juillet 1944* (Paris, 1974).

CHABAN-DELMAS, JACQUES, *L'Ardeur* (Paris, 1975).

CHAUTEMPS, CAMILLE, *Cahiers secrets de l'armistice, 1939–1940* (Paris, 1963).

CLOSON, FRANCIS-LOUIS, *Le Temps des passions: de Jean Moulin à la Libération. 1943–1944* (Paris, 1974).

—— *Commissaire de la République du général de Gaulle* (Paris, 1980).

COGNIOT, GEORGES, *Parti pris*, i. *D'une guerre mondiale à l'autre* (Paris, 1976).

COULET, FRANÇOIS, *Vertu des temps difficiles* (Paris, 1966).

DEBRÉ, MICHEL, *Trois républiques pour une France: mémoires* (Paris, 1984).

DENIS, PIERRE, *Souvenirs de la France Libre* (Paris, 1947).

DEWAVRIN, ANDRÉ—see PASSY, Colonel

FABRE-LUCE, ALFRED, *Journal de la France* (Paris, 1947).

FERNET, Vice-Amiral JEAN, *Aux côtés du maréchal Pétain: souvenirs, 1940–1944* (Paris, 1953).

FOUCHET, CHRISTIAN, *Au service du général de Gaulle* (Paris, 1971).

FRENAY, HENRI, *La Nuit finira* (Paris, 1973).

GALTIER-BOISSIÈRE, JEAN, *Mon journal pendant l'Occupation* (Paris, 1944).

GAULLE, CHARLES DE, *Le Fil de l'épée* (Paris, 1944).

—— *Vers l'armée de métier* (London, 1946).

—— *La France et son armée* (London, 1948).

—— *Mémoires de guerre*, 3 vols (Paris, 1954–9).

—— *Trois études* (Paris, 1970).

—— *Discours et messages, 1940–1946* (Paris, 1970).

—— *Discours et messages, 1946–1958* (Paris, 1970).

—— *Lettres, notes et carnets*, 6 vols, (Paris, 1980–4).

GAY, FRANCISQUE, *Les Démocrates d'inspiration chrétienne à l'épreuve du pouvoir: mémoire confidentiel* (Paris, 1951).

GIDE, ANDRÉ, *Pages de journal, 1939–1942* (New York, 1944).

GILLOUIN, RENÉ, *J'étais l'ami du maréchal Pétain* (Paris, 1966).

GUÉHENNO, JEAN, *Journal des années noires, 1940–1944* (Paris, 1947).

GUICHARD, OLIVIER, *Mon général* (Paris, 1980).

Hoover Institution, *France during the German Occupation, 1940–1944*, 3 vols. (Stanford, 1958).

HUSTON, JAMES A., *Across the Face of France* (London, 1984).

JEANNENEY, JULES, *Journal politique: septembre 1939–juillet 1942* (Paris, 1972).

JOXE, LOUIS, *Victoires sur la nuit 1940–1946: mémoires* (Paris, 1981).

LANIEL, JOSEPH, *Jours de gloire et jours cruels, 1908–1958* (Paris, 1971).

LARMINAT, EDGARD DE, *Chroniques irrévérencieuses* (Paris, 1962).

LEFRANC, PIERRE, *Avec qui vous savez: vingt-cinq ans avec de Gaulle* (Paris, 1979).

MALRAUX, ANDRÉ, *Antimemoirs* (London, 1968).

—— *Les chênes qu'on abat* (Paris, 1971).

MAURIAC, CLAUDE, *Le Temps immobile: un autre de Gaulle: journal, 1944–1954* (Paris, 1970).

MAYER, RENÉ, *Etudes, témoignages, documents* (Paris, 1983).

MENDÈS-FRANCE, PIERRE, *Œuvres complètes*, ii. *Une politique de l'économie, 1943–1954* (Paris, 1985).

MOCH, JULES, *Rencontres avec . . . de Gaulle* (Paris, 1971).

MONNET, JEAN, *Memoirs* (Garden City, NY, 1978).

MOULIN DE LABARTHÈTE, HENRI DU, *Le Temps des illusions: souvenirs (juillet 1940–avril 1942)* (Geneva, 1946).

PASSY, Colonel [pseudonym of ANDRÉ DEWAVRIN], *Souvenirs*, 2 vols. (Monte Carlo, 1947).

—— *Missions secrètes en France, novembre 1942–juin 1943* (Paris, 1951).
PÉTAIN, PHILIPPE, *Actes et écrits* (Paris, 1974).
PEYROUTON, MARCEL, *Du service public à la prison commune: souvenirs* (Paris, 1950).
PEZET, ERNEST, *Chrétiens au service de la cité* (Paris, 1965).
PINEAU, CHRISTIAN, *La Simple Vérité, 1940–1945* (Paris, 1960).
RÉVILLON, TONY, *Mes carnets (juin–octobre 1940)* (Paris, 1945).
REYNAUD, PAUL, *Le Destin hésite* (Paris, 1946).
RIST, CHARLES, *Une saison gâtée: journal de la guerre et de l'occupation, 1939–1945* (Paris, 1983).
SAUVY, ALFRED, *De Paul Reynaud à Charles de Gaulle* (Tournai, 1972).
SCHUMANN, MAURICE, *Un certain 18 juin* (Paris, 1980).
SOUSTELLE, JACQUES, *Envers et contre tout*, 2 vols. (Paris, 1947–50).
STÉPHANE, ROGER *Chaque homme est lié au monde*, 2 vols. (Paris, 1946–54).
TERRENOIRE, LOUIS, *De Gaulle 1947–1954: pourquoi l'échec?* (Paris, 1981).
TILLON, CHARLES, *Les FTP: témoignage pour servir à l'histoire de la Résistance* (Paris, 1962).
WEYGAND, MAXIME, *Mémoires: rappelé au service* (Paris, 1950).
ZAY, JEAN, *Souvenirs et solitude* (Paris, 1946).

VI. PUBLISHED PRIMARY SOURCES (Contemporary Plans, Treatises, etc.)

ALMIRA, JOSÉ, *Thèses pour la révolution nationale* (Paris, 1943).
ALPERT, PAUL, *Économie humaniste* (Paris, 1945)
AMELOT, PIERRE, *Structures françaises* (Paris, 1946).
ANTOINE, PHILIPPE, *A la recherche de la République* (Paris, 1945).
ARBEN, JACQUES, *Le Problème constitutionnel* (Paris, 1945).
ARON, RAYMOND, *L'Âge des empires et l'avenir de la France* (Paris, 1945).
—— *De l'armistice à l'insurrection nationale* (Paris, 1945).
—— and CLAIRENS, F., *Les Français devant la constitution* (Paris, 1945).
ASTIER DE LA VIGERIE, EMMANUEL D', *Rapport général sur la situation relative des partis et des mouvements de résistance, sur le rôle actuel de la Résistance et l'incidence des élections* (n.d.).
AUJOULAT, LOUIS, *La Vie et l'avenir de l'Union française* (Paris, 1947).
AURIOL, VINCENT, *Hier . . . demain*, 2 vols. (Paris, 1945).
BARATHON, CLAUDE, *Le Régionalisme d'hier et de demain* (Paris, 1942).
BARTHÉLÉMY, JOSEPH, *Provinces* (Paris, 1941).
BAYLE, FRANCIS, *Vers la disparition du salariat* (Paris, 1946).
BEAUCHAMP, MAURICE, *Pour la rénovation française: bases* (Paris, 1941).
BETTINGER, RAYMOND, *La Nouvelle Constitution (juillet 1940)* (Paris and Clermont-Ferrand, 1940).

BIJON, SÉBASTIEN, *La Lçeon des victoires perdues* (Toulouse, 1941).

BLOCQ-MASCART, MAXIME, *Chroniques de la Résistance* (Paris, 1945).

BLUM, LÉON, *L'Œuvre de Léon Blum, 1940–1945* (Paris, 1955).

—— *L'Œuvre de Léon Blum, 1945–1947* (Paris, 1958).

BONTE, FLORIMOND, *A l'échelle de la nation: réponse à l'auteur de 'A l'échelle humaine'* (Paris, 1945).

BOTHEREAU, ROBERT, *Applications actuelles du syndicalisme* (Paris, 1945).

BOURDEL, LÉONE, *La Mission de la France* (Paris, 1945).

BOURNAT, GILBERT DE, *Synthèses et réformes coloniales* (Paris, 1945).

BOUTILLIER, A., *Français, veux-tu refaire la France?* (Sarlat, 1940).

CAPITANT, RENÉ, *Pour une constitution fédérale* (Paris, 1946).

CARAGUEL, EDMOND, *La Nouvelle Constitution française* (Paris, 1941).

CASSIN, RENÉ, *18 mois de France Libre* (n.p., 1942).

CAZALIS, GEORGES, *La Révolution Nationale: réflexions pour le français à l'écoute* (Aurillac, 1941).

Centre des Jeunes Patrons, *Le Rôle des cadres dans l'entreprise* (n.p., 1942).

—— *Une étape* (Paris, 1945).

—— *Le Plan de sécurité sociale* (Paris, 1945).

CLOSON, FRANCIS-LOUIS, *La Région, cadre d'un gouvernement moderne* (Paris, 1946).

COGNIOT, GEORGES, *L'École et les forces populaires* (Paris, 1946).

COLLETTE-KAHN, SUZANNE, *Femme, tu vas voter: Comment?* (Paris, 1945).

Les Colonies pour la libération de la métropole (Paris, 1945).

Comité de l'Empire Français, *L'Action du Comité de l'Empire Français: principales interventions auprès des pouvoirs publics* (Paris, 1946).

Les Compagnons, *L'Université nouvelle*, 2 vols. (Paris, 1919).

Confédération Générale des Cadres, *Programme d'action et organisation générale* (Paris, n.d.).

Confédération Générale du Travail, *XXIIe Congrès National de Paris (26–29 septembre 1933)* (Paris, 1933).

—— *XXIIIe Congrès National de Paris (24–27 septembre 1935)* (Paris, 1935).

—— *XXVIe Congrès National de Paris (8–12 avril 1946)* (Paris, 1947).

CORCOS, FERNAND, *Suggestions pour la IVe République* (Quebec, 1944).

COURTIN, RENÉ, *Rapport sur la politique économique d'après-guerre* (Algiers, 1944).

DEBAT, F., *A chacun sa maison et non plus à chacun sa voiture* (Paris, 1941).

DEBRÉ, MICHEL, *La Mort de l'État républicain* (Paris, 1947). [See also Jacquier-Bruère.]

DEBRÉ, ROBERT, and SAUVY, ALFRED, *Des français pour la France* (Paris, 1946).

DEHON, R. P. ÉMILE, *La Nouvelle Politique coloniale de la France* (Paris, 1945).

DENAIS, JOSEPH, *La Réforme constitutionnelle* (Paris, 1945).

DETŒUF, AUGUSTE, *Passé, présent, avenir de l'organisation professionnelle* (Paris, 1946).

DUBOIS, ALEXANDRE, *Pourquoi et comment associer les travailleurs à leur entreprise* (Paris, 1946).

DUCLOS, JACQUES, *La Lutte des Communistes pour gagner la guerre et reconstruire la France* (Paris, 1944).

—— *Le Chemin de la renaissance française* (Paris, 1945).

—— *Union des forces démocratiques pour la renaissance de la France et la défense de la République* (Paris, 1945).

ESPERET, GÉRARD, *Essai sur la réforme de l'entreprise* (Paris, 1946).

Exposé et commentaires du projet syndical d'économie moderne dénommé Charte de la Démocratie, dressé et présenté par l'Union Départementale des Syndicats Confédérés de la région lyonnaise (Lyon, 1944).

FABIEN, JEAN, *Vers une réforme municipale* (Paris, 1945).

FABRY, JEAN, *Vers une constitution française* (Paris, 1945).

FERRAT, ANDRÉ, *La Peuple français devant le référendum* (Paris, 1945).

—— *La République à refaire* (Paris, 1945).

FLEURY, GEORGES, *Tirons les leçons des batailles perdues* (Thonon, 1941).

GADOFFRE, GILBERT, *Vers le style du XXe siècle* (Paris, 1945).

GARDEY, EMMANUEL [pseud. of Jean de Haas], *La Voie de l'avenir* (Paris, 1945).

GATTINO, JEAN, *Essai sur la révolution nationale* (Paris, 1941).

GIRAUDOUX, JEAN, *The France of Tomorrow* (Paris, 1940).

GRUNEBAUM-BALLIN, PAUL, *Vœux pour la quatrième république* (Paris, 1945).

GUÉRARD, ALBERT, *The France of Tomorrow* (Cambridge, Mass., 1942).

HAURIOU, ANDRÉ, *Vers une doctrine de la Résistance: le socialisme humaniste* (Algiers, 1944).

HERVÉ, PIERRE, *La Libération trahie* (Paris, 1945).

HUGOT, EMILE, *La IVe République* (London, 1944).

INSTITUT DE SCIENCE ECONOMIQUE APPLIQUÉE, *La Participation des salariés aux responsabilités et aux résultats de l'œuvre de production*, 2 vols. (Paris, 1945–6).

'JACQUES', *Soldat de France* (London, 1942).

JACQUIER-BRUÈRE [pseudonyms of Michel Debré and Emmanuel Monick], *Refaire la France* (Paris, 1945).

JOUHAUX, LÉON, *La CGT, ce qu'elle est, ce qu'elle veut* (Paris, 1937).

JOUSSET, BERNARD, *L'Accession des travailleurs au capital* (Paris, 1945).

JUNILLON, LUCIEN, *Réforme de l'administration française* (Paris, 1945).

LANGERON, ROGER, *Politique d'abord: souvenirs et anticipations* (Paris, 1943).

LARMINAT, EDGARD DE, *Que sera la France de demain?* (n.p., 1943).

LAURENTIE, HENRI, *L'Empire au secours de la métropole* (Paris, 1945).

LAVERGNE, BERNARD, *Le Problème des nationalisations* (Paris, 1946).

LEBLOND, MARIUS, *L'Empire de la France* (Paris, 1944).

LELACHE, S., *La Quatrième République* (Guéret, 1945).

LEMAIGNEN, ROBERT et al., *La Communauté impériale française* (Paris, 1945).

LOBSTEIN, JEAN, *La Révolution sociale et économique* (Paris, 1944).

LUCAS, ROBERT, *Un plan d'action économique et social* (n.p., n.d.).

MARTY, ANDRÉ, *Idées sur la nouvelle constitution de la République française* (Paris, 1946).

—— *La Question Algérienne* (Paris, 1946).

MATTERN, ERNEST, *Vers le bien-être et la paix sociale* (Paris, 1946).

MAYER, DANIEL, *Sur les ondes: discours prononcé à la radiodiffusion nationale* (Paris, 1945).

MENTHON, FRANÇOIS DE, *Notre politique économique* (Paris, 1946).

—— *Vers la quatrième république* (Paris, 1946).

MICHEL, HENRI, and MIRKINE-GUETZÉVITCH, BORIS (eds.), *Les Idées politiques et sociales de la Résistance* (Paris, 1954).

MOCH, FRANÇOIS, *La République du travail: order, justice et liberté* (Paris, 1944).

MOCH, JULES, *Arguments socialistes* (Paris, 1945).

—— *Guerre aux trusts: solutions socialistes* (Paris, 1945).

—— *Le Parti Socialiste au peuple de France* (Paris, 1945).

MOLINIÉ, HECTOR, *A la recherche d'une constitution* (Paris, 1945).

MONICK, EMMANUEL. See Jacquier-Bruère.

MORGUET, MARC, *Esquisse d'une constitution pour la IVe République* (n.d).

Mouvement de Libération Nationale, *Base d'un programme MLN* (Paris, 1944).

—— *1er congrès national, janvier 1945* (Paris, 1945).

Mouvement Populaire des Familles, *Pour en sortir: l'entreprise nouvelle* (Paris, 1946).

Mouvement Républicain Populaire, *Bâtir la France avec le peuple* (Paris, 1944).

—— *Congrès national du MRP 13–16 décembre 1945: motions adoptées* (Paris, 1945).

—— *Lignes d'action pour la Libération* (Paris, 1945).

—— *La Nationalisation* (Paris, 1945).

—— *Notre programme* (Lyon, 1945).

—— *Pour une réforme de l'enseignement* (Paris, 1945).

—— *Les Grandes Options de la politique économique* (Paris, 1946).

—— *Le MRP, parti de la quatrième République* (Paris, n.d.).

—— *Tracts de propagande* (BN collection, 1944–6).

NOGARO, BERTRAND, *Vues sur la réforme constitutionnelle* (Paris, 1946).

NOYELLE, HENRI, *Révolution politique et révolution économique* (Paris, 1945).

Parti Communiste Français, *École élémentaire du PCF* (Paris, 1944).

—— *Ce que veulent les communistes* (Paris, 1946).

—— *Deux années d'activité pour la renaissance économique et politique de la République française: rapports du Comité Central pour le XIᵉ congrès national du Parti Communiste Français* (Paris, 1947).

—— *La Politique économique de la France nouvelle* (n.p., n.d.).

—— *Tracts de propagande* (BN collection, 1944–6).

Parti Démocrate Populaire, *Xᵉ congrès national: déclaration de politique générale* (Paris, 1934).

—— *Ce que nous voulons* (n.p., n.d.).

—— *Tracts politiques* (BN collection, 1927–39).

Parti Républicain de la Liberté, *Les Idées essentielles du PRL* (Paris, 1946).

—— *Notes d'orientation à l'intention des orateurs du parti* (Paris, 1946).

—— *Le Programme du PRL: premier congrès national, 26, 27, 28 avril 1946* (Paris, 1946).

Parti Socialiste, *Les Décisions du congrès national extraordinaire des cadres des fédérations socialistes reconstituées dans la Résistance* (Paris, 1944).

—— *Le Parti Socialiste et l'unité française* (Paris, 1944).

—— *37ᵉ congrès national, 11–15 août 1945: rapports* (Paris, 1945).

—— *Pour les élections municipales et cantonales de 1945: le programme du Parti Socialiste* (Paris, 1945).

—— *Programme d'action du Parti Socialiste* (Paris, 1945).

—— *La Rénovation paysanne: programme socialiste d'action immédiate en agriculture* (Paris, 1945).

—— *L'Action socialiste à la seconde Constituante* (Paris, 1946).

—— *Conseil national du 9 juin 1946: compte-rendu des débats* (Paris, 1946).

—— *38ᵉ congrès national, 29 août–1ᵉʳ septembre 1946: rapports* (Paris, 1946).

—— *La Politique économique et financière d'André Philip et Albert Gazier, 26 janvier–2 juin 1946* (Paris, 1946).

—— *Programme d'action du Parti Socialiste 1946: assainir, produire, reconstruire, épurer, éduquer, libérer* (Paris, 1946).

—— *Tracts* (BN collection, 1944–6).

Patrons 46: cahiers de la Conféderation Française des Professions (Paris, 1946).

PERROUX, FRANÇOIS, and URVOY, Y., *Renaître* (Lyon, 1943).

PELIMLIN, PIERRE, *Perspectives sur notre économie* (Paris, 1948).

PHILIP, ANDRÉ, *Les Réformes de structure* (Algiers, n.d. [1944]).

—— 'Réformes économiques de structure' *Études et Documents*, 1 (Mar.–Apr. 1945), 3–58.

—— *Pour la IVᵉ République par les réformes de structure avec le MLN* (Paris, 1945).

Plan commun 44: contribution à une réforme de l'entreprise, 2nd edn. (Paris, 1945).

Plan commun 46: pour une organisation de la profession (Paris, 1946).

Le Plan Langevin–Wallon de réforme de l'enseignement (Paris, 1964).

PRÉAUD, ROBERT, *Sur la politique agricole et rurale de la France* (Paris, 1944).

Principes de la rénovation nationale (Paris, 1943).

Projet de constitution pour l'État Français (Paris, n.d.).

Projet de programme commun élaboré par le CGT, la Ligue des Droits de l'Homme, le Parti Socialiste, le Parti Communiste, en présence du Parti Radical (Paris, 1945).

RABIER, JACQUES-RENÉ, *La Participation ouvrière* (Paris, 1945).

REVAULT, L., *Pour reconstruire à neuf, il faut oser* (Paris, 1944).

SCELLE, GEORGES, and BERLIA, GEORGES, *La Réforme constitutionnelle: sa préparation, ses bases* (Paris, 1945).

SIMON, PIERRE-HENRI, *Préparer l'après-guerre* (Paris, 1940).

—— *De la République: essai sur la future constitution de la France* (Paris, 1945).

Société d'éditions économiques et sociales, *Les Conseils d'entreprises et les comités mixtes de production* (Paris, 1945).

SOYEZ, CHARLES, *Les Comités d'entreprises* (Lille, 1945).

SRIBER, JEAN, *La Reconstruction économique de la France* (Paris, 1946).

TANGUY-PRIGENT, FRANÇOIS, *Démocratie à la terre* (Paris, 1945).

TEXIER, HENRI, *Les Causes de la chute et les conditions de redressement* (Paris and Clermont-Ferrand, 1940).

VANVERTS, J., *La France de demain* (Paris, 1945).

VERDIER, ROBERT, *La Vie clandestine du Parti Socialiste* (Paris, 1944).

—— *Ecole laïque et liberté* (Paris, 1945).

Vers la révolution communautaire: les journées du Mont-Dore, 10–14 avril 1943 (Paris, 1943).

VIANNAY, PHILIPPE ('Indomitus'), *Nous sommes les rebelles* (Paris, 1945).

2. Secondary Sources

I. BOOKS

ADAM, GÉRARD, *La CFTC 1940–1958* (Paris, 1964).

ADDISON, PAUL, *The Road to 1945: British Politics and the Second World War* (London, 1975).

AGERON, CHARLES-ROBERT, *France coloniale ou parti colonial?* (Paris, 1978).

AMOUROUX, HENRI, *La Grande Histoire des Français sous l'Occupation*, 7 vols. (Paris, 1976–85).

ANDREW, CHRISTOPHER M., and KANYA-FORSTNER, A.S., *France Overseas: The Great War and the Climax of French Imperial Expansion* (London, 1981).

ANDRIEU, CLAIRE, *Le Programme Commun de la Résistance: des idées dans la guerre* (Paris, 1984).

—— LE VAN, LUCETTE, and PROST, ANTOINE (eds.), *Les Nationalisations de la Libération: de l'utopie au compromis* (Paris, 1987).

L'Année politique (Paris, 1945–7).

ARDAGH, JOHN, *The New French Revolution: a Social and Economic Survey of France, 1945–1967* (London, 1968).

ARNOULT, PIERRE, *Les Finances de la France et l'occupation allemande 1940–1944* (Paris, 1951).

—— *et al.*, *La France sous l'occupation* (Paris, 1959).

ARON, ROBERT, *Histoire de Vichy, 1940–1944* (Paris, 1954).

—— *Histoire de la libération de la France: juin 1944–mai 1945* (Paris, 1959).

—— *Dossiers de la seconde guerre mondiale* (Paris, 1976).

AUTRAND, AIMÉ, *Le Département de Vaucluse de la défaite à la libération, mai 1940–25 août 1944* (Avignon, 1965).

AZÉMA, JEAN-PIERRE, *De Munich à la Libération, 1938–1944* (Paris, 1979).

BANCAL, JEAN, *Les Circonscriptions administratives de la France* (Pairs, 1945).

BARRAL, PIERRE, *Les Agrariens français de Méline à Pisani* (Paris, 1968).

BAUCHARD, PHILIPPE, *La Mystique du Plan* (Paris, 1963).

—— *Les Technocrates et le pouvoir* (Paris, 1966).

BAUCHET, PIERRE, *Economic Planning: The French Experience* (London, 1964).

BAUDOIN, MADELEINE, *Histoire des groupes francs (MUR) des Bouches-du-Rhône, de septembre 1943 à la libération* (Paris, 1962).

BAUDOT, MARCEL, *L'Opinion publique sous l'occupation: l'exemple d'un département français, 1939–1945* (Paris, 1960).

310 *Bibliography*

BAUM, WARREN, *The French Economy and the State* (Princeton, 1958).

BECKER, JEAN-JACQUES, *Le Parti Communiste veut-il prendre le pouvoir? La stratégie du PCF de 1930 à nos jours* (Paris, 1981).

BECKER, JOSEF, and KNIPPING, FRANZ (eds.), *Power in Europe? Great Britain, France, Italy, and Germany in a Postwar World, 1945–1950* (Berlin and New York, 1986).

BÉDARIDA, RENÉE, *Les Armes de l'esprit: Témoignage Chrétien (1941– 1944)* (Paris, 1977).

BELLANGER, CLAUDE, *Presse clandestine, 1940–1944* (Paris, 1961).

BELLESCIZE, DIANE DE, *Les Neuf Sages de la Résistance: le Comité Général d'Études dans la clandestinité* (Paris, 1979).

BERL, EMMANUEL, *La Fin de la IIIᵉ République* (Paris, 1968).

BERTAUX, PIERRE, *Libération de Toulouse et de sa région* (Paris, 1973).

BICHET, ROBERT, *La Démocratie chrétienne en France: le Mouvement Républicain Populaire* (Besançon, 1980).

BLOCH-LAINÉ, FRANÇOIS, and BOUVIER, JEAN, *Le France restaurée, 1944– 1954* (Paris, 1986).

BOURDERON, ROGER, et al., *Le PCF: étapes et problèmes* (Paris, 1981).

BOURGI, ROBERT, *Le Général de Gaulle et l'Afrique noire, 1940–1969* (Paris, 1980).

BOURJOL, MAURICE, *Les Institutions régionales de 1789 à nos jours* (Paris, 1969).

BOUSSARD, ISABEL, *Vichy et la Corporation Paysanne* (Paris, 1980).

BRAUDEL, FERNAND, and LABROUSSE, ERNEST (eds.), *Histoire économique et sociale de la France*, iv, pts. 1, 2 (Paris, 1979–80).

BROGAN, DENIS, *French Personalities and Problems* (London, 1946).

BROSSOLETTE, GILBERTE, *Il s'appelait Pierre Brossolette* (Paris, 1976).

BROWER, DANIEL, *The New Jacobins: The French Communist Party and the Popular Front* (Ithaca, 1968).

BRUN, GÉRARD, *Technocrates et technocratie en France, 1918–1945* (Paris, 1985).

CALLOT, ÉMILE-FRANÇOIS, *Le Mouvement Républicain Populaire* (Paris, 1978).

CALMETTE, ARTHUR, *L'"OCM": histoire d'un mouvement de résistance de 1940 à 1946* (Paris, 1961).

CAMPBELL, PETER, *French Electoral Systems and Elections since 1789* (London, 1965).

CARITÉ, MAURICE, *Francisque Gay, le militant* (Paris, 1966).

CARON, FRANÇOIS, *An Economic History of Modern France* (London, 1979).

CARRÉ, JEAN-JACQUES, DUBOIS, PAUL, and MALINVAUD, EDMOND, *French Economic Growth* (Stanford, 1975).

CAUTE, DAVID, *Communism and the French Intellectuals, 1914–1960* (New York and London, 1964).

CENTRE DE DOCUMENTATION JUIVE CONTEMPORAINE, *La France et la question juive, 1940–1944* (Paris, 1981).

CÉPÈDE, MICHEL, *Agriculture et alimentation en France durant la IIe guerre mondiale* (Paris, 1961).

CHAPMAN, BRIAN, *Introduction to French Local Government* (London, 1953).

CHARDONNET, JEAN *Les Conséquences économiques de la guerre, 1939–1946* (Paris, 1947).

CHARLOT, JEAN, *Le Gaullisme d'opposition, 1946–1958* (Paris, 1983).

—— (ed.), *Les Français et de Gaulle: résultats des enquêtes menées par l'IFOP depuis 1944* (Paris, 1971).

CHAVARDÈS, MAURICE, *Un ministre éducateur: Jean Zay* (Paris, 1965).

CHENOT, BERNARD, *Organisation économique de l'Etat* (Paris, 1965).

COHEN-SOLAL, ANNIE, *Sartre: A Life* (New York, 1987).

CORBEL, PIERRE, *Le Parlement français et la planification* (Paris, 1969).

COTTA, MICHÈLE, *La Collaboration, 1940–1944* (Paris, 1964).

COURTIER, PAUL, *La Quatrième République* (Paris, 1975).

COURTOIS, STÉPHANE, *Le PCF dans la guerre: de Gaulle, la Résistance, Staline* (Paris, 1980).

COUTROT, ALINE, *Un courant de la pensée catholique: l'hebdomadaire 'Sept', mars 1934–août 1937* (Paris, 1961).

CRAWLEY, AIDAN, *De Gaulle: A Biography* (London, 1969).

CROZIER, BRIAN, *De Gaulle*, 2 vols. (London, 1973).

CROZIER, MICHEL, *Le Phénomène bureaucratique* (Paris, 1963).

—— *La Société bloquée* (Paris, 1970).

CULMANN, HENRI, *Les Principes de l'organisation professionnelle* (Paris, 1945).

DALLOZ, JACQUES, *La France de la Libération, 1944–1946* (Paris, 1983).

—— *La Guerre d'Indochine, 1945–1954* (Paris, 1987).

DANAN, YVES-MAXIME, *La Vie politique à Alger de 1940 à 1944* (Paris, 1963).

DANSETTE, ADRIEN, *Histoire de la libération de Paris* (Paris, 1946).

—— *Histoire religieuse de la France contemporaine* (Paris, 1965).

DEBRÉ, JEAN-LOUIS, *Les Idées constitutionnelles du général de Gaulle* (Paris, 1974).

DEBÛ-BRIDEL, JACQUES, *Les Partis contre Charles de Gaulle: naissance de la IVe République* (Paris, 1948).

—— *De Gaulle et le CNR* (Paris, 1978).

DECAUNES, LUC, *Réformes et projets de réforme de l'enseignement français de la Révolution à nos jours, 1789–1960* (Paris, 1962).

DEJONGHE, ÉTIENNE, and LAURENT, DANIEL, *Libération du Nord et du Pas-de-Calais* (Paris, 1974).

DENIS, HENRI, *Le Comité Parisien de la Libération* (Paris, 1963).

DePorte, Anton W., *De Gaulle's Foreign Policy, 1944–1946* (Cambridge, Mass., 1968).

Descamps, Henri, *La Démocratie chrétienne et le MRP: de 1946 à 1959* (Paris, 1981).

Domenach, Jean-Marie, *Gilbert Dru, celui qui croyait au ciel* (Paris, 1947).

Doueil, Pierre, *L'Administration locale à l'épreuve de la guerre (1939–1949)* (Paris, 1950).

Dreyfus, François-G., *De Gaulle et le gaullisme* (Paris, 1982).

Dupeux, Georges, *La France de 1945 à 1969* (Paris, 1983).

Duquesne, Jacques, *Les Catholiques français sous l'Occupation* (Paris, 1966).

Durand, Paul, *La Politique contemporaine de sécurité sociale* (Paris, 1953).

Durand, Yves, *Vichy, 1940–1944* (Paris, 1972).

Duroselle, Jean-Baptiste, *Deux types de grands hommes: le général de Gaulle et Jean Monnet* (Geneva, 1977).

—— *L'Abîme 1939–1945* (Paris, 1982).

Duverger, Maurice (ed.), *Partis politiques et classes sociales en France* (Paris, 1955).

Earle, Edward M. (ed.), *Modern France: Problems of the Third and Fourth Republics* (Princeton, NJ, 1951).

Ehrmann, Henry W., *Organized Business in France* (Princeton, NJ, 1957).

Einaudi, Mario, and Goguel, François, *Christian Democracy in Italy and France* (Notre Dame, Ind., 1952).

—— Byé, Maurice, and Rossi, Ernesto, *Nationalization in France and Italy* (Ithaca, NY, 1955).

Elections et référendums, 2 vols. (Paris, 1945–6).

Elgey, Georgette, *La République des illusions, 1945–1951, ou la vie secrète de la IVᵉ République* (Paris, 1965).

Fauvet, Jacques, *Les Partis politiques dans la France actuelle* (Paris, 1947).

—— *La France déchirée* (Paris, 1957).

—— *La IVᵉ République* (Paris, 1960).

—— *Histoire du Parti Communiste Français*, 2 vols. (Paris, 1964–5).

Foulon, Charles-Louis, *Le Pouvoir en province à la Libération: les commissaires de la République, 1943–1946* (Paris, 1975).

Fourastié, Jean, *Les Trente glorieuses: ou la Révolution invisible de 1946 à 1975* (Paris, 1979).

Fraser, W.R., *Education and Society in Modern France* (London, 1963).

Fridenson, Patrick, and Straus, André (eds.), *Le Capitalisme français 19ᵉ–20ᵉ siècle: blocages et dynamismes d'une croissance* (Paris, 1987).

FUNK, ARTHUR L., *Charles de Gaulle: the Crucial Years, 1943–1944* (Norman, 1959).

GALANT, HENRY C., *Histoire politique de la sécurité sociale française, 1945–1952* (Paris, 1955).

GARAS, FÉLIX, *Charles de Gaulle: seul contre les pouvoirs* (Paris, 1957).

GENDARME, RENÉ, *L'Expérience française de la nationalisation industrielle et ses enseignements économiques* (Paris, 1950).

GEORGES, BERNARD, and TINTANT, DENISE, *Léon Jouhaux: cinquante ans de syndicalisme*, 2 vols. (Paris, 1962–79).

GICQUEL, JEAN, and SFEZ, LUCIEN, *Problèmes de la réforme de l'État en France depuis 1934* (Paris, 1965).

GILLOIS, ANDRÉ, *Histoire secrète des Français à Londres de 1940 à 1944* (Paris, 1973).

GILPIN, ROBERT, *France in the Age of the Scientific State* (Princeton, NJ, 1968).

GIRARDET, RAOUL, *L'Idée coloniale en France de 1871 à 1962* (Paris, 1972).

GOGUEL, FRANÇOIS, *Géographie des élections françaises de 1870 à 1951* (Paris, 1951).

—— *France under the Fourth Republic* (Ithaca, NY, 1952).

GRAHAM, B.D., *The French Socialists and Tripartisme, 1944–1947* (London, 1965).

GRANET, MARIE, *Défense de la France: histoire d'un mouvement de résistance, 1940–1944* (Paris, 1960).

—— *Ceux de la Résistance, 1940–1944* (Paris, 1964).

—— and MICHEL, HENRI, *Combat: histoire d'un mouvement de résistance de juillet 1940 à juillet 1943* (Paris, 1957).

GRÉVISSE, SUZANNE, et al., *Succès et faiblesses de l'effort social français* (Paris, 1961).

GRUSON, CLAUDE, *Origine et espoirs de la planification française* (Paris, 1968).

GUN, NERIN, *Les Secrets des archives américaines: Pétain, Laval, de Gaulle* (Paris, 1979).

HACKETT, JOHN and ANNE-MARIE, *Economic Planning in France* (London, 1963).

HALLS, W.D., *The Youth of Vichy France* (Oxford, 1981).

HATZFELD, HENRI, *Du paupérisme à la sécurité sociale* (Paris, 1971).

HAYWARD, JACK and WATSON, MICHAEL (eds.), *Planning, Politics, and Public Policy: The British, French, and Italian Experience* (London, 1975).

HERVET, ROBERT, *Les Chantiers de la jeunesse* (Paris, 1962).

HIGONNET, MARGARET, et al. (eds.), *Behind the Lines: Gender and the Two World Wars* (New Haven, Conn., 1987).

HIRTLER, JEAN LUC, *Le Mouvement Républicain Populaire dans le Bas-Rhin en 1945–1946* (Strasburg, 1970).

Histoire du réformisme en France depuis 1920, 2 vols. (Paris, 1976).

HOFFMANN, STANLEY, *Decline or Renewal? France since the 1930s* (New York, 1974).

——*et al.*, *In Search of France* (New York, 1965).

HOSTACHE, RENÉ, *Le Conseil National de la Résistance* (Paris, 1958).

—— *De Gaulle 1944: victoire de la légitimité* (Paris, 1978).

HURSTFIELD, JULIAN, *America and the French Nation, 1939–1945* (Chapel Hill, NC, 1986).

INGRAND, HENRY, *Libération de l'Auvergne* (Paris, 1974).

International Labour Office, *Labour–Management Cooperation in France* (Geneva, 1950).

—— *International Labour Conventions and Recommendations, 1919–1981* (Geneva, 1982).

IRVING, R.E.M., *Christian Democracy in France* (London, 1973).

JACKSON, JULIAN, *The Politics of Depression in France, 1932–1936* (Cambridge, 1985).

JAFFRÉ, JÉRÔME, *La Crise du Parti Socialiste et l'avènement de Guy Mollet* (Paris, 1971). (BN microfiche)

JAMES, ÉMILE, *Les Comités d'entreprises: étude de l'ordonnance du 22 février 1945* (Paris, 1945).

JAMET, CLAUDE, *Le Rendez-vous manqué de 1944* (Paris, 1964).

JEANNENEY, JEAN-MARCEL, *Forces et faiblesses de l'économie française, 1945–1956* (Paris, 1956).

JOUVE, EDMOND, *Le Général de Gaulle et la construction de l'Europe, 1940–1966*, 2 vols. (Paris, 1967).

JULLIARD, JACQUES, *La IVe République, 1947–1958* (Paris, 1968).

KEDWARD, H.R., *Resistance in Vichy France: A Study of Ideas and Motivation in the Southern Zone, 1940–1942* (Oxford, 1978).

—— and AUSTIN, ROGER (eds.), *Vichy France and the Resistance: Culture and Ideology* (Totowa, NJ, 1985).

KERSAUDY, FRANÇOIS, *Churchill and de Gaulle* (London, 1981).

KINDLEBERGER, CHARLES P., *Economic Growth in France and Britain, 1851–1950* (Cambridge, Mass., 1964).

KRIEGEL, ANNIE, *Les Communistes français: essai d'ethnographie politique* (Paris, 1968).

KUISEL, RICHARD F., *Capitalism and the State in Modern France: Renovation and Economic Management in the Twentieth Century* (Cambridge, 1981).

KUPFERMAN, FRED, *Les Premiers Beaux Jours, 1944–1946* (Paris, 1985).

LABORIE, PIERRE, *Résistants, vichyssois et autres: l'évolution de l'opinion et des comportements dans le Lot de 1939 à 1944* (Paris, 1980).

LACOUTURE, JEAN, *De Gaulle*, 3 vols. (Paris, 1984–6).

LACROIX-RIZ, ANNIE, *La CGT de la Libération à la scission, de 1944 à 1947* (Paris, 1983).

LA GORCE, PAUL MARIE DE, *De Gaulle entre deux mondes* (Paris, 1964).

—— *L'Après-guerre, 1944–1952: naissance de la France moderne* (Paris, 1978).

LANZA, ALBERT, *Les Projets de réforme administrative en France de 1919 à nos jours* (Paris, 1968).

LAPIE, PIERRE-OLIVIER, *De Léon Blum à de Gaulle* (Paris, 1971).

LATREILLE, ANDRÉ, *De Gaulle, la Libération et l'Église catholique* (Paris, 1978).

LAUNAY, JACQUES DE, *Le Dossier de Vichy* (Paris, 1967).

—— *La France de Pétain* (Paris, 1972).

LEDWIDGE, BERNARD, *De Gaulle* (London, 1982).

LEFRANC, GEORGES, *Les Expériences syndicales en France de 1939 à 1950* (Paris, 1950).

—— *Le Mouvement Socialiste sous la Troisième République, 1875–1940* (Paris, 1963).

—— *Le Mouvement syndical sous la Troisième Republique* (Paris, 1967).

—— *Essais sur les problèmes socialistes et syndicaux* (Paris, 1970).

—— *Les Organisations patronales en France* (Paris, 1976).

LEGENDRE, PIERRE, *Histoire de l'administration de 1750 à nos jours* (Paris, 1968).

LEITES, NATHAN, *On the Game of Politics in France* (Stanford, 1959).

LÉVY, CLAUDE, *La Libération, remise en ordre ou révolution?* (Paris, 1974).

LICHTHEIM, GEORGE, *Marxism in Modern France* (New York, 1966).

LIGOU, DANIEL, *Histoire du socialisme en France, 1871–1961* (Paris, 1962).

LIPGENS, WALTER, *A History of European Integration, 1945–1947* (Oxford, 1982).

—— (ed.), *Documents on the History of European Integration*, 2 vols. (Berlin and New York, 1985–6).

LORWIN, VAL R., *The French Labor Movement* (Cambridge, Mass., 1954).

LOUBET DEL BAYLE, JEAN-LOUIS, *Les Non-conformistes des années 30* (Paris, 1969).

LÜTHY, HERBERT, *France against Herself* (New York, 1955).

MADJARIAN, GRÉGOIRE, *La Question coloniale et la politique du Parti Communiste Français, 1944–1947: crise de l'impérialisme colonial et mouvement ouvrier* (Paris, 1977).

—— *Conflits, pouvoirs et société à la Libération* (Paris, 1980).

MARABUTO, PAUL, *Les Partis politiques et les mouvements sociaux sous la IVe République* (Paris, 1948).

MARCHAL, ANDRÉ, *La Pensée économique en France depuis 1945* (Paris, 1953).

MARSEILLE, JACQUES, *Empire colonial et capitalisme français: histoire d'un divorce* (Paris, 1984).

MARSHALL, D. BRUCE, *The French Colonial Myth and Constitution-Making in the Fourth Republic* (New Haven, Conn., 1973).

MARTIN DU GARD, MAURICE, *La Carte impériale: histoire de la France outre-mer, 1940–45* (Paris, 1949).

MARWICK, ARTHUR, *War and Social Change in the Twentieth Century* (New York, 1974).

MAYER, DANIEL, *Les Socialistes dans la Résistance* (Paris, 1968).

MAYEUR, FRANÇOISE, *L'Aube: étude d'un journal d'opinion, 1932–1940* (Paris, 1966).

MAYEUR, JEAN-MARIE, *Des partis catholiques à la démocratie chrétienne* (Paris, 1980).

MERLE, MARCEL (ed.), *Les Eglises chrétiennes et la décolonisation* (Paris, 1967).

MEYNAUD, JEAN, *La Technocratie: mythe ou réalité?* (Paris, 1964).

MICAUD, CHARLES A., *Communism and the French Left* (London, 1963).

MICHEL, HENRI, *Les Courants de pensée de la Résistance* (Paris, 1962).

—— *Histoire de la France Libre* (Paris, 1963).

—— *Vichy Année 40* (Paris, 1966).

MILWARD, ALAN S., *The New Order and the French Economy* (Oxford, 1970).

—— *The Reconstruction of Western Europe 1945–51* (London, 1984).

MIOCHE, PHILIPPE, *Le Plan Monnet: genèse et élaboration, 1941–1947* (Paris, 1987).

MIQUEL, PIERRE, *La IVe République: hommes et pouvoirs* (Paris, 1972).

MONETA, JAKOB, *La Politique du Parti Communiste Français dans la question coloniale, 1920–1963* (Paris, 1971).

MONTASSIER, VALÉRIE ANNE, *Les Années d'après-guerre, 1944–1949: la vie politique en France, l'économie, les relations internationales, l'Union française* (Paris, 1980).

MORAZÉ, CHARLES, *La France bourgeoise* (Paris, 1946).

—— *Les Français et la République* (Paris, 1956).

MORGAN, KENNETH O., *Labour in Power, 1945–1951* (Oxford, 1984).

MORTIMER, EDWARD, *France and the Africans, 1944–1960: A Political History* (London, 1969).

—— *The Rise of the French Communist Party, 1920–1947* (London, 1984).

MOTTIN, JEAN, *Histoire politique de la presse, 1944–1949* (Paris, 1949).

MOULIN, LAURE, *Jean Moulin* (Paris, 1982).

NOGUÈRES, HENRI, *Histoire de la Résistance en France*, 5 vols. (Paris, 1967–81).

NORDENGREN, SVEN, *Economic and Social Targets for Postwar France* (Lund, 1972).

NOVICK, PETER, *The Resistance versus Vichy: The Purge of Collaborators in Liberated France* (London and New York, 1968).

Organisation Européenne de Coopération Economique, *Situation et problèmes de l'économie française* (Paris, 1955).

ORWELL, GEORGE, *The Collected Essays, Journalism, and Letters of George Orwell*, 4 vols. (New York, 1968).

PARODI, MAURICE, *L'Économie et la société française de 1945 à 1970* (Paris, 1971).

PARROT, JEAN-PHILIPPE, *La Représentation des intérêts dans le mouvement des idées politiques* (Paris, 1974).

PAXTON, ROBERT, *Vichy France: Old Guard and New Order, 1940–1944* (New York, 1972).

—— and MARRUS, MICHAEL R., *Vichy France and the Jews* (New York, 1981).

PETERSON, WALLACE C., *The Welfare State in France* (Lincoln, Nebr., 1960).

PHILIP, ANDRÉ, *Les Socialistes* (Paris, 1967).

PICKLES, DOROTHY, *France between the Republics* (London, 1946).

POLONSKI, JACQUES, *La Presse, la propagande et l'opinion publique sous l'occupation* (Paris, 1946).

PRIOURET, ROGER, *La République des partis* (Paris, 1947).

PROST, ANTOINE, *Histoire générale de l'enseignement et de l'éducation en France*, iv (Paris, 1981).

PURTSCHET, CHRISTIAN, *Le Rassemblement du Peuple Français, 1947–1953* (Paris, 1965).

QUILLIOT, ROGER, *La SFIO et l'exercice du pouvoir, 1944–1958* (Paris, 1972).

RACINE, NICOLE, and BODIN, LOUIS, *Le Parti Communiste Français pendant l'entre-deux-guerres* (Paris, 1972).

RAUCH, R. WILLIAM, *Politics and Belief in Contemporary France: Emmanuel Mounier and Christian Democracy* (The Hague, 1972).

RAYMOND-LAURENT, *Le Parti Démocrate Populaire, 1922–44* (Le Mans, 1966).

RÉMOND, RENÉ, *Les Droites en France* (Paris, 1982).

RIDLEY, FREDERICK, and BLONDEL, JEAN, *Public Administration in France* (London, 1964).

RIEBER, ALFRED J., *Stalin and the French Communist Party, 1941–1947* (New York, 1962).

Rioux, Jean-Pierre, *La France de la Quatrième République* i. *L'Ardeur et la nécessité, 1944–1952* (Paris, 1980).

Robrieux, Philippe, *Histoire intérieure du Parti Communiste*, 4 vols. (Paris, 1980–4).

Rossi, A. [pseudonym of Angelo Tasca], *Physiologie du Parti Communiste Français* (Paris, 1948).

Rude, Fernand, *Libération de Lyon et de sa région* (Paris, 1974).

Sadoun, Marc, *Les Socialistes sous l'occupation: résistance et collaboration* (Paris, 1982).

Sauvy, Alfred, *La Vie économique des Français de 1939 à 1945* (Paris, 1978).

Scritti di sociologia e politica in onore di Luigi Sturzo, iii (Bologna, 1953).

Sheahan, John, *Promotion and Control of Industry in Postwar France* (Cambridge, Mass., 1963).

Shonfield, Andrew, *Modern Capitalism: The Changing Balance of Public and Private Power* (London, 1965).

Siegfried, André, *De la IIIe à la IVe République* (Paris, 1956).

Sorum, Paul Clay, *Intellectuals and Decolonization in France* (Chapel Hill, NC, 1977).

Suleiman, Ezra, *Politics, Power, and Bureaucracy in France: The Administrative Elite* (Princeton, NJ, 1974).

Sweets, John F., *The Politics of Resistance in France, 1940–1944: A History of the Mouvements Unis de la Résistance* (De Kalb, Ill., 1976).

—— *Choices in Vichy France: The French under Nazi Occupation* (Oxford, 1986).

Talbott, John E., *The Politics of Educational Reform in France, 1918–1940* (Princeton, NJ, 1969).

Tarr, Francis de, *The French Radical Party: From Herriot to Mendès-France* (London, 1961).

Terrenoire, Elisabeth, *Un combat d'avant-garde: Francisque Gay et 'la vie catholique'* (Paris, 1976).

Tesson, Philippe, *De Gaulle 1er* (Paris, 1965).

Touchard, Jean, *Le Gaullisme, 1940–1969* (Paris, 1978).

Tournoux, Jean-Raymond, *Pétain et de Gaulle* (Paris, 1965).

—— *Jamais dit* (Paris, 1971).

—— *Le Feu et le cendre: les années politiques du général de Gaulle, 1946–1970* (Paris, 1979).

Ullmo, Yves, *La Planification en France* (Paris, 1974).

Vaudiaux, Jacques, *Le Progressisme en France sous la 4e République* (Paris, 1968).

Veillon, Dominique, *Le Franc-Tireur: un journal clandestin, un mouvement de résistance, 1940–1944* (Paris, 1977).

VISTEL, ALBAN, *La Nuit sans ombre: histoire des Mouvements Unis de Résistance, leur rôle dans la libération du Sud-Est* (Paris, 1970).

WALL, IRWIN M., *French Communism in the Era of Stalin: The Quest for Unity and Integration, 1945–1962* (Westport, Conn., 1983).

WEINSTEIN, BRIAN, *Éboué* (New York, 1972).

WERTH, ALEXANDER, *France: 1940–1955* (London, 1956).

WILLIAMS, PHILIP M., *Politics in Postwar France* (London, 1954).

WINOCK, MICHEL, *Histoire politique de la revue Esprit, 1930–1950* (Paris, 1975).

WORMSER, OLIVIER, *Les Origines doctrinales de la 'Révolution Nationale'* (Paris, 1971).

WRIGHT, GORDON, *The Reshaping of French Democracy* (New York, 1948).

—— *Rural Revolution in France: The Peasantry in the Twentieth Century* (Stanford, 1964).

ZÉVAÈS, ALEXANDRE, *Histoire du socialisme et du communisme en France de 1871 à 1947* (Paris, 1947).

II. ARTICLES

AMOYAL, JACQUES, 'Les Origines socialistes et syndicalistes de la planification en France', *Le Mouvement social*, 87 (1974), 137–69.

BELLESCIZE, DIANE DE, 'Le Comité Général d'Études de la Résistance', *Revue d'histoire de la Deuxième Guerre Mondiale*, 99 (1975), 1–24.

BERGER, SUZANNE, *et al.*, 'The Problem of Reform in France: The Political Ideas of Local Elites', *Political Science Quarterly*, 84 (1969), 436–60.

BOURDET, CLAUDE, 'La Politique intérieure de la Résistance', *Les Temps modernes*, 10 (1955), 1837–62.

BOUSSARD, ISABEL, 'État de l'agriculture française aux lendemains de l'Occupation (1944–1948)', *Revue d'histoire de la Deuxième Guerre Mondiale*, 116 (1979), 69–95.

—— 'Principaux aspects de la politique agricole française pendant la deuxième guerre mondiale', *Revue d'histoire de la Deuxième Guerre Mondiale,* 134 (1984), 1–25.

CAMERON, RONDO, and FREEDEMAN, CHARLES E., 'French Economic Growth: A Radical Revision', *Social Science History*, 7 (1983), 3–30.

CASSIN, RENÉ, 'Recent Reforms in the Government and Administration of France', *Public Administration*, 28 (1950), 179–87.

CHARLOT, JEAN, 'Les Élites politiques en France de la IIIe à la Ve République', *Archives européennes de sociologie*, 14 (1973), 78–92.

COQUERY-VIDROVITCH, C., 'Vichy et l'industrialisation aux colonies', *Revue d'histoire de la Deuxième Guerre Mondiale*, 114 (1979), 69–94.

COULET, FRANÇOIS, 'Indépendance et Libération, 1940–1945', *Espoir*, 27 (1979), 19–28.

DONEGANI, JEAN-MARIE, and SADOUN, MARC, 'La Réforme de l'enseignement secondaire en France depuis 1945: analyse d'une non-décision', *Revue française de science politique*, 26 (1976), 1125–46.

FOULON, CHARLES-LOUIS, 'Le Général de Gaulle et la libération de la France', *Espoir*, 9 (1975), 28–42.

GARRIGUE, M., 'L'Exécution du Plan dans l'industrie privée', *Collection droit social*, Mar. 1950, 29–37.

GERSCHENKRON, ALEXANDER, 'Social Attitudes, Entrepreneurship, and Economic Development', *Explorations in Entrepreneurial History*, 6 (1953), 1–19.

HOFFMANN, STANLEY, 'The Effects of World War II on French Society and Politics', *French Historical Studies*, 2 (1961), 28–63.

JEANNENEY, JEAN-NOEL, 'Hommes d'affaires au piquet: le difficile intérim d'une représentation patronale (septembre 1944–janvier 1946)', *Revue historique*, 263 (1980), 81–100.

JONES, JOSEPH, 'Vichy France and Post-war Economic Modernization: The Case of the Shopkeepers', *French Historical Studies*, 12 (1982), 541–63.

JOSSE, RAYMOND, 'L'École des Cadres d'Uriage (1940–1942)', *Revue d'histoire de la Deuxième Guerre Mondiale*, 61 (1966), 49–74.

KEDWARD, H.R., 'Patriots and Patriotism in Vichy France', *Royal Historical Society Transactions*, 5th ser., 32 (1982), 175–92.

KESLER, JEAN-FRANÇOIS, 'La Création de l'ENA', *La Revue administrative*, 178 (1977), 354–69.

KRAMER, STEVEN, P., 'La Stratégie socialiste à la Libération', *Revue d'histoire de la Deuxième Guerre Mondiale*, 98 (1975), 77–90.

—— 'La Crise économique de la Libération', *Revue d'histoire de la Deuxième Guerre Mondiale*, 111 (1978), 25–44.

KUISEL, RICHARD F., 'The Legend of the Vichy Synarchy', *French Historical Studies*, 6 (1970), 365–98.

—— 'Technocrats and Public Economic Policy: From the Third to the Fourth Republic', *Journal of European Economic History*, 4 (1973), 53–99.

—— 'Auguste Detœuf, Conscience of French Industry, 1926–47', *International Review of Social History*, 20 (1975), 149–74.

—— 'Vichy et les origines de la planification économique (1940–1946)', *Le Mouvement social*, 98 (1977), 77–101.

LABORIE, PIERRE, 'Opinion et représentations: la Libération et l'image de la Résistance', *Revue d'histoire de la Deuxième Guerre Mondiale*, 131 (1983), 65–91.

LACROIX-RIZ, ANNIE, 'Les Grandes banques françaises de la collaboration à l'épuration, 1940–1950: I. La collaboration bancaire', *Revue d'histoire de la Deuxième Guerre Mondiale*, 141 (1986), 3–44.

—— 'Les Grandes banques françaises de la collaboration à l'épuration: la non-épuration bancaire 1944–1950', *Revue d'histoire de la Deuxième Guerre Mondiale*, 142 (1986), 81–101.

LANDES, DAVID, 'Social Attitudes, Entrepreneurship, and Economic Development: A Comment', *Explorations in Entrepreneurial History*, 6 (1954), 245–72.

LAROQUE, PIERRE, 'Le Plan français de sécurité sociale', *Revue française du travail*, 1 (Apr. 1946), 9–20.

—— 'De l'assurance sociale à la sécurité sociale: l'expérience française', *Revue internationale du travail*, 57 (1948), 621–49.

—— 'La Sécurité sociale de 1944 à 1951', *Revue française des affaires sociales*, 25 (1971), 11–26.

LE COURIARD, DANIEL, 'Les Socialistes et les débuts de la guerre d'Indochine (1946–1947)', *Revue d'histoire moderne et contemporaine*, 31 (1984), 334–53.

LEFRANC, GEORGES, 'La Diffusion des idées planistes en France', *Revue européenne des sciences sociales: cahiers Vilfredo Pareto*, 12 (1974), 151–67.

LÉVY-LEBOYER, MAURICE, 'Le Patronat français a-t-il été malthusien?', *Le Mouvement social*, 88 (1974), 3–49.

—— 'Innovation and Business Strategies in Nineteenth- and Twentieth-Century France', in Edward C. Carter *et al.* (eds.), *Enterprise and Entrepreneurs in Nineteenth- and Twentieth-Century France* (Baltimore and London, 1976), 87–135.

—— 'Le Patronat français, 1912–1973', in Lévy-Leboyer (ed.), *Le Patronat de la seconde industrialisation* (Paris, 1979), 137–88.

L'HUILLIER, FERNAND, 'Les Gaullistes et l'Union française: action et réflexion, 1943–1953', *Études gaulliennes*, 6 (1978), 71–9.

LIEBMANN, LÉON, 'Entre le mythe et la légende: "L'anti-capitalisme" de Vichy', *Revue de l'Institut de Sociologie*, 37 (1964), 109–48.

LORWIN, VAL R., 'French Trade Unions since Liberation, 1944–1951', *Industrial and Labor Relations Review*, 5 (1952), 524–39.

MAIER, CHARLES, S., 'The Two Postwar Eras and the Conditions for Stability in Twentieth-Century Western Europe', *American Historical Review*, 86 (1981), 327–52.

MAILLARD, E., 'La Réforme de l'enseignement', *Revue d'histoire de la Deuxième Guerre Mondiale*, 56 (1964), 43–64.

MARSEILLE, JACQUES, 'L'Industrialisation des colonies: affaiblissement ou renforcement de la puissance française?', *Revue française d'histoire d'outre-mer*, 254 (1982), 23–34.

MICHEL, MARC, 'Decolonisation: French Attitudes and Policies, 1944–46', in Peter Morris and S. Williams (eds.), *France in the World* (1985), 81–6.

MIOCHE, PHILIPPE, 'Aux origines du Plan Monnet: les discours et les contenus dans les premiers plans français (1941–1947)', *Revue historique*, 265 (1981), 405–38.

—— 'Le Démarrage du Plan Monnet: comment une entreprise conjoncturelle est devenue une institution prestigieuse', *Revue d'histoire moderne et contemporaine*, 31 (1984), 398–416.

PETIT, RENÉE, 'Une loi nouvelle en matière de comités d'entreprises: la loi du 16 mai 1946', *Collection droit social*, Dec. 1946, 1–21.

PIROU, GAËTAN, 'Le Problème des trois secteurs', *Revue d'économie politique*, 54 (1940–1944), 447–66.

RABIER, JACQUES-RENÉ, 'Une expérience de planification souple en régime démocratique', *Collection droit social*, Mar. 1950, 1–10.

RÉMOND, RENÉ, 'Les Français voulaient-ils moderniser la France?', *L'Histoire*, 44 (1982), 94–5.

RIOUX, JEAN-PIERRE, 'A Changing of the Guard? Old and New Elites at the Liberation', in J. Howorth and P. Cerny (eds.), *Elites in France* (London, 1981), 78–92.

ROUSSO, HENRY, 'L'Organisation industrielle de Vichy (perspectives de recherches)', *Revue d'histoire de la Deuxième Guerre Mondiale*, 116 (1979), 27–44.

—— 'Les Élites économiques dans les années quarante', in *Le Elites in Francia e in Italia negli anni quaranta* (Italia Contemporanea, Dec. 1983/Mélanges de l'Ecole Française de Rome, Moyen Age-Temps Modernes, 95, 1983-2), 29–49.

—— 'La Mémoire et l'Histoire: l'exemple de Vichy', *French Politics and Society* 5/3 (1987), 7–13.

SEMIDEI, MANUELA, 'De l'empire à la décolonisation à travers les manuels scolaires français', *Revue française de science politique*, 16 (1966), 56–86.

SIMMONDS, J. C., 'The French Communist Party and the Beginnings of Resistance: September 1939–June 1941', *European Studies Review*, 11 (1981), 517–42.

WAHL, NICHOLAS, 'Aux origines de la nouvelle constitution', *Revue française de science politique*, 9 (1959), 30–66.

WRIGHT, GORDON, 'Reflections on the French Resistance (1940–1944)', *Political Science Quarterly*, 77 (1962), 336–49.

III. CONFERENCE PAPERS

[An asterisk denotes a citation of unpublished or partially unpublished conference papers. In this circumstance, the date indicates the year in which the conference was held.]

Approches de la philosophie politique du général de Gaulle à partir de sa pensée et de son action (Paris, 1983).
'L'Entourage' et de Gaulle (Paris, 1979).
La France en voie de modernisation (1944–1952) (Paris, 1981).
De Gaulle et la conférence de Brazzaville (Paris, 1987).
De Gaulle et la nation face aux problèmes de défense (1945–1946) (Paris, 1983).
De Gaulle homme d'État (Paris, 1978).
Le Général de Gaulle et l'Indochine, 1940–1946 (Paris, 1982).
Le Gouvernement de Vichy, 1940–42 (Paris, 1972).
Jean Moulin et le Conseil National de la Résistance (Paris, 1983).
La Libération de la France (Paris, 1976).
Nationalisations et formes nouvelles de participation des ouvriers à la Libération (1944–1951) (Paris, 1984).
Planification et société (Grenoble, 1974).
Les Prodromes de la décolonisation de l'empire français (1936–1956) (Paris, 1984).
La Quatrième République: bilan trente ans après la promulgation de la constitution du 27 octobre 1946 (Paris, 1978).

IV. UNPUBLISHED DISSERTATIONS

ALROY, GIL C., 'Radicalism and Modernization: the French Problem' (Princeton, 1962).
GAZET, MICHÈLE, 'L'Assemblée Consultative Provisoire: Alger 3 novembre 1943–25 juillet 1944' (Paris X, 1970).
JACKSON, JULIAN, 'The Politics of Depression in France, 1932–1936' (Cambridge, 1982).
KRAMER, STEVEN PHILIP, 'The Provisional Republic, the Collapse of the French Resistance Front and the Origins of Post-war Politics: 1944–1946' (Princeton, 1971).
LYNCH, FRANCES M.B., 'The Political and Economic Reconstruction of France, 1944–1947, in the International Context' (Manchester, 1981).
SHENNAN, ANDREW W.H., 'Rethinking France: The Liberation and Ideas of National Renewal' (Cambridge, 1987).
TOMLINSON, RICHARD, 'The Politics of Dénatalité during the French Third Republic, 1890–1940' (Cambridge, 1983).
WAHL, NICHOLAS, 'De Gaulle and the Resistance: The Rise of Reform Politics in France' (Harvard, 1956).

Index

Index

Hervé, Pierre 99, 130
higher education 178, 181, 184, 187
Hirsch, Étienne 236, 238
Hoffmann, Stanley 31
Houphouet-Boigny, Félix 145
Humanité, L' 95, 100, 130, 208, 219, 253

Indochina 151–2
Institut d'Études Corporatives et Sociales 22
Institut pour les Problèmes Humains 22
insurance industry 47, 244, 250, 252, 253, 254, 255
Intergroup of Native Deputies 165, 166
International Labour Organization 104, 215
Investment Fund for Economic and Social Development 159
Istel 264

Jamati, Georges 173
Jeanneney, Jules 62
Jeune République 78
Joint Production Committees 60, 191
Jouhaux, Léon 197, 203, 246
Jurgensen, J.-D. 41, 121

Kréher, Jean 173
Kuisel, Richard 31, 266

Labour Charter 27, 190, 274–5
Lacoste, Robert 226, 245, 255, 271, 272, 273
Laguionie, Pierre 21
Lamine-Guèye 145
Lampué, Professor 157, 158
Langeron, Roger 240–1
Langevin, Paul 183
Langevin–Wallon committee 180, 183–5
Lapie, P.-O. 144, 149, 160
Lapierre, Georges 173
Larminat, Edgard de 55, 66
Laroque, Pierre 215, 217, 223
Lassalle-Séré 150
Laurentie, Henri 143, 145, 147, 149–51, 155–6, 157, 158, 167
Laval, Pierre 110, 227
Le Brun, Pierre 246
Le Cour Grandmaison 110–11
Lebret, Father 23
Lente, Jacques 21
Lepercq, A. 245
Lescure, François de 173
Lettres Françaises Clandestines, Les 95
Lévy, Louis 88
liberalism 225, 229, 239, 240, 260, 269
Libération (Southern zone) 42, 45, 49
Libération-Sud 35, 37
Libérer et Fédérer 45, 192
Libérer et Fédérer 40
Loucheur, Louis 240
Loustau, Robert 20
Lozeray, Henri 159

machine tools 244, 250, 261–2
Maintenir 34
Maisonneuve, Pierre 59, 171
'malthusianism' vi, 48, 98, 100, 289–90
Man, Henri de 225
Marjolin, Robert 226, 236
Marquet, Adrien 227
Marrou, Henri 182
Marseillaise, La 57, 58, 66, 67, 143
Massis, Henri 20
maternity benefit 211, 216, 217
maurrasians 5, 20, 26, 29, 32
  see also Action Française
Mayer, Daniel 88, 89, 128, 256
Mayer, René 245, 280
Mendès-France, Pierre 44, 194, 233, 255, 266, 271, 278, 281, 285
  opposition to 244–5, 293
  reform plans 243–4, 252, 261, 270, 280
Menthon, François de 78, 131, 134
merchant shipping 244, 250, 252, 254
Mercier, André 149, 150, 163
Mercier, Ernest 226
Merleau-Ponty, Maurice 34
Michel, Henri 65, 97
milices patriotiques 2
Millerand, Alexandre 108
Ministry of the Family 204, 210
Ministry of Finance 220, 245, 278, 279, 280, 281
Ministry of Industrial Production 33, 194, 228, 234, 255, 279
Ministry of National Economy 226, 255, 260, 262
  operation of 233, 245
  proposals for reform of 225, 238, 240, 244, 278–83
Mireaux, E. 171
Moch, Jules 47, 88, 89, 115, 116,